Contents

KT-590-866

List of Contributors

Haakon B. Benestad MD
Senior Lecturer in Physiology, Institute of Physiology, Oslo, Norway

David Ivor Evans MA, MB(Ed), MRCP, DCH
Consultant Haematologist, Royal Manchester Childrens' Hospital, Booth Hall Childrens' Hospital and Monsall Hospital, Manchester; Honorary Lecturer in Child Health, University of Manchester, UK

C. G. Geary FRCP(Ed), FRCPath
Consultant Haematologist, Manchester Royal Infirmary; Honorary Lecturer in Haematology, University of Manchester, UK

E. C. Gordon-Smith MA, BSc, MSc, FRCP
Senior Lecturer in Haematology, Royal Postgraduate Medical School, Hammersmith Hospital, London, UK

H. Heimpel MD
Professor, Department of Internal Medicine, University of Ulm, Federal Republic of Germany

S. M. Lewis BSc, MD, FRCPath
Reader in Haematology, Royal Postgraduate Medical School, Hammersmith Hospital, London, UK

Gillian R. Milner MA, BM, PhD, MRCPath
Senior Registrar, Regional Blood Transfusion Centre, Sheffield, UK

Nydia G. Testa MD, PhD
Paterson Laboratories, Christie Hospital, Manchester, UK

Darryl M. Williams MD
Associate Professor of Medicine and Chief of the Section of Haematology–Oncology, Louisiana State University School of Medicine, USA

Preface

Although aplastic anaemia is a rarer disease than leukaemia, the clinical picture of bone marrow failure presented by severe aplasia is the more poignant when one recalls that at least 50% of all cases are a result of modern man's contact with his environment: indeed, as Dr Benestad points out on page 26, marrow damage is the most feared of all drug reactions since it is, so frequently, irreversible.

Ninety years have elapsed since Ehrlich's first graphic clinical and morphological description of aplastic anaemia, yet only in the last ten years have haematologists begun systematically to investigate and so comprehend the pathophysiology of the disease. Techniques which enable marrow progenitor cells to be grown in culture in the laboratory have permitted at least a semiquantitative analysis of the defect which exists in chronic marrow aplasia, while application of immunological methods is now providing clues as to how damage to stemcells might be provoked and sustained. While the enigma of the marrow defect in aplastic anaemia is slowly unravelled, management, whether simply supportive, or aimed at selecting patients for immuno-suppressive therapy or bone marrow transplantation, is gradually becoming more rational and effective.

This book represents a synthesis of the experience of eight experimental and clinical haematologists who have a particular interest in the disease in both adult and paediatric practice. The sections on red cell aplasia and the aplasia–leukaemia syndrome are included because the first, an intriguing 'partial' variant of aplastic anaemia itself, may yet provide us with understanding of immunological mechanisms at work in some cases of panhypoplasia, while the second is of importance in an era when marrow depression is increasingly frequently seen in patients treated with cytoxic immunosuppressant drugs, for many different conditions.

We hope that this detailed account of aplastic anaemia will provide an up-to-date and comprehensive account of the disease for all who are involved in its diagnosis and management.

October 1978   COLIN G. GEARY

Preface

1

Pathophysiology of Marrow Hypoplasia

C. G. GEARY and NYDIA G. TESTA

The association of fatty atrophy of the red marrow with cytopenia in the blood was first described by Ehrlich in 1888, though the term 'aplastic anaemia' was probably not used until Chauffard coined it to describe the clinical syndrome in 1904. Although these early descriptions, based on autopsy findings, emphasized hypoplasia of the marrow as a cardinal diagnostic feature, the terminology later became confused, because 'aplastic anaemia' became virtually synonymous with blood pancytopenia. Benzene—the first substance recognized to cause marrow damage—is indeed unusual in producing pancytopenia with both hypocellular and hypercellular marrows, and even extramedullary erythropoiesis (Hunter 1969; Saita 1973), but the main reason for confusion was the lack of a method for examining marrow cellularity during life, marrow puncture not becoming a routine procedure until the late 1930s. Patients with pancytopenia and cellular or hypercellular marrow pictures were subsequently classified as having hypersplenism, 'achrestic anaemia', 'refractory anaemia with cellular marrow' or, in kinetic terms, 'functional aplasia'. Although it is now recognized that many patients with aplastic anaemia have islands of intense, though frequently abnormal, haemopoietic activity, called 'hot pockets' (Kansu & Erslev 1976) (indeed, complete marrow 'aplasia' would be incompatible with life) there still seem to be good clinical grounds for distinguishing between pancytopenic patients with predominantly hypocellular marrows and those with cellular marrows. Thus isolated cytopenias are more common in the 'cellular' group, and the natural history is different: leukaemia may be a more common sequel in the latter group (Vilter et al. 1967), whilst others respond to immunosuppressants. Also, the aetiology probably differs. Apart from benzene, some antimetabolites and possibly chloramphenicol (Bithell & Wintrobe 1967), no substances are known to cause chronic marrow failure with both the hypercellular and hypocellular pictures; X-irradiation may produce the syndrome of pancytopenia with maturation arrest in a normocellular marrow, but this appears often to be a pre-leukaemic picture (Wendt 1971). Although drugs known to cause panhypoplasia also cause selective aplasias of one or other cell lines, the latter are more often reversible on stopping the drug.

Nevertheless, similar qualitative abnormalities of erythropoiesis are found in patients with hypoplastic marrows and those with hyperplastic, ineffective, marrows, while some children with constitutional aplasia present initially with pancytopenia and cellular marrows, and later develop hypoplasia (Fanconi 1967) (see Chapter 8), suggesting that too rigid a distinction should not be made.

DEFINITION AND CLASSIFICATION

Definition. Aplastic anaemia can be defined in morphological or in kinetic terms. The following definition is modified from one suggested by Heimpel and Kubanek (1975): 'a syndrome of peripheral blood pancytopenia, without dominant peripheral blood cell destruction, associated with hypocellularity of haemopoietic tissue, in both intramedullary and extramedullary sites, and without bone marrow fibrosis or invasion by malignant cells'. In kinetic terms, it can be defined as the failure of the early haemopoietic precursor cells (probably multipotential stem cells) to provide sufficient progeny for the maturing, morphologically identifiable cell compartments of the marrow. Dose-dependent transient aplasia does, of course, occur after irradiation or cytotoxic therapy, but, provided stem-cell damage is not profound, the haemopoietic tissue will regenerate and chronic aplasia will not occur (see p. 18). Heimpel and Kubanek have suggested, therefore, that these inevitable but usually rapidly reversible cases of iatrogenic aplasia should be excluded in defining aplastic anaemia, which is usually an 'unpredictable' disease.

Table 1.1. Classification of aplastic anaemia

I Ionizing radiation Cytotoxic chemicals	} dose-dependent

II Chemicals, drugs
     conditional
     immunological
	} largely dose-independent

III Viral cytotoxicity
     direct
     immunological	

IV Autoimmune cytotoxicity	
V Hereditary defect	

After Benestad (1974).

Table 1.2. Kinetic classification of aplasia

Pluripotent stem cells
   (*a*) reduced numbers
   (*b*) defective function

Environmental influences
   (*a*) defects in the bone marrow environment
   (*b*) abnormalities of short or long-range humoral
        factors influencing stem-cell growth
   (*c*) inhibitors of cell growth

Classification. No scheme for the classification of aplastic anaemia is completely satisfactory because the precise way in which marrow damage occurs in aplasia is unknown. In the majority, the disease arises as the result of an apparently idiosyncratic (genetically determined?) reaction to the environmental agent. The possible ways in which drugs might provoke this idiosyncratic response, and damage marrow cells, are discussed in Chapter 2. Table 1.1 summarizes possible pathophysiological mechanisms, and Table 1.2 shows a kinetic classification of aplastic anaemia.

HAEMOPOIETIC STEM CELLS

Stem cells occur in all rapidly dividing tissues and are customarily defined as those that can both maintain their own numbers and give rise to differentiated cells. The haemopoietic system, in fact, is a cell-renewal system in which a continued supply of differentiated non-dividing blood cells is sustained by the proliferation and differentiation of such ancestral, pluripotent cells (Fig. 1.1). The mouse spleen colony assay (Till & McCulloch 1961) detects cells, operationally defined as colony-forming units (CFU-S), which have the properties defined above: they have extensive self-renewal and differentiation capacity and give rise to clonal colonies which contain cells of the granulocytic, erythroid and megakaryocytic series (Siminovitch et al. 1963). Although there is, as yet, no assay available for human haemopoietic stem cells, recent reports of mixed colonies of unicellular origin derived from cultured mouse cells, and containing erythroid, granulocytic and megakaryocytic cells (Johnson & Metcalf 1977), suggest that clonal stem cell growth from human bone marrow haemopoietic tissue may be achieved in the near future.

There are, however, colony assays originally developed for mouse cells, which can be applied to the study of human haemopoiesis. Two different populations of cells give rise to *in vitro* colonies composed of recognizable erythroid cells. One type of colony-forming cell has been

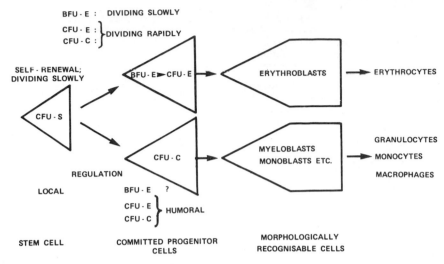

Fig. 1.1. The haemopoietic stem cell and some of its progeny. For an explanation of the abbreviations, see text. Populations of non-T lymphocytes are derived from a common 'myelolymphoid' stem cell, at least in some myeloproliferative syndromes (Fralkow 1978). This may explain the lymphopenia seen in severe aplastic anaemia.

named 'burst-forming unit, erythroid' (BFU-E) due to the character-istic arrangement of the cells in the fully developed colonies (Axelrad et al. 1974). A more mature cell, CFU-E ('colony forming unit, erythroid'), progeny of the former (Gregory & Heubelman 1977) gives rise to small colonies (Stephenson et al. 1971; Iscove et al. 1974). These two assays require the presence in the cultures of erythropoietin (Epo), a humoral regulator of erythropoiesis. Although, in contrast to the CFU-E, the BFU-E themselves do not appear to be regulated by Epo *in vivo*, their progeny became sensitive to Epo at some time during the growth of the bursts (Iscove 1977a).

Another method, also based on colony formation *in vitro*, permits the study of a cell population (CFU-C) which gives rise to colonies of granulocytes and/or macrophages when molecules with colony-stimulating activity (CSA) are present in the cultures (Bradley & Metcalf 1966; Pike & Robinson 1970). Examples of these different types of colonies are seen in Fig. 1.2.

In the generally accepted sequence of differentiation in the haemo-poietic system, the cell populations which give rise to these colonies are considered to be committed progenitor cells, subject to different regulatory mechanisms from those acting at the pluripotent stem-cell level (McCulloch et al. 1965; Curry & Trentin 1967; Lajtha & Schofield 1974). An enumeration and brief description of the assays available for the study of stem cells and committed progenitor cells is presented in

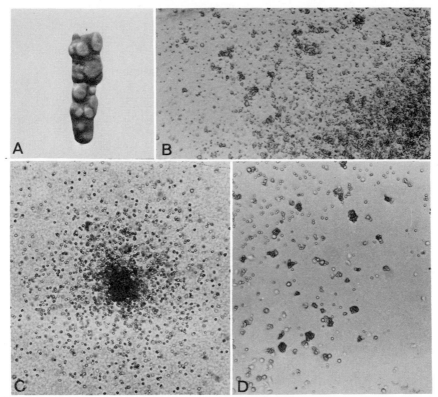

Fig. 1.2. A, Mouse spleen with surface colonies (CFU-S assay). B, Portion of an erythroid burst grown in methylcellulose (BFU-E assay). C, Granulocyte–macrophage colony grown in agar (CFU-C assay). D, Erythroid colonies grown in methylcellulose (CFU-E assay).

Table 1.3. Such colony assays have shown that bone marrow from patients with aplastic anaemia possesses reduced or undetectable numbers of progenitor cells, both for the granulocyte/macrophage series (CFU-C) (Kurnick et al. 1971; Greenberg & Schrier 1973; Kern et al. 1977) and for the erythroid series at both the CFU-E and the BFU-E levels (Hansi et al. 1977; Moriyama 1978). Other *in vitro* colony assays which detect progenitors of megakaryocytes, B-lymphocytes and T-lymphocytes have been developed recently (Metcalf et al. 1975*a, b*; Rozenszajn et al. 1975), but will not be discussed here.

Much clinical and experimental evidence indicates that the haemo-poietic system is capable of responding to a high demand for increased cell production, even over a whole lifetime, without failing. For example, aplastic anaemia is not more common in the elderly, nor in patients with chronic haemolytic anaemia, such as hereditary sphero-cytosis, in which the system is under continued stress. CFU-S are

Table 1.3. Assay system for stem and progenitor cells in haematopoieses

Cells	Nomenclature	Method	End point	Regulation	Applicable to man
Stem	CFU-S	Injection into potentially lethally irradiated mouse	Spleen colony	Local regulatory	—
Granulocyte-macrophage progenitor	CFU-C	Culture in agar or viscid medium in the presence of CSA	In vitro colony	Colony-stimulating activity (CSA)	Yes
Erythroid progenitors	BFU-E	Culture in viscid medium in the presence of Epo	In vitro colony	?	Yes
	CFU-E	Same	In vitro colony	Erythropoietin (Epo)	Yes
Megakaryocyte progenitor	CFU-Meg	Culture in agar in the presence of spleen conditioned medium		?	—
B-Lymphocyte progenitor	CFU-B	Culture in agar in the presence of β-mercaptoethanol	In vitro colony	?	—
T-Lymphocyte progenitor	CFU-T	Culture in agar in the presence of phytohaemagglutinin	In vitro colony	?	Yes

Factors present in serum, necessary for the growth of 'bursts' in vitro (Iscove) may be specific regulators.

capable of increasing their turnover, as evidenced by the high proportion undergoing DNA synthesis in experimental situations which require an increased rate of cell production: for example, during development, or regeneration after injury (Becker et al. 1965; Lajtha et al. 1969; Metcalf & Moore 1971). This property, together with an increased number of cell divisions in the more differentiated cell populations, producing an 'amplifying' effect (Lord 1965), makes it possible to maintain comparatively normal production of mature cells with substantially decreased numbers of stem cells. Although a compartment size exceeding 10% of the normal number of stem cells has been postulated as necessary before stem cells differentiate (Boggs et al. 1972; Boggs & Boggs 1976), experiments in which mice were exposed to continuous irradiation at a low dose rate indicate that 1–2% of the normal CFU-S and CFU-C numbers can still maintain femoral bone marrow cellularity at about 50% of the normal value (Testa et al. 1973).

Clearly, the condition necessary to avoid stem-cell exhaustion is that, in situations which provide maximum demand for differentiation, the proportion of stem cells that differentiate, as opposed to those which produce more stem cells, is no higher than 50%, irrespective of the absolute number of stem cells. In fact, it has been calculated that in bone marrow undergoing regeneration only about 40% of CFU-S per cell cycle are removed for differentiation (Lajtha et al. 1971). Physiological stem-cell 'exhaustion' therefore seems an unlikely cause of marrow aplasia if the stem cells are qualitatively normal, although it has been postulated in aplasia due to benzene toxicity (Benestad 1974) (see p. 39). If progressive stem-cell depletion leading to 'exhaustion' of the progenitor cell compartment were a common mechanism of aplastic anaemia, it would be anticipated that many patients with hypoplasia would proceed, inexorably, to total aplasia (Boggs & Boggs 1976), which does not, in fact, occur (see p. 108). However, the stem cell (CFU-S) population in mice is known to be very heterogeneous with regard to self-reproduction (Worton et al. 1969). Any selective damage to the most immature (i.e. those with the highest self-reproductive capacity), would be of more serious consequences than damage that affects either the most mature stem cells or the whole population in a random fashion.

Another example of the remarkable functional reserve of the marrow stem-cell compartment is provided by the work of Morley and Blake (1974a,b) who gave mice small doses of busulphan over long periods. Although marrow CFU-S and CFU-C were severely reduced, with CFU-S and CFU-C at less than 5% of their starting value (Morley

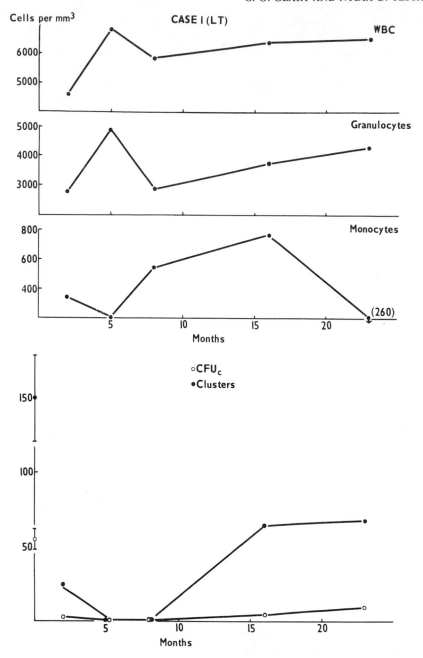

Fig. 1.3. Peripheral blood cell counts. CFU-C (more than 50 cells per colony and clusters (5 to 50 cells) in a patient who presented with thrombocytopenia, normal erythropoiesis, no sideroblasts and apparently normal granulopoiesis 3 years before these determinations. Values in ordinate represent the mean ± 1 sD in normal controls.

et al. 1975) the production of differentiated cells was maintained until haemopoiesis failed after a long period of up to 300 days. A similar situation exists in the W/W^v strain of mice in which the number of CFU-S is about 0·1% of that in normal mice (Russell & Bernstein 1966), yet the numbers of CFU-C and CFU-E are virtually normal (Bennett et al. 1968; Gregory et al. 1974). Evidently, then, a substantially reduced CFU-S compartment can sustain haemopoiesis at normal or nearly normal levels, for long periods. This concept may be of clinical importance, because it suggests that a latent bone marrow failure could exist for a long time without being detected clinically (Morley & Blake 1974a). Certainly some patients *without* granulocytopenia show a persistent defect in CFU-C numbers in the marrow (Fig. 1.3). This unrecognized defect may be of importance in patients undergoing treatment with cytotoxic agents, and could explain apparently idiosyncratic reactions to certain drugs (see Chapter 2).

APLASTIC ANAEMIA AS A DISORDER OF STEM CELLS

The evidence that aplastic anaemia is a disorder of haemopoietic stem cells derives from both clinical and experimental sources. The fact that marrow transplants can be achieved in many patients with aplastic anaemia (Storb & Thomas 1975) suggests a deficit which can be corrected by repopulation of marrow with normal haemopoietic stem cells. It has been shown in at least one case of successful marrow transplantation that, while the haemopoietic cells were identified as those of the donor, the stromal fibroblasts remained those of the patient (Wilson et al. 1978). Nevertheless, the possibility exists that a regulatory cell population (see below) is also transplanted and may correct a marrow defect in some cases. Moreover, the immunosuppressive treatment given to prepare the recipient for the graft might remove inhibitory factors, although this is not true of grafts between identical twins, which may be successful without such preparation (Pillow et al. 1966).

Other largely circumstantial evidence is as follows: the latent period, sometimes of several weeks, between exposure to the suspected toxic agent and onset of clinical aplasia suggests damage to a slowly replicating ancestral cell rather than its more mature progeny (Heimpel & Kubanek 1975) (though injury to a slowly dividing stromal cell might give a similar pattern); the presence of cytogenetic abnormalities in both lymphocytes and marrow cells from some children with constitutional aplasia and in marrow cells from occasional cases of acquired aplasia (El-Alfi et al. 1965; Castaldi &

Mitus 1968); the knowledge that some agents, such as chloramphenicol, benzene and the hepatitis virus, which undoubtedly produce aplasia, can cause chromosomal abnormalities in all marrow cells (Pollini & Combi 1964; Mitus & Coleman 1970); the observation that paroxysmal nocturnal haemoglobinuria and, less commonly, acute leukaemia develop in chronic aplasia, suggesting sequential mutations in an unstable clone. Finally, although it is not yet possible to quantify the ancestral stem cells in human marrow, most patients with aplasia show drastically reduced numbers of their closely related progeny, CFU-C (Table 1.4), and these have been shown to recover

Table 1.4. CFU-C numbers in aplastic anaemia

Reference	No. of cases	$CFU\text{-}C/10^5$ bone marrow cells[*]	
		Patients	Controls
Kurnick et al. (1971)	5	7 (4–8)	25 (16–34)
Greenberg and Shrier (1973)	5	7 (4–9)	26 (14–36)
Kern et al. (1977)	22	3 (0–18)	36 (16–52)

* Mean and range.

after successful marrow transplant (Haak et al. 1977) but rarely after other treatments (Kern et al. 1977), though CFU-E recover more readily (Hansi et al. 1977). Very low or undetectable CFU-C numbers are also observed in refractory cytopenias with cellular bone marrow (with or without increased blast cells) and pre-leukaemias (Greenberg et al. 1971; Senn & Pinkerton 1972; Moore 1974; Sultan et al. 1974; Milner et al. 1977).

The defect in the capacity of the stem-cell compartment to produce its differentiated progeny could arise in several ways. In addition to direct damage to stem cells (Heimpel & Kubanek 1975) defects in the marrow stroma (Knospe & Crosby 1971), regulatory disturbances (Stohlman 1972) or autoimmune damage to the marrow (Ascensao et al. 1976) have been postulated.

Marrow Environment

Aplastic anaemia could arise as a result of damage to the supporting marrow matrix, or 'microenvironment', rather than the haemopoietic stem cell itself. Although the influence of the cellular and humoral environment on the proliferation of developing blood cells is not well understood, there is abundant evidence of its importance (McCulloch et al. 1965; Russell & Bernstein 1966; Trentin 1970; Gidali & Lajtha 1972). The distribution of haemopoiesis in marrow and spleen of adult mice shows that these tissues possess specialized conditions essential for growth and differentiation of haemopoietic cells. Bone marrow, at least in mice, appears to be a highly organized tissue where the distribution of CFU-S and CFU-C is not random (Lord et al. 1975). Moreover, there is evidence that the microenvironment may exert different regulating influences on stem cells or may induce them to develop along one or other line of differentiation (Trentin 1970). The importance of the environment is illustrated by the defect in a genetically anaemic mouse, the $S1/S1^d$ (Steel) mouse, which possesses normal stem cells, as defined by the spleen colony assay, and by the capacity of its marrow to reconstitute haemopoiesis when injected into lethally irradiated mice, but appears to have a defect in its haemopoietic environment which impairs the proliferation of normal stem cells. The anaemia of this mouse is cured by an implant of spleen tissue which provides a normal environment into which the stem cells can migrate and differentiate (Russell & Bernstein 1966).

Microvasculature

Aplastic anaemia could arise because of direct damage to the marrow sinusoids: the only agent regularly causing aplasia in man which is known to injure blood vessels is X-irradiation (Kistler 1934) and this has been used as a tool to induce experimental aplasia in the marrow of normal rats, using gradually increasing doses (Knospe & Crosby 1971) (Fig. 1.4).

With the smallest dose (below 1000 rads), morphological aplasia occurred at 4 days but regeneration occurred within 14 days. This was interpreted as death of differentiated cells, and a proportion of stem cells; however, a prompt recovery occurred as a result of regeneration of undamaged stem cells in the irradiated area, migration of healthy cells from neighbouring unirradiated marrow, or possibly by heterotypic conversion of uncommitted cells normally resident in the cortex of the bone (Rubin et al. 1977). The microvasculature was presumably left relatively unscathed by such doses. However, at doses of 2000 rads or more, initial recovery was followed, 3 months later, by secondary aplasia: this was ascribed to damage to sinusoidal vascular cells, which have a much longer life cycle than the haemopoietic cells. Haemopoietic cells could not regenerate in this damaged environment.

Nevertheless, some recovery of the sinusoidal microcirculation eventually occurred with doses of less than 4000 rads, so that haemopoiesis was re-established in the irradiated site after about 6 months. When doses of 4000–6000 rads were used, however, aplasia appeared to be permanent, as is often found clinically in the sternal marrow of women receiving irradiation for breast carcinoma (p. 18). Nevertheless, regeneration was still possible, even in heavily irradiated areas, if

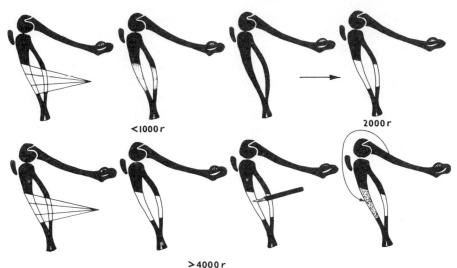

Fig. 1.4. Effects of various doses of local X-irradiation on rat bone marrow. At small doses of 1000 r or less, transient aplasia recovers within 2 weeks. At doses of 2000 r, recovery is followed by secondary aplasia at about 3 months, though this recovers at 6 months. At doses of more than 4000 r, aplasia appears permanent, but marrow implantation from healthy sites was possible if the irradiated site was prepared for the graft by curettage. For a discussion, see text.

the site was vigorously curetted before implantation of isogeneic marrow. These workers postulated that the curettage had provided a suitable matrix into which vascular cells could migrate from local sites, and eventually sustain growth of haemopoietic stem cells, transplanted from elsewhere. Both curettage and implantation of marrow were required before haemopoiesis was restored.

Experiments using this and other animal models in which local marrow injury is achieved by mechanical means (Patt & Maloney 1975), show that haemopoiesis cannot be sustained without an intact matrix, with its specialized sinusoidal architecture. Knospe and Crosby (1971) suggested that marrow sinusoidal damage might result, in the clinical situation, from drug sensitivity, which often has a vascular basis, whatever the target organ. The marrow hypoplasia following graft-versus-host reaction is one of the few clinical situations in which immunological damage to the marrow vasculature can be definitely invoked. Though it cannot be excluded in some cases of drug- or virus-induced aplasia, the evidence at present is that vascular damage is not a *common* cause of chronic aplasia; nevertheless, it might help to explain why 'hot pockets', which presumably contain pluripotent cells, are incapable of repopulating the whole marrow or establishing foci of extramedullary erythropoiesis. However, it is also possible that this inactivity reflects intrinsic abnormalities of such residual stem cells, of which dyserythropoiesis and increased fetal haemoglobin production are also evidence (Kansu & Erslev 1976).

The apparent radioresistance of stromal elements in intact marrow may be related to their low rates of replication, but latent radiation damage can be readily unmasked by conditions which promote their proliferation, such as mechanical injury or heterotopic implantation (Patt & Maloney 1975). Moreover, recent work (Dexter et al. 1978) shows that an *in vitro* environment, capable of maintaining CFU-S proliferation and differentiation for several weeks possesses a very radiosensitive component. In this system, haemopoiesis requires the presence of 'epithelioid' cells (which may be of endothelial origin) as well as fat cells (Fig. 1.5) and macrophages.

Other Components of the Environment

Although interference with the action of erythropoietin appears to be responsible for some cases of pure red cell aplasia (Jepson & Lowenstein 1966) it is unlikely that deficiency of postulated humoral 'poietins' produces panhypoplasia as it would be necessary to invoke simultaneous lack of factors controlling erythro-, granulo- and thrombopoiesis. Moreover, erythropoietin levels are usually raised in

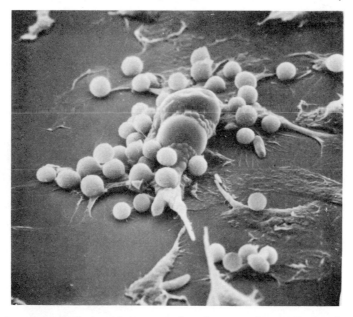

Fig. 1.5. Marrow cells in culture. Scanning electron micrograph showing a fat cell (centre) surrounded by colonies of granulocytic cells. The flat, attenuated 'epithelioid' cells are seen in the foreground and background. For a full description see Allen and Dexter (1976).

chronic aplasia (Hammond et al. 1962, 1968) and CSA production by cells from peripheral blood cells in patients with hypoplasia seems normal (Kern et al. 1977). Although some cases show decreased CSA production by circulating cells (Dicke et al. 1974), no information about production by bone marrow cells is available. However, other factors, produced locally in the bone marrow, may be disturbed in clinical aplasia. Experiments with local irradiation or shielding in mice indicate that CFU-S proliferation is regulated locally; when only one tibia, which contains about 5% of the total CFU-S in the body, is irradiated with 300 rads, the CFU-S surviving the irradiation have a high proportion of the population undergoing DNA synthesis (i.e. presumably proliferating at a higher rate) in spite of the fact that more than 95% of the body's bone marrow is normal. Conversely, when the 95% of the bone marrow is irradiated and 5% (one tibia) shielded, stem-cell proliferation in the shielded tibia remained normal (Gidali & Lajtha 1972). The genetic (see above) and functional, as well as anatomical considerations (Lord & Hendry 1972), indicate that short-range cell interactions play a role in the regulation of stem-cell proliferation. This interaction between stem cells and other, still poorly defined, associated cell populations may result in the induction of proliferation of stem cells, through the production and release of diffusible stimulator(s), which have been detected in bone marrow undergoing haemopoietic regeneration (Lord et al. 1977). Conversely, normal mouse bone marrow (in which the CFU-S are only turning over very slowly), specifically inhibits the proliferation of CFU-S obtained from regenerating bone marrow. It appears that these factors occur physiologically, and the rate of stem-cell proliferation may be adapted to satisfy different requirements by the balancing of stimulatory and inhibitory substances (Lord et al. 1977). As the production of these substances does not appear to be a prerogative of all the cell types in the marrow (Wright & Lord 1978), it is possible that only certain marrow cell subpopulations are responsible for their elaboration. If this is so, a regulatory role may be postulated for these cells and stem cell failure may conceivably be secondary to lesions affecting them. However, this remains at present a theoretical possibility, which could only be tested experimentally when in vitro assays for human haemopoietic stem cells become available. That a similar mechanism may operate at the level of the committed progenitor cells for granulocytes and macrophages has been proposed for certain patients with neutropenia (Senn et al. 1974): in vitro studies indicate that granulocytopenia may be due to a reduced CFU-C compartment, with normal function of the cells which produce an in vitro (and possible in vivo) humoral regulation of granulopoiesis (CSA).

Alternatively, both the CFU-C and the regulatory population may be decreased in numbers as a result of multiple defects or because of a secondary effect on the CFU-C population following a primary lesion on the cells which produce CSA. It is conceivable that, although humoral regulators of the stem cells have not so far been identified in human haemopoietic tissue, analogous lesions could cause aplasia.

A recent report (Jedrzejczak et al. 1977) shows that a cell population, sensitive to anti-theta antiserum, and therefore presumably a type of T-lymphocyte present in normal mouse bone marrow, is required at some stage of differentiation of the erythroid cell line. Although disturbances of these cells could be of relevance in the pathogenesis of red cell aplasia, it is unlikely that this could produce a panhypoplasia.

AUTOIMMUNITY

Immune mechanisms, involving both humoral antibodies and cell-mediated cytotoxicity, can injure proliferating haemopoietic precursor cells in the marrow. The damage may be restricted to a single cell type or involve several simultaneously. The resulting haematological syndrome reflects the cell line(s) involved. The best recognized of these is pure red cell aplasia (p. 195), where autoantibodies to erythroblast precursors are sometimes present, but antibodies to CFU-C, as well as more differentiated myeloid precursor cells, have been demonstrated in certain patients with granulocytopenia (for review, see Cline & Golde 1978). The evidence that aplastic anaemia itself has an auto-immune basis has been summarized by Benestad (1974). The patchy nature of marrow involvement, the absolute marrow lymphocytosis and plasmacytosis found in some cases and the occasional response to immunosuppressants is perhaps the most compelling. On the other hand, chronic marrow aplasia is only rarely found in the clinical setting of disorders known to have an autoimmune basis such as systemic lupus erythematosus or Sjogren's syndrome, though isolated or multiple peripheral blood cytopenias occur comparatively commonly; however, episodes of panhypoplasia have been recorded in the course of autoimmune haemolytic anaemia (Pirofsky 1969), while Cline and Golde (1978) described several patients in whom antibodies to CFU-C and/or CFU-E were associated with a variable marrow hypoplasia; one of these had systemic lupus erythematosus. With the exception of post-hepatitis aplasia and a few cases of thymoma associated with generalized marrow depression, autoantibodies to peripheral blood cells are rarely found in aplastic anaemia. However, it has been argued that an autoimmune attack might be directed against a 'private' antigen expressed only on haemopoietic stem cells and not their mature progeny (Benestad 1974). Thus specific antigens, restricted to one cell type, have already been identified on neutrophils, basophils, eosinophils, monocytes, B and T lymphocytes and myeloblasts; at least one cytopenia—isoimmune neonatal neutropenia—has been identified as due to antibodies reacting with such tissue-specific antigens. Very little is known about the antigenic characteristics of human haemopoietic stem cells, though in the mouse the pluripotent cell has been reported to possess antigens not present on CFU-C. A reliable method for detecting putative antibodies to pluripotent stem cells must await the development of an assay for human CFU-S.

Recently, the possibility of autoimmune cytotoxicity directed against haemopoietic cells has received support from *in vitro* experiments suggesting the presence of T-lymphocytes acting as suppressor cells in marrow hypoplasia. Kagan et al. (1976) observed that lymphocytes in the marrow of a patient with aplastic anaemia could suppress differentiation of granulocytes and proliferation of their own marrow cells in culture. Subsequent removal, by velocity sedimentation, of the lymphoid cells from the remaining marrow cells allowed spontaneous DNA synthesis to occur in these previously suppressed haemopoietic cells. When lymphocytes were removed, the ability of the patient's marrow to form granulocyte colonies in agar culture was much enhanced. In another experiment, treatment *in vitro* of marrow from an aplastic patient with antilymphocyte serum that was shown not to be toxic to CFU-C from normal bone marrow, allowed the aplastic marrow to increase granulocyte colony formation (Ascensao et al. 1976). These workers postulate that suppressor (T) lymphocytes in some patients with aplastic anaemia interfere with the proliferation and differentiation of marrow cells. It has also been shown that marrow lymphocytes from patients with aplastic anaemia can suppress granulopoiesis of normal marrow in agar culture. Kagan (quoted by Good 1977) showed that approximately one-third of patients with aplastic anaemia possessed lymphocytes in their marrows which were capable of suppressing granulocytic colony production when pre-incubated with normal marrow. Hoffman et al. (1976, 1977) also showed that peripheral blood lymphocytes from patients with aplastic anaemia were capable of suppressing erythropoiesis (though not granulopoiesis) *in vitro* in the CFU-E assay; this suppressor influence was found in small children with congenital erythroblastopenia (Blackfan–Diamond syndrome) and also in 5 of 7 adults with acquired aplastic anaemia. However, in their series of 7 children with Fanconi's anaemia, Saunders and Freedman (1978) were unable to show any inhibitory effect of their patients' blood lymphocytes on either CFU-C or CFU-E growth. Although it is tempting to believe that these findings suggest that some cases of aplastic anaemia are indeed due to the effects of cytotoxic lymphocytes on stem cells or at any rate on committed progenitor cells, Good (1977) has pointed out that the observed effects might not be of an immunological nature, but reflect the pathological operation of a normal control mechanism of haemo-poiesis; their presence may thus represent an epiphenomenon of the disease rather than its cause. The observation that removal of lympho-cytes from hypoplastic marrows enhances blood cell production *in vitro* might thus reflect manipulation of a lymphoid population that normally influences haemopoiesis, rather than abrogation of an auto-immune process. Moreover, one must recognize the role of blood transfusions in provoking humoral or cell-mediated immune reactions. Nevertheless, humoral factors which inhibit colony growth of normal marrow were found in two aplastic patients before transfusion (Gordon 1978), while Moore and Broxmeyer (1978) reported that marrow lymphoid cells from aplastic patients suppressed colony growth more effectively than morphologically similar cells from multi-transfused patients with other types of refractory anaemia.

Immunosuppressive Therapy

The occasional response of both drug-related and idiopathic aplastic anaemia to antilymphocyte serum, cytotoxic immuno-suppressants or even, rarely, corticosteroids alone, also suggests that inhibition of cell production is due to immunological processes in some cases. Sometimes chemotherapy has been given to prepare the patient for an allogeneic graft, when re-growth of the patient's own haemopoietic tissue has been observed (Territo 1977). Although one cannot exclude a transient permissive role of the transfused marrow, which might supply inducer substances stimulating stem-cell division, such an explanation is not valid in cases when remission has followed the use of antilymphocyte serum alone (Speck et al. 1978). An instructive case was reported by the Royal Marsden Hospital Bone Marrow Transplantation Team (1977). Two attempts to transplant marrow from an identical twin to a 15-year-old girl with posthepatitis aplasia were only transiently successful, but when the patient was prepared with high-dose cyclophosphamide therapy, as for a non-identical graft, haemopoiesis was re-established. The patient's serum contained a circulating humoral inhibitor which interfered with growth of the twin sister's marrow *in vitro*. This inhibitor was abolished by giving the patient azathioprine, though this drug did not permit a clinical remission; the presence of a cellular inhibitor was suggested by increased colony growth of marrow taken from the recipient after the second (abortive) graft when this was cultured in the presence of ATG.

The subject of immunosuppressive therapy in aplastic anaemia is discussed in Chapters 2 and 7.

APLASIA DUE TO IRRADIATION AND CYTOTOXIC DRUGS

Although the 'predictable' aplasia following X-irradiation and cyto-toxic drugs has a different natural history, compared with the idiosyn-cratic forms, it is briefly discussed here because mild forms of the syndrome are seen in oncological practice, while serious irradiation aplasia has followed industrial accidents, military nuclear tests and occasionally therapeutic irradiation.

The biological effects of irradiation depend on the amount of energy absorbed by the tissue exposed and its specific radiosensitivity. Those most vulnerable are bone marrow, germinal epithelium and intestinal epithelium. Radiation acts by killing cells directly, by reducing the survival time of the progeny of residual stem cells and by prolonging the interphase arrest (Cronkite 1967). The 'haemopoietic syndrome' follows whole body doses within the range of 100–450 rads, consider-ably lower than those required to produce an acute gastrointestinal syndrome. Only the more penetrating forms of external irradiation are likely to damage haemopoietic tissue; nevertheless, α- and β-particles with low penetration may produce serious effects if their carrier reaches the marrow in significant amounts, following ingestion or injection. The effects of irradiation on blood cells are dose-dependent and affect all cell lines, though lymphocytes and erythroblasts are more sensitive than granulocytes, which, in turn, are more sensitive than megakaryocytes.

A single large dose of whole body irradiation leads to profound bone marrow hypoplasia but recovery will normally ensue within weeks if the patient survives this critical period. There is a latent period, between the subsidence of any prodromal symptoms, im-mediately after exposure, and the onset of overt marrow depression, of 2–3 weeks. However, during this period, profound lymphopenia, starting within hours of exposure, and reversible atrophy of lymphoid tissue, are followed by granulocytopenia and thrombocytopenia. In the marrow, changes in erythroblast morphology and ferrokinetic patterns occur within hours of exposure, followed by abnormalities in granulocytes and megakaryocytes. Cell divisions show chromosomal breaks, bridges and abnormal mitoses, and eventually cease, and fatty atrophy ensues (Donati & Gartner 1973). During the period of clinical marrow depression, haemorrhage due to thrombocytopenia, direct vascular damage and, occasionally, circulating anticoagulants, is the most serious risk. Profound neutropenia and an impaired immune response are additional hazards. However, unless bleeding ensues, significant anaemia may not occur because the relatively long life-span of the mature erythrocytes, which are not damaged by doses of this order, will mask temporary cessation of erythropoiesis. Recovery, when it occurs, is usually evident within 6–7 weeks after exposure.

Although marrow doses of this magnitude are never intentionally incurred during whole body irradiation, segmental radiation, given for example for carcinoma of the breast, frequently results in permanent localized aplasia of sternal marrow, if doses exceed 3500 rads (Sykes et al. 1964). At this dose level, damage to the vascular stroma probably inhibits seeding of viable stem cells from other marrow sites (p. 12).

The delayed effects of irradiation are much more variable and unpredictable than the acute. After both acute and chronic exposure some individuals develop selective or combined cytopenias, sometimes associated with abnormalities of maturation in the marrow, and some of these probably constitute pre-leukaemic syndromes (Moloney & Lange 1954). Chromosomal abnormalities have been found in lymphocytes years after exposure to X-irradiation. The incidence of late aplastic anaemia, occurring many years after exposure to a single large or continuous low-dose irradiation, is difficult to estimate and is certainly much lower than that of leukaemia and myeloproliferative disorders (Wendt 1971). Cases have been described in survivors of the atomic bomb explosions and in individuals accidentally exposed to fall-out in nuclear tests (Conrad & Hickling 1965; for review see Betz et al. 1971). One difficulty has been to distinguish true aplasia cases from sub-leukaemic leukaemia with a hypoplastic marrow. However, Court-Brown and Doll (1965) reported that, in patients treated for ankylosing spondylitis with radiation doses above 100 rads, there was an increased incidence of marrow aplasia, while in a recent review, Johnson et al. (1977) found, amongst records of 50 cases of non-leukaemic marrow failure occurring as a late sequel of thorotrast administration, that some 20 were compatible with a diagnosis of aplastic anaemia.

CFU Studies

Although most cases of experimental aplasia induced by doses of irradiation, in the 100–450 rad range, appear to recover, serial measurements indicate that regeneration is never quite complete. After a single dose of irradiation to mice (450 rads) the numbers of CFU-S achieved are only slightly subnormal in the femur (Guzman & Lajtha 1970); but after 4 repeated doses of the same magnitude, given at monthly intervals, the stem-cell population reached only 10% of the control numbers. Furthermore, the CFU-S appear to have sustained persistent residual damage (Hendry et al. 1974). Residual damage, as measured by a decrease in their repopulation capacity, was also found in CFU-S from mice made aplastic by continuous busulphan treatment (Morley et al. 1975). However, although the main component of bone marrow damage was found in the stem cell compartment, environmental damage, of an unknown nature, was found both after repeated irradiation, and after busulphan treatment. Cyclophosphamide, at high dosage, also appears to damage haemopoietic stroma (Tavassoli 1975). This may have importance in patients having repeated courses of radiation, alone or combined with cytotoxic drugs. The regional variations in regenerative capacity at different marrow sites, seen after repeated courses of X-ray therapy, may reflect genetically determined differences, but a progressive disturbance of a humoral mechanism has also been postulated (Tavassoli 1975).

Chemotherapy

With some forms of chemotherapy, the pluripotent stem-cell compartment may be largely spared and temporary hypoplasia reflect damage to the more mature transit compartments of the marrow. For example, marrow cellularity in the mouse recovers to normal within 7 days of a single dose of methotrexate, a cycle-active (or 'S-phase dependent') drug. A single dose of cytosine arabinoside, another cycle-active agent, has little effect on transplantable mouse spleen colony-forming cells, while non-cycle-dependent agents such as nitrogen mustard and cyclophosphamide have profound effects (Valeriote & Tolen 1972; Boggs & Boggs 1973).

However, repeated doses of cycle-active drugs will eventually produce depletion of the stem-cell compartment (Bruce et al 1969) and this will be greatly enhanced if combined with 'pulses' of an alkylating agent, as often used in the treatment of malignant tumours. The long-term effect of such therapy may well be a chronic depletion of the stem-cell compartment. One example of such damage may be cited: the sudden onset of prolonged, or irreversible, marrow aplasia in a few patients with chronic myeloid leukaemia given continuous busulphan therapy.

SUMMARY

Aplastic anaemia is a haematological syndrome in which pancytopenia is associated with chronic fatty atrophy of the marrow and is due to depletion of, damage to or inhibition of haemopoietic stem cells or their supporting microenvironment. Damage affecting predominantly the rapidly dividing, maturing progeny of these ancestral cells, such as may occur with certain drugs and infections, will not usually lead to chronic aplasia. Moreover, the normal stem-cell compartment has substantial powers of recovery: profound marrow hypoplasia is frequently encountered following irradiation or treatment with cytotoxic drugs, but this predictable, largely dose-related marrow depression only rarely leads to chronic aplasia, although long-term depletion of stem cells and defects in the marrow environment are sometimes demonstrable after morphological recovery.

On the other hand, the uncommon, unpredictable type occurring after exposure to non-cytotoxic drugs, virus infections or as an 'idiopathic' disorder, is often irreversible and appears to accompany a permanent quantitative and/or qualitative change in the stem-cell compartment of the marrow. The pathogenetic factors at work may not always act directly on haemopoietic stem cells: damage or inhibition may be indirect, mediated through changes in the cellular or humoral environment of this ancestral cell; evidence is accumulating that, in some cases, these processes are of an autoimmune nature.

REFERENCES

ALLEN, T. D. & DEXTER, T. M. (1976) Cellular interrelations during in vitro granulopoiesis. *Differentiation*, 6, 191.

ASCENSAO, W., KAJAN, W., MOORE, M., PAKWA, R., HANSEN, J. & GOOD, R. (1976) Aplastic anaemia; evidence for an immunological mechanism. *Lancet*, i, 669.

AXELRAD, A. A., McLEOD, D. L., SHREEVE, M. M. & HEATH, D. A. (1974) Properties of cells that produce erythrocytic colonies in vitro. In *Hemopoiesis in Culture*, ed. W. Robinson, p. 226. Washington, D.C.: U.S. Government Printing Office.

BECKER, A. J., McCULLOCH, E. A., SIMINOVITCH, L. & TILL, J. E. (1965) The effect of differing demands for blood cell production on DNA synthesis by hemopoietic colony-forming cells of mice. *Blood*, 26, 296.

BENESTAD, H. B. (1974) Aplastic anaemia: considerations on the pathogenesis. *Acta med. scand.*, 196, 255.

BENNETT, H., CUDKOVICZ, R. S., FOSTER, J. R. & METCALF, D. (1968) Hemopoietic progenitor cells of W anemic mice studied in vivo and in vitro. *J. Cell Physiol.*, 71, 211.

BETZ, E. H., COTTIER, H., NAKAO, K. & ODARTCHENKO, N. (1971) Late effects on haemopoiesis and life-shortening. In *Manual on Radiation Haematology*, p. 181. Vienna: International Atomic Energy Agency.

BITHELL, T. C. & WINTROBE, M. M. (1967) Drug-induced aplastic anaemia. *Semin Hemat.*, 4, 208.

BOGGS, D. R. & BOGGS, S. S. (1976) The pathogenesis of aplastic anaemia; A defective pluripotent haematopoietic stem cell with inappropriate balance of differentiation and self-replication. *Blood*, 48, 71.

BOGGS, S. S. & BOGGS, D. R. (1973) Cell-cycling characteristics of exogenous spleen colony-forming units. *J. Lab. clin. Med.*, 82, 740.

BOGGS, S. S., CHERVENICK, P. A. & BOGGS, D. R. (1972) The effect of post-irradiation bleeding or endotoxin on proliferation and differentiation of hematopoietic stem cells. *Blood*, 40, 375.

BRADLEY, T. R. & METCALF, D. (1966) The growth of mouse bone marrow cells in vitro. *Aust. J. exp. Biol. med. Sci.*, 44, 87.

BRUCE, W. R., MEIKER, B. E., POWERS, W. E. & VALERIOTE, F. A. (1969) Comparison of the dose and time survival curves for normal hemopoietic and lymphoma colony-forming cells exposed to vinblastine, arabinosylcytosine and amethopterin. *J. natn. Cancer Inst.*, 42, 1015.

CASTALDI, G. & MITUS, W. J. (1968) Chromosome vacuolisation and breakage. *Archs intern. Med., Chicago, 121*, 177.

CHAUFFARD, M. (1904) Un cas d'anaemie pernicieuse aplastique. *Bull. Mém. Soc. méd. Hôp. Paris, 21*, 313.

CLINE, M. J. & GOLDE, D. W. (1978) Immune suppression of haematopoiesis. *Am. J. Med., 64*, 301.

CONRAD, R. A. & HICKLING, A. (1965) Medical findings in Marshallese people exposed to fall-out radiation: results from a 10 year study. *J. Am. med. Ass., 192*, 457.

COURT-BROWN, W. M. & DOLL, R. (1965) Mortality from cancer and other causes after radiotherapy for ankylosing spondylitis. *Br. med. J., 2*, 1327.

CRONKITE, E. P. (1967) Radiation-induced aplastic anaemia. *Semin. Hemat., 4*, 273.

CURRY, J. L. & TRENTIN, J. H. (1967) Hemopoietic spleen colony studies. I. Growth and differentiation. *Devl Biol., 15*, 395.

DEXTER, T. M., SPOONCER, E., HENDRY, J. H. & LAJTHA, L. G. (1978) Stem cells in vitro. In *Hematopoietic Cell Differentiation (ICN-UCLA Symposia on Molecular and Cellular Biology, Vol. X)*, ed. D. W. Golde, M. S. Cline, D. Metcalf & C. F. Fox. New York: Academic Press. in the press.

DICKE, K. A., VAN PUTTEN, L. M., OBER-KIEFTENBURG, V. & LOWENBERG, B. (1974) Standardization of human bone marrow cultures (Robinson assay) and its application in aplastic anaemia. In *Leukaemia and Aplastic Anaemia*, ed. D. Metcalf, M. Condorelli & C. Peschle. Rome: Il Pensiero Scientifico.

DONATI, R. M. & GARTNER, G. E. (1973) Haematological aspects of radiation exposure. In *Blood Disorders due to Drugs and Other Agents*, ed. R. H. Girdwood, p. 241. Amsterdam: Excerpta Medica.

EHRLICH, P. (1888) Uber einen Fall von Anämie mit Bemerkungen uber regenerative Veranderungen des Knochenmarks. *Charité-Annln, 13*, 300.

EL-ALFI, O. S., SMITH, P. M. & BIESELE, J. J. (1965) Chromosomal breaks in human leukocyte cultures induced by an agent in the plasma of infectious hepatitis patients. *Hereditas, 52*, 285.

FANCONI, G. (1967) Familial constitutional panmyelocytopathy, Fanconi's anaemia. *Semin. Hemat., 4*, 233.

FIALKOW, P. J. (1978) Stem cells and clonal evolution of myeloproliferative diseases studied with glucose-6-phosphate dehydrogenase (G-6-PD) maskers. *Proc. xviiith int. Congr. Haemat., Paris*, 236.

GIDALI, J. & LAJTHA, L. G. (1972) Regulation of haemopoietic stem cell turnover in partially irradiated mice. *Cell Tissue Kinet., 5*, 147.

GOOD, R. A. (1977) Aplastic anaemia: suppressor lymphocytes and haematopoiesis. *New Engl. J. Med., 296*, 41.

GORDON, S. (1978) Circulating inhibitors of granulopoiesis in patients with aplastic anaemia. *Br. J. Haemat., 39*, 491.

GREENBERG, P. L., NICHOLS, W. C. & SCHRIER, S. L. (1971) Granulopoiesis in acute myeloid leukaemia and preleukaemia. *New Engl. J. Med., 284*, 1225.

GREENBERG, P. L. & SCHRIER, S. L. (1973) Granulopoiesis in neutropenic disorders. *Blood, 41*, 753.

GREGORY, C. J. & HEUBELMAN, R. M. (1977) Relationships between early haemopoietic progenitor cells determined by correlation analysis of their numbers in individual spleen colonies. In *Experimental Haematology Today*, ed. S. J. Baum & G. D. Ledney, p. 93. Berlin: Springer Verlag.

GREGORY, C. J., TEPPERMAN, A. D., McCULLOCH, E. A. & TILL, J. E. (1974) Erythropoietic progenitors capable of colony formation in culture: response of normal and genetically anaemic W/W^v mice to manipulations of the erythron. *J. Cell Physiol., 84*, 1.

GUZMAN, E. & LAJTHA, L. G. (1970) Some comparisons of the kinetic properties of femoral and splenic haemopoietic stem cells. *Cell Tissue Kinet., 3*, 91.

HAAK, H. L., GOSELINK, H. M., VEENHOF, W., PELLINKHOF-STADELMANN, S., KLEIVERDA, J. K. & TE VELD, J. (1977) Acquired aplastic anaemia. IV. Histological and CFU studies in transplanted and non-transplanted patients. *Scand. J. Haemat., 19*, 159.

HAMMOND, G. D., ISHIKAWA, A. & KEIGHLEY, G. (1962) Relationship between erythro-poietin and severity of anaemia in hypoplastic and haemolytic states. In *Erythro-poiesis*, ed. L. O. Jacobson & M. Doyle, p. 351. New York: Grune & Stratton.

HAMMOND, G. D., SHORE, N. & MOVASSAGHI, N. (1968) Production, utilisation and excretion of erythropoietin. I. Chronic anaemia. II. Aplastic crisis. III. Erythro-poietic effects of normal plasma. *N.Y. Acad. Sci.*, *149*, 516.

HANSI, W., RICH, I., HEIMPEL, H., HEIT, W. & KUBANEK, B. (1977) Erythroid colony forming cells in aplastic anaemia. *Br. J. Haemat.*, *37*, 483.

HEIMPEL, H. & KUBANEK, B. (1975) Pathophysiology of aplastic anaemia. *Br. J. Haemat.*, *31* (suppl.), 57.

HENDRY, J. H., TESTA, N. G. & LAJTHA, L. G. (1974) Effect of repeated doses of x-rays of 14 MCV neutrons on mouse bone marrow. *Radiat. Res.*, *59*, 645.

HOFFMAN, R., ZANJANI, E. D., LUTTON, J. D., ZALUSKY, R. & WASSERMAN, L. R. (1977) Suppression of erythroid-colony formation by lymphocytes from patients with aplastic anaemia. *New Engl. J. Med.*, *296*, 10.

HOFFMAN, R., ZANJANI, E. D., VILA, J., ZALUSKY, R., LUTTON, J. D. & WASSERMANN, L. R. (1976) Diamond-Blackfan syndrome: lymphocyte-mediated suppression of erythropoiesis. *Science, N.Y.*, *193*, 899.

HUNTER, D. (1969) *Diseases of Occupations*, p. 514. London: English Universities Press.

ISCOVE, N. N. (1977a) The role of erythropoietin in regulation of population size and cell cycling of early and late erythroid precursors in mouse bone marrow. *Cell Tissue Kinet.*, *10*, 323.

ISCOVE, N. N. (1977b) Erythropoietin-independent regulation of early erythropoiesis. *Exp. Hemat.*, *5*, 6.

ISCOVE, N. N., SIEBER, F. & WINTERHALTER, K. H. (1974). Erythroid colony formation in culture of mouse and human bone marrow: analysis of the requirement for erythropoietin by gel filtration and affinity chromatography on agarose-concavalin A. *J. Cell Physiol.*, *83*, 309.

JEDRZEJCZAK, W. W., SHARKIS, S., AHMED, A. & SELL, K. W. (1977) Theta-sensitive cell and erythropoiesis: identification of a defect in W/W^v anaemic mice. *Science, N.Y.*, *196*, 313.

JEPSON, J. H. & LOWENSTEIN, L. (1966) Inhibition of erythropoiesis by a factor present in the plasma of patients with erythroblastopenia. *Blood*, *27*, 425.

JOHNSON, G. R. & METCALF, D. (1977) Pure and mixed erythroid colony formation in vitro stimulated by spleen conditioned medium with no detectable erythro-poietin. *Proc. natn. Acad. Sci., U.S.A.*, *74*, 3879.

JOHNSON, S. A. N., BATEMAN, C. J. T., BEARD, M. E. J., WHITEHOUSE, J. M. & WATERS, H. (1977) Long-term haematological complications of Thorotrast. *Q. Jl Med.*, *46*, 259.

KAGAN, W. A., ASCENSAO, J. A., PAKWA, R. N., HANSEN, J. A., GOLDSTEIN, G., VALERA, E. B., INCIFY, G. S., MOORE, M. A. S. & GOOD, R. A. (1976) Aplastic anaemia: presence in human bone marrow of cells that suppress myelopoiesis. *Proc. natn. Acad. Sci., U.S.A.*, *73*, 2890.

KANSU, E. & ERSLEV, A. J. (1976) Aplastic anaemia with 'hot-pockets'. *Scand. J. Haemat.*, *17*, 326.

KERN, P., HEIMPEL, H., HEIT, W. & KUBANEK, B. (1977) Granulocytic progenitor cells in aplastic anaemia. *Br. J. Haemat.*, *35*, 613.

KISTLER, G. H. (1934) Sequences of experimental infarction in the femurs of rabbits. *Archs Surg., Chicago*, *29*, 589.

KNOSPE, W. H. & CROSBY, W. H. (1971) Aplastic anaemia: a disorder of the bone marrow sinusoidal micro-circulation rather than stem-cell failure? *Lancet, i*, 20.

KURNICK, J. E., ROBINSON, W. A. & DICKEY, C. A. (1971) In vitro granulocytic colony formation potential of bone marrow from patients with granulocytopenia and aplastic anaemia. *Proc. Soc. exp. Biol. Med.*, *137*, 917.

LAJTHA, L. G., GILBERT, C. W. & GUZMAN, E. (1971) Kinetics of haemo-poietic colony growth. *Br. J. Haemat.*, *20*, 343.

LAJTHA, L. G., POZZI, L. V., SCHOFIELD, R. & FOX, M. (1969) Kinetic properties of haemopoietic stem cells. *Cell Tissue Kinet.*, *2*, 39.

LAJTHA, L. G. & SCHOFIELD, R. (1974) On the problem of differentiation in haemopoiesis. *Differentiation*, *2*, 313.

LORD, B. I. (1965) Cellular proliferation in normal and continuously irradiated rat bone marrow studied by repeated labelling with tritiated thymidine. *Br. J. Haemat.*, *11*, 130.

LORD, B. I. & HENDRY, J. H. (1972) The distribution of haemopoietic colony-forming units in the mouse femur and its modification by x-rays. *Br. J. Radiol.*, *45*, 110.

LORD, B. I., MORI, K. J. & WRIGHT, E. G. (1977) A stimulator of stem cell proliferation in regenerating bone marrow. *Biomedicine*, *27*, 223.

LORD, B. I., TESTA, N. G. & HENDRY, J. H. (1975) The relative spatial distribution of CFU-S and CFU-C in the normal mouse femur. *Blood*, *46*, 65.

McCULLOCH, E. A., TILL, J. E. & SIMINOVITCH, L. (1965) Genetic factors affecting the control of hemopoiesis. In *Canadian Cancer Conference*, ed. R. W. Begg, C. P. Leblond, R. L. Noble, R. J. Rossiter, R. M. Taylor & A. C. Wallace, p. 336. Oxford: Pergamon Press.

METCALF, D., MacDONALD, H. R., ODARTCHENKO, N. & SORDAT, B. (1975*a*) Growth of mouse megakaryocyte colonies in vitro. *Proc. natn. Acad. Sci., U.S.A.*, *72*, 1744.

METCALF, D. & MOORE, M. A. S. (1971) *Haemopoietic Cells*. Amsterdam: North Holland.

METCALF, D., NOSSAL, G. L. V., WARNER, N. L., MILLER, J. F. A. P., MANDEL, T. E., LAYTON, J. E. & GUTMAN, G. A. (1975*b*) Growth of B-lymphocyte colonies in vitro. *J. exp. Med.*, *142*, 1534.

MILNER, G. R., TESTA, N. G., GEARY, C. G., DEXTER, M. T., MULDAL, S., MacIVER, J. E. & LAJTHA, L. G. (1977) Bone marrow culture studies in refractory cytopenia and smouldering leukaemia. *Br. J. Haemat.*, *35*, 251.

MITUS, W. J. & COLEMAN, N. (1970) In vitro effect of chloramphenicol on chromosomes. *Blood*, *35*, 689.

MOLONEY, W. & LANGE, R. D. (1954) Leukaemia in atomic bomb survivors. II. Observations on early phases of leukaemia. *Blood*, *9*, 663.

MOORE, M. A. S. (1974) In vitro studies in the myeloid leukaemias. In *Advances in Acute Leukaemia*, ed. F. J. Cleton, D. Crowther & J. S. Malpas. Amsterdam: North Holland.

MOORE, M. A. S. & BROXMEYER, H. (1978) Possible role of suppressor cells in the pathophysiology of aplastic anaemia. *Proc. xviith int. Congr. Haemat., Paris*, 823.

MORIYAMA, Y. (1978) A lack of burst forming units in patients with aplastic anaemia. In *In Vitro Aspects of Erythropoiesis*, ed. M. J. Murphy. Berlin: Springer Verlag.

MORLEY, A. & BLAKE, J. (1974*a*) An animal model of chronic aplastic marrow failure. I. Late marrow failure after busulphan. *Blood*, *44*, 49.

MORLEY, A. & BLAKE, J. (1974*b*) Late changes in the number of stem and haemopoietic progenitor cells in experimental hypoplastic marrow failure. *Aust. J. exp. Biol. med. Sci.*, *52*, 909.

MORLEY, A., TRAINOR, K. & BLACK, J. (1975) A primary stem cell lesion in experimental hypoplastic marrow failure. *Blood*, *45*, 681.

PATT, & MALONEY, W. (1975) Marrow regeneration after local injury. *Exp. Hemat.*, *3*, 135.

PIKE, B. L. & ROBINSON, W. A. (1970) Human bone marrow colony growth in agar-gel. *J. Cell Physiol.*, *76*, 77.

PILLOW, R. P., EPSTEIN, R. B., BRUCKNER, C. D., GIBLETT, E. R. & THOMAS, E. D. (1966) Treatment of marrow failure by isogeneic marrow infusion. *New Engl. J. Med.*, *275*, 94.

PIROFSKY, B. (1969) *Autoimmunisation and the Autoimmune Haemolytic Anaemias*, p. 86. Baltimore: Williams & Wilkins.

POLLINI, G. & COLOMBI, R. (1964) In danno chromosomico midollare nell'anaemia aplastica benzolica. *Medna Lav.*, *55*, 241.

ROYAL MARSDEN HOSPITAL BONE-MARROW TRANSPLANTATION TEAM (1977) Failure of syngeneic bone-marrow graft without preconditioning in post-hepatitis marrow aplasia. *Lancet*, *ii*, 742.

ROZENSZAJN, L. A., SHOMAN, D. & KALECHMAN, I. (1975) Clonal proliferation of PHA-stimulated human lymphocytes in soft agar culture. *Immunology*, *29*, 1041.

RUBIN, P., ELBADAWI, N. A., THOMSON, R. A. E. & COOPER, R. A. (1977). Bone marrow regeneration from cortex following segmental fractionated irradiation. *Int. J. Radiation Oncol. Biol. Phys.*, *2*, 27.

RUSSELL, E. S. & BERNSTEIN, S. E. (1966) Blood and blood formation. In *Biology of the Laboratory Mouse*, ed. E. L. Green, 2nd ed., p. 351. New York: McGraw-Hill.

SAITA, G. (1973) Benzene induced hypoplastic anaemias and leukaemias. In *Blood Disorders due to Drugs and Other Agents.*, ed. R. H. Girdwood, p. 132. Amsterdam: Excerpta Medica.

SAUNDERS, E. F. & FREEDMAN, M. H. (1978) Constitutional aplastic anaemia: defective haematopoietic stem cell growth in vitro. *Br. J. Haemat.*, in the press.

SENN, J. S., MESSNER, H. A. & STANLEY, E. R. (1974). Analysis of interacting cell populations in cultures of marrow from patients with neutropenia. *Blood*, *44*, 33.

SENN, J. S. & PINKERTON, P. H. (1972) Defective in vitro colony formation by human bone marrow preceding overt leukaemia. *Br. J. Haemat.*, *23*, 277.

SIMINOVITCH, L., MCCULLOCH, E. A. & TILL, S. E. (1963) The distribution of colony-forming cells among spleen colonies. *J. Cell comp. Physiol.*, *62*, 327.

SPECK, B., GLUCKMAN, E., HAAK, H. L. & VAN ROOD, J. J. (1978) Treatment of aplastic anaemia by antilymphocyte globulin with and without marrow infusion. *Clin. Hemat.*, *7*, 611.

STEPHENSON, J. R., AXELRAD, A. A., MCLEOD, D. L. & SHREEVE, M. M. (1971) Induction of colonies of hemoglobin-synthesizing cells by erythropoietin in vitro. *Proc. natn. Acad. Sci., U.S.A..*, *68*, 1542.

STOHLMAN, F. (1972) Aplastic anaemia (editorial). *Blood*, *40*, 282.

STORB, R. & THOMAS, E. D. (1975) Bone marrow transplantation for aplastic anaemia. *Br. J. Haemat.*, *31* (Suppl.), 83.

SULTAN, C., MARQUET, M. & JOFFROY, Y. (1974) Etude de certains dysmyelopoieses acquises idiopatiques et secondaires par culture de moelle in vitro. *Ann. Med. intern.*, *125*, 599.

SYKES, M. P., SAVEL, H., CHU, F. C., BONADONNA, G., FARROW, J. & MATHIS, M. (1964) Long-term effects of therapeutic irradiation upon the bone marrow. *Cancer, N.Y.*, *17*, 1144.

TAVASSOLI, M. (1975) Studies on hemopoietic microenvironment. *Exp. Hemat.*, *3*, 213.

TERRITO, M. C. (1977) Autologous bone marrow repopulation following high dose cyclophosphamide and allogeneic marrow transplantation in aplastic anaemia. *Br. J. Haemat.*, *36*, 305.

TESTA, N. G., HENDRY, J. H. & LAJTHA, L. G. (1973) The response of mouse haemopoietic colony formers to acute or continuous gamma irradiation. *Biomedicine*, *19*, 183.

TILL, J. E. & MCCULLOCH, E. A. (1961) A direct measurement of the radiation sensitivity of normal mouse bone marrow cells. *Radiat. Res.*, *14*, 213.

TRENTIN, J. J. (1970) Influence of hematopoietic organ stroma (hematopoietic inductive microenvironment) on stem-cell differentiation. In *Regulation of Hematopoiesis*, ed. A. S. Gordon, p. 161. New York: Appleton-Century-Crofts.

VALERIOTE, F. A. & TOLEN, S. J. (1972) Survival of haematopoietic and lymphoma colony-forming cells in vivo following the administration of a variety of alkylating agents. *Cancer Res.*, *32*, 470.

VILTER, R. W., WILL, J. J. & JARROLD, T. (1967) Refractory anaemia with hyperplastic bone marrow. *Semin. Hemat.*, *4*, 175.

WENDT, F. (1971) Differential diagnosis of radiation injury. In *Manual on Radiation Haematology*, p. 298. Vienna: International Atomic Energy Authority.

WILSON, F. D., GREENBERG, B. R., KONRAD, P. N., KLEIN, A. K. & WALLING, P. A. (1978) Cytogenetic studies on bone marrow fibroblasts from a male–female hematopoietic chimera. *Transplantation*, *2*, 87.

WORTON, R. G., MCCULLOCH, E. A. & TILL, J. E. (1969) Physical separation of haemopoietic cells differing in their capacity for self renewal. *J. exp. Med.*, *130*, 91.

WRIGHT, E. & LORD, B. I. (1978) Personal communication.

2

Drug Mechanisms in Marrow Aplasia

HAAKON B. BENESTAD

Bone marrow aplasia is probably the most feared of all drug complications. Fortunately, it is a rare iatrogenic disorder. Marrow aplasia accounted for about 0·5% of all recent reports (1970–7) to the Norwegian Adverse Drug Reaction Committee (Lunde, personal communication). The disease may run an acute or chronic course, with an anticipated 5-year mortality of about 70% and a complete recovery rate of only 10% (Williams et al. 1973).

Approximately half the cases of marrow aplasia are idiopathic, and the majority of the remainder are caused by drugs. Most of us are constantly or intermittently exposed to a variety of drugs or other chemicals, present in our environment, of which we may not be aware. Therefore, many cases of idiopathic aplasias may, in fact, be caused by drugs or chemicals (see p. 50).

DRUGS IMPLICATED

Ehrlich was the first to describe a patient suffering from bone marrow aplasia in 1888. Since then, the reports reflect, to some degree, the changing patterns of exposure to drugs and chemicals. The aplasia caused by benzene was first described in 1897, that caused by arsene in 1916, by salvarsan in 1920 and by gold in 1924. Since the start of the chemotherapeutic and antibiotic era, chloramphenicol has been the drug most commonly implicated, though in many countries anti-inflammatory agents like the butazones seem to have taken the lead now (Table 2.1). However, as new drugs are developed and replace old ones, the causative drugs will certainly change. For example, several patients suffering from aplasia due to penicillamine have recently been reported, whereas this drug is, in general, not yet listed in the textbooks.

The incidence of drug-induced marrow aplasia clearly depends on properties of the drugs, as well as the frequency of their use. The calculated risk figures have varied somewhat, but 1:20 000 for

Table 2.1. Some of the currently most important drugs associated with marrow aplasia

Class	Drug(s)	Incidence* according to					
		Bithell and Wintrobe (1967)	Keiser and Walder (1970)	Speck (1975)	Böttiger and Westerholm (1973)	Williams et al. (1973)	de Gruchy (1975)
Antibiotics and chemotherapeutic drugs	Chloramphenicol	47	48	44	17	69	10
	Sulphonamides, etc.	8	4	—	7	16	5
Anti-inflammatory and antirheumatic drugs	Phenylbutazone	5	12	} 38	14	4	30
	Oxyphenbutazone	—	—		34	2	26
	Gold compounds	2	7	13	—	2	5
	Indomethacin	—	—	—	—	—	5
Anti-epileptic drugs	Diphenylhydantoin Troxidone (trimethadione) etc.	} 7	7	6	—	6	} 4 / 2
Antidiabetic drugs	Chlorpropamide, etc.	3	1	—	—	—	3
Antithyroid drugs	Potassium perchlorate Others	1 / —	} 2	—	—	—	—
Tranquillizers	Chlorpromazine etc.	4	—	—	—	—	—

* Expressed as a percentage of all drug-induced cases.

chloramphenicol and 1:100 000 for the butazones are probably
reasonable estimates. Nevertheless, the incidence of marrow aplasia
caused by the butazones was almost three times higher than that for
chloramphenicol in Sweden between 1966 and 1970, due to the more
frequent use of butazones than of chloramphenicol (Böttiger &
Westerholm 1973).

Many patients have been or are treated with several drugs at the
same time. Moreover, a complete and reliable drug history may be very
difficult to obtain. Therefore, reviewers tend to present long lists of
presumed and/or suspected drug aetiologies (Bithell & Wintrobe 1967;
Williams et al. 1973; de Gruchy 1975; Heimpel & Kern 1976) (see
Table 3.1). It has been pointed out, however, that the majority of cases
of drug-induced marrow aplasia are probably caused by a relatively
small number of drugs (de Gruchy 1975). Consequently, only the most
important or interesting ones are given in Table 2.1. In the following
discussion only a few drugs, which illustrate the different mechanisms
that may be involved in drug-induced marrow aplasia, will be
discussed in some detail.

POSSIBLE PATHOGENETIC MECHANISMS

Drug mechanisms in marrow aplasia may be analysed according to
the scheme given in Table 2.2 and Fig. 2.1. First, on the basis of

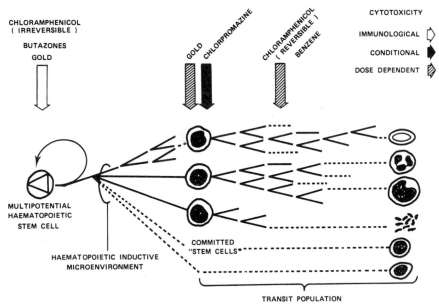

Fig. 2.1. Possible pathogenetic mechanisms involved in damage to bone marrow
cells by certain drugs.

Table 2.2 Scheme for the analysis of drug mechanisms

A. *Damage by*

1. Dose-dependent effects, e.g. cytotoxic drugs, benzene
2. Conditional or idiosyncratic effects (similar in principle to the haemolysis caused, for example, by primaquine in persons with glucose-6-phosphate dehydrogenase deficiency)
3. Immunological or lymphocyte-mediated effects

   a. Hapten cell mechanisms: cell-mediated or humoral immunity against drug (metabolite) complexed to macromolecule on cell surface

   b. Immune complex mechanisms: immune attack (including null lymphocytes, macrophages or complement activation) against a drug–carrier complex secondarily adsorbed to cell surface

   c. Autoimmune mechanisms

      i.   Cell-mediated or humoral immunity against drug-altered cell membranes ± cross reaction with normal cells. Including high-dosage 'spoiled membrane allergy'

      ii   Drug as hapten (see 3a), but cross reaction with normal cellular antigens in addition

      iii. Drug-induced production of auto-reactive clones

   d. Mechanisms involving altered regulatory lymphocytes

B. *Damage of*

1. Haematopoietic stem cells
2. Haematopoietic transit cells
3. Bone marrow stroma or 'microenvironment'

C. *Damage in the form of*

1. Cell killing, e.g. cytotoxic drugs
2. Inactivation of regulatory molecules, e.g. anti-erythropoietin antibodies
3. Other cellular effects, such as blockage of differentiation or maturation; impairment of stem cell self-renewal capacity; exhaustion of stem-cell proliferation capacity. These are all hypothetical mechanisms

---

clinical, laboratory and experimental findings, one must consider whether drug actions are (1) dose-dependent; (2) conditional (i.e. 'idiosyncratic', that is, they give rise to unusual effects or 'meta' reactions, or, in German literature, *pharmakogenetisch* (Gross & Hellriegel 1975)); or (3) immunological. Conditional mechanisms imply that either the target cells or drug metabolism are abnormal. Such defects are most likely to be of a hereditary nature, and they would render bone marrow cells susceptible to damage by the drug or its metabolites. Although such conditional reactions are unexpected, increasing doses will usually give more marked effects, which often occur in connection with drug intake. By contrast, the dose and time relationships are, in general, much more erratic in reactions having immunological causes.

Next, the target of the pathological process, whether stem cells, transit cells or stroma (microenvironment), must be considered. It must be noted that any pathogenetic factor that causes chronic aplasia by attacking the transit populations of the marrow must act continuously. A single damaging event, of strictly limited duration, may in principle be sufficient when the attack is directed against stem cells or stromal cells. Stem cells are, by definition, the ultimate source of blood cells, and stromal cells repair microenvironmental damage very slowly, if at all (Fried et al. 1976).

Finally, clues will be sought which might indicate whether damage is due to cell killing or to disturbed regulation of cell production, such as an impairment of the self-renewal capacity of stem cells.

CLINICAL, LABORATORY AND EXPERIMENTAL FINDINGS IN SELECTED DRUG-INDUCED APLASIAS

The most interesting and enigmatic cases of drug-induced marrow aplasia are those that cannot be explained by the expected, dose-dependent effect of the causative drug, such as occur with cytotoxic agents and antimetabolites. In most of these 'unpredictable' cases very little is known about the pathogenesis of the disease. This is largely due to the rarity of these diseases and to the lack of convenient and relevant animal models. Thus, the following discussion is merely an attempt to define the most likely drug mechanism in chloramphenicol, butazone, gold and chlorpromazine marrow aplasias. In addition, a short note on the marrow damage caused by benzene has been included. Strictly speaking benzene is not a drug, but benzene aplasia is still interesting, and not only for historical reasons. Here convenient animal models do exist, and the dependency of this form of aplasia on bad environmental hygiene and abuse of various organic solvents for 'sniffing' makes it difficult to eradicate totally (p. 46).

Chloramphenicol

Chloramphenicol aplasia has been the most frequent among drug-induced cases, and the one most studied. A dose-dependent and reversible pancytopenia may occur during chloramphenicol treatment, probably because the drug inhibits protein synthesis in mitochondria (Yunis 1973; see Benestad 1974 for additional references). This mechanism is similar to the effects of chloramphenicol on sensitive bacteria, and is a reminder of the hypothesis that mitochondria have evolved from a symbiotic inclusion of a bacterium in an ancestral cell. However, it is unlikely that the mechanism is the same in the dangerous, much rarer, and often irreversible form of bone marrow depression. Here, the aplasia often arises after a small total dose of chloramphenicol, or long after finishing the course of drug treatment.

Table 2.3. Comparison of acute reversible bone marrow suppression and chronic aplastic anaemia due to chloramphenicol

	Reversible suppression	*Aplastic anaemia*
Pathogenesis	Dose-dependent inhibition of mitochondrial protein synthesis, resulting in suppression of ferro-chelatase activity in erythroid precursors and decreased synthesis of cytochromes a + a$_3$ and b in all proliferating cells	Unknown. No relationship to total dose given. Possibly induction of cell-mediated autoimmunity against stem cells
Incidence	Occurs in most patients with blood level above 25 μg/ml	Various estimates: probably 1/20 000 to 1/40 000
Onset	Within days of administration	Commonly late onset, 2 weeks to 6 months after last dose. Most often 6–10 weeks. Previous exposure to chloramphenicol common
Outcome	Recovery on drug withdrawal	Usually fatal

Adapted in part from de Gruchy (1975) and Yunis (1973).

Evidence for the abnormal accumulation of chloramphenicol has been obtained for patients with dose-related bone marrow suppression (Weisberger 1969), but not for patients developing aplasia. The differences between the two types of chloramphenicol side effects are summarized in Table 2.3.

The two most probable mechanisms of damage seem to be drug idiosyncracy and immunity. There are a few reports of identical twins both suffering from chloramphenicol aplasia. Otherwise, there is no firm evidence for a genetic predisposition to chloramphenicol aplasia. Moreover, no consistent association between aplastic anaemia and HLA antigens or haplotypes has been found (Albert et al. 1976). Even if there were a genetic predisposition, this would not make the choice between an idiosyncratic and immune mechanism easier, because the immune response to specific antigens is also influenced by genetic factors.

Firm data establishing whether or not impaired, or aberrant, metabolism of chloramphenicol occurs in aplasia patients are lacking. An enzymatic defect of bone marrow cells, predisposing to chloramphenicol damage, might possibly be present in stem or stromal cells, or both. The transit cells in the marrow might also be susceptible to damage, but it seems that they are generally unaffected. One report (Yunis 1973) claimed that chloramphenicol at a concentration of 25–50 μg/ml *in vitro* decreased DNA synthesis in bone marrow from patients who had recovered from chloramphenicol aplasia. Concentrations above 100 μg/ml were needed significantly to depress DNA synthesis in normal control marrow. Others have found, however, that the susceptibility of normal marrow to chloramphenicol inhibition *in vitro* varies markedly (Morley et al. 1974), and that committed progenitor cells (CFU-C) from patients who have recovered from chloramphenicol aplasia are *not* abnormally sensitive to chloramphenicol *in vitro* (Howell et al. 1975a; Kern et al. 1975). Finally, the majority of stem and stromal cells probably do not engage, at least detectably, in DNA synthesis during such short periods of drug exposure *in vitro*. Therefore, the hypothesis that a defect in DNA metabolism determines the development of the aplasia, by rendering bone marrow cells susceptible to damage by chloramphenicol, has relatively little experimental evidence to support it.

The rare occurrence of chloramphenicol aplasia is compatible with an idiosyncratic reaction, but the apparent lack of relationship to drug dosage and duration of therapy, as well as the very variable interval between last dose taken and first symptom, is different from the situation in other idiosyncratic reactions, as for example drug induced haemolysis in G-6-PD deficient negroes (Allan 1973). Taken together, the evidence supporting idiosyncrasy is therefore meagre.

The case for an immunological mechanism is also problematic. Some findings certainly suggest a kind of allergy. For example Böttiger (1974) recorded an 87-year-old man, given a total dose of 15 g of chloramphenicol during two periods, with an interval of about 1 month between the two. The patient had a rash on both occasions and died from haemorrhage 1 week after diagnosis of aplasia was made. A 12-year-old boy had received chloramphenicol on several occasions during the previous 2 years; he then developed marrow aplasia after a course of chloramphenicol amounting to 1–2 g. Previous chloramphenicol courses without ill effects, the small total dose needed to induce the development of aplasia, and accumulation of lymphocytes and plasma cells in the affected marrow all favour an immune mechanism rather than idiosyncrasy. The variable course of the disease, ranging from an acute, lethal illness to a milder depression of cell formation in the marrow, continuing for several years, suggests the existence of an active uninterrupted process, probably of an immunological nature.

As discussed elsewhere (p. 17), autologous marrow repopulation has been reported in patients suffering from aplastic anaemia, including those possibly caused by chloramphenicol (Jeannet et al. 1976; Territo 1977). The patients were immunosuppressed with antilymphocyte globulin or cyclophosphamide and given allogeneic marrow, probably without engraftment. The most plausible explanation of these and similar cases is that the immunosuppressive preconditioning of the patients for marrow transplantation disrupted an immune process that was the cause of the aplasia. One alternative explanation, that the unsuccessful bone marrow graft still conferred some vital stimulatory factor or cell type needed by the diseased marrow, could not be excluded. Such an explanation could, however, be excluded in the single case reported by Baran et al. (1976), where recovery from aplastic anaemia, possibly caused by chloramphenicol, was associated with cyclophosphamide treatment of the patient.

Recently, several workers (see Good 1977 for references) have claimed that lymphocytes present in blood or bone marrow of patients with marrow aplasia, of both the idiopathic and the drug-induced varieties, may prevent autologous or normal, erythroid or granuloid–macrophage progenitor cells (CFU-E or CFU-C) from forming colonies in culture. This subject is discussed in greater detail in Chapter 1.

There are other clinical observations, however, that give indirect support for an immune pathogenesis of marrow aplasia in general. Some patients with a thymoma suffer from pure red cell anaemia, apparently caused by antibodies against erythropoietin or early erythroblasts. This anaemia may be associated with other diseases considered to be of an autoimmune nature. The isolated erythroid hypoplasia may, in a minority of patients, evolve into a generalized aplastic anaemia (see p. 195). Drugs suspected or known to cause aplastic anaemia also cause autoimmune haemolytic anaemia (α-methyldopa) (de Gruchy 1975), immunological thrombocytopcnia (e.g. diphenylhydantoin) (Petz & Fudenberg 1975), haemolytic anaemia (e.g. sulphonamides) (Petz & Fudenberg 1975), or agranulocytosis (e.g. sulphonamides, chlorpropamide and gold salts) (Petz & Fudenberg 1975), in which immunological mechanisms may be involved.

Some observations are difficult to reconcile with an immunological mechanism. Reactive lymphoid cells—'immunoblasts'—can be detected in the blood during immune and autoimmune reactions. Increased numbers of such cells have not generally been found in patients with drug-induced aplastic anaemia (Bacon et al. 1975). Corticosteroids often relieve symptoms of immune disorders, but they have in general been disappointing in aplastic anaemia. Even more significantly, early marrow transplantation has been successful as a treatment of severe aplastic anaemia (Camitta et al. 1976). This success would scarcely be expected if the transplanted stem cells contain the target antigen(s) of an immune reaction. However, these latter results would be compatible with an immunological pathogenesis if the immune reaction were directed against an antigen where the drug (metabolite) is an essential hapten. This possibility is unlikely, since the aplasia may occur so late after the last dose of chloramphenicol that the drug has probably been completely cleared from the body. The success of transplantation would also be explicable if the immune reaction had already burnt out, as it may do, for example, shortly after withdrawal of α-methyldopa in autoimmune haemolytic anaemia. However, there are often signs of a chronic, active, destructive process taking place in the bone marrow of these patients (see above). Finally, the immuno-suppressive treatment used to condition the patient for the transplant might prevent not only an immune response against minor histocompatibility antigens of the donor cells, but also the further operation of the pathogenetic immune reaction. It might be argued against this last explanation that, in a few cases, marrow transplantation to an aplastic patient from an identical twin has been successful without any immunosuppressive pretreatment (Pegg & Burns 1965; Harvey & Firkin 1968; Thomas et al. 1976). However, it is doubtful whether chloramphenicol could be incriminated in any of these.

Taken together, therefore, the balance of evidence appears to favour an immunological pathogenesis of marrow aplasia caused by chloramphenicol, but the issue is far from settled. On the evidence available, no definite statement can be made concerning the type of immune mechanism involved. However, the possibility of a long latent period between the last dose of chloramphenicol and the appearance of symptoms, and particularly the protracted course of active disease, make hapten cell mechanisms and immune complex mechanisms (Table 2.2 A/3/a and b) less likely ones. An altered function of the lymphocytes regulating stem cell proliferation, self-renewal and differentiation (Table 2.2 A/3/d) is conceivable but lacks experimental support. Among the hypothetical autoimmune mechanisms (Table 2.2) the high-dosage 'spoiled membrane allergy' of Nieweg (1973) can probably be ruled out by its dose requirements. Future development of assay systems applicable to multipotent human stem cells, and practical animal models for the kind of aplasia exemplified by chloramphenicol aplasia, may permit meaningful exploration of the remaining immune mechanisms.

The target of the pathogenetic process is probably the multipotent stem cells, and not stromal or transit cells. Successful bone marrow transfusion argues against a defective stroma. The findings that (a) the disease may appear a long time after completion of a course of drug treatment, (b) the few granulocyte macrophage progenitor cells (CFU-C) that can be retrieved from the patient's marrow seem to divide and mature normally in culture (Kern et al. 1977), and (c) the ^{3}H-thymidine labelling index of erythroblasts *in vitro* lies apparently within the normal range, are all difficult to reconcile with a primary damage of transit cells. The possibility that the 'soil' (haematopoietic micro-environment or stroma) is defective, rather than the 'seed' (stem cells) has been further discussed elsewhere (see Chapter 1; Benestad 1974). It cannot be totally dismissed, in particular if one believes in immune mechanisms. In any case, whether a putative immune attack is directed against stem cells or stromal cells, it is certainly puzzling that marrow transfusion can be therapeutically effective.

The simplest mechanism of depressing haematopoiesis in chlor-amphenicol aplasia would appear to be a direct killing of stem cells, whether by T-lymphocytes or by antibodies plus complement, null lymphocytes or macrophages. Experimentally, antibodies have been produced which react with mouse stem cells, but not with differen-tiated haematopoietic cells (Van den Engh & Golub 1974). Additional or alternative mechanisms have been proposed (Table 2.2). Available evidence does not support the possibility that established or putative regulatory molecules are being inactivated (see p. 13), except when antierythropoietin antibodies are present in pure red cell anaemia. In general erythropoietin levels and levels of granulocyte–macrophage colony-stimulating activity (CSA) are what would be expected from consideration of the degree of anaemia and number of CSA-producing mononuclear phagocytes present in the patients (Kern et al. 1977).

Theoretically, cell production may be decreased by blocking stem-cell differentiation (Kagan et al. 1976), by reducing stem-cell self-renewal capacity (Boggs & Boggs 1976), and by exhausting the proliferative capacity of the stem cells by placing excessive proliferative demands on them (see Chapter 1). The experimental evidence to date is rather meagre and circumstantial. To a large extent it stems from an animal model that may not be entirely relevant to human aplastic anaemia (Morley et al. 1975). Therefore, since experimental support for these hypothetical mechanisms is lacking, it should not be forgotten that simple concepts like immune 'killing' may well explain the relevant findings (Fig. 2.1).

Butazones (Pyrazolone Drugs)

Even though these drugs now seem to be the most commonly reported cause of marrow aplasia, relatively few detailed studies have been published on this type of aplasia. Characteristic features of phenylbutazone aplastic anaemia have been the occurrence of symptoms after a prolonged course of treatment ($\geqslant 4$ months), with total doses exceeding 50 g, and while the drug was still being taken

(Hale & de Gruchy 1960; McCarthy & Chalmers 1964): A normal 14-day course of treatment would give a total dose of about 6 g. A preponderance of females has been reported, probably reflecting the type of diseases treated (Fowler 1967). Most patients have been older than 50 years (McCarthy & Chalmers 1964). Hale and de Gruchy (1960) pointed out that the marrow aplasia was usually not associated with other known toxic or allergic side reactions of phenylbutazone. Some of these features have been contrasted with findings in phenyl-butazone-induced agranulocytosis, a disorder that is often rapidly reversible after withdrawal of the drug. The patients suffering from agranulocytosis are usually younger ones; the disease appears earlier after the start of drug therapy; there may be an associated skin rash and no apparent relation to dosage, which might be only a few grams. On the other hand, it appears that oxyphenbutazone, a metabolite of phenylbutazone, may induce marrow aplasia characterized by a lack of relationship to total dose given and duration of treatment. For example, two of the patients reported by Brownlie and Strang (1969) developed bone marrow hypoplasia in connection with the second of two short courses of oxyphenbutazone treatment, with total doses below 3 g.

Even in those cases where aplastic anaemia occurs after prolonged treatment with phenylbutazone, the disease was unexpected and could not have been foreseen from the total dose given. Moreover, it has not been possible to produce phenylbutazone marrow aplasia in rabbits and mice (Speck 1975). Therefore, the marrow damage is not dose-dependent, but must be idiosyncratic or immunological (Table 2.2). Here, as with chloramphenicol, a confident choice between the alternatives cannot be made. However, the long treatment periods before the aplasias became evident (phenylbutazone) and the occurrence of aplasia shortly after or during a second course of drug taking (oxyphenbutazone), make idiosyncrasy unlikely. On the other hand, it is known that a constant phenylbutazone dose will produce widely varying plasma concentrations in different patients, probably due to different capacities of oxidative enzymes in liver cell endoplasmic reticulum. The possibility that the marrow damage might be conditional or idiosyncratic, in the sense that a toxic accumulation of phenylbutazone takes place, caused by a defective paraoxidation in liver cells, was examined by Cunningham et al. (1974). They measured plasma clearance of acetanilide, which is metabolized by the liver in the same way as phenylbutazone, in normal volunteers and in phenylbutazone-induced and idiopathic hypoplasia. Even though plasma half-life of acetanilide was significantly prolonged in the phenylbutazone group (5·5 vs. 3·7 hours), the following features are noteworthy: (a) in any case the half-lives are short, making a marked accumulation of the drug improbable; (b) clearance and half-life data were overlapping for hypoplasia patients and controls; and (c) a defective liver oxidation cannot explain the hypoplasia induced by oxyphenbutazone.

Very circumstantial evidence for an immunological basis are the following features: (a) a marked chronic inflammatory infiltrate has been described in some patients with phenylbutazone-induced aplastic anaemia (Velde & Haak 1977); (b) the occurrence of aplasia after two short courses of oxyphenbutazone; (c) the finding that addition of phenylbutazone to blood lymphocyte cultures induced blastic transformation in one patient with a possible phenylbutazone-induced aplasia, but not in controls (Denman & Denman 1968); (d) phenylbutazone may perhaps cause a disease resembling disseminated lupus erythematosus, which is an immunological disorder (Assem 1977); and (e) the possibly beneficial effect of corticosteroid treatment in this disease (Hale & de Gruchy 1960).

Since it is very uncertain whether these types of marrow aplasia have an immunological basis, the possible immune mechanism (Table 2.2) cannot be more than guess-work. The clinical features mentioned do not invalidate any of the alternatives given in Table 2.2. It is an interesting possibility that some of the high-dose phenylbutazone aplasias may be due to 'spoiled membrane allergy' (Nieweg 1973). Nieweg claims that a high-dosage drug allergy may be induced by some drugs capable of altering cell membranes, possibly by affecting membrane sulphydryl groups. Then, either native membrane components are exposed or neoantigens are formed, both types provoking an immune response against the affected cells. The specificity of the response is thought to be for component(s) of the 'spoiled membranes' and not for the drug (metabolites). Cross-reactions may occur with agents with similar membrane effects, although the chemical structures of the drugs are dissimilar. The immune reaction may last as long as cells with affected membranes are present.

There is no rapid recovery of bone marrow function after withdrawal of the drug, suggesting that either stem cells or stroma have been damaged. As with chloramphenicol aplasia, there is no unequivocal evidence establishing which of the two is the target of the pathogenetic process, although most workers would probably favour the stem cells. Furthermore, there is, for the time being, no necessity to invoke more elaborate mechanisms (Table 2.2 C/2 and 3) than simple, perhaps prolonged, stem-cell killing to explain the relevant features of the disease.

Gold

There seems to be a larger group of patients where the aplasia developed at a total dose of sodium aurothiomalate or other organic gold salts in excess of 450 mg. In some of these patients a progressive fall in blood leucocyte and thrombocyte concentrations took place before the occurrence of frank marrow failure (Kay 1973). In a smaller group of patients marrow aplasia occurred without warning after small total doses of organic gold compounds, down to about 200 mg of the salt in the series reported by McCarty et al. (1962).

Sodium aurothiomalate added *in vitro* inhibited formation of granulocyte–macrophage colonies by normal human marrow cells in a dose-dependent manner. Significant inhibition was obtained by concentrations of gold salt that may well be reached *in vivo* during treatment (Howell et al. 1975*b*). Bone marrow cells from patients who had recovered from gold-induced neutropenia were not abnormally sensitive to gold *in vitro*. Others have found that the distribution or metabolism, or both, of gold salts may be abnormal in some anaemic patients, leading to accumulation and extremely slow excretion of the gold (Wohlenberg 1972). On the other hand, it has been claimed that marrow toxicity could not be predicted by measuring serum gold levels (for references see Baldwin et al. 1977). Furthermore, peripheral blood lymphocytes from 6 patients who had developed haematological side effects after gold therapy responded with blast transformation to *in vitro* challenge with sodium aurothiomalate (Denman & Denman 1968). At least 2 of these patients had aplastic anaemia. A minority of patients with skin rashes associated with gold therapy also had positive lymphocyte cultures, whereas lymphocyte transformation was not seen in the controls. Three patients who developed aplastic anaemia while receiving gold salts showed engraftment of bone marrow transplants from HLA-matched siblings (Baldwin et al. 1977).

These findings, taken together, are obviously confusing. A possible explanation is that some cases of gold-induced marrow aplasia may be due to idiosyncrasy, e.g. in the sense that an abnormal accumulation of gold takes place in some individuals. This would lead to a direct toxic effect on transit cells of the marrow, and possibly on stem and stromal cells as well. Here, occurrence and chronicity of the disorder late, after gold withdrawal, cannot exclude transit cells as target cells, since gold may remain in the body for years after withdrawal of the drug. In other cases the disease may be immunologically determined, conceivably by destruction of stem cells, transit cells or stromal cells. Again, there seems to be no need to postulate more 'sophisticated' mechanisms than simple cell killing to explain the various findings.

Chlorpromazine

The bone marrow hypoplasia caused by chlorpromazine is fairly common among patients in mental hospitals (Pisciotta 1971). It is a dose-dependent, but unexpected, disorder. Blood examinations disclose agranulocytosis and in some cases thrombocytopenia. The hypoplasia is easily reversible after withdrawal of the drug; therefore anaemia rarely develops. After normalization the patients can take moderate doses of chlorpromazine without serious relapse. These findings argue against immune mechanisms and rather indicate an idiosyncratic reaction. It has been shown that bone marrow from patients who have recovered from this hypoplasia still has apparently subnormal numbers of CFU-C (Pisciotta 1973) and also a subnormal uptake of ^{3}H-thymidine *in vitro*, even in the absence of the drug. This suggests that a constitutional error in marrow cells may form the basis for chlorpromazine idiosyncrasy. Furthermore, it is known that chlorpromazine normally inhibits growth in several types of tissues. It therefore appears that individuals with constitutionally defective bone marrow cells will not be able to compensate for the growth-depressing effect of chlorpromazine (Pisciotta 1971). The rapid reversibility of the disorder strongly suggests that the symptomatology may be explained by chlorpromazine effects on the transit populations of the bone marrow. Inhibition of proliferation would explain the findings as well as, or better than, any of the mechanisms listed under item C in Table 2.2.

Benzene

Benzene is an established cause of dose-dependent marrow aplasia. Pure toluene and xylene have not produced aplasia in experimental animals (Speck 1975). Benzene, toluene, xylene and other aromatic hydrocarbons are obtained primarily from coal and petroleum. It should be noted, however, that an extensive purification procedure is necessary to remove benzene from 'commercial' preparations of some of the other aromatic hydrocarbons. Preparations containing benzene have been used as solvents for glue, cement, insecticide, grease, fingernail polish, etc., and as diluents for paint, varnish and lacquer.

Clinically, pancytopenia in blood may be combined with both marrow hypoplasia and hyperplasia. The condition has in most cases been reversible after withdrawal from benzene exposure. Findings in animal experiments shed some light on these clinical features. In rabbits a connection was found between the dose of benzene given and degree of pancytopenia (Speck 1975). The marrow could be either hypoplastic or hyperplastic, with predominance of immature cell types and an apparent disorder of maturation. Marked chromosome abnormalities ('breaks and gaps', and, after long exposure to benzene, hyperploid mitoses) were also present. Radio-autographically, RNA and DNA synthesis were severely disturbed in basophilic normoblasts,

promyelocytes and myelocytes, but not in the less mature pronormo-
blasts. Neither were the multipotent stem cells (CFU-S) affected in a
mouse model (Speck 1975), in spite of the presence of an evident
marrow hypoplasia.

On the other hand, a long-lasting marrow aplasia in exposed
persons has also been reported, and claims have been made that little
correlation has been observed between the tissue levels of benzene and
the occurrence of aplastic anaemia (for references see Williams et al.
1973). The possibility, therefore, still exists that stem cells may be
damaged, for example by 'stem-cell exhaustion' (see Chapter 1), and
that individual idiosyncrasy may be involved to some extent. However, the main pattern apparently is dose-dependent damage of
haematopoietic transit cells, in the form of inhibition of cell
proliferation or cell killing.

SUMMARY

Drug mechanisms in the most important and interesting types of
marrow aplasia are still incompletely understood. Available evidence
suggests that the aplasia caused by chloramphenicol is probably due to
stem cell killing by an (auto?) immune mechanism (Fig. 2.1). The
butazones probably also damage stem cells, in some of the cases
conceivably by high-dosage 'spoiled membrane allergy', in others
possibly by hapten-cell or immune complex mechanisms (Table 2.2).
Gold salts may damage marrow cells both by direct cytotoxicity and by
immune mechanisms. Chlorpromazine aplasia is apparently due to
constitutionally defective DNA synthesis, so that a normal compensatory reaction cannot take place to remedy the inhibitory effects of the
drug on DNA synthesis. This aplasia is normally transient, since transit
cells and not stem cells are affected. Finally, benzene has a dose-
dependent suppressive effect on marrow transit cells, leading, possibly,
to stem cell exhaustion in some cases.

REFERENCES

ALBERT, E., THOMAS, E. D., NISPEROS, N. & STORB, R. (1976) HLA antigens and
    haplotypes in 200 patients with aplastic anemia. *Transplantation*, 22, 528.
ALLAN, N. C. (1973) Effects of drugs and other agents in erythrocyte enzyme
    deficiencies and haemoglobinopathies. In *Blood Disorders due to Drugs and Other
    Agents*, ed. R. H. Girdwood, p. 27, Amsterdam: Excerpta Medica.
ASSEM, E.-S. K. (1977) Drug allergy. In *Textbook of Adverse Drug Reactions*, ed. D. M.
    Davies. Oxford: Oxford University Press.
BACON, P. A., SEWELL, R. L. & CROWTHER, D. (1975) Reactive lymphoid cells ('immuno-
    blasts') in autoimmune and haematological disorders. *Clin. exp. Immunol.*, 19, 201.

BALDWIN, J. L., STORB, R., THOMAS, E. D. & MANNIK, M. (1977) Bone marrow transplantation in patients with gold-induced marrow aplasia. *Arthritis Rheum.*, 20, 1043.

BARAN, D. T., GRINER, P. F. & KLEMPERER, M. R. (1976) Recovery from aplastic anemia after treatment with cyclophosphamide. *New Engl. J. Med.*, 295, 1522.

BENESTAD, H. B. (1974) Aplastic anaemia: Considerations on the pathogenesis. *Acta med. scand.*, 196, 255.

BITHELL, T. C. & WINTROBE, M. M. (1967) Drug-induced aplastic anemia. *Semin. Hemat.*, 4, 194.

BÖTTIGER, L. E. (1974) Drug-induced aplastic anaemia in Sweden with special reference to chloramphenicol. *Postgrad. med. J.*, 50 (suppl. 5), 127.

BÖTTIGER, L. E. & WESTERHOLM, B. (1973) Drug-induced blood dyscrasias in Sweden. *Br. med. J.*, 2, 339.

BOGGS, D. R. & BOGGS, S. S. (1976) The pathogenesis of aplastic anemia: A defective pluripotent hematopoietic stem cell with inappropriate balance of differentiation and self-replication. *Blood*, 48, 71.

BROWNLIE, B. E. W. & STRANG, P. J. H. (1969) Oxyphenbutazone (Tanderil) and blood dyscrasia. *N.Z. med. J.*, 69, 77.

CAMITTA, B. M., THOMAS, E. D., NATHAN, D. G., SANTOS, G., GORDON-SMITH, E. C., GALE, R. P., RAPPEPORT, J. M. & STORB, R. (1976) Severe aplastic anemia: a prospective study of the effect of early marrow transplantation on acute mortality. *Blood*, 48, 63.

CUNNINGHAM, J. L., LEYLAND, M. J., DELAMORE, I. W. & PRICE EVANS, D. A. (1974) Acetanilide oxidation in phenylbutazone-associated hypoplastic anaemia. *Br. med. J.*, 2, 313.

DENMAN, E. J. & DENMAN, A. M. (1968) The lymphocyte transformation test and gold hypersensitivity. *Ann. rheum. Dis.*, 27, 582.

EHRLICH, P. (1888) Uber einen Fall von Anaemie mit Bemerkungen uber regenerative Veranderungen des Knochenmarks. *Charité-Annln*, 13, 300.

FOWLER, P. D. (1967) Marrow toxicity of the pyrazoles. *Ann. rheum. Dis.*, 26, 344.

FRIED, W., CHAMBERLIN, W., KEDO, A. & BARONE, J. (1976) Effects of radiation on hematopoietic stroma. *Exp. Hemat.*, 4, 310.

GOOD, R. A. (1977) Aplastic anemia-suppressor lymphocytes and hematopoiesis. *New Engl. J. Med.*, 296, 41.

GROSS, R. & HELLRIEGEL, H. P. (1975) Pathogenese und Klinik der aplastischen Syndrome. *Haemat. Bluttransfusion*, 16, 135.

DE GRUCHY, G. C. (1975) *Drug-induced Blood Disorders*, p. 39. Oxford: Blackwell Scientific.

HALE, G. S. & DE GRUCHY, G. C. (1960) Aplastic anaemia following the administration of phenylbutazone. *Med. J. Aust.*, 2, 449.

HARVEY, L. E. & FIRKIN, B. G. (1968) Repeated isogenic transplants in bone-marrow failure. *Med. J. Aust.*, 2, 538.

HEIMPEL, H. & KERN, P. (1976) Arzneimittelbedingte Panmyelopathien. *Blut*, 33, 1.

HOWELL, A., ANDREWS, T. M. & WATTS, R. W. E. (1975a) Bone-marrow cells resistant to chloramphenicol in chloramphenicol-induced aplastic anaemia. *Lancet*, i, 65.

HOWELL, A., GUMPEL, J. M. & WATTS, R. W. E. (1975b) Depression of bone marrow colony formation in gold-induced neutrophenia. *Br. med. J.*, 1, 432.

JEANNET, M., SPECK, B., RUBINSTEIN, A., PELET, B., WYSS, M. & KUMMER, H. (1976) Autologous marrow reconstitutions in severe aplastic anaemia after ALG pretreatment and HL-A semi-incompatible bone marrow cell transfusion. *Acta haemat.*, 55, 129.

KAGAN, W. A., ASCENCAO, J. A., PAHWA, R. N., HANSEN, J. A., GOLDSTEIN, G., VALERA, E. B., INCEFY, G. S., MOORE, M. A. S. & GOOD, R. A. (1976) Aplastic anemia: presence in human bone marrow of cells that suppress myelopoiesis. *Proc. natn. Acad. Sci.*, U.S.A., 73, 2890.

KAY, A. (1973) Depression of bone marrow and thrombocytopenia associated with chrysotherapy. *Ann. rheum. Dis.*, 33, 277.

KEISER, G. & WALDER, H. R. (1970) Die idiopathische und die medikamentös bedingte erworbene aplastische Anämie. *Schweiz. med. Wschr., 100*, 697.

KERN, P., HEIMPEL, H., HEIT, W. & KUBANEK, B. (1975) Bone-marrow cells resistant to chloramphenicol in chloramphenicol-induced aplastic anaemia. *Lancet, i*, 1190.

KERN, P., HEIMPEL, H., HEIT, W. & KUBANEK, B. (1977) Granulocytic progenitor cells in aplastic anaemia. *Br. J. Haemat., 35*, 613.

McCARTHY, D. D. & CHALMERS, T. M. (1964) Hematological complications of phenylbutazone therapy: Review of the literature and report of two cases. *Can. med. Ass. J., 90*, 1061.

McCARTY, D. J., BRILL, J. M. & HARROP, D. (1962) Aplastic anemia secondary to gold-salt therapy. *J. Am. med. Ass., 179*, 655.

MORLEY, A., FURNESS, M. & HIGGS, D. (1974) Inhibition of growth of marrow cells by chloramphenicol. *Aust. J. exp. Biol. med. Sci., 52*, 847.

MORLEY, A., TRAINOR, K. & BLAKE, J. (1975) A primary stem cell lesion in experimental chronic hypoplastic marrow failure. *Blood, 45*, 681.

NIEWEG, H. O. (1973) Aplastic anemia (panmyelopathy). A review with special emphasis on the factors causing bone marrow damage. In *Blood Disorders due to Drugs and Other Agents*, ed. R. H. Girdwood, pp. 83–106. Amsterdam: Excerpta Medica.

PEGG, D. E. & BURNS, J. E. (1965) A sex-dependent factor in aplastic anaemia? *Nature, Lond., 208*, 1187.

PETZ, L. D. & FUDENBERG, H. H. (1975) Immunological mechanisms in drug-induced cytopenias. *Progr. Hemat., 9*, 185.

PISCIOTTA, A. V. (1971) Drug-induced leukopenia and aplastic anemia. *Clin. Pharmac. Ther., 12*, 13.

PISCIOTTA, A. V. (1973) Immune and toxic mechanisms in drug-induced agranulocytosis. *Semin. Hemat., 10*, 279.

SPECK, B. (1975) Toxische Knochenmarkinsuffizienz. *Haemat. Bluttransfusion, 16*, 235.

TERRITO, M. C. (1977) Autologous bone marrow repopulation following high dose cyclophosphamide and allogeneic marrow transplantation in aplastic anaemia. *Br. J. Haemat., 36*, 305.

THOMAS, E. D., STORB, R., GIBLETT, E. R., LONGPRE, B., WEIDEN, P. L., FEFER, A., WITHERSPOON, R., CLIFT, R. A. & BUCKNER, C. D. (1976) Recovery from aplastic anemia following attempted marrow transplantation. *Expl Hemat., 4*, 97.

VAN DEN ENGH, G. J. & GOLUB, E. S. (1974) Antigenic differences between hemopoietic stem cells and myeloid progenitors. *J. exp. Med., 139*, 1621.

TE VELDE, J. & HAAK, H. L. (1977) Histological investigation of methacrylate embedded bone marrow biopsy specimens, correlation with survival after conventional treatment in 15 adult patients. *Br. J. Haemat., 35*, 61.

WEISBERGER, A. S. (1969) Mechanisms of action of chloramphenicol. *J. Am. med. Ass., 209*, 97.

WILLIAMS, D. M., LYNCH, R. E. & CARTWRIGHT, G. E. (1973) Drug-induced aplastic anemia. *Semin. Hemat., 10*, 195.

WOHLENBERG, H. (1972) Aplastische Anämie nach Goldbehandlung. *Medsche Welt, 23*, 971.

YUNIS, A. A. (1973) Chloramphenicol-induced bone marrow suppression. *Semin. Hemat., 10*, 225.

3

Clinical Features of Aplastic Anaemia

DARRYL M. WILLIAMS

In recent reports, aplastic anaemia has been defined as that disease associated with pancytopenia and a hypocellular bone marrow biopsy at some time in the course of the illness (Najean et al. 1965; Davis & Rubin 1972; Li et al. 1972; Williams et al. 1973). Such a definition permits the emergence of a specific clinical entity although similar features may be seen in other disease processes. For example, bone marrow failure is often transient, as in some infections. In some cases, an underlying cause, such as leukaemia or paroxysmal nocturnal haemoglobinuria, can be identified by careful study of the patient (Stohlman 1972). Genetic defects may also be seen in association with aplastic anaemia (Dawson 1955). Such congenital disorders as Fanconi's anaemia fulfill the criteria for aplastic anaemia, but because these diseases will be discussed in greater detail in other portions of this volume, they will not be considered further here.

There remains, however, a group of patients with acquired aplastic anaemia in whom no associated disease process can be identified. In many of these patients, onset of aplastic anaemia appears to follow a previous exposure to drugs, chemicals or certain infectious diseases, but in others, no such exposure history can be documented.

INCIDENCE

It is difficult to identify reliable figures for the incidence of acquired aplastic anaemia. It seems clear, however, that although aplastic anaemia remains an uncommon disorder, it is more prevalent now than at the beginning of the century (Smith 1919; Mohler & Leavell 1958).

Evidence has been presented that over the years there has been an increase in the number of patients reported in Switzerland (Donski & Bucher 1968). In the United States, some authors have observed increases in the numbers of patients admitted to their clinics during those recent years when chloramphenicol was distributed more widely

(Wallerstein et al. 1969; Williams et al. 1973). In one estimate, the population incidence of aplastic anaemia due to all causes was found to be 4·8 per million (Wallerstein et al. 1969). In a similar study in Sweden, the incidence approximated 13 per million (Böttiger & Westerholm 1972a). It cannot be determined whether these figures represent a difference in incidence between the two populations. From the available information there appear to be no differences in the underlying cause or in the laboratory features of the two patient groups (Böttiger & Westerholm 1972a). Whatever the incidence of the disease, it seems clear that it is increasing, and that at least in some situations this increase can be related to increased exposure of the population to toxic agents (Wallerstein et al. 1969).

AETIOLOGY

Only a few substances such as benzene have been clearly established as causing aplastic anaemia (Selling 1916). In most instances, determination of the cause of marrow injury is made difficult by a number of factors: (a) evidence of drug or chemical toxicity is usually only circumstantial; (b) there are no laboratory tests to establish a cause–effect relationship; (c) many patients are subjected to multiple exposures of several potentially toxic agents; and (d) reliable exposure history is often difficult or even impossible to obtain. Thus, it must be recognized that the history obtained is always the minimal exposure history. In many published series, about 50% of the cases of aplastic anaemia have been classified as secondary to a toxic exposure (Scott et al. 1959; O'Gorman Hughes 1969; Li et al. 1972; Davis & Rubin 1972; Williams et al. 1973).

An aetiological classification of the causes of drug and chemical induced aplastic anaemia is presented in Table 3.1. This classification is based in part on the American Medical Association Registry of Adverse Reaction (AMA 1967). Unfortunately, this registry was discontinued (Moser 1971) so that in recent years a number of additional suspect drugs, such as ibuprofen (Grype & Rubenzahl 1976) and D-penicillamine (Richards et al. 1976), have been reported but not collected in a readily accessible repository. Thus it is impossible to determine the potential toxicity of such agents. Accordingly, these and other agents reported in isolated case reports have not been included in Table 3.1.

Drugs

Many of the chemotherapeutic agents used in the treatment of neoplastic disease cause pancytopenia and marrow hypoplasia during the

Table 3.1. Aetiological classification of drug-induced aplastic anaemia

Drugs known to be associated with aplastic anaemia	Drugs possibly associated with aplastic anaemia	Aromatic hydrocarbons
Chloramphenicol	Amodiaquine	Benzene
Pyrazolones	Antihistamines	Stoddard solvent
Phenylbutazone	Chlorpheniramine	Quick-drying glues and cements
Oxyphenbutazone	Mepyramine (pyrilamine)	Trinitrotoluene
Amidopyrine	Tripelennamine	
Hydantoin analogues	Chlordiazepoxide	Insecticides
Methoin (mephenytoin)	Colchicine	Gammabenzene hexachloride
Phenytoin (diphenylhydantoin)	Meprobamate	Chlordane
Methylphenylhydantoin	Methicillin	Chlorphenothane (DDT)
Troxidone (trimethadione)	Phenothiazines	
Primidone	Promazine	
Phenacemide	Chlorpromazine	
Ethosuximide	Prochlorperazine	
Sulphonamides	Pecazine (mepazine)	
Sulphafurazole (sulfisoxazole)	Carbamazepine	
Sulphathiazole	Pyrimethamine	
Sulphadimethoxine	Quinidine	
Sulphonylureas	Salycylamide	
Tolbutamide	Streptomycin	
Chlorpropamide	Sulphamyl compounds	
Carbutamide	Acetazolamide	
Gold compounds	Chlorothiazide	
Organic arsenicals	Hydroflumethizide	
Potassium perchlorate	Thiocarbamates	
Mepacrine (quinacrine)	Carbimazole	
	Methimazole	
	Methylthiouracil	
	Propylthiouracil	
	Thiocyanate	
	Thiacetazone	

course of treatment. Except for these drugs, chloramphenicol accounts for the greatest number of cases of aplastic anaemia (Bithell & Wintrobe 1967; Donski & Bucher 1968; Böttiger & Westerholm 1972; Davis & Rubin 1972; Li et al. 1972; Williams et al. 1973; Modan et al. 1975). Moreover, in several series the incidence of aplastic anaemia seems to be related to the level of consumption of chloramphenicol by the population at risk (Wallerstein et al. 1969; Böttiger 1974; Hausmann & Skrandies 1974). In recent years both the use of chloramphenicol and the incidence of aplastic anaemia appear to be diminishing in many places throughout the world (Williams et al. 1973; Böttiger 1974; Hausman & Skrandies 1974). Other drugs which have been frequently associated with aplastic anaemia include phenylbutazone and related pyrazolene congeners, hydantoins, sulphonamides, sulphonylureas and gold compounds (see Chapter 2).

The drugs which are listed as possibly associated with aplastic anaemia have all been implicated in 2 or more cases of aplastic anaemia when given alone or with an innocuous drug. However, many of these drugs are widely prescribed and yet associated with few reported cases of aplastic anaemia. For example, antihistamines have been implicated as causing aplastic anaemia in at least 16 patients (Welch et al. 1954; AMA 1967; Deringer & Maniatis 1976) although the number of such cases compared with the number of patients taking antihistamines is extremely small. As has been pointed out, careful drug history may reveal that the patient has also taken a known toxic agent such as phenylbutazone (Spry 1976).

Aromatic Hydrocarbons

The aromatic hydrocarbons are obtained primarily from coal and petroleum. These products find widespread use in industry and commerce and include benzol, toluol, xylol and naphtha. Further refining results in the pure chemicals, benzene, toluene, xylene and naphthalene. Although only benzene has been clearly implicated as a cause of aplastic anaemia (Selling 1916), it is found as a contaminant of others of these distillates. These agents are found in a wide variety of commercial products such as solvents, paint thinners, insecticides, cement, glues, nail polish remover and petrol (Brandt et al. 1977). It is therefore usually impossible to be certain of the extent and duration of exposure to such agents. Furthermore, the patterns of exposure have changed over the years. Thus, the earliest documentations of the toxic effect of benzene were made in patients exposed to benzene products used in manufacturing processes (Santesson 1897; Selling 1910), whereas in recent years aplastic anaemia has been recognized as a complication of glue-sniffing by adolescents (Powars 1965). In view of the widespread use of these hydrocarbons, it is possible that their unsuspected or forgotten use may underlie the development of apparent idiopathic aplastic anaemia in many patients.

Insecticides

Insecticides have been associated with aplastic anaemia (Huguley 1963; Erslev 1964; Loge 1965; AMA 1967; Williams et al. 1973). Gammabenzene hexachloride (Lindane) has especially been implicated. Because insecticides are often distributed in an aerosol it is difficult to estimate the level of exposure. Moreover, they may be incorporated into soaps and powders that are used for many purposes around the household so that the user is not fully aware of their presence (Vodapeck 1975).

Hair Dyes

Although hair dye as a possible cause of aplastic anaemia had been reported as early as 1935 (Baldridge 1935), most reports of a causal relationship are anecdotal and concern patients in whom other exposures have been noted (Toghill & Wilcox 1976). In view of the widespread use of these agents (20% of women in the United Kingdom) (Jouhar 1976), there is little to suggest that hair dyes are an aetiological factor in aplastic anaemia.

Hepatitis

The association of viral hepatitis with transient mild anaemia, leuco-penia and thrombocytopenia has long been known, but the relation-ship of the disease with aplastic anaemia was not recognized until 1955 (Lorenz & Quaiser 1955). Even then, many authors viewed the association as either fortuitous or related through a toxic agent which causes both hepatic and bone marrow damage. Indeed, a syndrome of jaundice and aplastic anaemia following chloramphenicol treatment has been described (Hodgkinson 1971). In one series of 193 patients with aplastic anaemia and hepatitis, over 18% had received chlor-amphenicol (Hagler et al. 1975). Thus, in those patients who present the findings of combined hepatic and marrow dysfunction, the possibility of chloramphenicol toxicity must always be considered. However, there are now sufficient cases recorded of aplastic anaemia resulting from hepatitis, with no known drug exposures, that a typical clinical picture has begun to emerge.

The mechanisms which relate hepatitis and aplastic anaemia are unclear. Evidence has recently been presented that, at least in some cases, the viral infection might initiate an autoimmune reaction directed against haematopoietic cells (Royal Marsden Hospital Bone

Marrow Transplantation Team 1977) (see p. 17). Other mechanisms which have been considered include: failure of the liver to provide haematopoietic nutrients or to detoxify myelotoxic metabolic intermediates or drugs; acquisition of haematodepressive potential by the genome; direct virus-induced marrow damage; virus-induced chromosome damage; and individual susceptibility on an unexplained basis (Hagler et al. 1975).

Aplastic anaemia associated with hepatitis is primarily a disease of younger persons, and the age distribution is similar to that of uncomplicated infectious hepatitis (Ajlouni & Doeblin 1974). Men are more commonly affected than women (Ajlouni & Doeblin 1974; Hagler et al. 1975) but mortality among women is higher (Hagler et al. 1975). Typically, the aplastic anaemia has its onset within 10 weeks after the onset of the hepatitis. The severity of the aplasia has no relationship to the severity of the hepatitis, which is usually mild. In contrast, the aplastic anaemia is usually severe. In one series the mortality rate was 88% and the mean survival was 10 weeks after onset of marrow failure (Ajlouni & Doeblin 1974).

It is not known why the outlook is so sinister in aplastic anaemia associated with hepatitis, although the reason must certainly be found in the mechanisms by which the two diseases are causally related. Thus, it may be that the liver offers some undefined protective effect on the marrow which is impaired during the viral illness. Alternatively, the virus or the immune response which it evokes may be especially toxic to the marrow.

The risk of aplastic anaemia following hepatitis has not been well established, although in Sweden it has been estimated that the risk is between 1 and 2 cases of aplastic anaemia per thousand cases of hepatitis (Böttiger & Westerholm 1972b). There is no information concerning the frequency of aplastic anaemia during epidemics of hepatitis. It has been said that hepatitis A is more likely than hepatitis B to result in aplastic anaemia (Viala et al. 1970). There are insufficient serological data to define this issue. It has even been proposed that the hepatitis–aplastic anaemia syndrome may be the consequence of a viral agent not usually associated with human hepatitis (Hagler et al. 1975). With the recent awareness of other viruses as causal agents for hepatitis, there remains much work to be done to clarify the relationship of viral hepatitis to aplastic anaemia.

Pregnancy

Aplastic anaemia has been reported as a rare complication of pregnancy (Fleming 1973). Indeed, Ehrlich's patient was pregnant at the time of diagnosis (Ehrlich 1888). However, it is often unclear in the reported patients whether the blood disorder developed during pregnancy or was simply discovered because of increased medical surveillance (Knispel 1976). Furthermore, alternative diagnoses such as pernicious anaemia or possible exposure to agents such as chloramphenicol have not always been excluded (Scott et al. 1959). Moreover, the apparent rarity of aplastic anaemia as a complication of the rather common condition of pregnancy suggests that the association may only be coincidental! However, the prognosis of aplastic anaemia during pregnancy is grave. In 32 patients with demonstrated bone marrow hypoplasia, 61% died of haematological complications (Fleming 1973). Remissions have been reported following either delivery or abortion, but even in patients who survive to term, the mortality is comparable to that of patients with aplastic anaemia due to drugs or unknown causes (Knispel 1976).

Tuberculosis

Pancytopenia has been observed in a number of chronic systemic infections such as aspergillosis (Francombe & Townsend 1965), brucellosis (de Filippi 1942), bacterial endocarditis (Parsons et al. 1953) and, more commonly, miliary tuberculosis (Fountain 1954). In the latter, it is often possible to demonstrate either miliary tubercles or acid-fast bacilli in the spleen or in the bone marrow (Fountain 1954; Medd & Hayhoe 1955). Experimentally, development of pancytopenia in the peripheral blood has been shown to correspond to the development of tubercles within the bone marrow (Doan & Sabin 1927). However, in some patients, bone marrow examination by aspiration and biopsy has demonstrated hypoplasia, but no evidence of tubercles or tubercle bacilli (Medd & Hayhoe 1955; Fisher et al. 1966).

The importance of establishing the correct diagnosis has recently been emphasized (Bernard et al. 1975). Disappearance of pancytopenia has been observed in those patients given antibiotic treatment, but death has occurred in most patients because the diagnosis is unsuspected. Fever is almost invariably present and should provide a clinical clue. Splenomegaly is common but may develop only late in the course of the disease (Fountain 1954). Liver biopsy may be of particular value in the demonstration of miliary tubercles or of acid-fast organisms (Bernard et al. 1975).

Idiopathic

Although an increasing number of drugs and chemicals has been suspected to be of causal importance in aplastic anaemia, in most recent series an aetiological agent cannot be identified in about half of the cases (Scott et al. 1959; Lewis 1965; O'Gorman Hughes 1969; Davis & Rubin, 1972; Li et al. 1972). In some studies, however, as few as 20% (Böttiger & Westerholm 1972a) and as many as 86% (Williams et al. 1973) of patients have been found to have antecedent drug or chemical exposure. The reasons for these discrepancies are unclear. In large part they are due to the use of different criteria for the diagnosis of aplastic anaemia. There are differences of age in different study populations and advanced age has been proposed as a potential aetiological factor (Böttiger & Westerholm 1972a). There are no compelling data to support this hypothesis. It is possible that there are differences between populations in accessibility of toxic agents as well as in the means by which exposure history was obtained. Differences in the incidence of hepatitis in the study populations may also play a role (Hast et al. 1976). Whatever the explanation, it must be remembered that an exposure history is always a minimal estimate of exposure, since the entire population is exposed to insecticides, antibiotics and chemicals through its diet, and from many other non-medicinal sources. Idiopathic aplastic anaemia is therefore likely to be less common than the data would indicate. For although our understanding of aetiological factors has advanced since 1919, when Smith concluded that the aetiology of aplastic anaemia was 'nothing but speculation' (Smith 1919), much remains to be learned.

CLINICAL MANIFESTATIONS

Symptoms

The symptoms which cause the patient to consult a physician are most commonly related to bleeding, either alone or in combination with symptoms of anaemia or infection (Table 3.2) (Scott et al. 1959; Williams et al. 1973). Clinical manifestations due only to anaemia are less common, and those due only to infection are less common still. In a few patients, abnormal laboratory findings are discovered coincidentally during the course of a routine examination. Usually, the patient

Table 3.2. Mode of onset in 101 patients with aplastic anaemia

Related to	No. of patients
Bleeding	41
Anaemia	27
Bleeding and anaemia	14
Bleeding and infection	6
Infection	5
Routine examination	8

From Williams et al. (1973).

consults his physician shortly after the onset of symptoms. In our clinic, 62% of the patients were referred to us within 6 months of the onset of symptoms (Williams et al. 1973). However, some patients were not referred for more than 2 years after the onset of symptoms. This variation, of course, reflects not only differences in the rate of development of aplastic anaemia but also differences in referral patterns.

Other diseases may, of course, result in pancytopenia and, as a consequence, may be associated with similar symptoms. In some instances, such diseases can be distinguished by other clinical manifestations. For example, paroxysmal nocturnal haemoglobinuria may result in the symptoms of bleeding, anaemia or infection. In this setting, the correct diagnosis may be overlooked. However, when these features are observed in association with episodes of abdominal pain, thrombotic events or vascular occlusive catastrophes such as the Budd–Chiari syndrome, the physician should be alerted to the diagnosis. In many instances, however, the diagnosis may become apparent only after years of clinical observation and repeated laboratory evaluation.

Physical Findings

The most common physical findings are also related to the presence of bleeding. Petechiae, ecchymoses and fundal haemorrhages are prominent (Table 3.3). Splenomegaly is an unusual finding early in the course of the disease, and massive splenomegaly is against the diagnosis. Similarly, generalized lymphadenopathy is not a feature of aplastic anaemia and speaks strongly against the diagnosis (Williams et al. 1973).

Table 3.3. Initial physical findings in 101 patients with aplastic anaemia

	No. of patients	
	With	*Without*
Haemorrhagic manifestations	84	17
Splenomegaly	11	90
Hepatomegaly	3	98
Generalized adenopathy	0	101

From Williams et al. (1973).

Laboratory Studies

Although pancytopenia develops in all patients with aplastic anaemia, in some patients a reduction in only one of the formed elements may be observed at the time that the patient is first seen. Thus, the correct diagnosis does not become apparent until prolonged clinical evaluation is made. In one series, pancytopenia was observed in only 83% of patients at time of initial examination, even though all patients subsequently developed pancyotpenia. Thrombocytopenia was the most commonly noted laboratory abnormality at the time of initial presentation (Li et al. 1972). Neutropenia has been observed more frequently than leucopenia because the lymphocyte count may be normal or increased. However, lymphopenia is also commonly observed during the course of the disease (Lewis 1965; Williams et al. 1973) as are decreased numbers of monocytes (Williams et al. 1973; Twomey et al. 1973). Anaemia is usually severe and there is frequently an absolute reticulocytopenia which is unappreciated if the reticulocyte count is uncorrected for the degree of anaemia (Lewis 1965; Williams et al. 1973; Lohrmann et al. 1976; Hellreigal et al. 1977). Detailed analysis of the peripheral blood findings in aplastic anaemia will be found in Chapter 4.

Bone Marrow Findings

In most recent series, demonstration of marrow hypoplasia is essential to the diagnosis of aplastic anaemia (Lewis 1965; Najean et al. 1965; Davis & Rubin 1972; Li et al. 1972; Williams et al. 1973). However, it has been pointed out that, in as many as one-third of cases, a single aspiration may be misleading and the hypoplastic nature of the bone marrow may only be demonstrated by further aspirates or bone biopsy (Lewis 1965) (Chapter 4). In some patients with otherwise typical aplastic anaemia, persistent foci of intense haematopoietic activity ('hot pockets') have been identified. These observations have been taken as supportive evidence for the hypothesis that aplastic anaemia is a dyserythropoietic rather than a hypoactive process (Kansu & Erslev 1976) (see Chapter 1).

CLINICAL COURSE AND SURVIVAL

The overall mortality of aplastic anaemia is about 70% (Lewis 1965; Najean et al. 1965; Böttiger & Westerholm 1972a; Davis & Rubin 1972;

Table 3.4. Causes of death in patients with aplastic anaemia

Cause of death	No. of patients
Haemorrhage	22
Infection	16
Haemorrhage and infection	24
Other	2
Total	64

From Williams et al. (1973).

Li et al. 1972; Williams et al. 1973) and complete recovery can be expected in only about 10% of patients (Najean et al. 1965; Williams et al. 1973). The most common cause of death is haemorrhage, but in many patients both haemorrhage and infection are present at the time of death (Table 3.4). In most patients, bleeding is the result of thrombocytopenia. However, it is unusual for serious bleeding to occur when the platelet count is above 20 000/μl (van der Weyden & Firkin 1972). In recent years, the use of platelet transfusions to patients with severe haemorrhage or with platelet counts of less than 20 000/μl has resulted in more effective management of this complication, as discussed in Chapter 6.

Infection, which is usually associated with severe neutropenia, is also an important cause of morbidity and mortality (Lewis 1965; van der Weyden & Firkin 1972; Williams et al. 1973). In most instances, a specific bacterial organism can be identified (Williams et al. 1973). As with patients with neutropenia due to other haematological disorders,

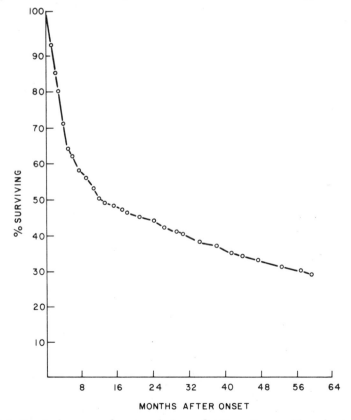

Fig. 3.1. Survival curve of a population of 101 patients with aplastic anaemia. (*Reproduced from Williams et al. 1973*)

scrupulous attention must be paid to seemingly innocent skin infections as well as to the possibilities of dental and perirectal abscesses. These observations and the relative infrequency of viral infections have suggested that there may be sparing of the lymphocyte system in aplastic anaemia. However, in a recent study, 8 of 19 patients with aplastic anaemia were found to have a decrease in one or more immunoglobulins suggesting that, at least in some patients, there is impairment of the immunological system (Mir et al. 1977).

It is thus apparent that aplastic anaemia is a serious disease, but one with a variable course. Some patients may live only a few days after the onset of their symptoms, while others may survive for years. In several studies, the shape of the survival curve has suggested that there may be at least two groups of patients with aplastic anaemia: one with a rapidly fatal course and a second with a slower rate of dying (Lewis 1965; Najean et al. 1965; Williams et al. 1973; O'Gorman Hughes 1973) (Fig. 3.1). The explanation for the biphasic shape of the survival curve remains unclear. It may be that the two populations have a different disease. Against this hypothesis are the observations that the two groups cannot be differentiated by age, aetiology or type of symptoms at onset (Williams et al. 1973). Alternatively, it may be that the relation between survival and the severity of marrow aplasia is itself biphasic. Thus, survival may decline only slightly until a threshold is reached beyond which survival declines sharply.

If the latter is correct, then it follows that a reliable measure of the level of severity of marrow aplasia might be useful in differentiating those patients who will experience a rapid evolution of their disease from those who will have a more indolent course. The search for such a measure of prognosis has become of increasing importance during recent years because of the introduction of new, effective, but potentially life-threatening treatments such as bone marrow transplantation (Thomas et al. 1972, 1975).

PROGNOSTIC INDICATORS

Clinical Factors

A number of workers have made attempts to define prognostic factors in aplastic anaemia. In early studies, the clinical condition of the patient was considered to be a useful guide to outcome. In particular, the presence of haemorrhage was viewed as an ominous sign (Israëls & Wilkinson 1961). More recently, a rapid onset of disease (Lewis 1965; Najean et al. 1965; Williams et al. 1973; Lynch et al. 1975) and the presence of haemorrhagic manifestations (Lewis 1965; Davis & Rubin 1972; Williams et al. 1973; Lynch et al. 1975) have been associated with diminished survival. In several studies, age had no bearing on outcome (Davis & Rubin 1972; Li et al. 1972; Williams et al. 1973; Lynch et al. 1975) while in one study, increased mortality was seen in those patients over 40 (Lewis 1965) and in another, younger patients were at a greater risk of dying (Najean et al. 1965). Women tend to have a more favourable outcome than men (Williams et al. 1973). However, the role of some of these factors in predicting outcome is unclear and none of them is a sufficiently direct measure of the extent of bone marrow injury to provide a reliable guide to the individual patient's clinical course.

Laboratory Studies

Blood studies. In many reports, efforts have been made to assess the severity of marrow aplasia from the degree of thrombocytopenia, neutropenia and reticulocytopenia. A lower reticulocyte count has been observed in patients who died than in survivors (Najean et al. 1965; Killander et al. 1969; Williams et al. 1973; Lohrmann et al. 1976; Hellriegel et al. 1977). This discrimination is especially useful when the reticulocyte count is expressed as an absolute (Lohrmann et al. 1976) or corrected (Williams et al. 1973) value (see p. 64). It has been pointed out that the reticulocyte count may provide a falsely pessimistic index in patients with acute infection (Geary 1976). In other studies, mortality has correlated with the severity of neutropenia (Lewis 1965; Najean et al. 1965; Killander et al. 1969; Davis & Rubin 1972) or thrombocytopenia (Lewis 1965; Killander et al. 1969) but seldom all three (Killander et al. 1969).

However, when the initial levels of peripheral cell reduction are compared between those patients who survive less than 4 months and those who survive longer than 4 months, reticulocytopenia, neutropenia and thrombocytopenia are all associated with a poor prognosis (Lynch et al. 1975).

Bone marrow studies. It is interesting that although functional hypoplasia of the bone marrow is considered to be the fundamental defect in aplastic anaemia, estimates of bone marrow cellularity in biopsy specimens do not correlate with prognosis (Lewis 1965; Frisch & Lewis 1974; te Velde & Haak 1977). However, an increase in the number of lymphocytes and/or plasma cells in either the aspirate or biopsy has been associated with a worse prognosis (Najean et al. 1965; Li et al. 1972; Williams et al. 1973; Frisch & Lewis 1974; Lynch et al. 1975; te Velde & Haak 1977). The reason for this is unknown. It may be that the lymphocyte count is raised simply as a consequence of erythroid and myeloid depletion. Against this are the observations that there is often an absolute increase in lymphocytes (Frisch & Lewis 1974), and that the presence of diffuse lymphoid infiltrates is associated with increased mortality (te Velde & Haak 1977). Such studies raise the speculative consideration that, at least in some cases, aplastic anaemia may have an autoimmune pathogenesis (see Chapter 1).

Radioisotope studies. Patients with aplastic anaemia have an impaired ability to incorporate iron into newly-forming red cells (p. 91). This reflects the hypoplasia of the marrow and can be demonstrated by ferrokinetic studies employing ^{59}Fe (Scott et al. 1959; Najean et al. 1965). In such investigations, plasma iron is increased, disappearance of ^{59}Fe is prolonged, plasma iron turnover is reduced, and iron incorporation into red blood cells is diminished. Interestingly, in some patients ferrokinetic data correlated better with the hypoplastic appearance of autopsy specimens than with earlier, more cellular aspirated specimens (Scott et al. 1959). Radio-iron utilization has also been employed as a useful measure of clinical course. The average radio-iron utilization in patients who died within 6 months was 11% while in patients who lived more than 1 year, it was 41%. Patients who survived between 6 and 12 months had an intermediate radio-iron utilization of 15·1%. Although there was considerable overlap between groups, the measurement of radio-iron utilization was more predictive of final outcome than any other prognostic factor measured (Najean et al. 1965). Unfortunately, ferrokinetic studies are often not of clinical utility. This is because the patient must be studied over several days during a time when clinical decisions must be made quickly and frequently and when transfusion therapy, infections and bleeding make the interpretation of such studies difficult or unreliable.

Recently, the use of indium scintigraphy has been advocated as a practical alternative to ferrokinetic studies (McNeil et al. 1976). Indium 111 chloride is bound and transported by transferrin in plasma. It has a favourable photopeak for scintigraphy and a relative lack of non-penetrating radiation (Hosain et al. 1969; McNeil et al. 1974). Although it differs chemically and kinetically from iron (Goodwin et al. 1971) indium chloride is also taken up by the marrow. Moreover, failure of indium 111 chloride uptake correlates with poor prognosis in aplastic anaemia (McNeil et al. 1976). The method has the advantage of providing useful information within 24 hours. As further experience is gained with this technique, it may prove to be an especially valuable addition to the assessment of the patient with aplastic anaemia.

Fetal haemoglobin. In early studies of acquired aplastic anaemia in children, fetal haemoglobin concentration was thought to have prognostic value. Survival was significantly greater in those patients with total fetal haemoglobin levels of 400 mg/dl or higher than in children with lower levels (Bloom & Diamond 1971). However, in a later study which incorporated some of the same patients, the measurement had limited prognostic value (Li et al. 1972). In a similar study of acquired aplastic anaemia in adults, fetal haemoglobin levels were found to be of no prognostic value (Aksoy & Erden 1973). A re-evaluation of the prognostic value of this variable is presently underway as part of the International Aplastic Anaemia Protocol.

Prognostic Index

Numerous studies have examined factors which may be of prognostic value in aplastic anaemia, but correlations have been inconsistent. In part this is because the course of aplastic anaemia is so variable that the interval between the prognostic measurement (such as a blood count) and the predicted event (mortality) may be separated by a long interval of time. However, when the survival curve of patients with aplastic anaemia is plotted, there are two distinct populations: those who die within 4 months after the onset of their illness and those who survive for longer periods of time (Lynch et al. 1975).

As has been previously described, the type of onset (bleeding manifestations *vs*. absence of bleeding), sex of the patient, interval between onset of first symptoms and first clinic visit, the level of initial reticulocytopenia, neutropenia and thrombocytopenia as well as the numbers of non-myeloid cells present in a bone marrow aspirate have all been found to have predictive value in separating those patients who will die within 4 months from those who will survive longer (Lynch et al. 1975).

By weighing these variables, it has been possible to develop a prognostic index that more reliably separates the two patient populations than does the use of any single variable by itself (Lynch et al. 1975). The formula by which this index was derived is as follows:

$$C = -0{\cdot}01796\,(B) + 0{\cdot}01272\,(S) - 0{\cdot}00008\,(OFV) \\ -0{\cdot}00359\,(R) - 0{\cdot}000002\,(N) - 0{\cdot}0018\,(P) \\ +0{\cdot}0046\,(NM)$$

where C is the prognostic index; B refers to onset of bleeding (graded 0 if bleeding was present at the onset of symptoms and graded 1 if bleeding was absent); S (sex) was graded 1 if the patient was female, 2 if the patient was male; OFV is the interval between onset of symptoms and first clinic visit in months; R is the corrected initial reticulocyte count (%); N is the initial neutrophil concentration (cells/mm^3); P is the initial platelet concentration (thousands/mm^3); and NM is the percentage of non-myeloid cells in the initial marrow aspirate.

In general, those patients whose prognostic index was a negative value had a more favourable outcome than those individuals whose index was positive. If the non-myeloid cells exceed 55%, this factor contributes the major portion of the positivity of the score. Thus, this variable appears to be of especially great importancè in predicting an unfavourable outcome. This relative weighing of the prognostic variables compares with other studies (Li et al. 1972; Williams et al. 1973). Recently, the prognostic index has been criticized as being no more and perhaps even less predictive of the patient's final outcome than is the clinical impression of the attending haematologist (Retief & Heyns 1976; te Velde & Haak 1977). Unfortunately, in these studies the numbers of patients were small and the numerical prognostic indices for patients were not reported. In one study, estimates of cellularity of the bone marrow were substituted for the percentage of non-myeloid cells in the bone marrow aspirate (Retief & Heyns 1976). Moreover, in that study, patients with other causes for pancytopenia were included in the study population. It is interesting to note, however, that in the second study, which employs the technique of plastic embedding of biopsy material, there was appreciation of morphological detail and anatomical relationships that was not possible with other embedding techniques, or with aspiration (te Velde & Haak, 1977) (p. 73). An increase in lymphoid infiltration was associated with poorer prognosis. This appears to be a confirmation of correlations made with aspirated material (Najean et al. 1965; Li et al. 1972; Williams et al. 1973; Lynch et al. 1975).

In a third study, the prognostic index was applied to 21 children with aplastic anaemia (Wehinger & Lencer 1977). The index was predictive of those patients who expired within 6 months after onset of their illness. Furthermore, there was grouping of patients so that the authors suggested that those patients with a prognostic index (C) of between 0·041 and 0·045 should be considered for bone marrow transplantation because of the severity of their aplasia. Those patients with C values less than 0 should probably not require therapy, while those patients with C values between 0 and 0·041 should be considered for alternate forms of therapy such as oxymetholone. Although these guidelines remain to be established firmly, other studies which use this approach to select patients for treatment will be awaited with great interest.

At present, our ability to predict those patients who will die from aplastic anaemia is inadequate. In part, this is because the methods we have available to measure the severity and duration of bone marrow aplasia are both insufficient and indirect. It is also because the clinical response of any single patient is subject to factors that are not quantifiable by laboratory determinations. Thus, we may be able to improve our ability to determine those patients at greatest and least risk as we become able to identify additional factors which influence the survival of patients with aplastic anaemia. For example, incorporation of data obtained from indium scintigraphy and thin section bone marrow histology might improve the selectivity of the presently available prognostic index. Continued efforts must be made to understand more clearly the factors which affect the survival of patients with aplastic anaemia if we are to make progress in developing and assessing new treatment programmes and in deciding appropriate treatment for the individual patient.

REFERENCES

AJLOUNI, K. & DOEBLIN, T. D. (1974) The syndrome of hepatitis and aplastic anaemia. *Br. J. Haemat.*, *27*, 345.

AKSOY, M. & ERDEN, S. (1973) Letter. *Blood*, *41*, 742.

AMERICAN MEDICAL ASSOCIATION (1967) Registry on Adverse Reactions, Panel on Hematology. Council on Drugs.

BALDRIDGE, C. W. (1935) Macrocytic anemia with aplastic features following the application of synthetic organic hair dye. *Am. J. med. Sci.*, *189*, 759.

BERNARD, J.-F., MERCIER, J.-C., RICHARD, B. & BOIVIN, P. (1975) Formes pancyto-péniques de la tuberculose aiguë. *Sem. Hôp. Paris*, *51*, 2239.

BITHELL, T. C. & WINTROBE, M. M. (1967) Drug-induced aplastic anemia. *Semin. Hemat.*, *4*, 194.

BLOOM, G. E. & DIAMOND, L. K. (1971) Prognostic value of fetal hemoglobin levels in acquired aplastic anemia. *New Engl. J. Med.*, *278*, 304.

BÖTTIGER, L. E. (1974) Drug-induced aplastic anaemia in Sweden with special reference to chloramphenicol. *Postgrad. med. J.*, *50* (Suppl. 5), 127.

BÖTTIGER, L. E. & WESTERHOLM, B. (1972a) Aplastic anaemia. I. Incidence and aetiology. *Acta med. scand.*, *192*, 315.

BÖTTIGER, L. E. & WESTERHOLM, B. (1972b) Aplastic anaemia. III. Aplastic anaemia and infectious hepatitis. *Acta med. scand.*, *192*, 323.

BRANDT, L., NILSSON, P. G. & MITELMAN, F. (1977) Non-industrial exposure to benzene as leukaemogenic risk factor. *Lancet*, *ii*, 1074.

DAVIS, S. & RUBIN, A. D. (1972) Treatment and prognosis in aplastic anaemia. *Lancet*, *i*, 871.

DAWSON, J. P. (1955) Congenital pancytopenia associated with multiple congenital anomalies (Fanconi type). *Pediatrics, Springfield*, *15*, 325.

DERINGER, P. M. & MANIATIS, A. (1976) Chlorpheneramine-induced bone-marrow suppression. *Lancet*, *i*, 432.

DOAN, C. A. & SABIN, F. R. (1927) Local progression with spontaneous regression of tuberculosis in bone marrow of rabbits, correlated with transitory anemia and leucopenia after intravenous innoculation. *J. exp. Med.*, *46*, 315.

DONSKI, S. T. & BUCHER, U. (1968) Increase of the number of pancytopenias between 1954 and 1964. *Helv. med. Acta*, *34*, 337.

EHRLICH, P. (1888) Ueber einen Fall von Anämie mit Beymerkringen über regenerative Veränderungen des Knochemarks. *Charité-Annln*, *13*, 300.

ERSLEV, A. J. (1964) Drug-induced blood dyscrasias: I. Aplastic anemia. *J. Am. med. Ass.*, *188*, 531.

DE FILIPPI, P. (1942) Mielosi globale aplastica in corso di melitense. *Haematologica*, *24*, 947.

FISHER, A. M., OSSMAN, A. G., jun., WILGIS, E. F. S. & KRAVITZ, S. C. (1966) Generalized tuberculosis with pancytopenia. *Bull. Johns Hopkins Hosp.*, *119*, 355.

FLEMING, A. F. (1973) Hypoplastic anemia. *Clinics Haemat.*, *2*, 477.

FOUNTAIN, J. R. (1954) Blood changes associated with disseminated tuberculosis. Report of four fatal cases and review. *Br. med. J.*, *2*, 76.

FRANCOMBE, W. H. & TOWNSEND, S. R. (1965) Pancytopenia and disseminated aspergillosis. *Can. med. Ass. J.*, *92*, 81.
FRISCH, B. & LEWIS, S. M. (1974) The bone marrow in aplastic anaemia: Diagnostic and
prognostic features. *J. clin. Path.*, *27*, 231.
GEARY, C. G. (1976) Selection for bone-marrow transplantation. *Lancet*, *ii*, 810.
GOODWIN, D. A., GOODE, R., BROWN, L. & IMBORNONE, C. J. (1971) ^{111}In-labelled
transferrin for the detection of tumours. *Radiology*, *100*, 175.
GRYPE, C. I. & RUBENZAHL, S. (1976) Agranulocytosis and aplastic anemia possibly due
to ibuprofen. *Can. med. Ass. J.*, *144*, 877.
HAGLER, L., PASTORE, R. A., and BERGIN, J. J. (1975) Aplastic anemia following viral
hepatitis: Report of two fatal cases and literature review. *Medicine, Balt.*, *54*, 139.
HAST, R., SKÅRBERG, K. O., ENGSTEDT, L., JAMESON, S., KILLANDER, A., LUNDH, B.,
REIZENSTEIN, P., UDÉN, A. M. & WADMAN, B. (1976) Oxymetholone treatment in
aregenerative anemia. II. Remission and survival—a prospective study. *Scand. J.
Haemat.*, *16*, 90.
HAUSMANN, K., & SKRANDIES, G. (1974) Aplastic anaemia following chloramphenicol
therapy in Hamburg and surrounding districts. *Postgrad. med. J.*, *50* (Suppl. 5),
131.
HELLRIEGEL, K. P., ZÜGER, D. & GROSS, R. (1977) Prognosis in acquired aplastic anemia.
An approach in the selection of patients for allogeneic bone marrow transplan-
tation. *Blut*, *34*, 11.
HODGKINSON, R. (1971) Infectious hepatitis and aplastic anaemia. *Lancet*, *i*, 1014.
HOSAIN, F., MCINTYRE, P. A., POULOSE, K., STERN, H. S. & WAGNER, H. N., jun. (1969)
Binding of trace amounts of ionic indium-113m to plasma transferrin. *Clinica
chim. Acta*, *24*, 69.
HUGULEY, C. M., jun. (1963) Drug-induced blood dyscrasias. *DM*, October, 1.
ISRAËLS, M. C. G. & WILKINSON, J. F. (1961) Idiopathic aplastic anaemia. Incidence and
management. *Lancet*, *i*, 63.
JANUARY, L. E. & FOWLES, W. M. (1940) Aplastic anemia. *Am. J. clin. Path.*, *10*, 792.
JOUHAR, A. J. (1976) Aplastic anaemia and hair dye. *Br. med. J.*, *i*, 1074.
KANSU, E. & ERSLEV, A. J. (1976) Aplastic anaemia with 'hot pockets'. *Scand. J. Haemat.*,
17, 326.
KILLANDER, A., LUNDMARK, K.-M. & SJÖLIN, S. (1969) Idiopathic aplastic anaemia in
children. Results of androgen treatment. *Acta paediat. scand.*, *58*, 10.
KNISPEL, J. W., LYNCH, V. A. & VIELE, B. D. (1976) Aplastic anemia in pregnancy: A
case report, review of the literature and a re-evaluation of management. *Obstetl
gynec. Surv.*, *31*, 523.
LEWIS, S. M. (1965) Course and prognosis in aplastic anaemia. *Br. med. J.*, *1*, 1027.
LI, F. P., ALTER, B. P. & NATHAN, D. G. (1972) The mortality of acquired aplastic
anemia in children. *Blood*, *40*, 153.
LOGE, J. P. (1965) Aplastic anemia following exposure to benzene hexachloride
(Lindane). *J. Am. med. Ass.*, *193*, 110.
LOHRMANN, H. P., NIETHAMMER, D., KERN, P. & HEIMPEL, H. (1976) Identification of
high-risk patients with aplastic anaemia in selection for allogenic bone-marrow
transplantation. *Lancet*, *ii*, 647.
LORENZ, E. & QUAISER, K. (1955) Panmyelopathie nach Hepatitis epidemica. *Wien.
med. Wschr.*, *105*, 19.
LYNCH, R. E., WILLIAMS, D. M., READING, J. C. & CARTWRIGHT, G. E. (1975) The
prognosis in aplastic anemia. *Blood*, *45*, 517.
MCNEIL, B. J., HOLMAN, B. L., BUTTON, L. N. & ROSENTHAL, D. S. (1974) Use of indium
chloride scintigraphy in patients with myelofibrosis. *J. nuclear Med.*, *15*, 647.
MCNEIL, B. J., RAPPEPORT, J. M. & NATHAN, D. G. (1976) Indium chloride scintigraphy: An index of severity in patients with aplastic anemia. *Br. J. Haemat.*, *34*,
599.
MEDD, W. E. & HAYHOE, F. G. J. (1955) Tuberculous miliary necrosis with pancytopenia. *Q. Jl. Med.*, *29*, 351.
MIR, M. A., GEARY, C. G. & DELAMORE, I. W. (1977) Hypoimmunoglobulinemia and
aplastic anemia. *Scand. J. Haemat.*, *19*, 225.

MODAN, B., SEGAL, S., SHANI, M. & SHEBA, C. (1975) Aplastic anemia In Israel: evaluation of the etiologic role of chloramphenicol on a community-wide basis. *Am. J. med. Sci.*, *270*, 441.
MOHLER, D. N. & LEAVELL, B. S. (1958) Aplastic anemia: An analysis of 50 cases. *Ann. intern. Med.*, *49*, 326.
MOSER, R. H. (1971) The obituary of an idea. *J. Am. med. Ass.*, *216*, 2135.
NAJEAN, Y., BERNARD, J., WAINBERGER, M., DRESCH, C., BOIEREN, M. & SELIGMANN, M. (1965) Evolution et prognostic des pancytopenies idiopathiques. *Nouv. Revue fr. Hémat.*, *5*, 639.
O'GORMAN HUGHES, D. W. (1969) Aplastic anemia in childhood: A reappraisal. I. Classification and assessment. *Med. J. Aust.*, *1*, 1059.
O'GORHAM HUGHES, D. W. (1973) Aplastic anaemia in childhood: A reappraisal. II. Idiopathic and acquired aplastic anemia. *Med. J. Aust.*, *2*, 361.
PARSONS, W. B., COOPER, T. & SCHEIFLEY, C. H. (1953) Occult subacute bacterial endocarditis manifested by hematologic abnormalities, including pancytopenia. *Ann. intern. Med.*, *39*, 318.
POWARS, D. (1965) Aplastic anemia secondary to glue sniffing. *New Engl. J. Med.*, *273*, 700.
RETIEF, F. P. & HEYNS, A. DU P. (1976) Pansitopenie en aplastiese anemie 'n retrospektieve beoordeling. *S. Afr. med. J.*, *50*, 1318.
RICHARDS, A. J., VELVIN, D. S., WHITMORE, D. N. & WILLIAMS, E. M. (1976) Fatal aplastic anaemia and D-penicillamine. *Lancet*, *i*, 646.
ROYAL MARSDEN HOSPITAL BONE MARROW TRANSPLANTATION TEAM (1977) Failure of syngeneic bone-marrow graft without preconditioning in post-hepatitis marrow aplasia. *Lancet*, *ii*, 742.
SANTESSON, C. G. (1897) Uber chronische Vergiftung mit Steinkohlen-Theerbenzin. Vier Todesfalle. *Arch. Hyg. Bakt.*, *31*, 336.
SCOTT, J. L., CARTWRIGHT, G. E. & WINTROBE, M. M. (1959) Acquired aplastic anemia: An analysis of thirty-nine cases and review of the pertinent literature. *Medicine, Balt.*, *38*, 119.
SELLING, L. (1910) A preliminary report of some cases of purpura haemorhagica due to benzol poisoning. *Bull. Johns Hopkins Hosp.*, *21*, 33.
SELLING, L. (1916) Benzol as a leucotoxin. Studies on the degeneration and regeneration of the blood and haematopoietic organs. *Johns Hopkins Hosp. Rep.*, *17*, 83.
SMITH, L. W. (1919) Report on an unusual case of aplastic anemia. *Am. J. Dis. Childh.*, *17*, 174.
SPRY, C. J. F. (1976) Chlorpheneramine-induced bone marrow suppression. *Lancet*, *i*, 545.
STOHLMAN, F., jun. (1972) Aplastic anemia. *Blood*, *40*, 282.
THOMAS, E. D., BUCKNER, C. D., STORB, R., NEIMAN, P. E., FEFER, A., CLIFT, R. A., SLICHTER, S. J., FUNK, D. D., BRYANT, J. I. & LERNER, K. E. (1972) Aplastic anaemia treated by marrow transplantation. *Lancet*, *i*, 284.
THOMAS, E. D., STORB, R., CLIFT, R. A., FEFER, A., JOHNSON, F. L., NEIMAN, P. E., LERNER, K. G., GLUCKSBERG, H. & BUCKNER, C. D. (1975) Bone marrow transplantation. *New Engl. J. Med.*, *292*, 832.
TOGHILL, P. J. & WILCOX, R. G. (1976) Aplastic anaemia and hair dye. *Br. med. J.*, *1*, 502.
TWOMEY, J. J., DOUGLASS, C. C. & SHARKEY, O., jun. (1973) The monocytopenia of aplastic anemia. *Blood*, *41*, 187.
TE VELDE, J. & HAAK, H. L. (1977) Aplastic anaemia. Histological investigation of methacrylate embedded bone marrow biopsy specimens; correlation with survival after conventional treatment in 15 adult patients. *Br. J. Haemat.*, *35*, 61.
VIALA, J. J., BRYON, P. A., CORDEL, J. C., REVEL, L. & CROIZAT, P. (1970) Discussions du role des hepatitis virales dans le declenchment des insuffisances medullaires chroniques. *Lyon méd.*, *223*, 1019.
VODAPECK, H. (1975) Cherchez la chienne. *J. Am. med. Ass.*, *234*, 850.
WALLERSTEIN, R. O., CONDIT, P. K., KASPER, C. K., BROWN, J. W. & MORRISON, F. R.

(1969) Statewide study of chloramphenicol therapy and fatal aplastic anemia. *J. Am. med. Ass.*, *208*, 2045.

WEHINGER, H. & LENCER, E. (1977) Zur Prognose der Panmyelophthise: Die Formel von Lynch. *Mschr. Kinderheilk.*, *125*, 561.

WELCH, H., LEWIS, C. N. & KERLAN, I. (1954) Blood dyscrasias a nationwide survey. *Antibiotics Chemother.*, *4*, 607.

VAN DER WEYDEN, M. & FIRKIN, B. G. (1972) The management of aplastic anaemia in adults. *Br. J. Haemat.*, *22*, 1.

WILLIAMS, D. M., LYNCH, R. E. & CARTWRIGHT, G. E. (1973) Drug-induced aplastic anemia. *Semin. Hemat.*, *10*, 195.

4

Laboratory Aspects of Aplastic Anaemia

H. HEIMPEL

The symptoms and clinical signs of aplastic anaemia are non-specific. They are all the expression of a lack of peripheral blood cells, leading to low oxygen transport capacity, loss of integrity of the vascular walls and impairment of defence mechanisms against a potentially harmful microbial environment. These consequences of haemopoietic failure are not only shared with other diseases of the haemopoietic organs such as megaloblastic anaemia, leukaemia, lymphoma, myelosclerosis and aplasia after cytostatics or irradiation, but are also influenced by the state of other organ systems, in particular the cardiovascular system. More specific are certain constellations of bone marrow histopathology and laboratory values, especially quantitative changes in the numbers of peripheral blood cells. The aim of this chapter is a critical evaluation of pertinent laboratory data in aplastic anaemia. A complete description of the symptomatology and natural history of the disease is not attempted, as this can be found in other chapters of the book.

PERIPHERAL BLOOD COUNTS

In typical aplastic anaemia, the number of red cells, granulocytes and platelets is significantly below the normal range. In the majority of cases, the number of these cells falls below the threshold necessary to guarantee their specific function. This is in agreement with the current pathophysiological concept of aplastic anaemia as a disorder of the pluripotent haemopoietic stem-cell pool (Heimpel & Kubanek 1975). However, a minority of cases of aplastic anaemia present with incomplete pancytopenias (Dreyfus 1959; Vincent & De Gruchy 1967; Williams et al. 1973; Heimpel et al. 1975; Huhn et al. 1975). In analysing such cases, the first point to be considered is the different kinetics of the haemopoietic cell lines. Decreased effective cell production is reflected more rapidly in the granulocytes and platelets than in red cells. Absolute reticulocyte counts are therefore a better parameter for evaluation of the erythroid series than the haematocrit or red cell count. This is just as true for acute aplastic anaemia as for more chronic cases which have received blood transfusions before diagnosis. A particular methodological problem is the relative inaccuracy of reticulocyte counts in the low normal or subnormal range. This is reflected by the observation that fluctuations in the absolute reticulocyte count in normal subjects are much greater than those in the red cell count. The accuracy of the reticulocyte count is especially low when a constant number of erythrocytes, e.g. 1000 cells, is examined. For clinical research and evaluation of prognosis, a method with a constant counting error should be used. One of these methods is the use of the Miller ocular, which allows enumeration of a constant number of a minor subpopulation of red cells (i.e. the reticulocytes) (Brecher & Schneiderman 1950). If at least 50 reticulocytes are counted, values of less than 25 000 reticulocytes/μl are significantly subnormal, suggesting decreased effective red cell production.

Fig. 4.1 shows the initial blood count constellations in patients with aplastic anaemia seen in our institution from 1967 to 1977. In all these patients, the diagnosis was established by bone marrow biopsies and subsequent clinical observation. The lower limits of normal were

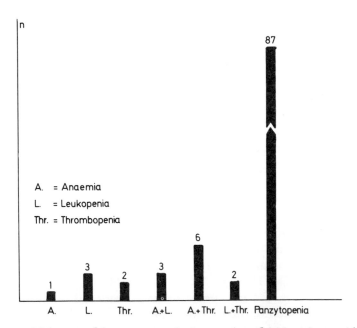

Fig. 4.1. Initial type of haemocytopenia in a series of 104 patients with aplastic anaemia.

defined as 3000 leucocytes/μl, 100 000 platelets/μl and 12 g haemo-globin/dl respectively. The distribution of the cell types involved is similar to the observations reported by Williams et al. (1973). In patients presenting without anaemia, reticulocytes were below normal in 4; all these patients became anaemic a few weeks later. Most of the patients showing initial cytopenia in only one or two cell lines developed complete pancytopenia within the following weeks or months. However, the prognosis of patients presenting with in-complete pancytopenia was better than that of the majority of patients with typical complete pancytopenia (Heimpel et al. 1975). This may be explained by the hypothesis that with a lesser degree of stem-cell damage the production of one cell line can be maintained due to physiological regulating mechanisms, at least in certain stages of the evolution of the disease.

Red Cells

Patients with severe aplastic anaemia require regular blood trans-fusions. Hence their blood always contains a mixture of autologous and transfused red cells, thereby preventing the detection of possible alterations in subpopulations of the patient's own cells. This has to be kept in mind when red cell abnormalities in aplastic anaemia are

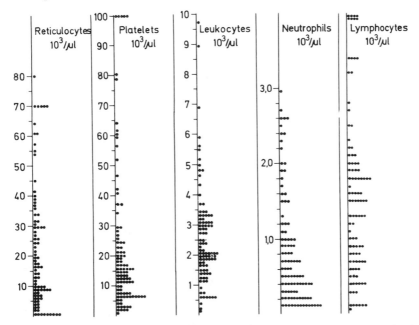

Fig. 4.2. Blood cell counts in a series of 104 patients with aplastic anaemia at the time of diagnosis.

interpreted. In non-transfused cases the MCV and MCH are normal
or increased (Scott et al. 1959). Moderate anisopoikilocytosis is
present, but there are no diagnostic morphological abnormalities.
Sporadic normoblasts may occasionally be found when a large number
of nucleated cells are surveyed (Scott et al. 1959; Hasselback & Thomas
1960); nevertheless an incidence of more than 5% in consecutive smears
militates against the diagnosis of aplastic anaemia and suggests
leukaemia, myelofibrosis or bone marrow metastasis.

The degree of anaemia—in the usual chronic case—is dependent
mainly on the frequency of red cell transfusions. Reticulocytes are
'absolutely' decreased, (i.e. below 25 000/μl) in about two-thirds of all
cases (Fig. 4.2). However, normal or moderately elevated reticulocyte
counts, as seen in a minority of cases (Lewis 1965; Vincent & De
Gruchy 1967; Williams et al. 1973; Heimpel et al. 1975), are
considered 'functionally' low because normal erythropoietic tissue
would respond to a comparable anaemic stimulus with a greater
reticulocytosis (i.e. the number of red cells newly formed per day). This
'relative' erythropoietic failure is not the result of subnormal
stimulation, because erythropoietin values are highly elevated in
aplastic anaemia (Alexanian 1973; Kubanek et al. 1975). Absolute
reticulocyte counts may be of higher prognostic value than any other
single laboratory result (Lohrmann et al. 1976) (see Chapter 3).

A few biochemical red cell abnormalities were observed in a
minority of cases with aplastic anaemia. HbF may be increased, especially in children, up to values of 12% (Shahidi et al. 1962; Bloom &
Diamond 1967). Low pyruvate kinase and glutathione reductase values
were found in some patients (Kleeberg et al. 1971). Such changes are
probably the metabolic expression of dyserythropoiesis of the remaining erythropoietic tissue and are more frequently found in pancytopenias with hyperplastic bone marrow, e.g. in pre-leukemia (Valentine
et al. 1973). Glutathione reductase activity has been normalized by
riboflavin injections without any change in the haematological picture
(Schröter 1969).

Somewhat more specific are PNH-like abnormalities in the red cell
membrane with positive acid serum and sucrose tests. The high
incidence of 15%, initially reported by Lewis and Dacie (1967), could
not be confirmed by other authors (Najean & Bernard 1965; Heimpel
et al. 1975). However, there is no doubt that patients starting as typical
cases of aplastic anaemia, with fatty marrow and negative acid serum
test, may show a positive test later and convert into a picture of
pancytopenia with hyperplastic erythropoiesis and typical haemolytic
and gastrointestinal manifestations. The course of such a patient is
depicted in Fig. 4.3. Increased complement sensitivity of a sub-

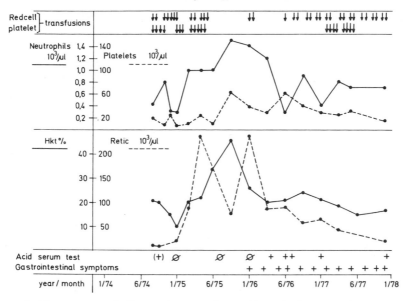

Fig. 4.3. The course of disease in a patient with aplastic anaemia-paroxysmal nocturnal haemoglobinuria syndrome. The marrow was initially hypoplastic with erythropoietic foci; later it showed moderate hyperplasia with an excess of erythroblasts and low numbers of megacaryocytes and granulopoietic cells.

population of young red cells, not detected by the acid serum test on unfractionated red cells, may be more frequent than overt PNH (Ben-Bassat et al. 1975) (see p. 98).

Red-cell survival was found to be shortened in some studies (Najean et al. 1959; Lewis 1962; Heimpel et al. 1964), but the significance of such data is reduced by the fact that there were only a few cases with true steady-state conditions of red cell turnover at the time of investigation. [51]Cr red cell survival studies are therefore not useful in evaluating aplastic anaemia, except for special cases such as in patients with PNH-like red cells or in secondary hypersplenism. The latter complication may be responsible for the favourable effect of splenectomy in a minority of patients with chronic aplastic anaemia. However, it has to be stressed that critical evaluation of our own series and of reports in the literature (Scott et al. 1959) did not yield conclusive evidence of benefit from splenectomy. On the other hand, Heaton et al. (1957) reported better survival in institutions including splenectomy in their therapeutic strategy, but did not find the usual histological features of hypersplenism in the spleens removed. In the individual case with preponderant chronic anaemia, decreased ^{51}Cr red cell survival, normal or increased plasma iron turnover, together with a palpable spleen, could support the decision to perform splenectomy.

Platelets

The number of platelets is below 30 000/μl in more than 70% of cases (Fig. 4.2). This is due to low platelet production; platelet life span as measured by ^{51}Cr in the absence of bleeding is usually normal (Najean et al. 1973; Adam et al. 1970). The distinct short-term oscillations of the platelet count which are seen in hypersplenism do not occur in aplastic anaemia. Platelets tend to fall and platelet transfusions to be required more often, when the patient suffers from septicaemia.

No useful metabolic or functional studies on platelets are available, partly because of methodological problems at low blood platelet concentrations. Megaplatelets as seen in the hyperdestructive type of thrombocytopenia, e.g. ITP, are not observed in aplastic anaemia.

Granulocytes

Granulocytes are usually below 1500/ml (Fig. 4.2) but normal granulocyte counts early in the disease are seen more often than normal values in platelets or red cells. An increased stab/seg ratio may be present. Occasionally immature forms are found (Scott et al. 1959), but more than 5% myelocytes and metamyelocytes are very unusual, except in the phase of active marrow regeneration. Neutrophil alkaline phosphatase scores may be elevated, up to values of 300 (normal 10–100). However, this finding has no diagnostic significance, because it may also occur in subleukaemic acute leukaemia. Granulocyte function has been investigated in some patients without clear-cut results (Clark et al. 1976; Territo et al. 1977).

Only a few useful data exist concerning the number of basophilic and eosinophilic granulocytes, again because of statistical problems in estimating low concentrations of the cell types concerned. Values derived from routine differential counts are erratic. For diagnostic purposes it is sufficient to state that basophilia is not present in aplastic anaemia and any degree of relative eosinophilia seldom present.

Monocyte counts are usually subnormal, their number being decreased in proportion to the number of neutrophilic granulocytes (Twomey 1973). Relative and even absolute monocytosis in pancytopenia always suggests pre-leukaemia with abnormal differentiation of the neutrophilic–monocytic series in the bone marrow.

Lymphocytes

Of particular interest is the low number of lymphocytes observed in some patients with severe aplastic anaemia (Fig. 4.2). Subnormal values of less than 1000/μl are described in 10–45% of patients in the literature

(Scott et al. 1959; Williams et al. 1973; Heimpel et al. 1975; Huhn et al. 1975). A similar lymphopenia is also observed in severe cases of acute drug-induced agranulocytosis. The morphology of the lymphocytes is normal. (Bacon et al. 1975), except for the occasional occurrence of plasma cells. An increase of DNA-synthesizing lymphocytes was reported by Cooper and Firkin (1964) but was not confirmed by the newer data from Bacon et al. (1975). Results of functional subclassification by Morley et al. (1974) and ourselves showed an absolute and relative decrease of B-cell and a relative increase of T-cell fraction using various marker techniques. This is in agreement with previous experiments by Flad et al. (1970), which showed a high and early increase of ^{3}H-TdR-incorporation in lymphocytes from patients with 'idiopathic' aplastic anaemia, stimulated with phytohaemagglutinin.

In contrast to other forms of lymphopenia, for instance in subjects receiving total body irradiation or in children with severe combined immunodeficiency disease, there are no observations pointing to clinically significant immunologic deficiencies in lymphopenic patients with aplastic anaemia. However, a distinct tendency towards low lymphocyte counts was predominantly seen in patients with subnormal immunoglobulin levels by Huhn et al. (1975).

At present, no satisfactory explanation for the concomitant lymphopenia in severe aplastic anaemia is possible. One may speculate that it results from failure of a common stem-cell pool necessary for the maintenance of both myelopoiesis and lymphopoiesis. That such a common stem-cell pool operates in post-fetal human beings is suggested by observations in chronic myeloproliferative disorders afflicting G-6-PDH-heterozygote females (Fialkow et al. 1978). Rare cases of an invariably fatal congenital combined immune and haemopoietic failure have been described (Gitlin et al. 1964). On the other hand, this hypothesis of damage to a common stem cell is difficult to equate with the observation that, in many cases of aplastic anaemia, bone marrow lymphocytes are present in normal or even increased numbers (Frisch & Lewis 1974; Te Velde & Haak 1977) (see p. 74).

However, the marrow lymphocytes may reflect a stromal defect associated with aggregates of T-cells (p. 15). Blood lymphopenia in aplastic anaemia is apparently a result of B-cell depletion, but data on lymphocyte sunpopulations in the marrow are not yet available.

BONE MARROW

Examination of suitable bone marrow specimens is still the clue for the diagnosis of aplastic anaemia and for the differential diagnosis of the pancytopenias without gross splenomegaly. The characteristic

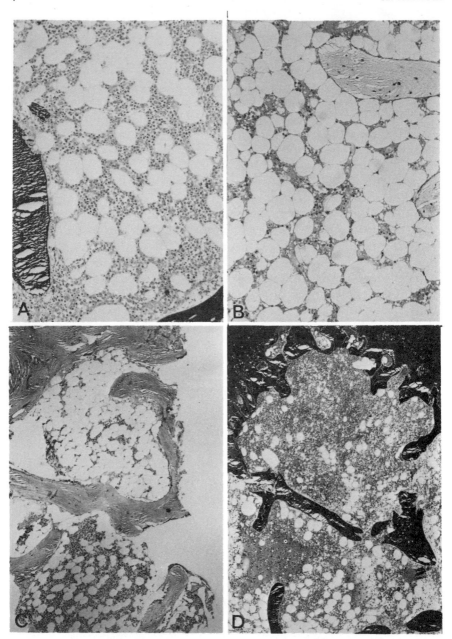

Fig. 4.4. Bone marrow biopsies. A, Normal. B, From a patient with severe aplastic anaemia. C, From a young patient with normal bone marrow. Note the 'pseudo-aplasia' in a subcortical marrow space. D, From a patient with severe chronic aplastic anaemia. Note the dense haemopoietic cells in one subcortical area. The marrow was aplastic in other parts of this biopsy cylinder and in consecutive biopsies. Methacrylate. Galliamin blue Giemsa. A, B, ×80. C, D, ×32.

PLATE I

Bone marrow biopsy from a patient with oligoblastic leukaemia. This patient developed acute leukaemia with peripheral blasts four months later.

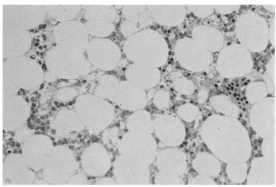

(*a*) Distinct hypoplasia. Overall cellularity was less than 20%. ×150

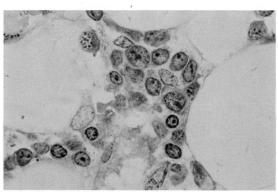

(*b*) A group of primitive cells, probably granulocytic precursors. One plasma cell (top left) shows a different structure. ×500

Methacrylate. Galliamin-blue-Giemsa

PLATE II

Bone marrow biopsies of patients with aplastic anaemia.

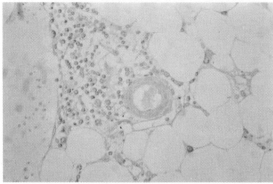

(a) Lymphocytes and plasma cells surrounding a small
artery.   ×150

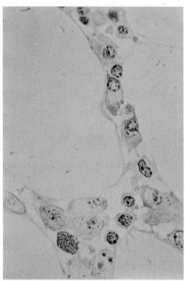

(b) Same patient. Plasma cells and
lymphocytes infiltrating
between fat cells.   ×500

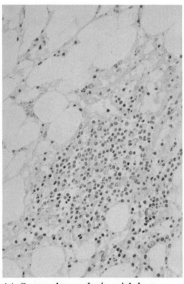

(c) Severe hypoplasia with larger
areas of lymphocytic
infiltration.   ×100

PLATE II (*continued*)

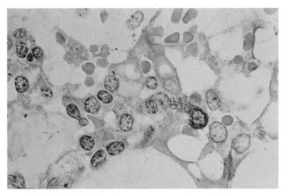

(*d*) Oedema and infiltration by lymphocytes and
tissue basophils in aplastic marrow.　×500

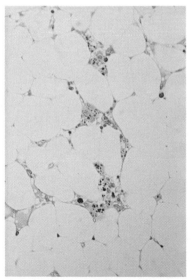

(*e*) Macrophages filled with coarse
material which stained blue in
Turnbull stain.　×100

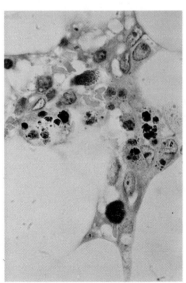

(*f*) Greater magnification of the
same area as in (*e*).　×500

Methacrylate. Galliamin-blue-Giemsa

PLATE III

Haemopoietic foci in aplastic marrow.

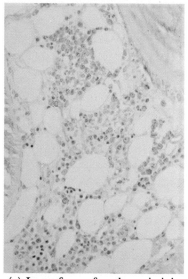

(a) Large focus of erythropoiesis in an aplastic marrow. ×150

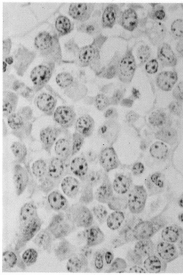

(b) Greater magnification of the same area. ×500

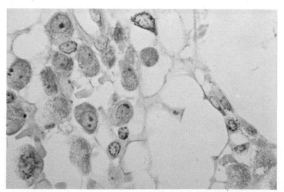

(c) Group of myelocytes and metamyelocytes. ×500

Methacrylate. Galliamin-blue-Giemsa

picture was described in the first case, published under the name 'aplastische Anämie', by Paul Ehrlich in 1888. It consists of the replacement by fat cells of the space normally filled with haemopoietic tissue and of various degrees of an 'inflammatory' infiltrate by lymphoid cells, plasma cells, mast cells and macrophages (Scott et al. 1959; Frisch & Lewis 1974; Burkhardt 1975; Te Velde & Haak 1977). The aplasia of haemopoietic cells can be seen macroscopically at autopsy or in large biopsy specimens and is easily demonstrated at low-power microscopy (Fig. 4.4). However, there are some pitfalls to bear in mind in evaluating the decrease of haemopoietic cells in the bone marrow:

1. In biopsies taken from the iliac crest or dorsal iliac spine, the subcortical areas may consist mainly of fat cells in normal subjects (Fig. 4.4A). The diagnosis of marrow aplasia or hypoplasia therefore requires a biopsy cylinder containing marrow in spongy bone at a length of at least 10 mm. It is mandatory that the marrow cavities enclosed by the bone trabeculae are not squeezed by the biopsy procedure. There are several methods of needle biopsy which fulfil these requirements if performed correctly. The best specimens are obtained by the technique of myelotomy as described by Burckhardt (1966). However, most clinicians prefer the biopsy needle of Jamshidi and Swaim (1971) for its simple, safe, fast and non-traumatic handling.

2. 'Normal' values of bone marrow cellularity are dependent on the technical details of the biopsy procedure, embedding, method of evaluation and age of the patient. If the area composed of fat and vascular lumina is compared to the area containing cells and intra-cellular material, a cellularity of about 20% is held to be the lower limit of normal by most investigators. In elderly individuals, 'moderately' decreased cellularities should be interpreted with great care and only if they are in agreement with the peripheral cell counts. On the other hand the diagnostic significance of the marrow cellularity is supported by the fact that in patients with distinct pancytopenia the marrow is in most instances either hypo- or hypercellular, depending on the localization of the disorder within the hierarchy of haemopoiesis, but seldom normocellular.

3. In patients with early remission from aplastic anaemia or with long-lasting partial remission, marrow cellularity may not be homo-genous, hypercellular foci of haemopoiesis being surrounded by larger areas of aplasia (January & Fowler 1940; Kansu & Erslev 1976). Such hypercellular foci of regenerating haemopoiesis may involve subcor-tical areas which are normally filled with fat cells (Fig. 4.4), simulating a hyperplastic marrow as in pre-leukaemia. Sufficiently long biopsy cylinders prevent such incorrect interpretation. In doubtful cases, one should not hesitate to take a second biopsy from the other iliac crest.

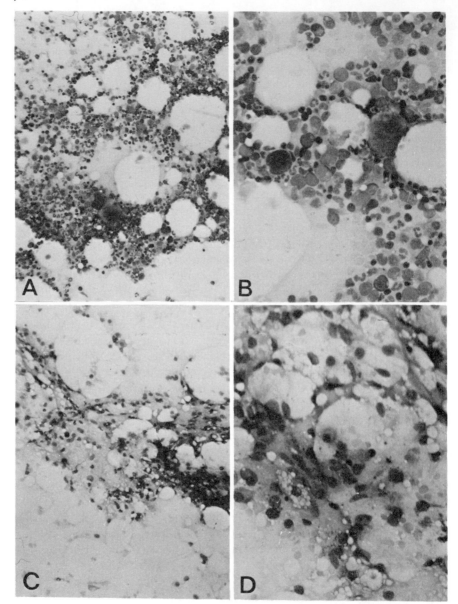

Fig. 4.5. Aspirated marrow particles. A, B, Normal marrow. C, D, From a patient with aplastic anaemia. Pappenheim. A, C, ×100. B, D, ×250.

4. For the reasons mentioned above, minor variations of cellularity in follow-up studies should not be 'over-interpreted' as evidence of deterioration or improvement in the state of haemopoiesis. Carefully recorded peripheral cell counts are, in the majority of patients, more reliable for monitoring the course of the disease. One exception is the

development of hypersplenism in long-standing aplastic anaemia with secondary haemochromatosis.

It is now generally accepted that bone marrow aspiration is insufficient for the diagnosis of aplastic anaemia (Lewis 1965; Gruppo et al. 1977), even though the appearance of fatty marrow particles containing stromal cells, lymphocytes, plasma cells and macrophages is very characteristic (Fig. 4.5). *Exclusion* of the diagnosis of aplastic anaemia in aspirated material is possible only if the marrow cytology is unequivocally diagnostic, e.g. in acute subleukaemic leukaemia or megaloblastic anaemia. Normocellularity or hypercellularity of aspirated specimens by itself does not rule out aplastic anaemia because of the possible variations in cellularity mentioned above. Hypocellularity is the most important diagnostic feature of the bone marrow in aplastic anaemia, but there are in addition a variety of other morphological details characteristic of aplastic anaemia which are interesting because they suggest pathophysiological mechanisms, and are also probably useful as prognostic indices (Frisch & Lewis 1974; Heimpel et al. 1975; te Velde & Haak 1977). More detailed histological descriptions, in the literature, of the marrow in aplastic anaemia are rare and often controversial; this is probably because the previously used techniques (decalcification and paraffin-embedding) lead to distortion of the fine bone marrow structure and shrinkage of the cells, preventing their proper identification. Embedding in plastic materials like methylacrylate allows better conservation of thinner sections and is now the method of choice for the histology of haemopoietic tissue (te Velde et al. 1977). If this method is not available, in addition to paraffin-embedded biopsies aspirated marrow should be used for diagnosis. One condition which may be overlooked in paraffin-embedded sections is the rare case of so-called 'low cell' (oligoblastic) leukaemia; here the diagnosis is based on the morphological appearance of small clusters of undifferentiated cells which are then falsely classified as belonging to one of the normal cell lines (Plate I).

In good sections of plastic-embedded bone marrow the following features may be observed in aplastic anaemia in addition to the overall hypocellularity:

1. Focal hyperplasia. This is seen predominantly in early remission, but such foci are also found in the marrow of severe cases not achieving remission. They often contain cells of either the erythroid or the granulocytic series. In contrast to the erythroid foci present in normal marrow they consist of cells of the same stage of maturity and may contain several mitoses (Heimpel 1974; te Velde et al. 1977) (Plate II). Dyserythropoietic features such as nuclear budding or other non-specific nuclear abnormalities are also present. Such features are also seen under the electron microscope and resemble

aberrations found in other congenital or acquired dyserythropoietic states (Frisch et al. 1975) (see Chapter 5).

2. Increase in lymphocytes, plasma cells and tissue basophils. An increase of these cells has been mentioned by many authors describing aplastic anaemia. However, many such reports, especially from children, are based on the evaluation of aspirated material and describe the percentage of lymphoid cells relative to the other marrow elements. It is probably not significant that such relative numbers increase with the severity of aplasia of the haemopoietic cells (Frisch & Lewis 1974). An absolute increase of lymphoid cells and plasma cells is observed also in the majority of patients with aplastic anaemia as estimated by the analysis of methylacrylate-embedded material (Plate II). The degree of lymphoid–plasmacytoid infiltration seems to be related to prognosis: high numbers of 'non-myeloid cells' (Williams et al. 1973), plasma cells (Heimpel et al. 1975) or lymphoid cells (te Velde et al. 1977) were found to be correlated with poor prognosis.

3. Increase of macrophages with excess amounts of diffuse and coarse non-haem iron. This is seen in almost all patients with aplastic anaemia but is most impressive in patients who have received large numbers of blood transfusions (Plate II).

4. Slight or moderate fibrosis has been observed in a few cases (Williams et al. 1973; Heimpel et al. 1975).

Marrow Scintigraphy

One problem discussed in many treatises on aplastic anaemia is the question of sampling error due to a possible abnormal or grossly heterogeneous distribution of haemopoietic and fatty marrow. The logical approach to solve this problem is the use of marrow scintigraphy. The best radiochemical for this purpose is ^{52}Fe, but this isotope is not commonly available. Others include ^{99}Tcm-sulphur-colloid and indium 111 chloride (Polycove & Tono 1975). The former is bound to plasma transferrin and the latter is taken up by the macrophages in the body, predominantly in liver, spleen and bone marrow. Decreased uptake in the bone marrow has been observed with all three methods. However, actual progress in diagnostic or prognostic evaluation has not been achieved by the use of these methods in aplastic anaemia. One main difficulty is the overlap of liver, spleen and bone marrow activity in the central region of the body. In addition, it was observed that ^{52}Fe, indium 111 and ^{99m}Tc-sulphur-colloid scans give similar marrow topography in normal, but not in aplastic, marrows (van Dyke et al. 1967; Merrick et al. 1974). In one study, ^{99}Tcm-sulphur-colloid scans were found normal in aplastic anaemia

(Schreiner 1974); in another investigation indium 111 chloride scans estimated semiquantitatively were held to be useful for prognosis, but data on distribution were not described (McNeil et al. 1976). In summary, further methodological progress providing techniques with higher specificity and better resolution is necessary before marrow scintigraphy can contribute to diagnosis and prognosis of aplastic anaemia.

IRON METABOLISM

Disturbance of erythroid cell proliferation and maturation is reflected in secondary changes of iron metabolism. These changes have been frequently investigated in aplastic anaemia, aided by the ideal features of the radioactive isotope ^{59}Fe for kinetic studies of erythropoiesis. The results are interesting in relation to the pathophysiology of the disease, but of limited diagnostic importance. Iron metabolism is influenced by increased loss from bleeding on the one hand, and increased input from transfusion on the other. Possibly iron absorption is increased, as in other forms of anaemia, but absorption data on well defined aplastic anaemia patients are lacking. In the majority of cases the iron balance is positive, resulting in haemosiderosis of liver and bone marrow. Increased bone marrow macrophage iron is seen even in fresh, non-transfused cases, as a result of normal or increased extravascular red cell destruction and a lack of reutilization for maturing erythroblasts. Serum iron and serum ferritin are usually elevated and serum transferrin is normal or low. In more than 90% of our own patients, the serum iron was higher than 140 μg/100 ml at the time of diagnosis. Plasma iron turnover is more often low or normal than high, radio-iron red cell utilization is always significantly reduced as result of aplasia and/or ineffective erythropoiesis (Fig. 4.6) (Giblett et al. 1956; Najean et al. 1959; Finch et al. 1970; Polycove & Tono 1975). In patients achieving partial remission with values of platelets and granulocytes compatible with long survival but with continuing transfusion requirements, secondary haemochromatosis may develop with all the secondary laboratory abnormalities, especially abnormal liver function tests (Pedoya et al. 1956).

Pancytopenia with hyperplastic bone marrow and ineffective erythropoiesis share with the true aplastic anaemias elevated plasma iron values and low red cell utilization; however, plasma iron turnover is elevated in such cases, as opposed to the low or normal values in aplastic anaemia. Increased uptake of radio-iron in liver and spleen, as detected by external counting, is characteristically present in both conditions. The degree of reduction in red cell utilization is, according

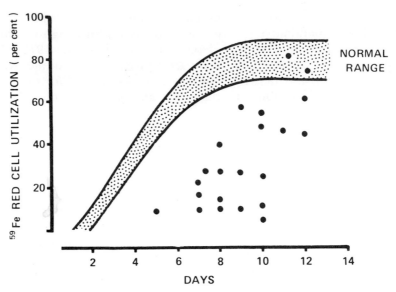

Fig. 4.6. Red cell utilization of ^{59}Fe in 22 patients with aplastic anaemia, compared with the normal range.

to Najean et al. (1965), correlated to the probability of spontaneous (or androgen-induced) remission. This fits with the prognostic value of the reticulocyte count, reflecting also the residual erythropoietic activity (see also p. 91).

HAEMOPOIETIC STEM CELLS

The number of granulocytic and erythrocytic colonies grown from mononuclear cell fractions of peripheral blood or bone marrow using the specific stimulators is markedly reduced. This is true not only for aplastic anaemia patients with severe pancytopenia but also for patients in partial or full clinical remission after severe aplastic disease (Greenberg & Schrier 1973; Kern et al. 1977; Haak et al. 1977; Hansi et al. 1978) (see Chapter 1). This is different from patients who reached a full remission by treatment of acute leukaemia. The only patients in which we found many granulocytic colonies shortly after the onset of haemopoietic recovery were children or adolescents with acute lymphatic leukaemia being treated successfully by cortico-steroids with an (erroneous) diagnosis of aplastic anaemia.

VARIOUS PLASMA COMPONENTS

It has been repeatedly noticed that the erythrocyte sedimentation rate (ESR) may be elevated to very high values and that in many cases this is not due to the anaemia alone (Vincent & De Gruchy 1967; Heimpel et al. 1975). Fibrinogen levels and acute phase proteins (Müller & Kluthe 1962) may be elevated, even in the absence of overt infection. Moderate polyclonal elevation of immunoglobulins was found in 40% of patients with aplastic anaemia by Huhn et al. (1975). This may be interpreted as being secondary to recurrent infections. Cases with acquired immunoglobulin deficiencies have been described (Huhn et al. 1975). The presence of monoclonal immunoglobulins or autoantibodies against red cells suggests other reasons for pancytopenia, for instance multiple myeloma or lupus erythematosus. Alloantibodies against HLA antigens are frequent and due to previous blood transfusions. They are probably responsible for early reports on 'autoantibodies' against leucocytes and platelets, observed with different serological techniques. Association of aplastic anaemia with certain blood groups or HLA antigens has not been observed (Albert et al. 1976). A variety of other abnormalities of serum components have been reported in single cases or retrospective surveys, but patterns of such changes are erratic and they are probably secondary due to complications of a blood disorder or concomitant diseases. Elevated GOT and GPT values are seen in about 10% of all patients with long-lasting aplastic anaemia, due to liver damage from secondary haemochromatosis or viral hepatitis transmitted by transfusions (Heimpel et al. 1975; Huhn et al. 1975).

COAGULATION

Plasma coagulation factors are normal except in situations of severe infection by the hepatitis virus or Gram-negative organisms. Coagulation factor XIII, which is frequently low in the leukaemias (Rasche 1976) has been found to be normal in aplastic anaemia. Disseminated intravascular coagulation is rare and may occur in Gram-negative septicaemia; in our experience, these are usually terminal patients where it is no longer possible to control the infection and the bleeding tendency.

DIFFERENTIAL DIAGNOSIS IN PATIENTS WITH PANCYTOPENIA

Table 4.1 shows the most frequent problems of differential diagnosis encountered in clinical practice. In our experience, subleukaemic leukaemia, extensive metastatic infiltration of the bone marrow and idiopathic thrombocytopenic purpura are the most frequent incorrect diagnoses made in aplastic anaemia and vice versa. Table 4.1

Table 4.1. The differential diagnosis of aplastic anaemia

	Disease	Discriminating features
Pancytopenia	Acute leukaemia	Usually some 'atypical' cells in blood Bone marrow diagnostic
	Severe vitamin B12 or folic acid deficiency	$MCV > 110\,\mu l$ $MCH > 40\,pg$ Bone marrow diagnostic Low folic acid or vitamin B12 plasma concentrations
	Hypersplenism	Large spleen; reticulocytosis Bone marrow hypercellular
	Aplasia induced by cytostatics	History Early haemopoietic regeneration
	Bone marrow metastases	Erythroblasts and immature granulocytes in blood Bone marrow: fibrosis, neoplastic infiltration
Anaemia and thrombocytopenia	Evans' syndrome	Marked reticulocytosis, positive antiglobulin-test Megaplatelets
	Bleeding from ITP	Reticulocytosis Megaplatelets Low plasma iron
Anaemia and leucopenia	Acute agranulocytosis	Platelets normal or high Very low neutrophil count Bone marrow: absence or maturation arrest of granulocytes
	Preleukaemia	Bone marrow: hyperplastic, often Pelger-cells, micromegakaryocytes

emphasizes the importance of obtaining a second bone marrow specimen of sufficient quality and quantity, if there is any doubt as to the definitive diagnosis.

REFERENCES

ADAM, W., HEIMPEL, H. & KRATT, E. (1970) Die Bestimmung der Thrombozyten-lebenszeit mit ^{51}Cr. II. Untersuchungen über die Lebenszeit autologer Thrombo-zyten bei Patienten mit ausgeprägter Thrombozytopenie. *Blut*, *21*, 9.
ALBERT, E., THOMAS, D., NISPEROS, B. & STORB, R. (1976) HLA-Antigens and haplo-types in 200 patients with aplastic anemia. *Transplantation*, *22*, 528.

ALEXANIAN, R. (1973) Erythropoietin excretion in bone marrow failure and hemolytic anemia. *J. Lab. clin. Med.*, *82*, 438.
BACON, P. A., SEWELL, R. & CROWTHER, D. (1975) Reactive lymphoid cells ('immunoblasts') in autoimmune and haematological disorders. *Clin. exp. Immunol.*, *19*, 201.
BEN-BASSAT, J., BROK-SIMONI, F. & BRACHA, R. (1975) Complement-sensitive red cells in aplastic anemia. *Blood*, *46*, 357.
BLOOM, G. E. & DIAMOND, L. K. (1967) Prognostic value of fetal hemoglobin levels in acquired aplastic anemia. *New Engl. J. Med.*, *278*, 304.
BRECHER, G. & SCHNEIDERMAN, M. (1950) A time-saving device for the counting of reticulocytes. *Am. J. clin. Path.*, *20*, 1079.
BURKHARDT, R. (1966) Technische Verbesserungen und Anwendungsbereich der Histo-Biopsie von Knochenmark und Knochen. *Klin. Wschr.*, *44*, 326.
CLARK, R. A., JOHNSON, F. L., KLEBANOFF, S. J. & THOMAS, E. D. (1976) Defective neutrophil chemotaxis in bone marrow transplant patients. *J. clin. Invest.*, *58*, 22.
COOPER, J. A. & FIRKIN, B. G. (1964) The presence of desoxyribonucleic acid synthesizing cells in patients with refractory anaemia. *Blood*, *24*, 415.
DREYFUS, B. (1959) A propos de 81 observations de pancytopénies idiopathiques chroniques sans splénomégalie. *Revue Hémat.*, *14*, 62.
EHRLICH, P. (1888) Über einen Fall von Anämie mit Bemerkungen über regenerative Veränderungen des Knochenmasks. *Charité-Annln*, *13*, 300.
FIALKOW, P. J., DENMAN, A. M., SINGER, J. & LOWENTHAL, M. N. (1978) Human myeloproliferative disorders: clonal origin in human pluripotent stem cells. *Proc. 5th Cold Spring Harbor Conf. Cell Proliferation*, in the press.
FINCH, C. A., DEUBELBEISS, K., COOK, J. D., ESCHBACH, J. W., HARKER, L. A., FUNK, D. D., MARSAGLIA, G., HILLMAN, R. S., SLICHTER, S., ADAMSON, J. W., GANZONI, A. & GIBLETT, E. R. (1970) Ferrokinetics in man. *Medicine, Balt.*, *49*, 17.
FLAD, H. D., HOCHAPFEL, G., FLIEDNER, T. M. & HEIMPEL, H. (1970) Blastentransformation und DNS-Synthese in Lymphozytenkulturen von Patienten mit aplastischer Anämie (Panmyelopathie). *Acta haemat.*, *44*, 21.
FRISCH, B. & LEWIS, S. M. (1974) The bone marrow in aplastic anaemia: Diagnostic and prognostic features. *J. clin. Path.*, *27*, 231.
FRISCH, B., LEWIS, S. M. & SHERMAN, D. (1975) The ultrastructure of dyserythropoiesis in aplastic anaemia. *Br. J. Haemat.*, *29*, 545.
GIBLETT, E. R., COLEMAN, D., PIRZIO-BIROLI, G., DONOHUE, M., MOTULSKY, A. G. & FINCH, C. A. (1956) Erythrokinetics: Quantitative measurements of red cell production and destruction in normal subjects and patients with anemia. *Blood*, *11*, 291.
GITLIN, D., VAWTER, G. & CRAIG, J. M. (1964) Thymic alymphoplasia and congenital aleukocytosis. *Pediatrics, Springfield*, *33*, 184.
GREENBERG, P. L. & SCHRIER, S. L. (1973) Granulopoiesis in neutropenic disorders. *Blood*, *42*, 753.
GRUPPO, R. A., LAMPKIN, B. C. & GRANGER, S. (1977) Bone marrow cellularity determination: Comparison of the biopsy, aspirate, and buffy coat. *Blood*, *49*, 29.
HAAK, H. L., GOSELINK, H. M., VEENHOF, W., PELLINKHOF-STADELMANN, S., KLEIVERDA, J. K. & TE VELDE, J. (1977) Acquired aplastic anaemia in adults. IV. Histological and CFU studies in transplanted and non-transplanted patients. *Scand. J. Haemat.*, *19*, 159.
HANSI, W., RICH, I., HEIMPEL, H., HEIT, W. & KUBANEK, B. (1978) Erythroid colony forming cells in aplastic anaemia. *Br. J. Haemat.*, *37*, 483.
HASSELBACK, R. C. & THOMAS, J. W. (1960) Aplastic anaemia. *Can. med. Ass. J.*, *82*, 1253.
HEATON, L. D., CROSBY, W. H. & COHEN, A. (1957) Splenectomy in the treatment of hypoplasia of the bone marrow. *Ann. Surg.*, *146*, 637.
HEIMPEL, H. (1974) Aplastische und hypoplastische Knochenmarkserkrankungen. *Med. Klin.*, *69*, 404.
HEIMPEL, H., DOBLER, J. & KEIDERLING, W. (1964) Blutumsatzuntersuchungen mit ^{51}Cr bei 50 Patienten mit primärer Panmyelopathie. *Klin. Wschr.*, *42*, 680.
HEIMPEL, II. & KUBANEK, B. (1975) Pathophysiology of aplastic anaemia. *Br. J. Haemat.*, *30* (Suppl.), 57.

HEIMPEL, H., REHBOCK, C. & VON EIMEREN, A. (1975) Verlauf und Prognose der Panmyelopathie und der isolierten aplastischen Anämie. *Blut, 30,* 235.

HUHN, D., FATEH-MOGHADAM, A., DEMMLER, K., KRONSEDER, A. & EHRHART, H. (1975) Hämatologische und immunologische Befunde bei der Knochenmarkaplasie. *Klin. Wschr., 53,* 7.

JAMSHIDI, K. & SWAIM, W. R. (1971) Bone marrow biopsy with unaltered architecture: a new biopsy device. *J. Lab. clin. Med., 77,* 335.

JANUARY, L. E. & FOWLER, W. M. (1943) Aplastic anemia. *Am. J. clin. Path., 10,* 792.

KANSU, E. & ERSLEV, A. J. (1976) Aplastic anaemia with 'hot pockets'. *Scand. J. Haemat., 17,* 326.

KERN, P., HEIMPEL, H., HEIT, W. & KUBANEK, B. (1977) Granulocytic progenitor cells in aplastic anaemia. *Br. J. Haemat., 35,* 613.

KLEEBERG, U., HEIMPEL, H., KLEIHAUER, E. & OLISCHLÄGER, A. (1971) Relativer Glutathion- und/oder Pyruretkinasemangel in den Erythrozyten bei Panmyelopathien und akuten Leukämien. *Klin. Wschr., 49,* 557.

KUBANEK, B., HEIT, W. & BOCK, E. (1975) Regelmechanismen der Hämopoiese bei der Knochenmarkinsuffizienz. *Hämat. Bluttransfusion, 16,* 76.

LAJTHA, L. G. (1975) Haemopoietic stem cells. *Br. J. Haemat., 29,* 529.

LEWIS, S. M. (1962) Red cell abnormalities and haemolysis in aplastic anaemia. *Br. J. Haemat., 8,* 322.

LEWIS, S. M. (1965) Course and prognosis in aplastic anemia. *Br. med. J., i,* 1027.

LEWIS, S. M. & DACIE, J. V. (1967) The aplastic anemia—paroxysmal hemoglobinuria syndrome. *Br. J. Haemat., 13,* 236.

LOHRMANN, H.-P., KERN, P., NIETHAMMER, D. & HEIMPEL, H. (1976) Identification of high-risk patients with aplastic anaemia in selection for allogeneic bone-marrow transplantation. *Lancet, ii,* 647.

MCNEIL, B., RAPPEPORT, J. M. & NATHAN, D. (1976) Indium chloride scintigraphy: An index of severity in patients with aplastic anemia. *Br. J. Haemat., 34,* 599.

MERRICK, M. V., GORDON-SMITH, E., LAVENDER, J. & SZUR, L. (1974) A comparison of In-111 with Fe-52 and Tc-99m-sulfur colloid for bone marrow scanning. *J. nucl. Med., 16,* 66.

MORLEY, A., HOLMES, K. & FORBES, J. (1974) Depletion of B-lymphocytes in chronic hypoplastic marrow failure (aplastic anemia). *Aust. N.Z. J. Med., 4,* 538.

MÜLLER, W. & KLUTHE, R. (1962) Serumeiweißveränderungen bei Panmyelopathien. *Proc. 8th Congr. europ. Soc. Haemat., Wien, 1961,* 184.

NAJEAN, Y., ARDAILLON, CAEN, J., LARRIEN, M. J. & BERNARD, J. (1966) Survival of radiochromium labelled platelets in thrombocytopenias. *Blood, 22,* 718.

NAJEAN, Y. & BERNARD, J. (1965) Prognosis and evolution of the idiopathic pancytopenias. *Ser. Haemat., 5,* 1.

NAJEAN, Y., ARDAILLOU, N. & FAILLE, S. (1973) Étude retrospective de 135 cas de thrombopénie chronique avec durée de vie normale des plaquettes. *Nouv. Revue fr. Hémat., 13,* 529.

NAJEAN, L., MEEUS-BITH, L., BERNARD, C. & BOIRON, M. (1959) Exploration isotopique de l'erythrocinetique dans 31 cas de pancytopénie idiopathique à moelle histologiquement normale ou riche. *Sang, 30,* 101.

PEDOYA, C., MOLINIER, A., DUCHESNE, G. & AZORIN, D. (1956) Hémosidérose posttransfusionelle, au cours d'une anémie chronique polytransfusee (444 transfusions sanguines en dix ans). *Bull. Mém. Soc. méd. Hôp. Paris, 4,* 304.

POLYCOVE, M. & TONO, M. (1975) Studies of the erythron. *Semin. nucl. Med., 5,* 11.

RASCHE, H. (1975) Blutgerinnungsfaktor XIII und Fibrinstabilisierung. *Klin. Wschr., 53,* 1137.

SCHREINER, D. P. (1974) Reticuloendothelial scans in disorders involving the bone marrow. *J. nucl. Med., 15,* 1158.

SCHRÖTER, W. (1969) Glutathione reductase deficiency and riboflavin in hypoplastic anemia. *New Engl. J. Med., 281,* 651.

SCOTT, J. L., CARTWRIGHT, G. E. & WINTROBE, M. M. (1959) Acquired aplastic anemia: An analysis of 39 cases and review of the pertinent literature. *Medicine, Balt., 38,* 119.

SHAHIDI, N. T., GERALD, P. S. & DIAMOND, L. K. (1962) Alkali-resistant hemoglobin in aplastic anemia of both acquired and congenital types. *New Engl. J. Med.*, *266*, 117.

TERRITO, M. C., GALE, R. P. & CLINE, M. J. (1977) Neutrophil function in bone marrow transplant recipients. *Br. J. Haemat.*, *35*, 245.

TWOMEY, J. J., DOUGLAS, C. C. & SHARKEY, O. (1973) The monocytopenia of aplastic anemia. *Blood*, *41*, 187.

VALENTINE, W. N., KONRAD, P. N. & PAGLIA, D. D. (1973) Dyserythropoietis, refractory anemia and preleukemia: metabolic features of the erythrocytes. *Blood*, *41*, 857.

TE VELDE, J., BURKHARDT, R., KLEIVERDA, K., LEENHEERS-BINNENDIJK, L. & SOMMERFELD, W. (1977) Methyl-methacrylate as an embedding medium in histopathology. *Histopathology*, *1*, 319.

TE VELDE, J. & HAAK, H. L. (1977) Aplastic anaemia. Histological investigation of methacrylate embedded bone marrow biopsy specimens; correlation with survival after conventional treatment in 15 adult patients. *Br. J. Haemat.*, *35*, 61.

VINCENT, P. C. & DE GRUCHY, G. C. (1967) Complications and treatment of acquired aplastic anemia. *Br. J. Haemat.*, *13*, 977.

WILLIAMS, D. M., LYNCH, R. & CARTWRIGHT, G. E. (1973) Drug-induced aplastic anaemia. *Semin. Hemat.*, *10*, 195.

5

Dyserythropoiesis in Aplastic Anaemia

S. M. LEWIS

The term 'ineffective erythropoiesis' was originally used by Giblett et al. (1956) and by Haurani and Tocantins (1961) to describe haematological disorders in which there is an abnormality of the developing cells which results in their intramedullary destruction. The term 'dyserythropoiesis' was introduced in recognition of the fact that, even when erythroblasts are functionally abnormal, some do survive, proliferate and mature, albeit that they are abnormal and their dependent erythrocytes are likely to have a shortened life span. Initially, the term dyserythropoiesis was used to describe a congenital defect which has subsequently become known as the congenital dyserythropoietic anaemias. The wider use of the term was proposed by Lewis and Verwilghen (1972) in order to draw attention to the fact that there is a wide range of conditions—both congenital and acquired—with the morphological and kinetic features which characterize disturbed erythropoiesis.

In the context of aplastic anaemia, dyserythropoiesis should be considered from three points of view:

1. Aplastic anaemia and dyserythropoiesis may occur simultaneously as an effect of injury or 'insult' to the erythropoietic stem cell.

2. Dyserythropoiesis may occur during regeneration in a marrow which is recovering from aplasia; paroxysmal nocturnal haemoglobinuria (PNH) is a notable illustration of the way in which an abnormal clone may arise in this disease.

3. Dyserythropoiesis is a phenomenon in various refractory cytopenias, including the myelodysplastic syndrome which manifests features of aplastic anaemia but which in reality may be a preleukaemic disorder.

In all these, the term dyserythropoiesis is, perhaps, too restrictive, as damage of the bone marrow which affects erythropoiesis will, as a rule, also extend to the granulocyte leucocytes and the platelets, leading to dyshaemopoiesis. Of course, in aplastic anaemia the features of dyserythropoiesis are usually overshadowed by the hypoplasia but it is important to recognize the extent to which dyserythropoiesis may occur and realize that, in aplastic anaemia, there is not only a *quantitative* decrease in erythropoiesis with the production of insufficient numbers of blood cells, but also invariably a *qualitative* disturbance. This results in ineffective erythropoiesis, with intramedullary destruction of some cells before maturation, failure of release of a proportion of the erythrocytes into the peripheral blood, and a shortened life span of those which do enter the circulation.

DIAGNOSIS OF DYSERYTHROPOIESIS

In establishing the diagnosis, there are five approaches which correlate morphological and functional aspects (Lewis & Verwilghen 1977):

1. Demonstration of morphological features at level of light microscopy.

2. Ultrastructural features.

3. Assessment of erythropoietic production and destruction with special reference to intramedullary cell death; this requires ferrokinetic studies, red cell survival studies and measurement of various biochemical parameters of ineffective erythropoiesis and haemoglobin synthesis.

4. Identification of defects in nucleic acid metabolism associated with abnormal erythropoiesis.

5. Demonstration of antigenic and biochemical modifications of the erythrocytes.

Morphological Features

Morphological abnormalities which characterize dyserythropoiesis include binuclearity and multinuclearity, internuclear chromatin bridging, megaloblastosis with asynchrony between nuclear and cytoplasmic maturation and premature nuclear extrusion, nuclear degeneration (blurred nuclear outlines, irregular shapes, budding and fragmentation) and mitotic abnormalities. There may be persistence of intercellular cytoplasmic connections and abnormalities of the cytoplasm itself, with vacuolation, basophilic stippling, and excessive numbers of siderotic granules (Lewis & Verwilghen 1973). Ring sideroblasts are sometimes seen in the marrows of patients with aplastic anaemia (MacGibbon & Mollin 1965) and evolution into a syndrome resembling primary sideroblastic anaemia has occurred

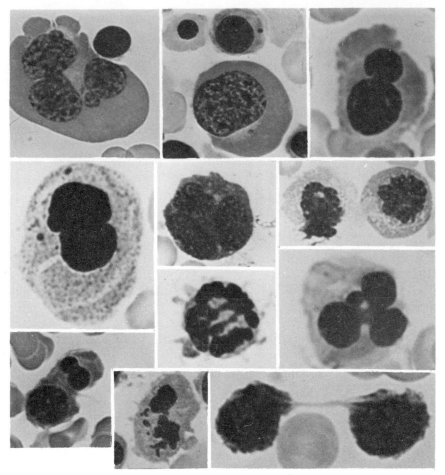

Fig. 5.1. Morphological features of dyserythropoiesis as seen in bone marrow smears from patients with aplastic anaemia.

after partial recovery from aplasia (Geary et al. 1974). Ring sideroblasts are believed to be the hallmark of mitochondrial damage or dysfunction, and it is significant that a reversible ring sideroblastosis has been reported after exposure to chloramphenicol (Beck & Ludin 1967), since the reversible erythroid depression seen with this drug (p. 31) is also believed to be associated with mitochondrial damage to the cell.

These features were originally thought to be identified specifically with congenital dyserythropoietic anaemias but it has been demonstrated (Lewis & Frisch 1976) that some or even all occur, to a greater or lesser extent, in a wide range of acquired dyserythropoietic anaemias. The paucity of cells in smears from aspirated marrows in aplastic anaemia may make it difficult to appreciate the extent of dyserythropoiesis in this condition in the first instance but it is readily apparent in cellular foci or when a thorough survey is carried out (Fig. 5.1). In a study of 100 bone marrows from cases of aplastic anaemia, Frisch and Lewis (1974) found evidence of dyserythropoiesis in every case. In a few only 5% of the erythroid cells were abnormal but in the majority of cases more than half of the erythroid cells and in some cases as many as 90% were affected. The occurrence of dyserythropoiesis in relation to the stages of cell development is shown in Table 5.1. This suggests that dyserythropoiesis may occur as a result

Table 5.1. Dyserythropoiesis in the bone marrow in aplastic anaemia

Type of cell	Mean (%)
Normal	
Early erythroblasts	15·6
Late erythroblasts	18·1
Dyserythropoietic	
Early erythroblasts	14·8
Late erythroblasts	49
Binucleate	
Early	0·4
Late	0·8
Mitoses	2·3

All the erythroblasts seen in 100 bone marrow preparations are included in the analysis.

of disturbance at any stage of erythropoiesis or that non-lethally injured cells may mature, albeit with a persistent abnormality. It is not certain whether a quantitative study of the dyserythropoiesis might have prognostic value but it is possible that the presence of a mixed population of normal and abnormal erythroid cells signifies that a proportion of stem cells were unaffected by the causal agent and, when remission occurs, the marrow contains the progeny of these unaffected stem cells which have survived to repopulate the marrow, as well as descendants of non-lethally injured cells which manifest a persistent abnormality.

Ultrastructure

The light microscope features described above are reflected in the ultrastructural appearances. These have been extensively illustrated by

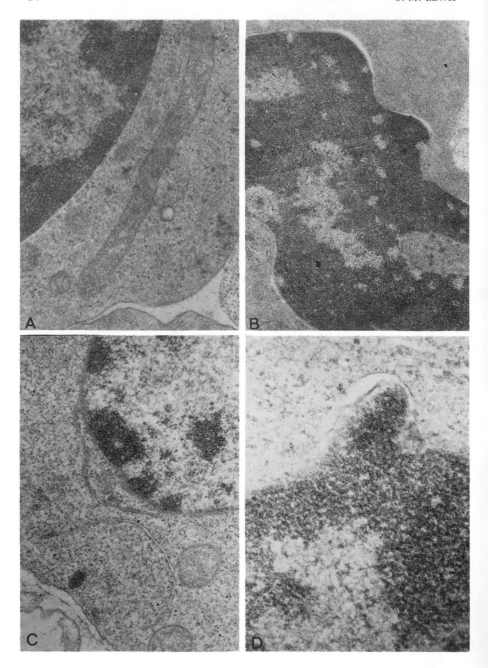

Fig. 5.2. Some ultrastructural features of dyserythropoiesis seen in bone marrow preparations from patients with aplastic anaemia. A, Abnormal elongated mitochondria, ×24 000. B, Loss of nuclear membrane formation, ×18 000. C, Sheets

Frisch et al. (1975) and their observations are summarized here. The abnormalities are numerous and complex. They include the binucleated and multinucleated cells which are visible by light microscopy, with internuclear chromatin bridges and intercellular bridges containing microtubules. Mitochondria vary in size, and many show disintegration of their cristae and/or heavy loading with ferritin. Ribosomes vary considerably in both quantity and distribution at all stages of cell development: some erythroid cells have few ribosomes; in others the ribosomes are present either singly as monosomes or heavily clustered and distributed unevenly. The nuclei are irregular in shape, some with clefts in both euchromatin and heterochromatin. But the most striking anomalies relate to the nuclear membrane and appear to arise from defective formation of the nuclear envelope following mitotic division. Attachment of membrane sheets to chromosomes is incomplete and the membrane-lined nuclear clefts or splits can be followed around the circumference of the nucleus,

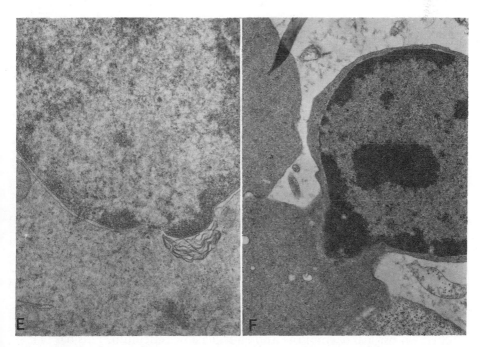

of endoplasmic reticulum near the nucleus with disintegration of the nuclear membrane, ×24 000. D, Nuclear bulge with breakdown of the nuclear envelope, ×48 000. E, Whorl formation and widened nuclear pore, ×24 000. F. Premature extrusion of immature nucleus, ×12 000. Further illustrations may be found in Frisch et al. (1975).

parallel to the nuclear membrane or more often located in the chromatin at right angles to the nuclear membrane and sometimes in communication with the nuclear cisternae. There are also prominent peripheral cisternae which can sometimes be traced back to cytoplasmic reticulum in direct continuity with the outer layer of the nuclear membrane. Other evidence of nuclear membrane disturbance is the presence of confluence of its inner and outer layers, as well as localized disintegration, myelinization and whorl formation. Outpouchings of nuclear substance and, conversely, the presence of ferritin, ribosomes, vesicles and even mitochondria within the nucleus emphasize the functional failure of the nuclear membrane (Fig. 5.2).

Interpretation of ultrastructural features. The dynamic functions of the nuclear membrane and its close relationship to endoplasmic reticulum have been described in several reviews (Feldherr 1972; Wischnitzer 1973; Franke 1974). The nuclear membrane is more than a static partition between the nucleus and the cytoplasm. Ordered arrangement of nuclear chromatin during interphase is maintained by the attachment of DNA fibrils to the nuclear membrane and it has been postulated that membrane attachment of heterochromatin and chromosomes is a prerequisite of an orderly arrangement during prophase prior to mitotic division, so that membrane integrity is necessary for normal mitosis. DNA replication is initiated at specific sites within the inner nuclear membrane which also has close association with production of histones and RNA whilst ribosome production is based on the outer membrane (Harris et al. 1974). Nuclear pores are concerned with nucleocytoplasmic interchange at macromolecular level and especially with RNA transport, and they are implicated in the formation of polyribosomes, as the ribosomes leave the nucleus at the pores (Mephan & Lane 1969). The annulate lamellae seem to have a role in RNA transport and they are involved in protein synthesis (Wischnitzer 1970).

An end result of nuclear membrane defect would thus be failure of normal mitosis and of normal DNA and RNA synthesis and of RNA transport; this will lead to a profound disturbance in protein synthesis and all the manifestations of dyserythropoiesis. This complication is hardly surprising in aplastic anaemia since a number of drugs and toxins which may cause marrow depression are known to have a direct effect on nuclear membrane and endoplasmic reticulum. This has been described in liver cells under the influence of toxic agents by Verbin et al. (1969) and by Salomon (1962) who demonstrated that the response of endoplasmic reticulum to thioacetamide is to form concentric or parallel arrays of replicated membrane resembling myelin figures or whorls; similar whorls and distension of nuclear membrane have been induced experimentally in liver cells by cycloheximide, chloramphenicol and other drugs which inhibit various stages of protein synthesis (Hwang et al. 1974) and also in cells affected by viruses. Endoplasmic reticulum is a primary site for detoxification and metabolism (Bangham 1964; Siekevitz 1972). When a cell is exposed to an overwhelming toxin it is possible that the detoxification function may extend to the nuclear membrane, with resultant damage to it. This is especially likely to occur with erythroblasts as they have relatively little endoplasmic reticulum and all the more so with the later erythroblasts which are generally devoid of endoplasmic reticulum; and it is relevant to note that these cells are more frequently affected by dyserythropoiesis than are their progenitors (Frisch et al. 1974). Earlier studies had led Gregg and Morgan (1959) to speculate that membrane replication represents a basic type of cellular response to infection and injury. Alternatively, it may be that in the process of repair during recovery from an injury, rogue molecules of atypical composition may penetrate the membrane and complex with some of its normal ingredients and thus cause its disruption (Bangham 1964) and prevent restoration of the normal relationships between nuclear envelope and intranuclear structures which are necessary for subsequent cell division.

However, in the case of dyserythropoiesis associated with aplastic anaemia it is not possible, from present evidence, to be sure whether the nuclear membrane anomaly is the primary defect or whether it results from a biochemical disturbance in cell synthesis which may affect the nuclear membrane and thus give rise to dyserythropoiesis. For example, Zentgraf and Franke (1974) have suggested that disruption of nuclear membrane can result from a positive charge caused by the action of positively charged histones or ribosomes which accumulate in sufficient amounts to cause this effect when there is an arrest of DNA synthesis, for whatever reason. Thus, toxic agents acting at different levels can bring about an apparently similar end result of aplastic anaemia and dyserythropoiesis. These ultrastructural observations do not solve the conundrum of which comes first, but they do illustrate how the effects may express themselves.

One ultrastructural abnormality which perhaps deserves special note is the nuclear clefting described above and illustrated in Fig. 5.3. The clefts are most probably caused by derangements of nuclear membrane formation and fusion during mitosis, but they may also be due to deep infoldings of the nuclear envelope. They are closely reminiscent of the clefts which occur in cancer cells (Bernhard 1972; Tani et al. 1971). This, together with the abnormal mitotic figures

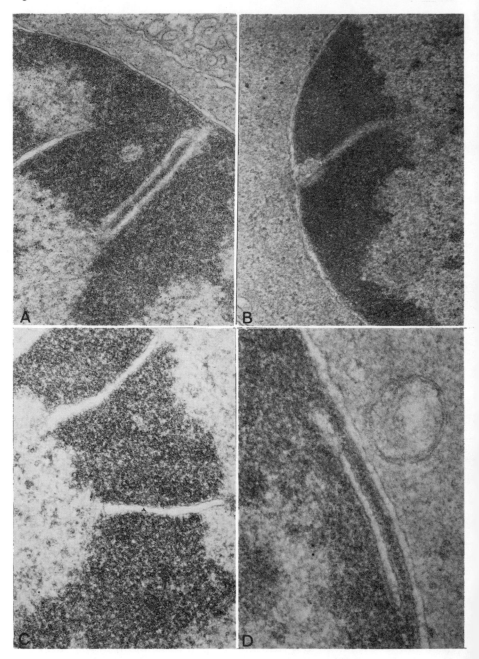

Fig. 5.3. Nuclear clefts in erythroblasts in aplastic anaemia. A, ×42 000. B, ×42 000. C, ×48 000. D, ×72 000.

illustrated in both light microscopy and electron microscopy, supports the speculation that aplastic anaemia might give rise to an abnormal clone with predisposition to leukaemia.

Assessment of Erythropoietic Production and Destruction

Ferrokinetic studies. In aplastic anaemia there is a prolonged plasma clearance half-time of injected radio-iron with an iron utilization of less than 20–25%. By contrast, in dyserythropoiesis plasma clearance half-time is accelerated with utilization in the order of 25–50%. In aplastic anaemia where there is a significant dyserythropoietic element the patterns may overlap, but in general ferrokinetic studies enable one to identify which condition predominates. A useful parameter is the ratio of plasma clearance (as $T\frac{1}{2}$ in minutes) to utilization (as %); this provides a more clear-cut separation. In aplastic anaemia the ratio is high, frequently 10–100, whereas in dyserythropoiesis it is low, usually less than 1 (Lewis & Verwilghen 1977) (Fig. 5.4).

Plasma clearance time does not always reflect marrow iron turnover and thus cannot be relied on as an expression of the degree of erythropoiesis (Ricketts et al. 1977). More meaningful information may be obtained by using complex compartmental analysis of plasma clearance (Ricketts et al. 1975) from which red cell iron turnover, together with total marrow iron turnover, can be calculated and thus measurement of both effective and ineffective erythropoiesis obtained. Using this procedure, Ricketts et al. (1975) obtained the following results in 3 patients with erythroid hypoplasia.

				Normal
Marrow iron turnover (μmol/litre blood/day)	14	5	52	104 (SD 20)
Red cell iron turnover (μmol/litre blood/day)	0	0	32	82 (SD 13)
Ineffective erythropoiesis (%)	100	100	38	

Such very profound failure of red cell production is rare in panhypoplasia, though it is a feature of pure red cell aplasia.

Surface counting during a radio-iron study also provides useful information. In aplastic anaemia radio-activity is confined to the liver where the iron is taken up as storage material; in dyserythropoiesis there is accumulation and retention of the iron in bone marrow where it is taken up by erythroblasts and retained there because of subsequent failure of erythropoietic development. Radio-iron studies are usually performed with [59]Fe. A short-lived cyclotron-produced isotope [52]Fe, which is available in some centres, is suitable for measuring the relative contributions of erythropoiesis and iron storage by quantitative scanning (Pettit et al. 1976). Surface counting and scanning may be of particular help in distinguishing aplastic anaemia from refractory anaemias (Fig. 5.5).

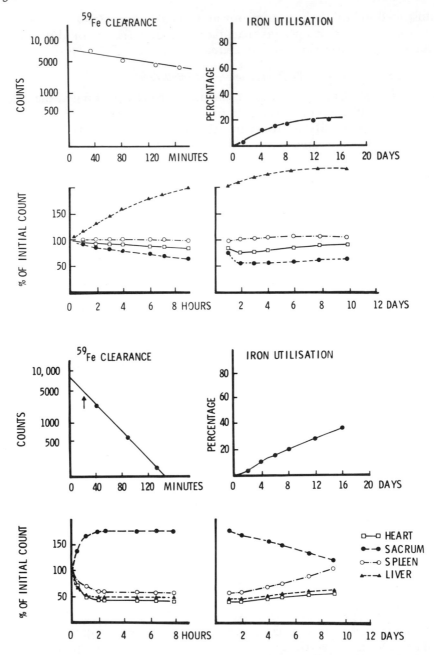

Fig. 5.4. Ferrokinetic studies with ^{59}Fe. *Above*, Aplastic anaemia: plasma clearance half-time 230 minutes and plasma iron turnover 5·4 mg/litre/day. *Below*, Dyserythropoiesis: plasma clearance half-time 20 minutes and plasma iron turnover 63 mg/litre/day.

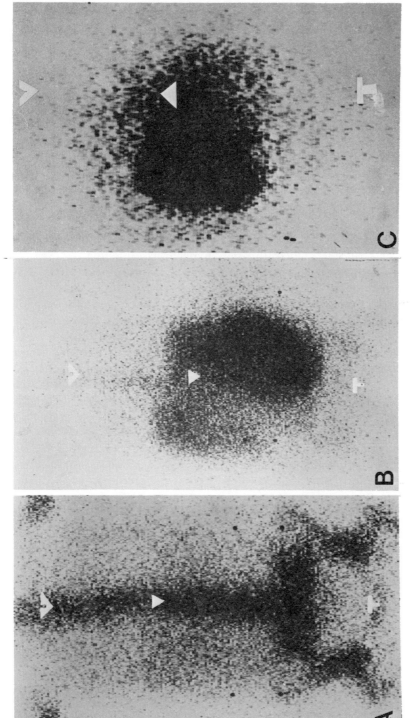

Fig. 5.5. ^{52}Fe scans characteristic of polycythaemia vera (A), myelosclerosis with extramedullary erythropoiesis (B) and aplastic anaemia (C).

Red cell survival. Random labelling is carried out usually with ^{51}Cr, less frequently with DF ^{32}P. The normal red cell life span is 100–120 days, with a Cr $T\frac{1}{2}$ of 25–33 days. In dyserythropoiesis there is usually a reduced survival, of the order of 20–50 days (Lewis & Verwilghen 1977). In a study of 16 patients with aplastic anaemia, the Cr $T\frac{1}{2}$ was found to be 10–19 days (Lewis 1962). As labelling had been carried out in all these patients before or long after transfusion, and there was no detectable haemorrhage at the time of study, it seems likely that the increased cell elimination was due to reduced red cell survival. This demonstration of a possible intrinsic defect in the red cells supports the view that significant dyserythropoiesis exists. In about one-third of the cases the spleen was implicated as the site of haemolysis.

Nucleic acid metabolism and other indicators of inefficient erythropoiesis and haemoglobin synthesis. Unconjugated hyperbilirubinaemia, increased faecal urobilin, appearance of an early bilirubin peak after administration of labelled haem precursors and endogenous carbon monoxide production are useful parameters of decreased efficiency of haemoglobinopoiesis. The best markers for identifying destruction of erythroblast cytoplasm are lactic dehydrogenase and aldolase; excessive production of LDH type B is particularly marked when erythroblasts are destroyed, and some authors have suggested that an increase of aldolase is an even better sign of destruction of immature erythroblasts (Lewis & Verwilghen 1977). There are no published data on these parameters specifically in aplastic anaemia and it is likely that the increase due to dyserythropoiesis will be minimized by the overall lower level of erythropoiesis. DNA synthesis can be investigated *in vitro* by means of labelled nucleotides, e.g. tritiated thymidine; dyserythropoiesis is suggested when there is proliferative arrest of the erythroblasts. In aplastic anaemia it is important to distinguish this from erythroblast arrest as a result of the marrow failure *per se*. By the same token, an increased level of uric acid, which is considered to be due to increased catabolism of nucleotides in an ineffective bone marrow, is not a feature of aplastic anaemia.

Antigenic Modification of Red Cell Membrane

Increased sensitivity to lysis by anti-I serum (the so-called cold antibody lysis test) was demonstrated by Lewis et al. (1961) in the red cells from patients with a wide variety of dyserythropoietic haematological disorders, including aplastic anaemia, untreated megaloblastic anaemia, myelosclerosis, sideroblastic anaemia, leukaemia and haemoglobinopathies. There was also some increased agglutination and, in a subsequent study, Lewis et al. (1970) showed that the red cells of patients with dyserythropoiesis could bind up to six times the amount of anti-I bound by normal red cells. This phenomenon is especially well seen in aplastic anaemia.

Lysis also occurs in paroxysmal nocturnal haemoglobinuria (PNH). In dyserythropoiesis, lysis is mainly or entirely due to the increased antibody binding without increased complement sensitivity, by contrast to PNH, where lysis is much greater than could be accounted for by a slightly increased antibody uptake (Table 5.2). Furthermore,

Table 5.2. Antibody binding capacity and complement sensitivity*

Condition	Antibody uptake (% Anti-I)		Complement sensitivity (titre for 50% lysis)	
Normal	1·10	0·3–2·0	1·42	0·7–2·4
Paroxysmal nocturnal haemoglobinuria	1·57	1·3–2·0	11·67	2·9–27·0
Aplastic anaemia	2·94	1·0–6·0	2·41	1·3–3·3

* Mean and range.

acidified serum lysis—the diagnostic test for PNH—is negative in dyserythropoiesis with two exceptions: (a) in one form of congenital dyserythropoietic anaemia, CDA Type II, or HEMPAS, where there is a unique antigen (Crookston et al. 1969) and (b) when PNH or a PNH-like defect occurs in aplastic anaemia (see below). Lysis in the cold antibody lysis test has been shown to correlate sufficiently well with other manifestations of dyserythropoiesis to permit its use as a screening procedure (Lewis 1969; Catovsky et al. 1971). The pattern of lysis *in vitro* is summarized in Table 5.3. Increased agglutinability by anti-i has been shown by Cooper et al. (1968) in sideroblastic anaemia, untreated megaloblastic anaemia and malignant blood disease, and the red cells of patients with aplastic anaemia may show similar abnormalities (Worlledge 1977).

Red Cell Enzymes

In a study on 10 cases of aplastic anaemia, Boivin et al. (1975) noted a number of red cell enzyme abnormalities although they were not as frequent or as striking as in 'refractory anaemias' and other types of dyserythropoiesis (Boivin 1977). They found decreased phosphofructokinase in 2, decreased 2,3-DPG mutase in 1, PK deficiency in 1 and decreased adenylate kinase in 1. Conversely, one case had increased hexokinase and one had markedly increased G-6-PD. In Faconi's anaemia and in 2 cases of Blackfan–Diamond disease, they recorded similar varied alterations. The most constant findings, in both

Table 5.3. *In vitro* tests of diagnostic value

Condition	Acidified serum lysis	Sucrose lysis	Anti-I lysis	Anti-i lysis	Anti-I agglutination	Anti-i agglutination
Normal	–	–	–	–	+	–
Paroxysmal nocturnal haemoglobinuria	+++	+++	+++	±	+	±
Aplastic anaemia (with dyserythropoiesis)	–	–	++	+	+++	++
Aplastic–PNH syndrome	± to +++	± to +++	+++	+	+++	++

acquired and congenital aplastic anaemias, appeared to be the increases in hexokinase and G-6-PD and the PK deficiency.

The increase in red cell enzymes had been ascribed to a prolonged synthetic period during maturation or, where there is failure of cell division, to concentration of the synthesized enzyme protein in one cell instead of it being distributed amongst two or more cells (Valentine et al. 1972). There are similarities in the enzyme pattern to that found in neonatal erythrocytes (Rochant et al. 1972; Boivin et al. 1974). Similarly, the antigenic modifications described above have features characteristic of neonatal cells. This may be due to disturbed synthesis of membrane protein or it may reflect membrane immaturity due to an abnormally short marrow transit time, or reactivation of fetal erythropoiesis. In this connection it is of interest to note that in aplastic anaemia HbF is elevated in the 2–20% range (Shahidi et al. 1962). A burst of HbF production may occur after bone marrow transplantation during the period of marrow regeneration (Alter et al. 1976) and following remission from aplastic anaemia, but the HbF level is not related to the prognosis. Elevated HbF levels have also been reported in Fanconi's anaemia (Beard et al. 1973; Beard 1976). In this latter situation the glycine/alanine composition of the fetal haemoglobin is that of normal neonates (Beard 1976), whereas variable ratios have been reported in acquired aplastic anaemia (Schroeder & Huisman 1974).

There has been much speculation on the synthesis of HbF in dyserythropoietic conditions and there is no clear causal relationship. The suggested mechanisms fall into two main groups; the 'mistake hypothesis' and the 'clonal selection of F cells' hypothesis (Weatherall 1977).

According to the 'mistake hypothesis', if the rate of erythropoiesis is increased and the maturation pattern abnormal there may be more opportunities for mistakes to occur in the mechanisms which suppress the γ-chain loci, and HbF production happens more or less by chance in an abnormal marrow. This is, however, unlikely to be the explanation in non-regenerating aplastic anaemia and Weatherall (1977) favours the clonal selection hypothesis as a much more likely mechanism for HbF synthesis in aplastic anaemia, as well as in other dyserythropoietic states; his observation that, in these disorders, cells which contain HbF have different turnover rates compared with those which make HbA suggests that the stem cells involved in producing the F-cell lines, possibly by mixture of their turnover properties, are less susceptible to whatever agents are responsible for the aplastic anaemia or other form of marrow damage. There are, however, differences in the enzyme patterns between normal fetal and dyserythropoietic red cells which emphasize the fact that the occurrence of fetal erythropoiesis in aplastic anaemia does not account for the various manifestations of dyserythropoiesis which occur.

PNH IN APLASTIC ANAEMIA

Paroxysmal nocturnal haemoglobinuria (PNH) is a remarkable disease by virtue of its variability in presentation, mechanism of lysis and complex interrelationship with aplastic anaemia. It has been extensively reviewed (recently, *inter alia,* by Dacie & Lewis 1972; Sirchia & Lewis 1975). The frequent coexistence of marrow hypoplasia and haemolysis due to the PNH red cell defect is well documented in individual case reports and reviews from several centres, including those by Lewis and Dacie (1967), Gardner and Blum (1967), Hunter and Nelson (1967), Sakamoto et al. (1967), Zurwehme and Pixberg (1970), Tay and Chia (1971), Wasi et al. (1970), Dacie and Lewis (1972), and Hartmann and Arnold (1977).

In typical PNH the characteristic findings are anaemia, leucopenia and thrombocytopenia. There is a neutropenia with less than 1.5×10^9/litre in over half the patients (Polli et al. 1973). The platelet count is lower than 150×10^9/litre in about two-thirds and less than 80×10^9/litre in a quarter of the patients (Polli et al. 1973). The anaemia is accompanied by a reticulocytosis but this is 2–4 times lower than in other haemolytic anaemias relative to the degree of anaemia (Lewis & Dacie 1967). Notwithstanding the peripheral blood pancytopenia, the bone marrow, in typical cases, is hypercellular due to increased erythropoiesis, and although the myeloid : erythroid ratio may be reversed, the bone marrow is not devoid of myeloid cells and megakaryocytes, too, are present. In such cases it seems possible that there is some peripheral blood destruction, as both PNH granulocytes and platelets can be shown, at least *in vitro,* to undergo complement lysis in a way similar to PNH red cells (Gardner & Murphy 1972). Similarly, the relatively low reticulocyte count can be explained by the fact that PNH reticulocytes are especially sensitive to lysis both *in vitro* and *in vivo* (Metz et al. 1960; Kan & Gardner 1965).

On the other hand, hypoplastic or even aplastic marrow is not infrequently encountered in PNH patients either at the onset or later in the course of their illness. Marrow hypoplasia and PNH may be associated in one of two ways:

1. The patient presents with signs of active haemolysis, has a reticulocytosis and a hyperplastic bone marrow, and is diagnosed as PNH by an unequivocally positive acidified serum lysis test. In the course of the illness an episode of marrow hypoplasia may develop and

give rise to pancytopenia. In such cases it is difficult to exclude the possibility that the patient may have had a transient episode of marrow hypoplasia at the start of the illness from which he made a partial recovery, only to relapse at a later stage after PNH has developed.

2. More usually the patient presents with pancytopenia and marrow hypoplasia. The acidified serum test is negative or weakly positive. At a variable time after the onset this test becomes positive. The marrow may continue to be hypoplastic and the clinical features are those of aplastic anaemia, or the marrow recovers to a variable extent, the acidified serum test becomes more strongly positive and the patient eventually presents all the clinical and haematological features of classical haemolytic PNH. In some patients, however, recovery from the aplastic anaemia does not occur, the PNH does not develop beyond a positive acidified serum test and thus, in these cases, PNH is

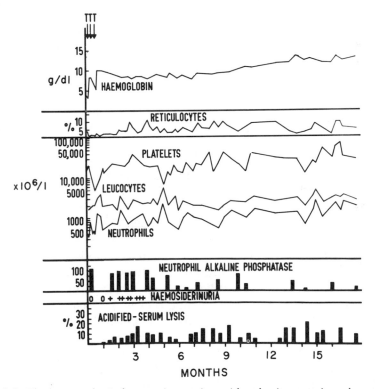

Fig. 5.6. The haematological course in a patient with aplastic anaemia and paroxysmal nocturnal haemoglobinuria. The patient was a 37-year-old woman who developed aplastic anaemia possibly after exposure to weedkiller. The graph illustrates the onset of paroxysmal nocturnal haemoglobinuria, which persisted as a laboratory phenomenon for several years after recovery from aplasia, but has now disappeared completely.

a laboratory phenomenon only, without significant effect on the patient's clinical condition. Examples of the clinical and haematological courses are shown in Figs 4.3 and 5.6.

Because of the variable presentation, the fact that the relationship between PNH and aplastic anaemia has become well recognized only in recent years, and that acidified serum tests are not always carried out routinely in aplastic anaemia, it is difficult to define the incidence accurately. In the series of 80 patients studied by Dacie and Lewis (1972) 29% were first diagnosed as aplastic anaemia, and half the patients with diagnosed PNH had marrow hypoplasia to a greater or lesser extent during the course of the disease. Conversely, about 15% of patients with aplastic anaemia have a demonstrable PNH defect at some stage.

One test of some value in detecting the changing condition is the neutrophil alkaline phosphatase score, which is extremely high in aplastic anaemia, and low or even negative in PNH; intermediate scores are found in the aplastic anaemia–PNH syndrome (Lewis & Dacie 1965).

The phenomenon of the aplastic anaemia–PNH syndrome is of interest in studying the evolution of both diseases. Most workers agree that a likely cause of PNH is the establishment, by somatic mutation within the marrow, of a clone of stem cells which have some biological advantages over normal stem cells and produce the dyshaemopoietic cells of PNH. The supporting evidence has recently been reviewed by Hartmann and Arnold (1977). The cause of the postulated mutation leading to the development of the PNH clone remains obscure. In aplastic anaemia the PNH clone may develop in patients whose marrow injury has apparently a 'toxic' aetiology. These have included aplasia due to chloramphenicol (Beal et al. 1964; Quagliana et al. 1964; Seaman 1969; Wasi et al. 1970), resorcin (Schubothe 1958), benzene (Aksoy et al. 1975), and other toxins and drugs, including various antibiotics, antihistamines, sedatives, tranquillizers, insecticides and weed-killers (Quagliana et al. 1964). However, it occurs also in idiopathic aplastic anaemia (Lewis & Dacie 1967) as well as the familial (Fanconi's) type (Dacie & Lewis 1961). It thus seems less likely that the aetiological factors which lead to aplastic anaemia may also cause PNH, and more likely that the link between aplastic anaemia and PNH is the occurrence of marrow hypoplasia *per se*, with its associated dyshaemopoiesis. The existence of two populations of red cells in PNH, those readily lysed and those more resistant to lysis, suggests that PNH may be a two-step disorder, with aplastic anaemia or at least marrow hypoplasia as the first step. It appears that PNH clones are more likely to arise in patients recovering from aplastic anaemia. In such cases PNH cells (as judged by the *in vitro* lysis tests) form only a small part of the cell population and thus do not constitute the full extent of stem cell repopulation.

LEUKAEMIA

The development of leukaemia in aplastic anaemia is an uncommon complication (see p. 230). It may be analogous to the development of PNH, as leukaemia has occurred in patients suffering from idiopathic aplastic anaemia as well as in those with Fanconi's type. A few patients with PNH have developed acute leukaemia, and Gordon Smith (1977) refers to a patient with chloramphenicol-induced aplastic anaemia in whom the PNH defect occurred, to be followed two years later by myeloblastic leukaemia. Previously, a similar case had been recorded by Seaman (1969) and by Wasi et al. (1970) who reported the case of a 17-year-old boy who developed aplastic anaemia after taking chloramphenicol; 18 months later he developed myeloblastic leukaemia. The acidified serum lysis test, previously negative, was now positive. These cases suggest that the leukaemic clone represents a further mutation in an abnormal tissue, although it is not clear why there should be this predisposition to new mutations. Dameshek (1969) suggested that individual bone marrows might react in different ways to the similar insults and that the variability in reaction, resulting in aplastic anaemia, leukaemia or PNH, might be explained by genetic differences.

REFRACTORY (DYSPLASTIC) CYTOPENIAS

There are two types of chronic refractory cytopenia which have an important relationship to aplastic anaemia: (*a*) refractory anaemia with medullary myeloblastosis and (*b*) refractory anaemia with proliferative dysplasia. Their relevance to this chapter is that in both conditions dyserythropoiesis, or rather dyshaemopoiesis, is a major feature.

Refractory Anaemia with Medullary Myeloblastosis

This condition, also referred to as refractory anaemia with excess of myeloblasts (RAEM or RAEB), was first described by Dreyfus et al. (1968, 1969) and has recently been reviewed by Sultan et al. (1977). The syndrome occurs equally in men and women older than 50 years, who present with the symptoms of chronic anaemia without palpable lymph nodes or enlarged spleen and liver. There is a peripheral blood pancytopenia although the platelet count may be only slightly reduced or even normal. Qualitative abnormalities of all cell lines are present—poikilocytosis with basophilic stippling, agranular poly-morphs with a Pelger-like anomaly, and abnormally large and hypogranular platelets. The bone marrow is of normal or increased cellularity. Erythroblasts show all the features of dyserythropoiesis including multinuclearity, nuclear bridging, megaloblastosis, basophilic stippling and cytoplasmic vacuolation.

The characteristic feature is an increase of up to 35% in immature forms of the myeloid series (i.e. myeloblasts and promyelocytes). These cells are, moreover, qualitatively abnormal: the promyelocytes have blast-like nuclei without chromatin condensation and with one or more nucleoli. The cytoplasm is basophilic, sometimes with large azurophilic granules and (sometimes) deficient in granules. Auer rods are not a feature of the blasts. Megakaryocytes too may be morphologically abnormal with small round nuclei and scanty basophilic cytoplasm surrounded by a few giant platelets.

The dyserythropoietic pattern is confirmed by other features: HbF is often found in excess; a decrease in blood group antigens, especially A, B and H, and an increase of I have been observed (Dreyfus et al. 1969) and a number of red cell enzyme abnormalities have been found, notably decreased pyruvate kinase, and the same contrast between increased and decreased activities of different enzymes which has been noted in aplastic anaemia and other acquired dyserythropoietic states (Dreyfus et al. 1969; Boivin 1977).

The relationship of this condition to aplastic anaemia on the one hand and to leukaemia on the other has not been clearly established. Cases which fulfil these criteria have been described by several authors who have labelled them 'smouldering leukaemia' or 'pre-leukaemia' (for references, see Sultan et al. 1977). It is important, however, to recognize the syndrome as such, because the dysplastic phase may be stable for a considerable period provided that chemotherapy is not administered. Dreyfus (1976) believes that, in many patients, the bone marrow situation remains steady for months or years without evidence of acute leukaemia, although Najean et al. (1976) in a study of 79 patients observed that 63% had died from acute myeloblastic leukaemia with a 15-month median survival; these patients had been treated with high-dose androgen regimen. The variable course, itself reminiscent of the variable course in aplastic anaemia, suggests that the underlying marrow disorder may not be identical in all cases, and there may be different pathogenetic mechanisms, albeit with similar morphological features. Cytochemical reactions, serum lysozymes, red cell antigen and enzyme patterns, and cytogenetic studies have all been studied but they do not distinguish the cases adequately. On the other hand, there is evidence that bone marrow culture studies of colony forming capacity may be of value in distinguishing non-leukaemic RAEB from pre-leukaemia or at least for monitoring the progress of the dysplastic condition. Change in the growth pattern or a modification of cluster to colony ratio is said to precede, often for many months, the evolution towards leukaemic proliferation (Sultan et al. 1977; Milner et al. 1977).

Proliferative Dysplasia

This condition also occurs in older patients. The peripheral blood is indistinguishable from aplastic anaemia, with pancytopenia and reticulocytopenia. The bone marrow is of normal or increased cellularity, but aspirated marrow often shows a paucity of cells in the 'trails'. The reticulin content is increased, but fibroblast proliferation and fibrosis are not prominent features. There is dyserythropoiesis with a significant number of erythroblasts affected by binuclearity, karyorrhexis, etc. There is no increase in the proportion of myeloblasts and promyelocytes, and megakaryocytes are present usually in approximately normal numbers.

The first impression is of a myeloproliferative disorder but clinically the features are not those of myelofibrosis, as splenomegaly does not occur, the peripheral blood does not show a leuco-erythroblastic reaction, poikilocytosis is no more marked than in classical aplastic anaemia and there is no extramedullary haemopoiesis. Ferrokinetic studies demonstrate a marked reduction in red cell utilization of the same order as in aplastic anaemia, while by contrast plasma clearance is normal and rapid. This pattern is essentially that of dys-erythropoiesis with hypoplasia. The most suitable term to describe these cases seems to be 'refractory anaemia with proliferative dysplasia' (Gordon Smith 1972). Their managment should be along lines similar to that for aplastic anaemia.

REFERENCES

AKSOY, M., ERDEM, S. & DINCOL, G. (1975) Two rare complications of chronic benzene poisoning: myeloid metaplasia and paroxysmal nocturnal haemoglobinuria. Report of two cases. *Blut, 30*, 255.

ALTER, B. P., RAPPEPORT, J. M., HUISMAN, T. H. J., SCHROEDER, W. A. & NATHAN, D. G. (1976) Fetal erythropoiesis following bone marrow transplantation. *Blood, 48*, 843.

BANGHAM, A. D. (1964) Interactions producing injury or repair of cellular membranes. *Cellular Injury*, p. 167. London: Churchill Livingstone.

BEAL, R. W., KRONENBERG, H. & FIRKIN, B. G. (1964) The syndrome of paroxysmal nocturnal haemoglobinuria. *Am. J. Med., 37*, 899.

BEARD, M. E. J. (1976) *Congenital Disorders of Erythropoiesis*, pp. 103–25. Amsterdam: Elsevier.

BEARD, M. E. J., YOUNG, D. E., BATEMAN, C. J. T., McCARTHY, G. T., SMITH, M. E., SINCLAIR, L., FRANKLIN, A. W. & BODLEY SCOTT, R. (1973) Fanconi's anaemia. Q. Jl. Med., 42, 403.

BECK, E. A. & LUDIN, H. (1967) Reversible sideroachrestic disorder after treatment with chloramphenicol. Helv. med. Acta, 34 (Suppl. 47), 139.

BERNHARD, W. (1972) Ultrastructure of the cancer cell. Handbook of Molecular Cytology. Amsterdam: North Holland.

BOIVIN, P. (1977) Red blood cell enzyme abnormalities in dyserythropoietic anaemias. In: Dyserythropoiesis, ed. S. M. Lewis & R. L. Verwilghen, pp. 221–46. London: Academic Press.

BOIVIN, P., GALAND, C., HAKIM, J. & KAHN, A. (1975) Acquired erythroenzymopathies in blood disorders. Br. J. Haemat., 31, 531.

BOIVIN, P., HAKIM, J. & KAHN, A. (1974) Anomalies biochimiques des cellules sanguines au cours des anémies réfractaires. Ann. Med. intern., 125, 627.

CATOVSKY, D., LEWIS, S. M. & SHERMAN, D. (1971) Erythrocyte sensitivity to in-vitro lysis in leukaemia. Br. J. Haemat., 21, 541.

COOPER, A. G., HOFFBRAND, A. V. & WORLLEDGE, S. M. (1968) Increased agglutinability by anti-i of red cells in sideroblastic and megaloblastic anaemia. Br. J. Haemat., 15, 381.

CROOKSTON, J. H., CROOKSTON, M. C., BURNIE, K. L., FRANCOMBE, W. H., DACIE, J. V., DAVIS, J. A. & LEWIS, S. M. (1969) Hereditary erythroblastic multinuclearity associated with a positive acidified-serum test: a type of congenital dyserythropoietic anaemia. Br. J. Haemat., 17, 11.

DACIE, J. V. & LEWIS, S. M. (1961) Paroxysmal nocturnal haemoglobinuria: variation in clinical severity and association with bone-marrow hypoplasia. Br. J. Haemat., 7, 442.

DACIE, J. V. & LEWIS, S. M. (1972) Paroxysmal nocturnal haemoglobinuria: clinical manifestations, haematology, and nature of the disease. Ser. Hemat., 5, 3.

DAMESHEK, W. (1969) Foreword and a proposal for considering paroxysmal nocturnal hemoglobinuria (PNH) as a 'candidate' myeloproliferative disorder. Blood, 33, 263.

DREYFUS, B. (1976) Preleukemic states. I. Definition and classification. II. Refractory anemia with an excess of myeloblasts in the bone marrow (smouldering acute leukaemia). Blood Cells, 2, 33.

DREYFUS, B., ROCHANT, H., SALMON, CH., BOIVIN, P., SULTAN, C., MANNONI, P., GALAND, C. & CARTRON, J. P. (1968) Anémies réfractaire états preleucemiques et anomalies enzymatiques multiples. C. r. hebd. Séanc. Acad. Sci. Paris, 267, 1627.

DREYFUS, B., SULTAN, C., ROCHANT, H., SALMON, CH., MANNONI, P., CARTRON, J. P., BOIVIN, P. & GALAND, C. (1969) Anomalies of blood group antigens and erythrocyte enzymes in two types of chronic refractory anaemia. Br. J. Haemat., 16, 303.

FELDHERR, C. M. (1972) Structure and function of the nuclear envelope. Adv. Cell molec. Biol., 2, 273.

FRANKE, W. W. (1974) Nuclear envelopes. structure and biochemistry of the nuclear envelope. The electron microscopy and composition of biological membranes and their ultrastructure. Phil. Trans. R. Soc. Lond. B, 268, 67.

FRISCH, B. & LEWIS, S. M. (1974) The bone marrow in aplastic anaemia: diagnostic and prognostic features. J. clin. Path., 27, 231.

FRISCH, B., LEWIS, S. M. & SHERMAN, D. (1975) The ultrastructure of dyserythropoiesis in aplastic anaemia. Br. J. Haemat., 29, 545.

FRISCH, B. LEWIS, S. M., SHERMAN, D., WHITE, J. M. & GORDON SMITH, E. C. (1974) The ultrastructure of erythropoiesis in two haemoglobinopathies. Br. J. Haemat., 28, 109.

GARDNER, F. H. & BLUM, S. F. (1967) Aplastic anemia in paroxysmal nocturnal haemoglobinuria. Mechanisms and therapy. Semin. Hemat., 4, 250.

GARDNER, F. H. & MURPHY, S. (1972) Granulocyte and platelet functions in paroxysmal nocturnal hemoglobinuria. Ser. Haemat., 5, 78.

GEARY, C. G., DAWSON, D. W., SITLANI, P. K., ALLISON, H. A. & LEYLAND, M. J. (1974) An association between aplastic anaemia and sideroblastic anaemia. *Br. J. Haemat.*, 27, 337.

GIBLETT, E. R., COLEMAN, D. H., PIRZIO-BIROLI, G., DONOHUE, D. M., MOTULSKY, A. G. & FINCH, C. A. (1956) Erythrokinetics: quantitative measurements of red cell production and destruction in normal subjects and patients with anemia. *Blood*, 11, 291.

GORDON-SMITH, E. C. (1972) Bone marrow failure: diagnosis and treatment. *Br. J. Haemat.*, 23 (Suppl), 167.

GORDON-SMITH, E. C. (1977) Aplastic anaemia: speculation on pathogenesis. In: *Dyserythropoiesis*, ed. S. M. Lewis & R. L. Verwilghen. London: Academic Press.

GREGG, M. B. & MORGAN, C. (1959) Reduplication of nuclear membrane in HeLa cells infected with adenovirus. *J. biophys. biochem. Cytol.*, 6, 539.

HARRIS, J. R., PRICE, M. R. & WILLISON, M. (1974) A comparative study on rat liver and hepatoma nuclear membranes. *J. Ultrastruct. Res.*, 48, 17.

HARTMANN, R. C. & ARNOLD, A. B. (1977) Paroxysmal nocturnal haemoglobinuria (PNH) as a clonal disorder. *A. Rev. Med.*, 28, 187.

HAURANI, F. I. & TOCANTINS, L. M. (1961) Ineffective erythropoiesis. *Am. J. Med.*, 31, 519.

HUNTER, J. & NELSON, M. G. (1967) Paroxysmal nocturnal haemoglobinuria following 'aplastic anaemia'. *Acta haemat.* 38, 57.

HWANG, K. M., YANG, L. C., CARRICO, C. K., SCHULTZ, R. A., SCHENKMAN, J. B. & SARTORELLI, A. C. (1974) Production of membrane whorls in rat liver by some inhibitors of protein synthesis. *J. cell Biol.*, 62, 20.

KAN, S. Y. & GARDNER, F. H. (1965) Lifespan of reticulocytes in paroxysmal nocturnal hemoglobinuria. *Blood*, 25, 759.

LEWIS, S. M. (1962) Red cell abnormalities and haemolysis in aplastic anaemia. *Br. J. Haemat.*, 8, 322.

LEWIS, S. M. (1969) Studies of the erythrocyte in aplastic anaemia and other dyserythropoietic states. *Nouv. Revue fr. Hémat.*, 9, 49.

LEWIS, S. M. & DACIE, J. V. (1965) Neutrophil (leucocyte) alkaline phosphatase in paroxysmal nocturnal haemoglobinuria. *Br. J. Haemat.*, 11, 549.

LEWIS, S. M. & DACIE, J. V. (1967) The aplastic anaemia–paroxysmal nocturnal haemoglobinuria syndrome. *Br. J. Haemat.*, 13, 236.

LEWIS, S. M., DACIE, J. V. & TILLS, D. (1961) Comparison of the sensitivity to agglutination and haemolysis by a high-titre cold antibody of the erythrocytes of normal subjects and of patients with a variety of blood diseases including paroxysmal nocturnal haemoglobinuria. *Br. J. Haemat.*, 7, 64.

LEWIS, S. M. & FRISCH, B. (1976) Congenital dyserythropoietic anaemias: electron microscopy. In: *Congenital Disorders of Erythropoiesis*. Amsterdam: Elsevier/Excerpta Medica/North Holland.

LEWIS, S. M., GRAMMATICOS, P. & DACIE, J. V. (1970) Lysis by anti-I in dyserythropoietic anaemias: role of increased uptake of antibody. *Br. J. Haemat.*, 18, 465.

LEWIS, S. M. & VERWILGHEN, R. L. (1972) Dyserythropoiesis and dyserythropoietic anaemia. *Br. J. Haemat.*, 23, 1.

LEWIS, S. M. & VERWILGHEN, R. L. (1973) Dyserythropoiesis and dyserythropoietic anemias. *Progress Hemat.*, 8, 99.

LEWIS, S. M. & VERWILGHEN, R. L. (1977) Dyserythropoiesis: Definition, diagnosis and assessment. *Dyserythropoiesis*, pp. 3–20. London: Academic Press.

MACGIBBON, B. H. & MOLLIN, D. L. (1965) Sideroblastic anaemia in man: observations on seventy cases. *Br. J. Haemat.*, 11, 59.

MEPHAN, R. H. & LANE, G. R. (1969) Nucleospores and polyribosome formation. *Nature, Lond.*, 221, 288.

METZ, J., BRADLOW, B. A., LEWIS, S. M. & DACIE, J. F. (1960) The acetylcholinesterase activity of the erythrocytes in paroxysmal nocturnal haemoglobinuria in relation to the severity of the disease. *Br. J. Haemat.*, 6, 372.

MILNER, G. R., TESTA, N. G., GEARY, C. G., DEXTER, T. M., MULDAL, S., MACIVER, J. E. & LAJTHA, L. G. (1977) Bone marrow culture studies in refractory cytopenia and 'smouldering leukaemia'. *Br. J. Haemat.*, *35*, 251.

NAJEAN, Y., PECKING, A. & BROQUET, M. (1976) Anémies réfractaires avec myéloblastose partielle. Analyse d'un protocol, groupant 79 cas. I. Caractères cliniques et évolution sous androgénothérapie. *Nouv. Revue fr. Hémat.*, *16*, 67.

PETTIT, J. E., LEWIS, S. M., WILLIAMS, E. D., GRAFTON, C. A., BOWRING, C. S. & GLASS, H. I. (1976) Quantitative studies of splenic erythropoiesis in polycythaemia vera and myelofibrosis. *Br. J. Haemat.*, *34*, 465.

POLLI, E., SIRCHIA, G., PERRONE, S., MERCURIALI, F. & ZANELLA, A. (1973) *Emoglobinuria Parrossistica Notturna—Revisione Critica*. Milan: Cilag-Chemie Italiana.

QUAGLIANA, J. M., CARTWRIGHT, G. E. & WINTROBE, M. M. (1964) Paroxysmal nocturnal hemoglobinuria following drug-induced aplastic anemia. *Ann. intern. Med.*, *61*, 1045.

RICKETTS, C., CAVILL, I., NAPIER, J. A. F. & JACOBS, A. (1977) Ferrokinetics and erythropoiesis in man: an evaluation of ferrokinetic measurements. *Br. J. Haemat.*, *35*, 41.

RICKETTS, C., JACOBS, A. & CAVILL, I. (1975) Ferrokinetics and erythropoiesis in man: The measurement of effective erythropoiesis, ineffective erythropoiesis and red cell lifespan using ^{59}Fe. *Br. J. Haemat.*, *31*, 65.

ROCHANT, H., DREYFUS, B., BOUGUERRA, M. & TONT-HAT, H. (1972) Refractory anaemias, preleukemic conditions and fetal erythropoiesis. *Blood*, *39*, 721.

SAKAMOTO, S., SHIBATA, A., TAKASE, S., ONODERA, S., MIURA, A. B., SUZUKI, A., SUZUKI, C., OIKAWA, A. & OKUYAMA, M. (1967) A case of paroxysmal nocturnal hemoglobinuria which has shown a picture of hypoplastic anemia for a long time. *Acta haemat. jap.*, *30*, 462.

SALOMON, J. C. (1962) Modifcations des cellules du perenchyme hépatique du rat sous l'effet de la thioacétamide. Etude au microscope electronique des lésions observées à la phase tardive d'une intoxication chronique. *J. ultrastruct. Res.*, *7*, 293.

SCHROEDER, W. A. & HUISMAN, T. H. J. (1974) Multiple cistrons for fetal haemoglobin in man. *Ann. N.Y. Acad. Sci. U.S.A.*, *241*, 70.

SCHUBOTHE, H. (1958) Bone marrow aplasia and paroxysmal nocturnal haemoglobinuria following administration of resorcin and metacresol. In: *Sensitivity Reaction to Drugs: A Symposium*, ed. M. L. Rosenheim & R. Moulton. Oxford: Blackwell Scientific.

SEAMAN, A. J. (1969) Sequel to chloramphenicol aplastic anaemia: acute leukaemia and paroxysmal nocturnal hemoglobinuria. *NW Med.*, *69*, 831.

SHAHIDI, N. T., GERALD, P. S. & DIAMOND, L. K. (1962) Alkali-resistant hemoglobin in aplastic anaemia of both acquired and congenital types. *New Engl. J. Med.*, *266*, 117.

SIEKEVITZ, P. (1972) Biological membranes: the dynamics of their organisation. *A. Rev. Physiol.*, *34*, 117.

SIRCHIA, G. & LEWIS, S. M. (1975) Paroxysmal nocturnal haemoglobinuria. *Clin. Haemat.*, *4*, 199.

SULTAN, C., IMBART, M., RICARD, M. F. & MARQUET, M. (1977) Myelodysplastic syndromes. In: *Dyserythropoiesis*, ed. S. M. Lewis & R. L. Verwilghen, pp. 171–81. London: Academic Press.

TANI, E., TAKEUCHI, J., ISHIJIMA, Y., HIGASHI, N., FUJIHARA, E., AMENTANI, T. & ANDO, K. (1971) Elongated nuclear sheet and intranuclear myelin figure of human medullablastoma. *Cancer Res.*, *31*, 2120.

TAY, H. H. & CHIA, B. L. (1971) Paroxysmal nocturnal haemoglobinuria following aplastic anaemia—case report. *Med. J. Aust.*, *1*, 139.

VALAENTINE, W. N., CROOKSTON, J. H., PAGLIA, D. E. & KONRAD, P. N. (1972) Erythrocyte enzymatic abnormalities in HEMPAS (hereditary erythroblastic multinuclearity with a positive acidified serum test). *Br. J. Haemat.*, *23*, 107.

VERBIN, R. S., GOLDBLATT, P. J. & FARBER, E. (1969) The biochemical pathology of inhibition of protein synthesis in vivo. *Lab. Invest.*, *20*, 529.

WASI, P., KRUETRACHUL, M. & NA-NAKORN, S. (1970) Aplastic anemia—paroxysmal nocturnal hemoglobinuria syndrome—acute leukaemia in the same patient: The first record of such occurrence. *J. med. Ass. Thailand*, *53*, 656.

WEATHERALL, D. J. (1977) Foetal-haemoglobin production or foetal erythropoiesis in dyserythropoietic anaemias. In: *Dyserythropoiesis*, ed. S. M. Lewis & R. L. Verwilghen, pp. 247–269. London: Academic Press.

WISCHNITZER, S. (1970) The anulate lamellae. *Int. Rev. Cytol.*, *27*, 65.

WISCHNITZER, S. (1973) The submicroscopic morphology of the interphase nucleus. *Int. Rev. Cytol.*, *34*, 1.

WORLLEDGE, S. M. (1977) Red cell antigens in dyserythropoiesis. In: *Dyserythropoiesis*, ed. S. M. Lewis & R. L. Verwilghen, pp. 191–208. London: Academic Press.

ZENTGRAF, H. & FRANKE, W. W. (1974) Preferential breakdown of the nuclear envelope in hen erythrocytes after phenylhydrazine treatment. *Beitr. path. Anat.*, *151*, 167.

ZURWEHME, D. & PIXBERG, H. U. (1970) Paroxysmale nachtliche Hämoglobinurie in der Differentialdiagnose aplastisches Knochenmarkeskrankungen. *Med. Klin.*, *65*, 63.

6

Treatment of Aplastic Anaemia, I. Conservative Management

E. C. GORDON-SMITH

Aplastic anaemia is not a malignant or progressive disease. It may be regarded as a deficiency disease involving blood cells. Death results from a failure of replacement therapy, not directly from failure to control the disease. Some patients with aplastic anaemia, even with severe disease, may recover. It is not known whether all or even most patients have this capacity for recovery, but ideally all efforts should be made to keep the patient alive long enough for this recovery to take place. This obvious goal is nevertheless most difficult to achieve in practice. Replacement therapy requires multiple transfusions of red cells, platelets and white cells. Bone marrow transplantation is a special form of replacement therapy which is discussed in the next chapter. The problems encountered in aplastic anaemia are those pertaining to any patient who needs frequent transfusions but exaggerated by the continuous, as opposed to intermittent, requirement for blood products, and by the susceptibility of the patient to local and systemic infections. The long-term protection of patients from infection puts a huge demand on resources, both medical and emotional.

The second aim of conservative management is to accelerate the recovery of the bone marrow or to utilize such function as remains. The best way to achieve such accelerated recovery must be removal of the cause of the aplasia, and perhaps the first few tentative steps have been made along this particular road with the identification of possible inhibitory factors to stem cell and committed cell proliferation (see Chapter 1). This chapter considers first the general support measures needed for the treatment of all patients with aplastic anaemia and secondly therapeutic means used to try and accelerate autologous recovery.

TRANSFUSIONS IN APLASTIC ANAEMIA

Methods of Intravenous Infusion

Patients with aplastic anaemia may require frequent, often daily, transfusions of blood products for long periods, sometimes months. The preservation of veins for infusion, the prevention of local infection and the choice of intravenous cannulae are of paramount importance. Keeping veins open for repeated infusions is mainly a matter of care. Nursing and medical staff must be aware of the patient's total dependence on intravenous blood products and so treat drip sites with great respect. Short intravenous cannulae inserted into peripheral veins should be changed every 24 hours (Collin et al. 1975). Metal and Teflon cannulae are less irritant to blood vessels than polystyrene, but the choice of cannula will depend upon the preference of the person who has to put up the drip. During acute episodes, as may occur at presentation or when an infection develops, it may be convenient to have a central venous line inserted. A catheter introduced into the subclavian vein, under platelet cover and aseptic conditions, is most convenient. The entry site of the catheter is treated with antiseptic cream and the catheter may be left *in situ* for 2 weeks, or longer, providing the patient is in a sterile environment. Central lines should be used when irritant solutions such as cephalothin, antilymphocyte globulin or potassium in high doses are used. Long catheters introduced via veins in the antecubital fossa may also be used, but the risk of infection developing if the catheter remains in place for a long time is greater than with a subclavian line because of the shorter subcutaneous tunnel.

Red Cell Transfusions

Red cell transfusions are used to keep the haemoglobin at such a level that the patient is comfortable. It has been suggested that the haemoglobin should be kept between about 6 g/dl and 9 g/dl so that a maximum erythropoietic drive is exerted on the marrow and hence accelerates recovery. On the other hand, it may be that the Hb level should be kept high because there is a reciprocal relationship between granulopoiesis and erythropoiesis (Morley et al. 1970). There is no evidence that the level of Hb influences recovery in aplasia and common sense dictates that as few transfusions as possible should be given. Transfusions of red cells may exacerbate thrombocytopenia, with an increased risk of haemorrhage, unless platelets are given as well. The choice of red cell preparation is probably not important for the patient who is not likely to receive a bone marrow transplant. Packed cells are suitable for most patients, white-cell poor or washed blood being reserved for patients who develop transfusion reactions. Blood which has been stored by freezing has certain advantages; it is less viscous than 'conventional' blood and therefore is less trouble to infuse, while the absence of lymphocytes and other white cells in the reconstituted blood means that reactions are rare and possibly that there is less risk of developing antibodies to platelets (Pepper 1976). Virus infections are also less likely to be transmitted in frozen blood (Meryman 1974).

Platelet Transfusions

The policy for platelet transfusions is much more difficult to decide than for red cells. The development of platelet antibodies, either antiplatelet or HLA antibodies, may be a disaster for the patient. Theoretically special care should be taken to keep the risk to a minimum but it is no good keeping transfusions to a minimum if the patient dies! There are three factors to consider in the use of platelet transfusions: first, the clinical indications, secondly the platelet preparations to use and thirdly the prevention and management of platelet sensitization.

Clinical indications for platelet transfusions. There is no way in which the possibility of a major haemorrhage in a thrombocytopenic patient can be predicted with certainty. The following points should be borne in mind when deciding upon the need for transfusion: buccal haemorrhages, retinal haemorrhages, haematuria and rapidly progressive purpura are all associated with a high risk of major haemorrhage, while unexplained headache and gastrointestinal haemorrhage are absolute indications for transfusion. Platelet counts below 10×10^9/litre are associated with a high risk, especially if the patient has an infection. Haemorrhage into the alveolar lung spaces is a serious problem in some patients, especially when associated with pneumonia. The changes on the radiograph are indistinguishable from pneumonia but the condition may be distinguished from oedema by the carbon monoxide transfer test (Ewan et al. 1976). Menstrual blood loss may be a difficult problem in aplastic anaemia, both because of the anaemia resulting and because platelets are consumed in the bleeding. It is reasonable to suppress menstruation, completely if possible, using oestrogens and norethisterone, even though there is a theoretical risk of suppressing marrow function with the former and the latter may cause headaches which are difficult to distinguish from early cerebral haemorrhage. Recurrent menstrual blood loss, gastrointestinal bleeding and haematuria may sometimes be indications to use platelets on a regular rather than clinically justified basis, despite the risk of sensitization.

Choice of platelet donor. There are three possible sources of platelets: random donors collected by the National Blood Transfusion Service, family members and unrelated donors specifically selected after HLA or other antigen matching. Family members must not be used if the patient is to receive a full bone marrow transplant (see Chapter 7). Random donations, collected either from pooled ABO-matched platelet-rich plasma in normal blood transfusion practice, or from single donors following separation of platelets on a cell centrifuge, may be available from blood transfusion centres. Development of antibodies is to be expected after a number of such transfusions, refractoriness usually appearing from about 8 weeks onward following random platelet transfusion (Grummet & Yankee 1970). The development of antiplatelet antibodies, either specific HLA antibodies or antibodies directed against other platelet components, may be a disaster for the patient but the ready availability of random donor platelets is an obvious advantage. HLA-matched platelets provide a source from which sensitization is unlikely (Yankee et al. 1973) but as yet there are insufficient panels to provide enough platelets for all aplastic patients.

Avoidance of antiplatelet antibody formation. Two different preparations of platelets may avoid sensitization of the patient and delay, or even prevent, the production of platelet antibodies. As mentioned above, the use of HLA-compatible platelets from the start may prevent antibody formation (Yankee et al. 1973; Mittal et al. 1976). Such platelets would have to be provided from individual donors using a cell-separator method. Since a successfully managed aplastic patient may require platelet transfusions for many months the difficulties in providing platelets in sufficient numbers are obvious. The National Blood Transfusion Service is building up panels of HLA-typed donors and provision of such platelets in the future is feasible. Nevertheless, centres caring for aplastic patients in this way would need facilities for collecting platelets from suitable donors at night, weekends and holidays when the Transfusion Service would find difficulty in making collections.

A second, promising, approach to the problem of sensitization to platelet transfusions is the use of white-cell-free platelets. Some transfusion reactions may occur even when HLA matched platelets are given but removal of 'contaminating' leucocytes may restore the effectiveness of such platelets (Herzig et al. 1975). A prospective clinical trial of leucocyte-poor platelet preparations carried out in Leiden seems to support the idea that the antibody response is, at least, long delayed (Eernisse & Brand 1977). The preparation of white-cell-free platelets requires extra centrifugation procedures or the use of nylon filter (Diepenhorst et al. 1972) but such washing could be made semi-automated and hence a practical procedure at National Blood Transfusion centres or even at the managing hospital.

Identification of sensitization to platelets. The first indication that a patient has developed significant platelet antibodies is a failure to control minor bleeding with platelets which were previously effective. This is usually mirrored by a fall in the average platelet count seen in the haematological chart. Sometimes the development of platelet antibodies may be associated with a fall in the neutrophil count as well (Hertzig et al. 1974). Direct estimation of antiplatelet antibodies is possible but the difficulties of the techniques available mean that only a few centres are at present able to measure them. A functional indication of antibody formation may be gained by measuring the increment in circulating platelet counts at 5, 15 and 60 minutes after transfusion of platelets. In the presence of antibody, no rise is seen in the circulating count. The type of antibody, whether HLA antibody or one directed against platelet antigens, should be identified if possible because the future management of the patient may be different in the two cases.

Management of patient who has developed antiplatelet antibodies. If the antiplatelet antibody has HLA specificity, it may be possible to improve the effectiveness of platelet transfusions by using HLA-compatible platelets (Yankee et al. 1973; Mittal et al. 1976). When antibodies are directed against other platelet antigens there is little prospect at present of obtaining compatible platelets (Hoak & Koepke 1976). It may be possible, using the increment test outlined above, to find specific donors whose platelets survive better than others, but such success is uncommon and puts particular strain on the donors in a long-continued disease. Despite the presence of antibodies, platelet transfusions may control bleeding, even though no increment is found in the peripheral blood and no change in bleeding time detected (Hoak & Koepke 1976). Fig. 6.1 shows the haematological chart of such a patient in whom development of antiplatelet antibodies was heralded by laryngeal haemorrhage. She was given an increased dose of prednisolone (80 mg/day) together with platelets from 20 random donors daily. Fortunately this controlled haemorrhage and eventually her own marrow recovered sufficiently to produce platelets of her own. Such success is unfortunately rare and platelet antibodies are a disaster.

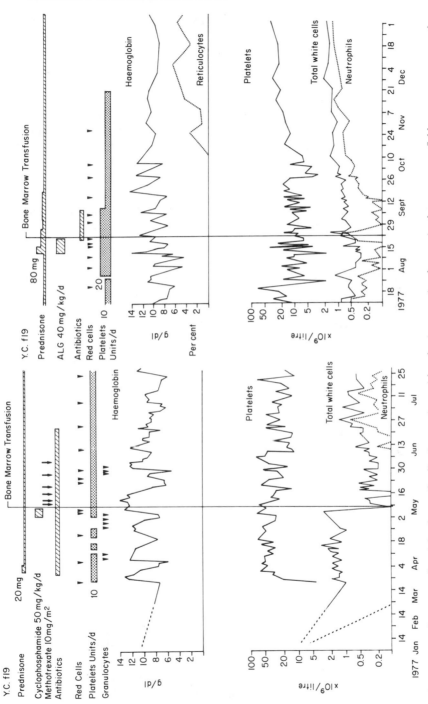

Fig. 6.1. Development of antiplatelet antibodies in a patient with aplastic anaemia who received an unsuccessful bone marrow transplant. The left-hand side shows haematological response to platelet support in the transplant period. Platelets from 10 donors per day contained an average platelet count of 40×10^9/litre. The right-hand part shows the fall in platelet count despite increased support. The patient eventually recovered autologous marrow function after ATG and repeat marrow transfusion from the same donor.

INFECTION

Infection is a major cause of death in aplastic anaemia. In the severely neutropenic patients organisms which are not usually pathogenic to man may become so, particular problems arising with *Pseudomonas aeruginosa*, *Proteus* and *Klebsiella* species (Spiers et al. 1974). Infection may develop at great speed and the time between initial fever and irreversible Gram-negative shock may be a matter of hours. There are, therefore, two important principles employed in the prevention of death from infection in aplastic anaemia. The first is that infection should if possible be prevented and the second that if there are clinical indications of infection, either fever or morphological features, the putative infection is treated immediately, before bacteriological confirmation is obtained.

Prevention of Infection

The main source of infection in neutropenic patients is endogenous, bacteria entering from various sites, particularly the gastrointestinal tract and upper respiratory air passages, including the mouth. Exogenous infections are a problem mainly in patients who are in hospital for a long time.

Endogenous infection. Whilst a neutropenic, aplastic patient is in hospital, certain methods may be employed to reduce the amount of potential endogenous pathogens. Some form of decontamination of the gastrointestinal tract is essential. Broad-spectrum antibiotics which are not absorbed from the gastrointestinal tract are usually employed, a suitable combination being framycetin, colistin and nystatin (FRACON), though nystatin syrup is unpleasant to take and may be nauseating. Amphotericin syrup is a suitable but more expensive alternative. An antifungal agent (nystatin or amphotericin) is usually given for 48 hours before the antibacterial drugs in order to eradicate yeasts before the bacteria, since absence of bacteria may encourage fungal overgrowth. The non-absorbable antibiotics, are used in association with low bacterial content food. If only short periods of gut sterilization are comtemplated, for example for bone marrow transplant patients, then sterile food may be used, though the preparation of such a diet requires great efforts on the part of dieticians and the sterile supply department. The food is not very appetizing and is not well tolerated by conservatively managed patients with aplastic anaemia; for these patients it is reasonable to supply well cooked food, served hot, freshly cooked and tinned foods, avoiding such obvious sources of bacterial and fungal contamination as salads, fresh fruit and so on.

Vitamin supplements with folic acid, vitamin C and pyridoxine should be given.

There seems no doubt that gut decontamination reduces the incidence of febrile episodes in neutropenic patients, though the evidence comes from studies of patients with acute leukaemia, not aplastic anaemia, where the situation differs because of the relatively short periods of neutropenia in the former (Storring et al. 1977). There is debate as to the best method of decontamination. The scheme outlined above, FRACON, takes no account of any idiosyncratic pathogens which may be present in the gut flora, being designed simply to reduce the bacterial and fungal content to a minimum. In some centres specially designed regimens of antibiotics, determined by the existing gut flora, are being used (Guigot & van Furth 1977). The effort required of microbiological departments is large. In experimental animal situations the 'tailored' courses have advantages but the clinical benefit over 'blunderbuss' therapy has not been proved.

Equal attention must be paid to the other major source of pathogens: the oral cavity and upper respiratory airways. Scrupulous oral toilet with ·a suitable antiseptic mouthwash (chlorhexidine is satisfactory) together with antifungal lozenges is essential. The mouthwash should be used after any food, drink or snacks are taken and at least 2-hourly throughout the day. Special attention should be paid to keeping the teeth clean; normal tooth-brushes may be unsuitable because of gum bleeding. Experience suggests that such mouth care reduces the incidence not only of mouth ulcers but also of gum bleeding and other haemorrhagic manifestations. Most patients can manage such oral toilet on their own but children have to be encouraged to carry out the procedures frequently.

The nose should be kept clean as far as possible and antibiotic creams may be used as necessary. The skin itself requires careful cleaning; antiseptic lotions may be useful and any small break or lesion in the skin should be taken very seriously. The axillae and groins are particularly likely to harbour pathogens and to develop pustules.

Exogenous infection. In hospital, patients should be in a protected environment out of contact with other patients. In the conservative management of aplastic anaemia it is impractical to maintain isolation in a sterile environment other than in exceptional circumstances. The patient should have his own room or cubicle; clean (preferably sterile) personal utensils should be used and staff entering the room should remove outer clothing likely to be contaminated (for example, doctors' white coats) or cover their outer clothes with a sterile gown or disposable plastic apron. A special stethoscope should remain permanently inside the room so that doctors and nurses do not have to use their own. The patient need not be totally confined to his room but whether he should be allowed to visit the general toilet or bathroom will depend upon the standards of cleanliness and the availability of special facilities in different hospitals.

Treatment of Established or Presumed Infection

As with all severely neutropenic patients (neutrophil count less than 0.2×10^9/litre) there is no time to await bacteriological reports before starting antibiotic therapy when a fever develops (Schimpff et al. 1971). Broad-spectrum antibiotics are given intravenously if any fever above 38°C persists for more than 2 hours (a 'guideline', not a rule). A suitable combination is an aminoglycoside (gentamicin or tobramycin) plus carbenicillin in full doses, a combination which covers most organisms apart from some anaerobic organisms such as *Bacteroides*. Lincomycin or clindamycin, which cover *Bacteroides*, are out of favour as 'blind' drugs because of the apparent association with pseudo-membranous colitis (Tedesco et al. 1974). The aminoglycoside and carbenicillin must be given separately since the latter inactivates the former *in vitro* and the aminoglycoside levels in the serum should be monitored to find the optimum dose. Carbenicillin is given as the sodium salt (27 mmol/5 g infusion) so salt overload is a possible consequence unless anticipated. Hypokalaemia is usual and potassium supplements, often more than 100 mmol/day, are required (Tattersall et al. 1972). If positive bacteriological evidence is obtained later, the broad-spectrum antibiotics should be discontinued and the appropriate antibiotics substituted. A difficult problem in aplastic anaemia is the decision to stop broad-spectrum antibiotics. A reasonable approach is to aim for a period of at least 5 days without fever before the antibiotics are stopped. Even so, if there is established infection it is likely that the same infection will recur after stopping antibiotics. Another problem is failure of fever to respond to broad-spectrum antibiotics. The use of granulocyte transfusions (see below) may be effective, or it may be necessary to treat as if the patient had an unusual organism, for example *Pneumocystis carinii* (pentamidine), fungal infection (amphotericin B with or without 5-fluorocytosine) or possible anaerobic organism (metronidazole). There is evidence that cotrimoxazole (trimethoprim and sulphonamide) will prevent the proliferation of *Pneumocystis*. Trials of this drug used prophylactically in acute leukaemias and bone marrow transplant patients are under way but results are not yet available. In conservatively managed aplastic anaemia, the problems of the duration of neutropenia remain and the indications or role of prophylactic antibiotics are less clear cut.

Granulocyte Transfusions

Antibiotics may be less active in the neutropenic patient than in those with normal neutrophils. This is thought to apply particularly to the aminoglycosides. Furthermore, drugs which are bacteriocidal in the presence of neutrophils may be only bacteriostatic in their absence so that recurrent infection with the same organism may occur. There are various methods of collecting granulocyte donations and these, together with their effects on granulocyte function, have been reviewed (Freireich 1975a, 1977). The method of collection will depend upon the available resources of a particular centre.

Indications and use. There is no place for prophylactic granulocyte transfusions in the conservatively managed patient with aplasia. Granulocytes should be given if fever persists for more than 24 hours after starting antibiotics and immediately if there is a localized cellulitic lesion associated with fever. Antibiotics seem to penetrate poorly into the oedema fluid of cellulitic lesions and even apparently trivial lesions, if associated with fever, should be treated with granulocyte transfusions. The effectiveness of granulocyte transfusions has not been proven beyond doubt in controlled trials, but such data as are available are very suggestive of their beneficial action (Higby 1977). There is good evidence that granulocytes have to be given on at least four successive days to be effective. One of the difficulties in assessing the effectiveness of granulocyte transfusions is that of deciding which effects to monitor. From the clinical point of view removal of fever or regression of infective lesion is clearly the most important. Increments in peripheral neutrophil counts at 30 and 180 minutes after infusion are also used (Goldstein et al. 1971; McCullough et al. 1976) but the effectiveness of neutrophils may be related to their ability to leave the circulation rather than to remain in it.

Choice of donors. Donors are usually obtained from family members, friends or volunteer panels (Graw et al. 1972) or from patients with chronic granulocytic leukaemia who are being treated by cytoreduction (Morse et al. 1961; Eyre et al. 1970). Donors should be ABO-compatible with the recipient (though ABO-incompatible granulocytes are effective, the problems of red cell contamination make incompatible transfusions slightly hazardous). Ideally, HLA compatibility should be obtained since the closer the A and B loci match the better the granulocytes survive (Hester & Rossen 1974). However, it is not always possible to obtain a sufficiently large panel of HLA-compatible donors. Patients may develop antibodies to granulocytes, either HLA or specific, as a result of transfusions with platelets or white cell contaminated blood. The management of such patients, as with those who develop platelet antibodies, is difficult and requires a search for compatible donors. It is theoretically desirable to use only a single donor for each course of granulocyte transfusions, particularly if they are HLA-matched. Successive donations can be given without detriment to the donor or yield of granulocytes but in practice it is often difficult to achieve this aim.

Complications. Apart from the development of antibodies, there are two major side effects of granulocyte transfusions. The infusion often produces fever, and sometimes rigors and more severe systemic complications, either because of antigen–antibody reactions or because of complement damage to the granulocytes during collection. Transfusions should be covered by hydrocortisone and piriton injections. The second problem is the engraftment of stem cells which are present in the transfusion which may produce graft-versus-host disease. Theoretically a conservatively managed aplastic patient should be able to reject such a graft but graft-versus-host disease has been reported when CGL cells are given (Schwarzenberg et al. 1967; Lowenthal et al. 1975) and at least on one occasion when a normal donor was used (Ford et al. 1976). Some authorities suggest that all granulocyte donations should be irradiated to 1000–1500 rads before transfusion to abolish stem cell activity (Bussel et al. 1975). Others take the opposite view that graft-versus-host disease is very rare in this circumstance and that a temporary graft is beneficial to the patient (Freireich 1975b). Our practice is to irradiate CGL cells, but not those from normal donors, unless the patient is immunosuppressed for bone marrow transplantation, when all blood products are irradiated.

OUT-PATIENT MANAGEMENT OF APLASTIC ANAEMIA

It will be appreciated that the conservative management of aplastic anaemia at its best is very demanding upon resources—economic, personal and emotional—far more so than radical treatments such as bone marrow transplantation. Most patients with aplasia will present with symptoms which require hospitalization for a varying period of time and which require the measures outlined in the preceding sections. In a few fortunate patients such measures may produce a period of stability where the patient is well but requires support with red cell and platelet transfusions and is at risk from infection but uninfected. With such patients a decision will have to be made whether to manage them as out-patients. The two major problems of infection and haemorrhage remain, and it is the arrangements which may be made to cope with these which help with the decision.

Infection

It is considered that patients at home are relatively safe from antibiotic-resistant pathogens compared with hospital environment. Gut decontamination is withdrawn before discharge. The safest way of stopping decontamination and recolonizing the gastrointestinal tract is a matter for considerable debate. It is our practice to use *Lactobacillus* at the time of withdrawal of antibiotics but other centres recommend the use of stored, encapsulated faecal material from the patient so that they are recolonized with their original flora. The patient is advised to keep to a cooked diet as mentioned above. Indoctrination of the patient into the importance of apparently trivial infections is intense and they continue with oral toilet. The most important measure is that they contact either the primary or secondary centre directly they notice any fever or septic lesion. They are advised to avoid crowds or potential sources of infection.

Bleeding

If the patient requires platelet transfusions before leaving hospital he will continue to need them as an out-patient. Our experience is that it is unsatisfactory to leave problems of bleeding to the patient or, indeed, to a local hospital because out-patient management produces inevitable delays before platelet transfusions can be obtained. This leads to the concept of a secondary centre in the management of out-patient aplastic anaemia patients. Before the patient is discharged arrangements are made, and their practicality confirmed, with a local hospital for the patient to receive platelet transfusions at regular intervals, in some cases on a daily basis. The blood transfusion centre serving the secondary centre is approached before discharge if they are to supply platelets, warning of the probable load and ascertaining that suitable donors will be available. If the patient lives reasonably close to the primary centre and transport arrangements can be made in a satisfactory fashion (i.e. not in a communal ambulance full of infected patients), then the patient is seen at frequent intervals (perhaps weekly) at the primary centre. This scheme seems to be very cumbersome and demanding on the patient but most prefer it to spending months in a protected environment in hospital. The use of regular platelets from random donors in this situation may be criticized on the grounds that the risk of platelet antibody production is increased but in practice this has proved the most satisfactory method so far. Six patients were discharged from this hospital with the above criteria of low platelet count and were managed 'on demand'. Four of these died from haemorrhage which occurred before platelet transfusion could be given. There is one survivor in this group. Of four patients managed with regular platelet transfusions, two have partial remissions and no longer require transfusions, two others are well but the follow-up is rather short (3 months in those still requiring transfusion).

ACTIVE MEASURES USED TO IMPROVE MARROW FUNCTION

Androgens

Testosterone was first used in the treatment of childhood aplastic anaemia by Shahidi and Diamond in 1959. This therapeutic approach was chosen because previous observations had shown that testosterone increased the haemoglobin in patients under treatment for breast cancer (Kennedy & Nathanson 1953) and some patients with myeloid metaplasia (Pringle & Gardner 1959). In addition, Shahidi and Diamond had observed spontaneous remission of childhood aplasia in two boys at puberty. The authors recorded the effect of testosterone 3 mg/kg weekly, given by intramuscular injection, on five patients with aplastic anaemia. There was no evidence that they had congenital aplastic anaemia and four patients fulfilled the criteria of severe aplastic anaemia. All five patients improved significantly following treatment with testosterone; in particular granulocyte and platelet counts rose over a period of 6–8 months. All patients received corticosteroids in addition to testosterone, either for some time prior to starting androgens or simultaneously. Corticosteroids alone produced no benefit. The main problems with continued testosterone therapy were the virilizing effects and the repeated intramuscular injections. Further development in the pharmacology of androgens produced the 17-α alkylated androgens, which could be absorbed from the gastrointestinal tract, and of other drugs which had more anabolic and fewer androgenic properties. A number of these have been tried in aplastic anaemia but the results of therapy are difficult to assess. First, there has been no double-blind control trial in aplastic anaemia of androgens compared with no androgens. The initial excellent results of Shahidi and Diamond in a disease which was almost universally fatal made workers reluctant to deny any patients this therapy. Since 1959, however, the support available for patients with aplastic anaemia has developed enormously, as outlined in the first part of this chapter, and controlled trials should now be possible. The trial would have to be rigidly controlled and involve more than one centre because it now seems clear that the advantages of androgen

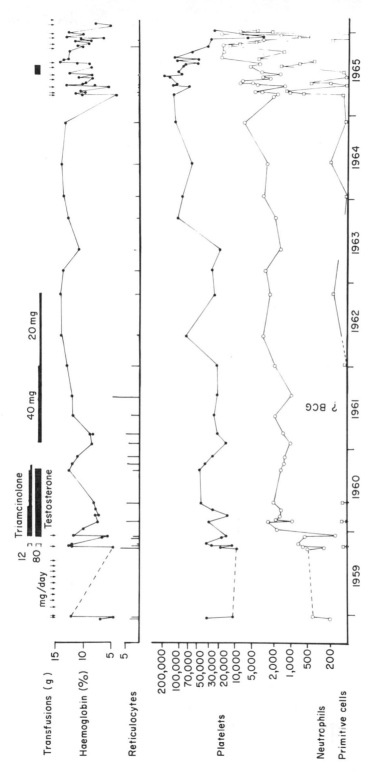

Fig. 6.2. Apparent response to anabolic steroids in a patient with hypoplastic anaemia. The response is dependent on a continuing small dose of anabolic steroid. The patient ultimately died with acute myeloblastic leukaemia 6 years after onset of aplasia.

therapy are small, if present, and large numbers of patients would be needed to show any effect. Naturally, the support care given to patients in both treated and untreated groups would have to be of the same standard. Further, aplastic anaemia may not have a uniform pathogenesis and it could be that a small proportion of the whole group may benefit from androgens whilst the majority suffer only the side effects.

Occasionally individual patients with acquired aplastic anaemia appear to respond to androgens and the response is dependent upon continuing therapy (Fig. 6.2), suggesting cause and effect. More commonly, recovery, either partial or complete, is reasonably stable and is independent of continuing androgen therapy.

Androgens increase plasma erythropoietin levels, but their effects in aplastic anaemia probably depend on direct stimulation of the haemopoietic stem-cell. The androgenicity of the steroid is not critical in determining its effectiveness though women and children tend to show a greater response than men (Shahidi 1973).

Evidence for and against androgen therapy. Shahidi and Diamond's results with testosterone were supported by the clinical experience of Sanchez-Médal et al. (1964) in Mexico using the 17-α alkylated androgen, oxymetholone. These authors found a 46·7% response to oxymetholone in patients with various degrees of severity of disease and of different aetiologies. Allen et al. (1968) in the USA treated five consecutive cases of childhood aplasia (four idiopathic, one constitutional) with oxymetholone (2·5–4 mg/kg/day) and achieved beneficial responses in all five despite previous resistance to testosterone therapy in two of them. Ten patients with aplastic anaemia (one with Fanconi's anaemia) were treated with the intramuscular androgen, nandrolone decanoate (1–1·5 mg/kg/week) by workers in Chile (Daiber et al. 1970). Two patients died, six achieved normal haematological results (including the Fanconi's) and two improved significantly. These authors included a list of historical controls, 12 patients immediately preceding the anabolic trial, of whom six died, two showed no improvement, two showed partial improvement and two became normal. These beneficial results, especially in children, were not confirmed by workers at the Boston Children's Hospital (Li et al. 1972). Of 58 children under 16 with aplastic anaemia all but one received androgens and corticosteroids; 41 (71%) were dead at the time of publication with a median survival of the whole group less than 6 months. The authors conclude that androgens produced no obvious benefit in the management of aplasia. Similarly Williams et al. (1973) in Salt Lake City were unable to find any significant difference between the survivors of patients treated with or without androgens in a retrospective survey of 101 patients with aplastic anaemia. Retrospective analysis of 76 adult patients with aplastic anaemia treated at Hammersmith Hospital showed that the 42 patients treated with androgens (30 with oxymetholone 2·5–4 mg/kg/day, six with methandienone 1 mg/kg/day, four with methyltestosterone 1 mg/kg/day and two with nandrolone phenylproprionate 1 mg/kg/week) had a marginally better survival than the 34 who did not receive androgens (Fig. 6.3) but that the difference in overall survival was not of great statistical significance ($0·05 > P > 0·02$). The survey suffers from the problems of all uncontrolled retrospective surveys: changes in support measures may contribute to the differences in survival. The two groups were comparable in other respects, namely granulocyte counts, platelet counts, aetiology and age. A comparison of survival in 26 androgen-

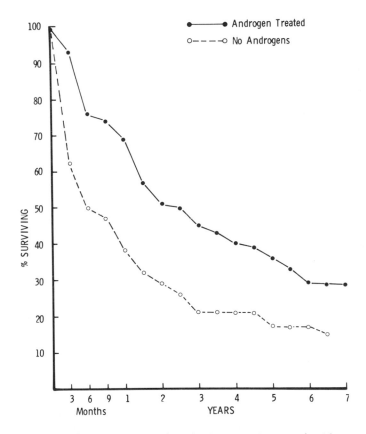

Fig. 6.3. Survival of 30 patients with aplastic anaemia treated without anabolic steroids compared with 32 who received them. The two groups are comparable for neutrophil, platelet and reticulocyte counts and for age and sex. The survey was retrospective. There is no significant difference in long-term survival.

treated patients (oxymetholone 17, methrenolone 3 and methandro-stenolone 2) with 14 treated without androgens in Leiden (Haak 1978) also showed no significant difference between the two groups. A small prospective trial of androgen treatment with three 'arms' (oral androgens *vs.* intramuscular androgens *vs.* no androgens) involving several centres in the USA and UK, showed no advantage for androgen therapy (Camitta et al. 1977).

The effectiveness of androgen therapy in aplastic anaemia remains unclear. Some emphasis has been given, in the preceding paragraphs, to the origins of the various reports because it may be that the aetiology of aplastic anaemia varies in different parts of the world and that the good results of treatment with androgens found in Central and South America reflect a different type of disease. Those patients in all groups, who do recover in association with androgen therapy, do so 2 or 3 months after starting the treatment; thus if androgens are used they should be used in high dosage for at least 3 months. If no effect has been achieved at 6 months, the androgens will probably not be effective. The possible synergy of androgen therapy with anti-lymphocyte globulin in promoting recovery in aplasia is discussed in the next chapter.

Side effects of androgens. The side effects of androgens may be divided into two groups: those which are an inherent part of the androgenic nature of the steroids, and those which arise from structural changes in the basic steroid.

Androgenic side effects. Virilization occurs with all androgenic steroids though modification of the testosterone molecule may promote anabolic effects and decrease the androgenic effects. Deepening of the voice, due to changes in the larynx, and hirsutism are particularly troublesome for female patients. Virilization in young male children produces physical and emotional problems. Early bone fusion may be less severe than was earlier feared (see p. 184). Acne may be extremely troublesome and even life-threatening in neutropenic, thrombocytopenic patients. Tetracycline should be given on a regular basis if acne occurs. Prostatic hypertrophy should be anticipated in older male patients. Hypercholesterolaemia and hypertrigly-ceridaemia occur in patients treated with all androgens, particularly oral androgens. Salt retention is an inevitable consequence of high-dose androgens and needs to be considered in patients who have high transfusion requirements and possible myocardial damage. There are minor differences between different androgenic steroids but the differences are probably not significant (Najean & Pecking 1975).

Liver toxicity. The 17-α substituted androgens, which are absorbed from the gastrointestinal tract, also cause a cholestatic jaundice. The reaction is dose-dependent but there is considerable individual variation in susceptibility. Conjugated bilirubin levels are elevated and there may also be rises in transaminase levels. Serum alkaline phosphatase levels are less commonly raised. If the 17-α alkylated androgens are used in combination with other drugs which may cause cholestastis or if there is any previous impairment of hepatic function (for example post-hepatic aplasia) then the jaundice and disordered liver function is likely to be much worse. The biochemical changes are usually reversible, though with the high-dose androgens used in aplasia the reversal is slower than is usually suggested (Sherlock 1975).

Hepatocellular carcinoma. Malignant tumours of the liver have been described in patients with aplastic anaemia treated with androgens (Johnson et al. 1972). The tumours may be multifocal or single and occasionally regress when androgens are withdrawn. The development of a tumour is indicated by a change in liver function tests and may be with a deterioration in haematological condition. The α-fetoprotein is usually not elevated. Occasionally patients who have not received androgens develop carcinoma, the tumour developing in a liver already damaged by haemosiderosis consequent on multiple blood transfusions. The opposite, namely hepatocellular carcinoma arising in a patient treated with androgens, but who received very few transfusions, is also reported. It seems certain that hepatocellular carcinoma is a small but definite risk in patients who receive high-dose androgens for a long time, probably over a year or more. The risk in the use of short-term androgens is less clear-cut.

Peliosis hepatitis. The development of multiple venous lakes, peliosis hepatitis, has also been reported in patients receiving long-term androgens (Bagheri & Boyer 1974). The disorder is characterized by enlargement of the liver with relatively mild biochemical changes. Sometimes there is local pain or tenderness. The disorder is apparently benign though may be associated with a hepatocellular carcinoma (Bagheri & Boyer 1974) or possibly independent. Peliosis hepatitis appears on ^{99m}Tc colloid liver scan as multiple filling defects which are also present when selenomethionine is used, whereas selenomethionine is taken up by hepatic carcinoma. Withdrawal of androgens leads to a slow disappearance of the venous lakes.

Acute leukaemia. Occasional reports have appeared of acute leukaemia developing in patients with aplastic anaemia who received androgens (Delamore & Geary 1971). In our series of 76 patients with acquired aplastic anaemia two developed acute myeloid leukaemia and both had received androgens. However, the acute leukaemia developed over a year after recovery from aplasia in one of these patients and other reports suggest that acute leukaemia may develop without the addition of androgens in acquired aplasia (Vincent & de

Gruchy 1967; Brauer & Dameshek 1967). Acute leukaemia is a well recognized complication of Fanconi's anaemia with or without androgen therapy (see Chapter 8). It is not possible to implicate androgens definitely in the genesis of acute leukaemia following aplastic anaemia.

Splenectomy

Removal of the spleen is rarely attempted for the treatment of aplastic anaemia. The spleen is not enlarged in these patients and isotope studies seldom indicate a particular role of the spleen in sequestering or destroying cells in these patients. Before the introduction of androgens for therapy, splenectomy was used in the management of some of these patients. Scott et al. (1959) reviewed the management of 39 patients with aplasia of whom 15 underwent splenectomy. Six of these patients died, two probably as a result of the surgery. Of the nine survivors, one failed to improve, three had partial and five substantial improvement. Heaton et al. (1957) had earlier reported their experience with aplastic anaemia. Four of eight patients with acquired aplastic anaemia improved after splenectomy. These authors collected a further 35 cases from the literature. Scott et al. (1959) compared the survival of their 15 patients in one group, the 43 patients of Heaton et al. in another and their own 24 non-splenectomized aplastic patients and found what appeared to be a significantly better prognosis in the splenectomized groups. The authors, however, counselled caution in the interpretation of the results. When more sophisticated statistical analysis was applied to the results there was no significant difference in the splenectomized and non-splenectomized patients. Furthermore, there are difficulties in interpreting data on patients whose case reports have been collected from the literature and it is important that carefully matched controls are considered. As Stohlman (1972) pointed out in relation to the use of androgens, differences in the severity of the disease may be crucial in the effects of treatment. As with androgens, the case for splenectomy has not yet been proved and perhaps the hazards of failed therapy are even greater. Splenectomy does not influence refractoriness to platelet transfusion in sensitized patients (Grummet & Yankee 1970).

Corticosteroids

Corticosteroids alone do not seem to shorten the period of aplasia (Erslev et al. 1952) and may be dangerous if given in high doses because of the increase in infection. Scott et al. pointed out this risk in 1959 and it remains true. Patients, particularly children, who do respond rapidly to high-dose corticosteroids nearly always turn out to have acute lymphoblastic leukaemia (Melhorn et al. 1970) (see p. 76). Low-dose corticosteroids, 10–15 mg prednisolone or equivalent per day for an adult, are traditionally used in an attempt to reduce the purpura caused by a low platelet count. The practice arose following observations that patients receiving ACTH had a higher capillary resistance as measured by negative pressure than controls (Robson & Duthie 1950). These authors gave ACTH to three patients with idio-pathic thrombocytopenic purpura and observed an increase in capillary resistance which preceded the rise in platelet count. Whilst the data on which the treatment is based are scanty, such low-dose cortico-steroids probably do no harm and may reduce skin bleeding complications.

Other Treatment

The most recent methods of treating aplastic anaemia, bone marrow transplantation and the use of antilymphocyte globulin are considered in the next chapter. Cobalt salts have been used in the past but produce no improvement in survival. Recently, Besa et al. (1977) have reported on the use of aetiocholanolone (a 5-β hydroxy steroid) and predniso-lone in patients with various disorders causing pancytopenia. This metabolite of testosterone, which is non-virilizing, stimulates mouse marrow precursor cells to enter cell cycle *in vitro* (Byron 1970), increases iron incorporation *in vivo* in mice (Gordon et al. 1970; Gorshein & Gardner, 1970) and stimulates haem synthesis in animals *in vitro* (Levere et al. 1970; Gorshein et al. 1975). Three of the patients in this series had aplastic anaemia. In two of them there was a partial response to this treatment. The platelet count rose slowly (months) but the neutrophils, particularly in one patient, rose rapidly. [59]Fe clearance was also accelerated in one patient. Aetiocholanolone will raise the granulocyte count by release of marrow reserve cells (Vogel et al. 1967) but Besa and his colleagues claim a more sustained increase in granulocyte count than can be accounted for by this mechanism.

CONCLUSIONS

Conservative management of aplastic anaemia depends mainly on support for the patient with transfusions and avoidance of infection. Androgens in high dose may have some beneficial effect in a few patients but probably do not affect the outcome in severe aplastic anaemia. Low-dose corticosteroids may be used. To some extent the outcome may be influenced by the enthusiasm with which supportive care is pursued.

REFERENCES

ALLEN, D. M., FINE, M. H., NECHELES, T. F. & DAMESHEK, W. (1968) Oxymetholone therapy in aplastic anaemia. *Blood, 32*, 83.

BAGHERI, S. A. & BOYER, J. L. (1974) Peliosis hepatitis associated with androgenic–anabolic steroid therapy. A severe form of hepatic injury. *Ann. intern. Med., 81*, 610.

BESA, E. C., WOLFF, S. M., DALE, D. C. & GARDNER, F. H. (1977) Aetiocholanolone and prednisone therapy in patients with severe bone-marrow failure. *Lancet, i*, 728.

BRAUER, M. J. & DAMESHEK, W. (1967). Hypoplastic anemia and myeloblastic leukaemia following chloramphenicol therapy. Report of 3 cases. *New Engl. J. Med., 277*, 1003.

BUSSEL, A., BÉRUBUMAN, M., GRANGE, M. J., BOIRON, M. & BERNARD, J. (1975) Comparison of results induced by irradiated and non-irradiated chronic myelocytic leukaemia cell transfusions and the relationship in vitro studies. In: *Leukocytes: Collection, Separation and Transfusion*, ed. J. M. Goldman & R. M. Lowenthal, p. 395. London: Academic Press.

BYRON, J. W. (1970). Effect of steroids on the cycling of haematopoietic stem cells. *Nature, Lond., 228*, 1204.

CAMITTA, B., THOMAS, E. D., NATHAN, D. G., SANTOS, G., GORDON-SMITH, E. & RAPPEPORT, J. (1977) Severe aplastic anemia: effect of androgens on survival. American Society of Hematology, San Diego, December, 1977.

COLLIN, J. COLLIN, C., CONSTABLE, F. L. & JOHNSTON, I. D. A. (1975) Infusion thrombophlebitis and infection with various cannulae. *Lancet, ii*, 150.

DAIBER, A., HERVE, L., CON, I. & DONOSO, A. (1970) Treatment of aplastic anemia with nandrolone decanoate. *Blood, 36*, 748.

DELAMORE, I. W. & GEARY, C. G. (1971) Aplastic anaemia, acute myeloblastic leukaemia and oxymetholone. *Br. med. J., 2*, 743.

DIEPENHORST, P., SPROKHORST, R. & PRINS, H. K. (1972) Removal of leukocytes from whole blood and erythrocyte suspensions by filtration through cotton wool filtration techniques. *Vox Sang., 23*, 308.

EERNISSE, J. G. & BRAND, A. (1977) Postponement (or prevention?) of immunization against HLA-antigens by blood and platelet transfusions. *Br. J. Haemat., 35*, 674.

ERSLEV, A. J., IVESON, C. K. & LAWRASON, F. D. (1952) Cortisone and ACTH in hypoplastic anemia. *Yale J. Biol. Med., 25*, 44.

EWAN, P. W., JONES, H. A., RHODES, C. G. & HUGHES, J. M. B. (1976) Detection of intrapulmonary haemorrhage with carbon monoxide uptake. Application to Goodpasture's syndrome. *New Engl. J. Med., 295*, 1391.

EYRE, E. H., GOLDSTEIN, M. & PERRY, S. (1970) Leukocyte transfusions: function of transfused granulocytes from patients with classic myelocytic leukaemia. *Blood, 36*, 432.

FORD, J. M., LUCEY, J. J., CULLEN, M. H., TOBIAS, J. S. & LISTER, T. A. (1976) Fatal graft-versus-host disease following transfusion of granulocytes from normal donors. *Lancet, ii*, 1167.

FREIREICH, E. J. (1975a) Leucocyte collection and transfusion: A historical perspective. In: *Leucocytes: Collection, Separation, and Transfusion*, ed. J. M. Goldman & R. M. Lowenthal, p. 27. London: Academic Press.

FREIREICH, E. J. (1975b) General discussion. In: *Leucocytes: Collection, Separation and Transfusion*. ed. J. M. Goldman & R. M. Lowenthal, p. 403. London: Academic Press.

FREIREICH, E. J. (1977) Prospects for the future of the separation and collection of blood cells. *Expl Hemat.*, 5 (suppl. 1), 3.

GOLDSTEIN, I., EYRE, H., HENDERSON, E., TERASAKI, P. & GRAW, R. G. (1971) Leukocyte transfusions: role of leukocyte alloantibodies in determining transfusion response. *Transfusion, 11*, 19.

GORDON, A. S., ZANJAM, E. D., LEVERE, R. D. & KAPPAS, A. (1970) Stimulation of mammalian erythropoiesis by 5β-H steroid metabolites. *Proc. natn. Acad. Sci., U.S.A., 65*, 919.

GORSHEIN, D. & GARDNER, F. H. (1970) Erythropoietic activity of steroid metabolites in mice. *Proc. natn. Acad. Sci., U.S.A.*, *65*, 564.

GORSHEIN, D., REISNER, E. H. & GARDNER, F. H. (1975) Tissue culture of bone marrow v. effect of 5 beta (H) steroids and cyclic AMP on heme synthesis. *Am. J. Physiol.*, *228*, 1024.

GRAW, R. G. HERZIG, G. P., PERRY, S. & HENDERSON, E. S. (1972) Normal granulocyte transfusion therapy. *New Engl. J. Med.*, *287*, 367.

GRUMMET, F. C. & YANKEE, R. A. (1970) Long term platelet support of patients with aplastic anemia. Effect of splenectomy and steroid therapy. *Ann. intern. Med.*, *73*, 1.

GUIGOT, H. F. L. & VAN FURTH, R. (1977) Partial antibiotic decontamination. *Br. med. J.*, *i*, 800.

HAAK, H. L. (1978) *Acquired Aplastic Anaemia in Adults: A Clinical, Histological and Experimental Study of Diagnosis and Treatment*. Proefschift. Dutch Efficiency Bureau—Pijnacker.

HEATON, L. D., CROSBY, W. H. & COHEN, A. (1957) Splenectomy in the treatment of hypoplasia of the bone marrow, with a report of twelve cases. *Ann. Surg.*, *146*, 637.

HERTZIG, R. H., HERTZIG, G. P., BULL, M. I., DECTER, J. A., LOHRMANN, H. P., STOUT, F. G., YANKEE, R. A. & GRAW, R. G. (1975) Correction of poor platelet transfusion response with leukocyte-poor HL-A matched platelet concentrates. *Blood*, *46*, 743.

HERTZIG, R. H., POPLAK, D. G. & YANKEE, R. A. (1974) Prolonged granulocytopenia from incompatible platelet transfusions. *New Engl. J. Med.*, *290*, 1220.

HESTER, J. P. & ROSSEN, R. O. (1974) Multiple PMN transfusions: rôle of HLA compatibility and leukoagglutinins. *Proc. Am. Ass. Cancer Res.*, paper 211.

HIGBY, D. J. (1977) Controlled prospective studies of granulocyte transfusion therapy. *Expl Hemat.*, *5* (Suppl. 1), 57.

HOAK, J. C. & KOEPKE, J. A. (1976) Platelet transfusions. *Clinics in Haematology*, Vol. 5. *Blood Transfusion and Blood Products*, ed. J. D. Cash, p. 69. Philadelphia and London: Saunders.

JOHNSON, L. F., FEAGLER, J. R., LERNER, K. G., MAJERUS, P. W., SIEGEL, M., HARTMANN, J. R. & THOMAS, E. D. (1972). Association of androgenic-anabolic steroid therapy with the development of hepatocellular carcinoma. *Lancet*, *ii*, 1274.

KENNEDY, B. J. & NATHANSON, I. T. (1953) Effects of intensive sex steroid hormone therapy in advanced breast cancer. *J. Am. med. Ass.*, *152*, 1135.

LEVERE, R. D., KAPPAS, A. & GRANICK, S. (1967) Stimulation of hemoglobin synthesis in chick blastoderms by certain 5β androstane and 5β megnane steroids. *Proc. natn. Acad. Sci., U.S.A.*, *58*, 985.

LI, F. P., ALTER, B. P. & NATHAN, D. G. (1972) The mortality of acquired aplastic anemia in children. *Blood*, *40*, 153.

LOWENTHAL, R. M., GROSSMAN, L., GOLDMAN, J. M., STORRING, R.A., BUSKARD, N. A., PARK, D. S., MURPHY, B. C. & GALTON, D. A. G. (1975) Granulocyte transfusion therapy: a comparison of the use of cells obtained with normal donors with those from patients with chronic granulocytic leukaemia. In *Leukocytes: Collection, Separation and Transfusion*, ed. J. M. Goldman & R. M. Lowenthal, p. 363. London: Academic Press.

McCULLOUGH, J., WEIBLEN, B. J., DEINARD, A. R., BOEN, J., FORTNING, I. E. & OINE, P. G. (1976) In vitro function and post-transfusion survival of granulocytes collected by continuous-flow centrifugation and by filtration leukapheresis. *Blood*, *48*, 315.

MELHORN, D. K., GROSS, S. & NEWMAN, A. J. (1970) Acute childhood leukaemia presenting as aplastic anemia: the response to corticosteroids. *J. Pediat.*, *77*, 647.

MERYMAN, H. T. (1974) Low temperature storage of red cells. In: *The Human Red Cell in Vitro*, ed. J. J. Greenwalt & G. A. Jamieson, p. 323. New York: Grune & Stratton.

MITTAL, K. K., ALANNAH RUDER, E. & GREEN, D. (1976) Matching of histocompatibility (HL-A) antigens for platelet transfusion. *Blood*, *47*, 31.

MORLEY, A., HOWARD, D., BENNETT, B. & STOHLMAN, F. (1970) Studies on the regulation of granulopoiesis, 11. Relationship to other differentiation pathways. *Br. J. Haemat.*, *19*, 523.

MORSE, E. E., BRONSON, W., CARBONE, P. P. & FREIREICH, E. S. (1961) Effectiveness of granulocyte transfusions from donors with chronic myelocytic leukemia to patients with leukopenia. *Clin. Res.*, *9*, 332.

NAJEAN, Y. & PECKING, A. (1975) Androgen therapy of aplastic anaemia. *IIIrd Meeting, int. Soc. Haemat., Europ. Afr. Div., Lond, 11*, 18.

PEPPER, D. S. (1976) Frozen red cells. In: *Clinics in Haematology, Vol. 5. Blood Transfusion and Blood Products*, ed. J. D. Cash, p. 53. Philadelphia and London: Saunders.

PRINGLE, T. C. & GARDNER, F. H. (1959) Treatment of myeloid metaplasia with testosterone. *Clin. Res.*, *7*, 210.

ROBSON, H. N. & DUTHIE, J. J. R. (1950) Capillary resistance and adrenocortical activity. *Br. med. J., ii*, 971.

SANCHEZ-MEDAL, L. B., PIZZUTO, J., TORRE-LOPEZ, E. & DERBEY, R. (1964) Effect of oxymetholone in refractory anaemia. *Archs intern. Med.*, *113*, 721.

SCHIMPFF, S., SATTERLEE, W., YOUNG, V. M. & SERPICK, A. (1971) Empiric therapy with carbenicillin and gentamycin for febrile patients with cancer and granulocytopenia. *New Engl. J. Med.*, *284*, 1061.

SCHWARZENBERG, L., MATHE, G., AMIEL, J. L., COTTON, A., SCHNEIDER, M. & SCHLUMBERGER, J. R. (1967) Study of factors determining the usefulness and complications of leukocyte transfusions. *Am. J. Med.*, *43*, 206.

SCOTT, J. L., CARTWRIGHT, G. E. & WINTROBE, M. M. (1959) Acquired aplastic anaemia: an analysis of thirty-nine cases and review of the pertinent literature. *Medicine, Balt., 38*, 1959.

SHAHIDI, N. T. (1973) Androgens and erythropoiesis. *New Engl. J. Med.*, *289*, 72.—

SHAHIDI, N. T. & DIAMOND, K. K. (1959) Testosterone-induced remission in aplastic anemia. *Am. J. Dis. Child., 98*, 293.

SHERLOCK, S. (1975) Drugs and the liver. *Diseases of the Liver and Biliary System,* p. 345. Oxford: Blackwell Scientific.

SPIERS, A. S. D., TATTERSALL, M. H. & GAYA, H. (1974) indications for systemic antibiotic prophylaxis in neutropenic patients. *Br. med. J., iii*, 440.

STOHLMAN, F. (1972) Editorial: aplastic anemia. *Blood, 40*, 282.

STORRING, R. A., JAMESON, B., McELWAIN, T. J., WILTSHAW, E., SPIERS, A. S. D. & GAYA, H. (1977) Oral non-absorbed antibiotics prevent infection in acute non-lymphoblastic leukaemia. *Lancet, ii*, 837.

TATTERSALL, M. H. N., BATTERSBY, G. & SPIERS, A. S. D. (1972) Antibiotics and hypokalaemia. *Lancet, i*, 630.

TEDESCO, F. J., BARTON, R. W. & ALPERS, E. H. (1974) Clindamysin associated colitis. A prospective study. *Ann. intern. Med., 81*, 429.

VINCENT, P. C. & DE GRUCHY, G. C. (1967) Complications and treatment of acquired aplastic anaemia. *Br. J. Haemat., 13*, 1977.

VOGEL, J. M., YANKEE, R. A., KIMBALL, H. R., WOLFF, W. M. & PERRY, S. (1967) The effect of etiocholanolone on granulocyte kinetics. *Blood, 30*, 474.

WILLIAMS, D. M., LYNCH, R. E. & CARTWRIGHT, G. E. (1973) Drug-induced aplastic anemia. *Semin. Hemat., 10*, 195.

YANKEE, R. A., GRATT, K. S., DOWLING, R. & HENDERSON, E. S. (1973) Selection of unrelated compatible platelet donors by lymphocyte HL-A matching. *New Engl. J. Med., 288*, 760.

7

Treatment of Aplastic Anaemia, II. Bone Marrow Transplantation and the Use of Antilymphocyte Globulin

E. C. GORDON-SMITH

BONE MARROW TRANSPLANTATION

Many attempts were made in the 1950s and 1960s to reconstitute marrow in patients with hypoplastic anaemia, both the idiosyncratic type and that secondary to cytotoxic or radiation therapy, using allogeneic marrow from various sources. The marrow donors were ABO-compatible but, except in the case of identical twins, no attempt was made to match any other tissue antigens. With very few exceptions, the result was failure (Bortin 1970). Animal experiments had shown that mice and guinea-pigs could be rescued from the lethal effects of irradiation on bone marrow by infusion of syngeneic and allogeneic marrow (Lorenz et al. 1951) and that irradiation and nitrogen mustards were immunosuppressive as well as cytotoxic (Schwab et al. 1950). There was evidence that marrow could be given intravenously without harmful effect. In 1957 Thomas and colleagues at Cooperstown (Thomas et al. 1957) reported the effects of marrow infusion in six patients who had received irradiation or cytotoxic drug therapy for malignant disease. In one patient, who was treated with 450 rad total body irradiation (TBI) over 8 days and who received stored frozen marrow taken *post mortem* from a patient who died of cerebral haemorrhage, there was evidence for a temporary take of the marrow as indicated by appearance of C+ cells in the C− recipient. In Paris, Mathé and his colleagues achieved temporary grafts in five patients accidentally exposed to whole body irradiation using aspirated marrow from ABO-compatible volunteers (Mathé et al. 1959). These patients survived with reconstitution of their own marrow function. These early attempts at marrow transplantation showed that intravenous marrow infusion could be given with safety to patients and that grafting was possible in immunosuppressed subjects. Animal work with monkeys had indicated that a special problem would be encountered in bone marrow transplantation, namely the reaction of immunocompetent cells from the donor against the recipient's tissues, causing graft-versus-host disease similar to, though more severe than, the secondary syndrome of rodents (van Bekkum et al. 1959; de Vries et al. 1961). The graft-versus-host disease in monkeys was characterized by damage to the skin, liver and gastrointestinal tract and a marked increase in the risk of infection (Crouch et al. 1961). Thus three problems were identified associated with allogeneic bone marrow transplantation: rejection of the graft, support for the recipient during engraftment and graft-versus-host disease. Evidence that marrow grafting could succeed in the majority of patients with aplastic anaemia was obtained from grafts between identical twins (syngeneic grafts) suggesting that in some cases, at least, replacement of stem cells was sufficient to cure the disease.

Syngeneic Bone Marrow Grafts

Bone marrow obtained from an identical twin is not affected by immunological 'barriers' when transfused into the recipient. Syngeneic marrow may thus be effective in reconstituting normal haematological function in aplastic anaemia, but there are some anomalies in the effectiveness of this treatment which may be relevant to the pathogenesis of aplastic anaemia (see Chapter 1). The first successful transplant of this type was reported by Robins and Noyes (1961). A 7-year-old girl received marrow from her proven identical twin sister. There was a prompt improvement in her blood count, starting 5 days after the transfusion, particularly in the white cell count. The platelet count rose in two stages, to about 30×10^9/litre some two weeks after the graft, and then to just below normal levels about 150 days later. The recipient was receiving prednisone 40 mg daily at the time of the transfusion. Fernbach and Trentin (1962) had reported an unsuccessful attempt at treating drug-induced aplastic anaemia in this way despite two transfusions of $3 \cdot 6$ and $2 \cdot 8 \times 10^9$ bone marrow cells and they concluded that there was an abnormality of the environment which prevented the bone marrow proliferation. Mills et al. (1964) and Thomas et al. (1964) reported two further successfully treated cases. In both these patients the haematological response was rapid, the first indication of success appearing about 7 days after infusion and eventually normal haematological values were obtained. Pegg et al. (1964) reported an unsuccessful attempt at treating a 54-year-old man with pure red cell aplasia with marrow from a presumed identical twin. There was a transient reticulocyte response but this failure is scarcely surprising in view of the probable autoimmune aetiology in most cases of red cell aplasia (see p. 201). Melvin and Davidson (1964) reported partial success with syngeneic marrow transfusion in a 66-year-old woman with chloramphenicol-induced aplasia. As with the case of Robins and Noyes, granulocyte counts and the haematocrit improved but the platelet count remained low, though there was a transient rise following splenectomy. Thomas' group, now at Seattle, reported another success in a patient with idiopathic aplastic anaemia in whom there was a prompt rise of platelets and granulocytes to normal values, followed by partial relapse about 3 months later, with eventual spontaneous rise back to normal levels (Pillow et al. 1966). The authors included in their report two other patients who died soon after the transplant (15 hours and 4 days) without time for any improvement in blood count to show itself. Harvey and Firkin (1968) reported an interesting response to syngeneic marrow infusion in a 32-year-old woman with phenylbutazone- and/or chloramphenicol-induced aplasia who required three marrow transfusions before substantial improvement occurred. Following the first, there was no change in blood count; after the second, temporary recovery occurred, while the third transfusion was followed by a sustained, though incomplete, rise in all cells, least marked in the platelet count which remained at 20–30 × 10^9/litre despite a splenectomy. The Royal Marsden Hospital Bone Marrow Transplant Team (1977) reported a case in whom two transfusions of adequate numbers of cells failed to restore marrow function but haemopoiesis returned to normal when the recipient was treated with cyclophosphamide, 50 mg/kg, before a third infusion (see p. 17).

Table 7.1 summarizes the various published syngeneic transplants which have been performed for aplastic anaemia. Responses fall into three groups; patients who died before the procedure could be evaluated, those who became haematologically normal and those in whom recovery was incomplete (the last group following the pattern most frequently seen in the conservatively managed patient, namely, a persistent thrombocytopenia).

If an identical twin is available, marrow infusion from the healthy twin to the patient is clearly the treatment of choice, preferably before the recipient becomes very ill. Several transfusions may be required before the patient recovers and it is possible that those who do not respond to an adequate infusion of marrow cells will nevertheless recover if given immunosuppression first.

Allogeneic Bone Marrow Transplantation

Rejection. The importance of the major histocompatibility system (MHS) in prolonging acceptance of various types of tissue graft,

Table 7.1. Syngeneic twin bone marrow transfusions for aplastic anaemia

Group	Author	Age/Sex	Probable cause	Transfused cells (×10⁹)	Result
I Died before graft could be evaluated	Pillow et al (1966)	15, M 9, F 23, F	Unknown Unknown ?Chloramphenicol	2·2 2·6 1·2	Died in 1 month Died in 15 hours Died in 4 days
II Normal haemopoietic reconstitution	Robins and Noyes (1961)	7, F	Various anticonvulsants	5·5	Delayed platelet recovery
	Thomas et al. (1964) Mills et al. (1964) Royal Marsden Hospital Bone Marrow Transplant Team (1977)	9, F 9, F 15, F	Unknown Unknown Hepatitis	6·1 7·3 6·5 16·3 ?	Steady return to normal (11 years+) Prompt return to normal (6 years +) Transient, partial Transient, partial Immunosuppressed with cyclophosphamide. Normal haematological reconstitution
III Partial haemopoietic reconstitution	Fernbach and Trentin (1962)	3, M	Chloramphenicol ± sulphonamide	3·6 (1st) 2·8 (2nd) 6.6 (3rd)	Patient remained severely thrombocytopenic. Third attempt 5 years after the first
	Melvin and Davidson (1964)	66, F	Chloramphenicol	6	Platelets approx. 30 × 10⁹/litre
	Harvey and Firkin (1968)	32, F	Chloramphenicol and many other drugs	4·2 (1st) 10.7 (2nd) 17.1 (3rd)	No graft Transient Sustained. Platelets 100 × 10⁹/litre

particularly skin and kidney, was shown by various groups once sero-logical identification of some histocompatibility antigens and lymphocyte determination of others became possible (van Rood et al. 1966; Singal et al. 1969).

In dogs, it was shown that histocompatibility between donor and recipient, as indicated by serological testing and the mixed lymphocyte reaction (MLR), reduced the incidence of rejection and of graft-versus-host disease (Storb et al. 1968). However, matching of these major histocompatibility systems is insufficient, of itself, to protect against rejection. 'Minor' antigen systems are also involved. Some of the special problems of bone marrow rejection were indicated by experiments in mice where it was shown that F_1 hybrid strains rejected marrow from homozygous inbred parents, despite the sharing of one major histocompatibility system (Cudkowicz & Bennett 1971). This hybrid resistance could be partially overcome by immunosuppression as could the rejection of DLA identical marrow in outbred dogs (Storb et al. 1969). The methods of immunosuppression used were total body irradiation (Santos et al. 1958) and/or cyclophosphamide (Santos et al. 1970). Using the latter agent the Seattle group found that they could improve the acceptance rate by preceding the immunosuppression with an antigenic stimulus from the donor in the form of a buffy coat transfusion of leucocytes (Storb et al. 1969). Cyclophosphamide acts efficiently as an immunosuppressive agent after such a stimulus but irradiation is ineffective (Santos 1974), so that buffy coat should not be used when total body irradiation is employed in immunosuppression of a recipient. Further attempts to improve the acceptance rate, particularly following sensitization by prior transfusion (see below), involved the use of increased immunosuppression with antilymphocyte globulin (ALG), prepared in animals against human T lymphocytes, and procarbazine, a powerful immunosuppressant of unknown mechanism (Storb et al. 1974a; Weiden et al. 1976). When applied to man, the schedules and dosages shown in Table 7.2 were obtained. Early results from Seattle indicated that total body irradiation was less effective than cyclophosphamide alone in obtaining long-term survival in aplastic patients, so that Regimen III is now rarely used for this purpose (Storb et al. 1974c).

Apart from matching the major histocompatibility systems of donor and recipient and immunosuppression of the recipient, other factors probably influence acceptance of the graft. In dogs, prior transfusions of blood products increase the chances of rejection, particularly if a transfusion from a related dog is used (Storb et al. 1970a; Weiden et al. 1975). The evidence in man is less clear-cut. In a detailed analysis of factors which influenced rejection, Storb et al. (1977a) found that the

Table 7.2. Immunosuppressive regimens

Days before transplant	Regimen I	Regimen II	Regimen III
7		ALG*	
6	Buffy coat 1 unit	Procarb 12·5 mg/kg	
5	Cyclophosphamide 50 mg/kg	ALG* Cyclophosphamide 50 mg/kg	
4	Cyclophosphamide 50 mg/kg	Procarb 12·5 mg/kg Cyclophosphamide 50 mg/kg	Cyclophosphamide 60 mg/kg
3	Cyclophosphamide 50 mg/kg	ALG* Cyclophosphamide 50 mg/kg	Cyclophosphamide 60 mg/kg
2	Cyclophosphamide 50 mg/kg	Procarb 12·5 mg/kg Cyclophosphamide 50 mg/kg	Total body irradiation 100 rads
1			

* Antilymphocyte globulin. Dose varies according to source and potency.
Regimen III is not generally used for aplastic anaemia but is used for acute leukaemia.

marrow cell dose given and the degree of histocompatibility, as measured by the relative response index in the mixed lymphocyte reaction, were the two most strongly influencing success. Patients with aplastic anaemia who have received no blood products before transplant are uncommon but successful engraftment appears to be much more readily obtained in such patients, compared with those who have received many transfusions (Thomas, Storb, personal communication). There is also some suggestion, though not statistically significant, that there is a correlation between the number of transfused units and rejection. It is important, therefore, to select patients for transplantation before they have been sensitized to unknown tissue antigen systems by multiple transfusions. Furthermore, as discussed in the next section, refractoriness to platelet transfusions is associated with an increased risk of graft-versus-host disease.

Graft-versus-host disease

As with the prevention of rejection, the most important factor in avoiding graft-versus-host disease is the degree of histocompatibility between recipient and donor. Unidentified antigens play a part in susceptibility to graft-versus-host disease in man, and immunosuppression is partially successful in reducing the incidence. After the graft the cytotoxic properties of immunosuppressive drugs must be taken into account, for the engrafting marrow is likely to be highly susceptible to such assaults. Experimentally, methotrexate was found to reduce the incidence of graft-versus-host disease in dogs (Storb et al. 1970*b*) and this drug is predominantly used in man. The Seattle protocol consists of methotrexate 15 mg/m² on day 1, 10 mg/m² on days 3, 6, 11, and then weekly for 100 days (Thomas et al. 1971). Theoretically, graft-versus-host disease can be prevented by removal of immunocompetent cells from the transfused marrow and this is experimentally possible; successful transplants in monkeys following removal of immunocompetent cells by density gradient centrifugation have been reported (Dicke & van Bekkum 1971). Unfortunately, only acute graft-versus-host disease is prevented and delayed; chronic disease may still occur. Moreover in man, such procedures have not yet proved effective in reducing the problem of graft-versus-host disease.

Decontamination of the microflora of gut may be important in reducing graft-versus-host disease. In mice, the secondary syndrome, which is similar, though perhaps not identical, to graft-versus-host disease, can be prevented if germ-free or colonization-resistant mice are given allogeneic transplants (van Bekkum et al. 1974; Pollard et al. 1976). Decontamination is obviously desirable for other reasons in human patients with aplastic anaemia, but whether these measures influence human graft-versus-host disease is uncertain.

Analysis of 73 transplants carried out for aplastic anaemia in Seattle suggest that two other factors are important in reducing the incidence of graft-versus-host disease (Storb et al. 1977*b*). Refractoriness to random platelet transfusions was associated with a high risk of graft-versus-host disease and, surprisingly, transplants between opposite sexes also increased the risk, which suggests some immunological function in the human Y chromosome.

It is important, in these immunosuppressed patients, that no further immunocompetent cells should be introduced, since graft-versus-host disease or even 'graft-versus-graft' disease may then result. Irradiation with 1500 rad of all blood products likely to contain such cells is necessary (Glucksberg et al. 1974).

Clinical and histological manifestations. Graft-versus-host disease is manifest mainly in the gut, liver and skin, though other organs may be affected. The disease varies from a mild self-limiting and transient disorder to a severe form which may become chronic.

Histopathologically, graft-versus-host disease is characterized by degenerative and necrotic changes in the affected organs with increasing lymphocyte infiltration as the disease progresses (Lerner et al. 1974). This has been termed the aggressor lymphocyte response by Woodruff et al. (1976). It is preceded or accompanied by a lymphoid response which takes place in most lymphoid tissue and marked by a proliferative phase of lymphoblasts followed by lymphorhexis and, finally, atrophy.

The histological changes which occur in the main target organs have been graded as indicated in Table 7.3 by the Seattle group (Thomas et al. 1975). Graft-versus-host disease is frequently associated with infection and the histological changes are not always readily separated from those which may accompany viral or fungal infections, or from drug eruptions. Serial skin biopsies are possible and helpful in transplant patients as a guide to the development of graft-versus-host disease.

Table 7.3. Histopathological staging of graft-versus-host disease according to organ systems

Stage	Skin	Liver	Intestinal tract
1+	Basal vacuolation and/or necrosis	Small interlobular bile ducts abnormal <25%	Dilation of glands: single cell necrosis of epithelial cells
2+	As 1+ with spongiosis, dyskeratosis and eosinophilic necrosis of epidermal cells	25–50%	As 1+ with necrosis and dropout of entire glands
3+	As 2+ with microscopic epidermal–dermal separation	50–75%	As 2+ with microscopic mucosal desquamation
4+	Frank epidermal loss	>75%	Diffuse microscopic denudation

Fever, skin rash, jaundice and gastrointestinal disturbance are the normal accompaniments (Fig. 7.1). The skin rash is the most constant feature and begins as a maculopapular rash which frequently involves the palms and soles but spares the upper trunk, at least in the early stages. This distribution is unlike that of a drug-induced eruption. The lesions may be itchy. As the disease becomes more severe, the rash becomes confluent and exfoliative and bullous formation may occur. If the disease becomes chronic a scleroderma-like syndrome may develop, with either generalized (Masters et al. 1975) or localized (van Vloten et al. 1977) lesions, or lichen-planus-like lesions may appear (Saurat et al. 1975). Increasing jaundice with evidence of hepatocellular disease indicates liver involvement, while diarrhoea, becoming severe and watery, together with abdominal pain, indicates gut involvement. The clinical staging of graft-versus-host disease and organ involvement according to organs affected are shown in Tables 7.4 and 7.5 (Thomas et al. 1975). The common cause of death in patients so affected is infection, particularly virus or opportunistic infections of the lungs producing interstitial pneumonitis (Neiman et al. 1973).

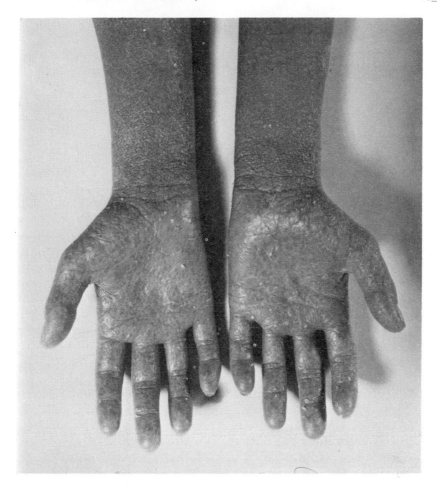

Fig. 7.1. Severe cutaneous manifestations in a patient with chronic graft-versus-host disease. There was a generalized scleroderma-like reaction, particularly marked on the hands and feet. (*By courtesy of Dr R. L. Powles, Royal Marsden Hospital*)

Table 7.4 Clinical staging of graft-versus-host disease, 1. Organ systems

Stage	Skin	Liver	Intestinal tract
1+	Maculopapular rash <25% body surface	Bilirubin 25–40 μmol/litre	Diarrhoea of 0·5–1·0 litre/day
2+	Rash on 25–50% body surface	Bilirubin 40–75 μmol/litre	Diarrhoea of 1·0–1·5 litres/day
3+	Generalized erythroderma	Bilirubin 75–200 μmol/litre	Diarrhoea of >1·5 litres/day
4+	Erythroderma with bullous vesicles and exfoliation	Bilirubin >200 μmol/litre	Severe abdominal pain ± ileus

Table 7.5. Clinical staging of graft-versus-host disease, 2. Overall
clinical grading

Grade	Skin	Liver	Intestinal tract	Clinical performance
I	1+ to 2+	0	0	Normal
II	1+ to 3+	1+	and/or 1+	Mild decrease
III	2+ to 3+	2+ to 3+	and/or 2+ to 3+	Marked decrease
IV	2+ to 4+	2+ to 4+	and/or 2+ to 4+	Incapacitated

Treatment. No treatment available at present is particularly effective
in the management of graft-versus-host disease. Antilymphocyte
globulin has shown some promise (Storb et al. 1974*b*) though, at least
in some patients, ALG abrogates the reaction but when the treatment
is stopped the graft-versus-host disease returns with unabated severity.
Corticosteroids in high dose may also temporarily control the disease,
but the effect is not usually sustained, for most patients relapse when
the high doses are reduced or stopped. There is a close relationship
between the disease and virus infections and in one case involving the
skin graft-versus-host disease occurred in a region previously affected
by measles virus, unaffected areas being spared (Fenyk et al. 1978). The
preparation and administration of ALG is discussed briefly later but it
should be remembered that ALG may have some antiplatelet activity
and that its administration must be covered with additional platelet
transfusions if the patient is thrombocytopenic. The dose of ALG
required varies considerably between different preparations and
possibly even batches. The only effect easily measured in the recipient
is the lymphocyte count, which should be suppressed almost to zero,
particularly the T-cell population.

Method of Marrow Collection and Transfer

The method of marrow collection used in many transplantation
centres is that described by Thomas and Storb (1970). This method has
remained virtually unchanged since its first reported use by Thomas on
the patient of Robins and Noyes (1961). The donor is rendered pain-
free by general or spinal anaesthesia. Bone marrow is aspirated from
the posterior iliac crests through multiple aspiration sites. The marrow
is transferred to siliconized stainless steel beakers which contain tissue
culture medium (Tc 199) with 40 units of heparin per ml. The collected
marrow is passed through stainless steel wire meshes to break up any
marrow fragments into single cells, transferred to a blood-giving pack
and transfused into the recipient using a giving set without a filter.
Complications include febrile reactions and the possible danger of

micro-emboli in the lungs. The recipient should be monitored continuously whilst the marrow infusion is taking place and resuscitation equipment should be instantly available. In practice the procedure is simple and trouble-free. There are a number of variations of this simple procedure. Some centres use a completely closed system for marrow collection (Pegg & Kemp 1966) to reduce further the risk of infecting the marrow. Not all centres use Tc 199 and some use a filter in the giving set, though this may reduce the number of cells reaching the recipient. Very few problems arise with the donor. There may be some temporary soreness at the site of aspiration but most donors are able to leave hospital the following day and some hardy donors leave the same day!

Quantity of marrow required. The quantity of marrow transferred is of the utmost importance. In animal experiments there is a definite relationship between the amount of marrow transferred and graft acceptance, the volume of allogeneic marrow required being considerably greater than the amount of syngeneic marrow (van Bekkum 1976). As mentioned earlier in this chapter, the Seattle group (Storb et al. 1977a) found a strong negative correlation between marrow dose and rejection, recipients receiving 3×10^8 cells/kg having significantly fewer rejections than those who received less. The dose of marrow cells given is crudely calculated by measuring the total nucleated cells present in the marrow transfusion and subtracting the number estimated as attributable to peripheral blood, as calculated from the neutrophil count. These measurements are made whilst the donor is still in theatre so that the final volume required can be calculated. Recently the Seattle group have suggested that the maximum amount of marrow possible, obtained by aspiration from the sternum and anterior iliac crests as well as posterior crests, plus peripheral cells, including circulating stem cells obtained by cell separator techniques, should be given (Storb et al. 1977a). The total volume of marrow required is usually of the order of 1–1·5 litres so the donor may require transfusion. It is prudent to remove 500 ml of blood from the donor for autologous transfusion about 10 days before the marrow harvest.

Selection of Donor

The marrow donor should be physically healthy, willing without pressure to donate marrow and histocompatible with the recipient. ABO compatibility is not essential though preparation of the recipient for an ABO-incompatible graft is more difficult. If more than one donor is available a donor of the same sex should be chosen because of the increased risk of graft-versus-host disease when donors of opposite sex are used (Storb et al. 1977*b*). At present histocompatibility is tested by serological methods to determine the HLA A and B antigens, and by the mixed lymphocyte reaction to determine the D locus identity. It appears that the D locus is the major determinant of graft compatibility (van Rood 1974); a successful graft in a patient with severe combined immune deficiency (SCID) has been obtained using a MLR non-reactive individual who was HLA A and B non-identical (Dupont et al. 1973). The mixed lymphocyte reaction is not a suitable screening test for random donors so at present the chances of finding an unreactive individual have to be increased by using A and B identity. Since the A, B and D loci are closely linked in the same chromosome, the sixth (van Someren et al. 1974), siblings who have A and B identity have a greater than 95% chance of being MLR-unreactive because cross-over at these loci is rare. The same is not true of unrelated donors (see below). Serological tests for the D locus determined antigens may become available, in which case screening for unrelated donors may be made easier.

The mixed lymphocyte reaction is measured using donor and recipient lymphocytes in culture, first with both sets of lymphocytes viable (two-way test) and then with one or other prevented from dividing by irradiation or mitomycin (one-way test). A deliberately mismatched control is used. Tritiated thymidine is added to the culture medium. When one set of lymphocytes is stimulated by the other the cells divide and take up thymidine. The result may be expressed in various ways including the 'relative response index':

$$RRI = \frac{R + ID - R + IR}{R + IX - R + IR} \times 100\%$$

where R is the cpm taken up by recipient lymphocytes in culture with irradiated donor (ID), irradiated recipient (IR) and irradiated mismatched (IX) cells. Several mismatches should be used to obtain a mean value for mismatched cells. The Seattle group found that an RRI of less than 1·6% was associated with greater graft acceptance (Storb et al. 1977*a*).

Selection of Recipient

The results of bone marrow transplantation for aplastic anaemia are given later but, briefly, about 40–50% of the grafts are successful. The 50–60% of patients who die do so mainly as a result of the grafting procedure, usually from infection following rejection or graft-versus-host disease. Since it is possible that some of these patients might have survived if treated conservatively, it is clearly essential to establish criteria by which only patients with the most severe aplasia, who have a very poor chance of survival, are selected for transplantation. Clearly, only those who have a fully compatible sibling donor will be considered at all, the chances of any one sibling being compatible being 1 in 4. Various attempts have been made to determine criteria which separate patients with a poor prognosis from those with a better chance of survival. These factors are discussed in detail in Chapter 3. The various definitions of severity are shown in Table 7.6; in each case a previous diagnosis of aplastic anaemia is mandatory. Aplastic

Table 7.6. Criteria of severe aplastic anaemia

Lewis (1965)	Neutrophils $<0.1 \times 10^9$/litre Platelets $<20 \times 10^9$/litre	Single factor analysis
Lynch et al. (1975)*	Duration of symptoms to presentation (OFV) Haemorrhagic manifestations (B) Platelet count (P) Neutrophils (N) Reticulocytes (R) Non-myeloid cells in marrow (NM) Sex (S) (male = 1, female = 2)	Prognostic Index, $C = -0.01796(B) + 0.01272(S)$ $-0.00008(OFV) -$ $0.000002(N) - 0.00018(P) +$ $0.00046(NM)$ $C \geqq 0.033 = $ Severe $C \leqq 0.0 = $ Benign
Camitta et al. (1975)	Neutrophils $<0.5 \times 10^9$/litre Platelets $<20 \times 10^9$/litre Reticulocytes (corrected) $<1\%$	Two out of 3 features present
Lorhmann et al. (1976)	Reticulocytes $<10 \times 10^9$/litre	In severely neutro- and thrombocytopenic patients
Mathé and Schwartzenburg (1977)	High peripheral blood lymphocyte count	

* See discussion in Chapter 3.

anaemia following infectious hepatitis usually falls into the severe group. The mortality in this fairly well defined group of aplastics is 85% (Camitta et al. 1974) and the association may be taken as an absolute indication for transplantation providing the liver function tests have returned nearly to normal. If the patient is considered to be in the severely affected group and has a compatible sibling, transplantation should be carried out as soon as possible (Camitta et al. 1976) in order to minimize the risk of sensitization by transfusions, and while the patient is in a good clinical state, preferably uninfected. Certainly, in transplantation for acute leukaemia, uninfected reasonably healthy patients do better than sick patients (Thomas et al. 1977).

Support for the Transplant Patient

Once the decision to transplant has been taken, preparation for the procedure begins. The patient begins gut decontamination and oral and skin hygiene, as described in the previous chapter. Sterile food is started. Once the patient is 'clean' and in a sterile environment immunosuppression is started with the appropriate regimen (Fig. 7.2).

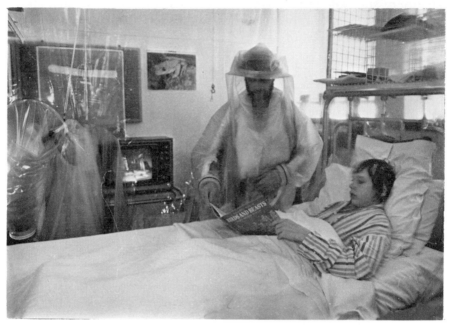

Fig. 7.2. Trexlec Vickers plastic isolation tent. The patient is rendered as clean as possible before entering. All equipment in the tent is sterilized before entry.

It is our practice to introduce a subclavian catheter under strictly sterile conditions before starting immunosuppression and to leave it in place for as long as possible. Cyclophosphamide in the doses used has well recognized side effects, of which haemorrhagic cystitis is the most worrying in the pancytopenic patient. This may be avoided by giving a high fluid load and keeping the urine alkaline. The administration of cyclophosphamide and the fluid intake given are shown in Table 7.7, a protocol based on the advice of Thomas and his colleagues. Anti-emetics may be required, and diarrhoea may occur, but generally the drug is surprisingly well tolerated. The patient must be warned of the side effects of cyclophosphamide, particularly alopecia, and arrangements for a wig should be made before starting treatment.

Table 7.7. Administration of cyclophosphamide 50 mg/kg in an adult patient

Time	Infusion	Additions
06·00–10·00	1 litre dextrose/saline	50 mmol NaHCO₃ + 20 mmol KCl
10·00–10·30	Cyclophosphamide 50 mg/kg in 250 ml dextrose/saline	
10·30–14·00	1 litre dextrose	50 mmol NaHCO₃ + 20 mmol KCl
14·00–18·00	1 litre dextrose/saline	50 mmol NaHCO₃ + 20 mmol KCl
18·00–22·00	1 litre dextrose	20 mmol KCl
22·00–02·00	1 litre dextrose/saline	10 mmol KCl
02·00–06·00	1 litre dextrose	10 mmol KCl

Frusemide 40 mg or acetazolamide 250 mg to be given intravenously 1 hour before cyclophosphamide and frusemide 40 mg intravenously 6 hours after cyclophosphamide.

Following the immunosuppression platelet and, to a lesser extent, red cell requirements are frequently increased above the pre-immuno-suppression level. Blood products should be irradiated to 1500 rad as already discussed (p. 137) to avoid graft-versus-host disease from engraftment of immunocompetent cells from this source. If there is evidence that the recipient was free of cytomegalovirus infection before transplantation it is desirable that cytomegalovirus-free donors be used, though cryopreserved red cells are free of this virus infection (Chapter 6). Indications for broad-spectrum antibiotics are the same as for any neutropenic patient, though once started in the post-transplant patient they should be continued until the graft is established. Granulocyte transfusions may be given prophylactically or to treat known or presumed infections. Trials of prophylactic granulocyte transfusions versus 'demand' transfusions are under investigation in the USA but definitive results are not yet available.

Evidence for engraftment normally appears between 15 and 30 days after the graft. Apart from a general sense of well-being in the patient the first signs are usually the appearance of peripheral blood reticulocytes or granulocytes. Platelet response is more delayed. Fig. 7.3 shows the typical course in an uncomplicated, successful transplant. Graft-versus-host disease is usually heralded by the appearance of fever, followed by a skin rash, but any manifestation may develop first, making the diagnosis difficult. Reactive lymphocytes appear in the peripheral blood in increasing numbers and a marked lympho-cytosis, particularly if it can be demonstrated that the cells are of donor origin, is an ominous sign. There is no clear-cut indication for starting treatment for graft-versus-host disease. The Seattle group recommend that clinical stages III and IV should be treated with ALG (Storb et al. 1974b). but it may be that treatment should be started at an earlier

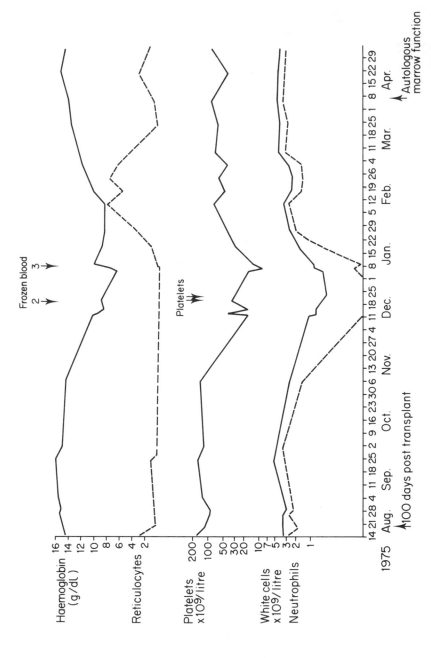

Fig. 7.3. Autologous recovery of bone marrow function 8 months after failure of previously successful bone marrow transplant. Red cell markers showed that the recovered marrow was unlike the donor marrow and therefore presumably of patient origin. The patient remains well after a further 18 months.

stage. Because of the risk of graft-versus-host disease, and its possible aggravation by bacterial contamination, gut decontamination should be continued until the major hazard is past, that is for at least 60 days. It is not clear whether the patient should remain in strict isolation for this period and social and medical pressures often demand that strict isolation be abandoned soon after the granulocyte count becomes normal.

Management of virus infections. Virus infections are a particular hazard in transplanted patients, especially, though not exclusively, if graft-versus-host disease is present. The virus may be endogenous or exogenous. Latent endogenous viruses may be activated following transplantation, particularly those of the herpes and papova groups (Rinaldo et al. 1976). Cytomegalovirus is the most commonly activated of the herpes group and is associated with interstitial pneumonitis, particularly in patients transplanted for acute leukaemia (Clift et al. 1974). Of 50 patients who received allogeneic transplants for either aplastic anaemia or haematological malignancy in Seattle one-third of those obtaining satisfactory grafts died with cytomegalovirus-associated interstitial pneumonitis (Neiman et al. 1973). A subgroup who received syngeneic marrow had a lower incidence (Neiman et al. 1976). The incidence is less in patients with aplasia than in those with malignant disease. Nevertheless, about 50% of transplant patients show some evidence of cytomegalovirus infection, using serological, cultural isolation or histological methods (Neiman et al. 1976). Lethal cyto-megalovirus infection occurred earlier in these patients than non-fatal disease and a good prognosis was accompanied by a rise in comple-ment-fixing antibodies.

Herpes simplex infections may be activated and in these patients disseminated spread is a special danger. The pathogenicity of other viruses, for example the polyoma group, is still a matter for specu-lation (Henry et al. 1977).

The treatment of virus infection is difficult but should be started as soon as evidence of pathogenic infection becomes available. Herpes-virus infections are treated with adenosine arabinoside (ara-A) in maximally tolerated doses—20 mg/kg. Unfortunately this agent is relatively insoluble and has to be given in a large volume of fluid. Local lesions due to herpes simplex or zoster should be treated with idoxuridine, 40%, in dimethylsulphoxide. For exogenous infections which may be encountered, for example a high risk of varicella or measles, immune serum or gamma-globulin should be given. Inter-feron has been used, with apparently good effect, to treat cytomegalo-virus infection in a patient with severe combined immunodeficiency disease and a trial of the same agent in a patient transplanted for acute myeloblastic leukaemia produced benefit, though the trial was limited by lack of availability of interferon (O'Reilly et al. 1976). Interferon apparently had some effect against graft-versus-host disease and modified the activity of oncogenic viruses in F_1 (Galb/c × A/J) mice in whom the disease was induced by transfer of parent Balb/c spleen cells (Hirsch et al. 1973). Interferon, however, inhibits T-cell function and its prophylatic use in transplanted patients would have to be monitored carefully.

Other infections. Other opportunistic infections, such as *Pneumocystis carinii* and fungal infections, also occur in the post-transplant period. Cotrimoxazole may be effective in preventing infection with the former. Regular screening for fungal antigens, antibodies and organisms should be carried out weekly on the patient.

Treatment of rejection. An allogeneic marrow transplant may fail to take, produce a transient graft or occasionally be rejected after a period of months. Failure to take may be assumed when no increase in marrow cellularity or peripheral blood count occurs within 30 days of the transfer. Temporary transplants may be inferred from a rise in granulocyte counts unaccounted for by transfusions, which subsequently disappears. Most rejection occurs within the first 50 days after the transplant but occasionally delayed rejection occurs. Rejection is also a dangerous time with regard to infection.

Evidence for engraftment. It is important in allogeneic transplant patients to determine which marrow has grown, since autologous recovery sometimes follows marrow transplantation (Thomas et al. 1976; Speck et al. 1976b). Where there is a sex difference between donor and recipient, XY chromosome markers are used. Where the sex is the same, blood groups and isoenzyme patterns in red cells or white cells are used, though a considerable period may elapse before elimination of all transfused red cells makes this method valid. Fluorescent chromosome banding techniques for autosomal chromosomes may eventually prove to be another useful method of proving early allogeneic engraftment. The presence of graft-versus-host disease is usually taken to indicate engraftment (Storb et al. 1976b) and a rise in marrow cellularity and the appearance of peripheral blood cells within the initial 15–30-day period may be taken as presumption of graft, at least in those patients who do not survive long enough to have red cell markers examined. Patients who may come to transplantation should have the minor blood group systems determined before any transfusions are given, if this is possible, for then an appropriate antigen may be chosen which, by excluding it from transfused red cells, may be used as an early marker of engraftment.

Results of Bone Marrow Transplantation

The first series of successful transplants for aplastic anaemia comprised four patients reported by the Seattle group in 1972 (Thomas et al. 1972); in 1974 they reviewed results in the first 24 patients so treated. Six of the patients received total body irradiation, the remainder cyclophosphamide only (Storb et al. 1974c). Eleven (45%) of the patients obtained haematological reconstitution though two had chronic graft-versus-host disease. Failure to take and rejection accounted for seven deaths, graft-versus-host disease for four, cyto-megalovirus infection for one, and one further patient died of a mysterious infection over a year later (Table 7.8). These were patients

Table 7.8. Bone marrow transplantation for aplastic anaemia

| Author | No. of patients | Death associated with | | Survivors |
		Rejection/ No take	GVHD	
Storb et al. (1974c)	24	7 (29%)	4 (17%)	11 (45%)
Storb et al. (1976b)	49	15 (30%)	12 (25%)	20 (41%)
Camitta et al (1976)	36	11 (28%)	2 (6%)	24 (67%)
UCLA (1976)	12	4 (33%)	1 (8%)	7 (55%)
European Bone Marrow Transplant Group (1977, unpublished)	73	41 (56%)	5 (7%)	27 (35%)

treated between November 1970 and March 1973. In a second series of 49 patients, transplanted between April 1973 and March 1976 (Storb et al. 1976b), 20 survived (41%) with 15 deaths from rejection or no take and 12 from graft-versus-host disease. It was recognized that at least some of the mortality might be accounted for by the delay in referral for bone marrow transplantation, so that patients arrived for trans-plant sensitized by many transfusions and in poor clinical condition. For this reason it was decided to start a prospective multi-centre trial of transplantation versus conservative management with patients accep-ted for transplant as early as possible on the basis of fairly simple criteria (Camitta et al. 1976). Of the 36 patients transplanted, 24 (67%) obtained complete response 3–12 months after grafting, though it is interesting that two patients eventually recovered autologous marrow function, one following preparation for regrafting with ALG and pro-

carbazine alone, the other (the patient shown in Fig. 7.3) spontaneously. Thirty-one patients were managed conservatively, seven
without androgens, 24 with. Only one patient became haematologically normal, five had partial response and six showed no
improvement (survival 39%). The differences between the groups when
survival was plotted against time by life table analysis was significant (P
$= 0.006$, Wilcoxon) (Fig. 7.4). It must be remembered that this was not

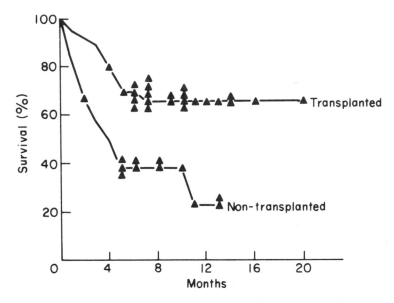

Fig. 7.4. Survival of 36 patients who received early allogeneic transplants compared
with 34 patients managed conservatively. The difference in survival is significant
($P = 0.001$). Results updated from Camitta et al. (1976). (*By courtesy of Dr B. Camitta and
Dr R. Storb*)

a time randomized trial and that the conservative management of
patients probably varied between different centres. It may be that total
commitment to conservative support increases the chances of survival
in this group (Mathé & Schwarzenberg 1977). The UCLA group
compared 12 patients transplanted soon after diagnosis with nine
patients of similar severity who received equivalent support. There
were seven normal survivors in the first group (55%), but none in the
second (Table 7.8). Combined (unpublished) results from European
centres, reported to the European Bone Marrow Transplant Group in
1977, showed 27 survivors from 73 transplanted patients. Rejection
and failure to take accounted for 41 (56%) of the deaths. Results from
other series are also included in Table 7.8.

Regrafting and the treatment of rejection. Rejection or failure to take is the major problem in transplanting in aplastic anaemia, graft-versus-host disease being a smaller problem. This is the opposite of the problems encountered in transplantation for acute leukaemia using total body irradiation and cyclophosphamide (Thomas et al. 1977). Rejection of a marrow graft presents many of the problems seen in sensitization by family member transfusions and, to overcome this sensitization, the Seattle group proposed the use of ALG and procarbazine as well as cyclophosphamide as preparation for a second graft. The results of second grafting have not been very encouraging (Wright et al. 1976) but there is a very interesting group of patients who recover autologous function, occasionally spontaneously, sometimes following further immunosuppression. In these patients the temporal relationship between rejection and autologous recovery suggests a causative link. One of the major problems with second grafts is that the recipients are often infected following the rejection and are not suitable candidates for transplantation. As emphasized previously, most rejection occurs within the first 5 weeks of grafting so patients should be in strict isolation, if possible, for at least this length of time. As soon as it is known that the graft has failed, preparations for regrafting should be made using ALG and additional immunosuppression; at the same time a careful watch is maintained for any signs of spontaneous recovery, especially after the ALG is given, so that the procedure can be halted at any time. Needless to say, the prospect of regrafting puts an enormous strain on the patient, relatives and nursing staff and the maintenance of morale is an essential part of a transplant team's duties.

Late consequences of transplantation. There are, as yet, no clear data on the late consequences of transplantation. Cyclophosphamide produces aspermia in some circumstances (Fairley et al. 1972) but this may not be inevitable. It is reasonable to offer the services of a sperm bank to appropriate men before starting the cyclophosphamide. The incidence of genetic abnormalities in subsequent children is unknown but does not seem yet to be markedly increased in children of patients who have been treated for cancer with comparable cytotoxic regimens (Li & Jaffe 1974). It is likely that there will be an increased risk of malignant disease but this has not yet become apparent. The major problems seem to last for about 2 years after transplantation, during which time patients are still at risk from infection. Death occurred from bacteriological infection in two of our adult patients who had apparently fully functional grafts, at 86 and 89 days, after they had been discharged. The main reason for such overwhelming infections was the refusal of both patients to enter hospital again as soon as fever developed, emphasizing again the importance of good morale in transplant patients.

Immunological status of transplanted patients. Immunological defects are demonstrable in patients who have received allogeneic bone marrow transplants for at least one year following the procedure (Elfenbein et al. 1976; Storb et al. 1976a). Total immunoglobulin levels usually return fairly rapidly to normal but it is possible to show impaired primary and secondary response to antibody *in vivo* for the first year. Patients are, however, able to mount antibody responses to cytomegalovirus or herpes zoster virus during this period. *In vitro* testing of lymphocyte function is normal after about 3 months but response to skin test antigens remains impaired for many months. Generally, *in vitro* tests do not correlate well with function *in vivo*, and transplanted patients must be considered susceptible to fungal, viral and protozoal, as well as bacterial infections for up to 2 years after transplantation. An explanation of such susceptibility, and the need for prompt management of even trivial infections, must be given to the patient, his relatives and the local medical team following successful transplantation.

Transplants from Unrelated Donors

The chances of any particular sibling being HLA-identical and MLR-compatible is about 1 in 4. Given the size of families in the Western world the chances of a patient having a compatible donor are about 1 in 3. This leaves 60–70% of patients without a suitable donor. Since the collection of marrow from a healthy donor is relatively simple and free of risk, the organization of panels of volunteers would seem a reasonable way to overcome this problem. Unfortunately, the difficulties of building up such panels are enormous. The close relationship of the HLA A, B and D genes on the 6 chromosome does not mean that in *random* donors the D locus is likely to be identical if the A and B are identical. The matching of the A and B loci produces about a 1 in 10 chance of finding a D locus compatible donor amongst unrelated individuals so that screening by the mixed lymphocyte reaction becomes difficult. Besides the difficulty of screening for the D locus there are problems of unidentified loci which may be important. Storb et al. (1976) found that graft-versus-host disease was a greater problem following transplants from unrelated dog donors compared with littermates, in each case matched for the major dog leucocyte antigen systems.

The theoretical donor pool sizes needed to provide HLA matched donors for different numbers of recipients have been calculated by Opelz et al. (1974). If only HLA A and B identity are required, panels of 40 000 donors would provide for most recipients but if MLR-compatibility is needed, on present typing methods, some ten times that number would be required, even assuming that there was no marked linkage disequilibrium. In practice much smaller donor numbers would probably provide compatible sources for most recipients who have common HLA groups. If specific serological techniques become universal for D locus matching, then pool sizes of less than 20 000 may be sufficient, but this assumes that only the D locus is important.

Transient engraftment of a patient with aplastic anaemia from an HLA identical MCL non-reactive donor has been reported (Lohrmann et al. 1975). Graft-versus-host disease occurred and the patient rejected the graft. Two attempts to produce grafts from histocompatible unrelated donors, one in a patient with Fanconi's anaemia and one for acute leukaemia, failed to show any evidence of engraftment (Gordon-Smith, unpublished observations). Other attempts using phenotypically identical unrelated donors have also been unsuccessful (Speck et al. 1973).

Bone Marrow Transplantation for Other Types of Aplastic Anaemia

Fanconi's anaemia. Patients with Fanconi's anaemia may be successfully transplanted providing a compatible sibling donor is available (Barrett et al. 1977). Because of the recessive inheritance of the disease, the likelihood of a suitable donor is reduced though there is no evidence for segregation of the disease with the histocompatibility genes. There appear to be no special problems relating to transplantation in this disorder though it is not known whether the high incidence of leukaemia and epithelial cancers in this disorder is reduced by this transplantation. It is hoped that the former would be, but presumably not the latter.

Paroxysmal nocturnal haemoglobinuria (PNH). PNH is amenable to treatment by grafting though the procedure should be confined to those patients in whom the marrow failure predominates over haemolysis as the cause of anaemia. Complete haematological normality may be restored following a graft (Storb et al. 1974c) though, clearly, a long follow up is required to be sure that the thrombotic tendency which accompanies this disease (Peytremann et al. 1972) is eliminated.

ANTILYMPHOCYTE GLOBULIN (ALG) IN THE TREATMENT
OF APLASTIC ANAEMIA

Bone marrow transplantation offers hope for severely affected patients with aplastic anaemia but only for those who have suitable donors. In 1970 Mathé et al. reported the effect of immunosuppression with ALG (prepared in horses by injection of human peripheral blood lymphocytes collected by continuous flow centrifugation) on four patients with aplastic anaemia who received marrow transfusions, in three cases from HLA identical siblings and in the fourth case from a daughter. In two cases of sibling transplants both recipient and donor received ALG. Both patients died without engraftment. The other two were well 3 and 4 months later with evidence of mixed chimerism in the red cell population. A further case was added in 1974 (Jeannet et al. 1974). Encouraged by these results Speck et al. (1976*a*) investigated the effect of xenogeneic ALG on survival of marrow grafts from unmatched donors in rabbits and found that chimeras could be produced with donor haemopoietic cells and recipient lymphocytes. A similar technique was used in seven patients with acquired severe aplastic anaemia who received one-haplotype-identical marrow following conditioning with ALG (Lymphöse, Berne; Serum- und Impfinstitut). Three patients had a good response though in two thrombocytopenia persisted. In each of these patients there was no evidence of engraftment and autologous recovery was thought probable. Three other patients died and the seventh was followed for too short a period to assess results. It cannot be deduced from these observations that the marrow transfusion contributed to the recovery in the three patients.

On the other hand, Mathé and Schwarzenberg (1976) reported on 20 patients managed with ALG and mismatched marrow. Three out of four who obtained temporary grafts survived more than 5 years whereas only one of 16 who showed no evidence of engraftment survived that long.

The possibility of using the relatively benign conditioning with ALG and moderately hopeful results warranted further investigation of this method of treatment. Two centres, one in Leiden and one in Basel, continued to use ALG and marrow transfusion whilst a third, Hôpital St Louis in Paris, used ALG alone. The results were reported in a joint paper (Speck et al. 1977): 15 patients received ALG alone, six had a good response and one a partial response. Five died of sepsis and one of haemorrhage. Two showed no response but remained alive more than 90 days later. Fourteen patients received ALG and haploidentical marrow: six had a good response, five died and two remained alive more than 2 years without response. Follow-up ranged from more than 150 days to more than 1000 days in the survivors. The majority of the patients in these groups had severe aplastic anaemia. A good response was indicated by a rise in peripheral white count such that the patient could return to normal life without transfusion but complete haematological reconstitution was exceptional. The response to ALG and marrow was slow, occurring over several months. The response to ALG alone, when it occurred, was more rapid. Two different sorts of ALG were used; in Leiden and Basel ALG prepared in horses using thoracic duct lymphocytes was provided by Schweizerisches Serum- und Impfinstitut, in Paris a similar preparation from Merieux (Lyon) was used.

Synergy of ALG with Androgens

All the patients reported in the Basle Study (Speck et al. 1977) received androgens as well as ALG. An analysis of response to ALG and infused marrow, both in patients and in rabbits, suggests that androgens increase the chances of a successful graft, though this remains a clinical impression.

Preparation and Use of ALG

One of the major difficulties with ALG is the lack of standardization, quality control and specificity in the final product. Most ALG is produced with either thoracic duct lymphocytes or lymphoblast cultures as the antigens, various animals being used to raise the anti- bodies. Thoracic duct lymphocytes are of T-cell origin and therefore have a theoretical advantage but lymphoblast cultures are more readily available commercially. Some of the problems were discussed in London in 1976 (*Postgraduate Medical Journal*, 1976). Even the dosage of ALG is open to discussion. The present policy (1977) in using ALG with or without infused marrow in a trial of patients with aplastic anaemia is to use 40 mg/kg intravenously on each of four successive days followed by marrow transfusion if indicated. Side effects are plentiful, especially on the first day. Apart from anaphylactic reactions, which should be avoided by testing with appropriate animal serum, thrombocytopenia, headache, vomiting and haemorrhage are frequent. These reactions may be minimized by intravenous cortico- steroids and analgesics such as pethidine. For reasons that are not clear the second to fourth day infusions are usually without trouble. Even if the ALG has been absorbed with platelets to remove antiplatelet anti- bodies, maximum available platelet support should be given with the infusion. Serum sickness occurs in about one-third to half of the patients, appearing 10 days after the ALG. Although no fatalities have yet been reported with this substance its use should be very carefully monitored.

CONCLUSIONS

Bone marrow transplantation is the treatment of choice for patients with severe aplastic anaemia with a suitable donor and preferably before the patient has been transfused. The success of this procedure has stimulated a search for other methods of treating those patients who do not have a donor. Total support for the duration of the illness is probably the best conservative arrangement available but it is very costly in terms of money and morale. ALG and androgens probably have a role to play in the treatment of some patients. The former is still an experimental method of treatment and the accumulation of new data on its effectiveness or otherwise is awaited.

REFERENCES

BARRETT, A. J., BRIGDEN, W. D., HOBBS, J. R., HUGH-JONES, K., HUMBLE, J. G., JAMES, D. C., RETSAS, S., ROGERS, T. R., SELWYN, S., SNEATH, P. & WATSON, J. G. (1977) Successful bone marrow transplant for Fanconi's anaemia. *Br. med. J.*, *i*, 420.

BORTIN, M. M. (1970) A compendium of reported human bone marrow transplants. *Transplantation*, *9*, 571.

CAMITTA, B. M., NATHAN, D. G., FORMAN, E. N., PARKMAN, R., RAPPEPORT, J. M. & ORELLANA, T. D. (1974) Post hepatitic severe aplastic anemia—an indication for early bone marrow transplantation. *Blood*, *43*, 473.

CAMITTA, B. M., THOMAS, E. D., NATHAN, D. G., SANTOS, G., GORDON-SMITH, E. C., GALE, R. P., RAPPEPORT, J. M. & STORB, R. (1976) Severe aplastic anemia: a prospective study of the effect of early marrow transplantation on acute mortality. *Blood*, *48*, 63.

CLIFT, R. A., BUCKNER, C. D., FEFER, A., LERNER, K. G., NEIMAN, P. E., STORB, R., MURPHY, M. & THOMAS, E. D. (1974) Infectious complications of marrow transplantation. *Transplant. Proc.*, *6*, 389.

CROUCH, B. G., VAN PUTTEN, L. M., VAN BEKKUM, D. W. & DE VRIES, M. J. (1961) Treatment of total-body X-irradiated monkeys with autologous and homologous bone marrow. *J. natn. Cancer Inst.*, *27*, 53.

CUDKOWICZ, G. & BENNETT, M. (1971) Peculiar immunobiology of bone marrow allografts. II. Rejection of parental grafts by resistant F1 hybrid mice. *J. exp. Med.*, *134*, 1513.

DICKE, K. A., VAN PUTTEN, L. M., OBER-KIEFTENBURG, V. E. & LOWENBERG, R. (1976) Standardisation of human bone marrow cultures and its application in aplastic anaemia. In: *Leukaemia and Aplastic Anaemia*, ed. D. Metcalf, M. Condovelli & C. Peschle. Rome: Il Pensiero Scientifico.

DICKE, K. A. & VAN BEKKUM, D. W. (1971) Allogeneic bone marrow transplantation after elimination of immunocompetent cells by means of density gradient centrifugation. *Transplant. Proc.*, *3*, 666.

DUPONT, B., ANDERSON, V. & ERNST, P. (1973) Immunologic reconstruction in severe combined immunodeficiency with HL-A incompatible bone marrow graft: donor selection by mixed lymphocyte culture. *Transplant. Proc.*, *5*, 905.

ELFENBEIN, G. J., ANDERSON, P. N., HUMPHREY, R. L., MULLINS, G. M., SENSENBRENNER, L. L., WANDS, J. R. & SANTOS, G. W. (1976) Immune system reconstitution following allogeneic bone marrow transplantation in man: a multiparameter analysis. *Transplant. Proc.*, *8*, 641.

FAIRLEY, K. F., BARRIE, J. U.& JOHNSON, W. (1972) Sterility and testicular atrophy related to cyclophosphamide therapy. *Lancet*, *i*, 568.

FENYK, J. R., SMITH, C. M., WARKENTIN, P., KRIVIT, W., GOLTZ, C. W., NEELY, J. E., NESBIT, M. E., RAMSAY, N., COCCIA, P. F. & KERSEY, J. H. (1978) Sclerodermatous graft-versus-host disease limited to an area of measle exanthem. *Lancet*, *i*, 472.

FERNBACH, D. J. & TRENTIN, J. J. (1962) Isologous bone marrow transplantation in identical twin with aplastic anemia. *Proc. 8th int. Congr. Haemat.*, *1*, 150.

GLUCKSBERG, H., STORB, R., FEFER, A., BUCKNER, C. D., NEIMAN, P. E., CLIFT, R. A., LERNER, K. G. & THOMAS, E. D. (1974) Clinical manifestations of graft-versus-host disease in human recipients of marrow from HLA-matched sibling donors. *Transplantation*, *18*, 295.

HARVEY, L. E. & FIRKIN, B. G. (1968) Repeated isogeneic transplants in bone-marrow failure. *Med. J. Aust.*, *ii*, 538.

HENRY, K., BIRD, R., WATSON, G. & HUGH-JONES, K. (1977) Aplastic anaemia, bone marrow transplantation and polyoma and other virus infections (letter). *Lancet*, *i*, 195.

HIRSCH, M. S., ELLIS, D. A., PROFFITT, M. R. & BLACK, P. H. (1973) Effects of interferon on leukaemia virus activated graft-versus-host disease. *Nature New Biol.*, *244*, 102.

JEANNET, M., RUBINSTEIN, A., PELIT, B. & KUMMER, H. (1974) Prolonged remission of severe aplastic anemia after ALG pretreatment and HLA-semiincompatible bone-marrow cell transfusion. *Transplant. Proc.*, *6*, 359.

LERNER, K. G., KAO, G. F., STORB, R., BUCKNER, C. D., CLIFT, R. A. & THOMAS, E. D. (1974) Histopathology of graft-*vs*-host reaction (GvHR) in human recipients of marrow from HL-A-matched sibling donors. *Transplant. Proc.*, *6*, 367.

LEWIS, S. M. (1965) Course and prognosis in aplastic anaemia. *Br. med. J.*, *i*, 1027.

LI, F. P. & JAFFE, N. (1974) Progeny of childhood cancer survivors. *Lancet*, *ii*, 707.

LOHRMANN, H. P., DIETRICH, M., GOLDMANN, S. F., KRISTENSEN, T., FLIEDNER, T. M., ABT, C., PFLIEGER, H., FLAD, H. D., KUBANECK, B. & HEIMPEL, H. (1975) Bone marrow transplantation for aplastic anaemia from a HL-A and MLC identical unrelated donor. *Blut*, *31*, 347.

LOHRMANN, H. P., KERN, P., NIETHAMMER, D. & HEIMPEL, H. (1976) Identification of high-risk patients with aplastic anaemia in selection for allogeneic bone marrow transplantation. *Lancet*, *ii*, 647.

LORENZ, E., UPHOFF, D. & REID, T. R. (1951) Modification of irradiation injury in mice and guinea pigs by bone marrow infusions. *J. natn. Cancer Inst.*, *12*, 1951.

LYNCH, R. E., WILLIAMS, D. M., READING, J. C. & CARTWRIGHT, S. E. (1975) The prognosis in aplastic anaemia. *Blood*, *45*, 517.

MASTERS, R., HOOD, A. F. & COSINI, B. (1975) Chronic cutaneous graft vs host reaction following bone marrow transplantation. *Archs Dermat.*, *111*, 1526.

MATHÉ, G., AMIEL, J. L., SCHWARZENBERG, L. CHOAY, J., TROLARD, P., SCHNEIDER, M., HAYAT, M., SCHLUMBERGER, J. R. & JASMIN, C. L. (1970) Bone marrow graft in man after conditioning by antilymphocyte serum. *Br. med. J.*, *ii*, 131.

MATHÉ, G., JEANNET, H. & PENDIC, B. (1959) Transfusions et greffes de moelle osseuse homologue chez des humans irradiés à hautes dose accidentellement. *Revue fr. Étud. clin. biol.*, *4*, 226.

MATHÉ, G. & SCHWARZENBERG, L. (1976) Treatment of bone marrow aplasia by mismatched marrow transplantation after conditioning with antilymphocyte globulin: long term results. *Transplant. Proc.*, *8*, 595.

MATHÉ, G. & SCHWARZENBERG, L. (1977) Selection of bone-marrow aplasia patients for allogeneic bone-marrow transplantation. *Lancet*, *i*, 1361.

MELVIN, K. E. W. & DAVIDSON, J. N. G. (1964) Aplastic anaemia treated by transplantation of isologous bone marrow. *N.Z. med. J.*, *63*, 93.

MILLS, S. D., KYLE, R. A., HALLENBECK, G. A., PEASE, G. L. & GREE, I. C. (1964) Bone marrow transplant in identical twin. *J. Am. med. Ass.*, *188*, 1037.

NEIMAN, P., WASSERMAN, P. B., WENTWORTH, B. B., KAO, G. F., LERNER, K. G., STORB, R., BUCKNER, C. D., CLIFT, R. A., FEFER, A., FASS, L., GLUCKSBERG, H. & THOMAS, E. D. (1973) Interstitial pneumonia and cytomegalovirus infection as complications of human marrow transplantation. *Transplantation*, *15*, 478.

NEIMAN, P. C., THOMAS, E. D., REEVES, W. C., RAY, C. G., SALE, G., LERNER, K. G., BUCKNER, C. D., CLIFT, R. A., STORB, R., WEIDEN, P. L. & FEFER, A. (1976) Opportunistic infection and interstitial pneumonia following marrow transplantation for aplastic anemia and hematologic malignancy. *Transplant. Proc.*, *8*, 663.

OPELZ, G., MICKEY, M. R. & TERASAKI, P. I. (1974) Unrelated donors for bone-marrow transplantation and transfusion support: pool sizes required. *Transplant. Proc.*, *6*, 405.

O'REILLY, R. J., EVERSON, L. K., EMÖDI, G., HENSEN, J., SMITHWICK, E. M., GRIMES, E., PAKWA, S., PAKWA, R., SCHWARTZ, S., ARMSTRONG, D., SIEGEL, F. P., GUPTA, S., DUPONT, B. & GOOD, R. A. (1976) Effects of exogenous interferon in cytomegalovirus infections complicating bone marrow transplantation. *Clin. Immunol. Immunopath.*, *6*, 51.

PEGG, D. E., FLEMING, W. J. D. & COMPSTON, N. (1964) A case of aplastic anaemia treated by isologous bone marrow infusion. *Postgrad. med. J.*, *40*, 213.

PEGG, D. E. & KEMP, N. H. (1960) Collection, storage, and administration of autologous human bone marrow. *Lancet*, *ii*, 1426.

PEYTREMANN, R., RHODES, R. S. & HARTMANN, R. C. (1972) Thrombosis in paroxysmal nocturnal haemoglobinuria (PNH) with particular reference to progressive diffuse hepatic vein thrombosis. *Ser. Hemat.*, *3*, 115.

PILLOW, R. P., EPSTEIN, R. B., BUCKNER, C. D., GIBLETT, E. R. & THOMAS, E. D. (1966) Treatment of bone marrow failure by isogeneic marrow infusion. *New Engl. J. Med.*, *275*, 94.

POLLARD, M., CHANG, C. F. & SRIVASTARA, K. K. (1976) The rôle of microflora in development of graft-versus-host disease. *Transplant. Proc.*, *8*, 533.

Postgraduate Medical Journal (1976) Antilymphocyte globulin in clinical practice. *52*, Suppl. 5.

RINALDO, C. R., HIRSCH, M. S. & BLACK, P. H. (1976) Activation of latent viruses following bone marrow transplantation. *Transplant. Proc.*, *8*, 669.

ROBINS, M. M. & NOYES, W. D. (1961) Aplastic anemia treated with bone-marrow transfusion from an identical twin. *New Engl. J. Med.*, *265*, 974.

ROYAL MARSDEN HOSPITAL BONE MARROW TRANSPLANT TEAM (1977) Failure of syngeneic bone-marrow grafting without preconditioning in post hepatitis marrow aplasia. *Lancet*, *ii*, 742.

SANTOS, G. W. (1974) Immunosuppression for clinical bone marrow transplantation. *Sem. Hemat.*, *11*, 341.

SANTOS, G. W., BURKE, P. J. & SENSENBRENNER, L. L. (1970) Rationale for the use of cyclophosphamide as immunosuppression for marrow transplants in man. In: *International Symposium on Pharmacologic Treatment in Organ and Tissue Transplantation*, ed. A. Bertelli and A. P. Monaco. Amsterdam: Excerpta Medica.

SANTOS, G. W., COLE, L. J. & ROAN, P. L. (1958) Effect of X-ray dose on the protective action and persistence of rat bone marrow in irradiated penicillin treated mice. *Am. J. Physiol.*, *194*, 23.

SAURAT, J. H., GLUCKMAN, E., BUSSEL, A., DIDERJEAN, L. & PERISSANT, A. (1975) The lichen planus like eruption after bone marrow transplantation. *Br. J. Dermat.*, *92*, 675.

SCHWAB, L., MOLL, F. C., HALL, T., BREAN, H., KIRK, M., HANON, C. VAN Z. & JANEWERY, C. A. (1950) Experimental hypersensitivity in the rabbit. Effect of inhibition of antibody formation by X-radiation and nitrogen mustards on the histologic and serologic sequences and on the behaviour of serum complement, following large injections of foreign proteins. *J. exp. Med.*, *91*, 505.

SINGAL, D. P., MICKEY, M. R. & TERASAKI, P. I. (1969) Serotyping for homotransplantation. XXIII. Analysis of kidney transplants from parental versus sibling donors. *Transplantation*, *7*, 246.

SPECK, B., BUCKNER, C. D., CORNU, P. & JEANNET, M. (1976a) Rationale for the use of ALG as sole immunosuppressant in allogeneic bone marrow transplantation for aplastic anemia. *Transplant. Proc.*, *8*, 617.

SPECK, B., CORNU, P., JEANNET, M., NISSEN, C., BURRI, H. P., GROFF, P., NAJEL, G. A. & BUCKNER, C. D. (1976b) Autologous marrow recovery following allogeneic bone marrow transplantation in a patient with severe aplastic anemia. *Expl Hemat.*, *4*, 131.

SPECK, B., GLUCKMAN, E., HAAK, H. L. & VAN ROOD, J. J. (1977) Treatment of aplastic anaemia by antilymphocyte globulin with and without allogeneic bone marrow infusions. *Lancet*, *2*, 1145.

SPECK, B., ZWAAN, F. E., VAN ROOD, J. J. & GERNISSE, J. G., (1973) Allogeneic bone marrow transplantation in a patient with aplastic anemia using a phenotypically HLA-identical unrelated donor. *Transplantation*, *16*, 24.

STORB, R., EPSTEIN, R. B., BRYANT, J., RAJDE, H. & THOMAS, E. D. (1968) Marrow grafts by combined marrow and leukocyte infusions in unrelated dogs selected by histocompatibility typing. *Transplantation*, *6*, 587.

STORB, R., EPSTEIN, R. B., GRAHAM, T. C. & THOMAS, E. D. (1970a) Methotrexate regimens for control of graft-versus-host disease in dogs with allogeneic marrow grafts. *Transplantation*, *9*, 240.

STORB, R., EPSTEIN, R. B., RANDOLPH, R. H. & THOMAS, E. D. (1969) Allogeneic canine marrow transplantation following cyclophosphamide. *Transplantation*, *7*, 378.

STORB, R., FLOERSHEIM, G. L., WEIDEN, P. L., GRAHAM, T. C., KOLB, H. J., LERNER, K. G., SCHROEDER, M. L. & THOMAS, E. D. (1974a) Effect of prior blood transfusion on marrow grafts; Abrogation of sensitization by procarbazine and antilymphocyte serum. *J. Immunol.*, *112*, 1508.

STORB, R., GLUCKMAN, E. & THOMAS, E. D. (1974b) Treatment of established human graft-versus-host disease by antilymphocyte globulin. *Blood*, *44*, 57.

STORB, R., OCHS, H. D., WEIDEN, P. L. & THOMAS, E. D. (1976a) Immunologic reactivity in marrow graft recipients. *Transplant. Proc.*, *8*, 637.

STORB, R., PRENTICE, R. L. & THOMAS, E. D. (1977a) Marrow transplantation for aplastic anemia: factors associated with rejection. *New Engl. J. Med.*, *296*, 61.

STORB, R., PRENTICE, R. L. & THOMAS, E. D. (1977b) Treatment of aplastic anemia by marrow transplantation from HLA identical siblings: Prognostic factors associated with graft-versus-host disease and survival. *J. clin. Invest.*, *59*, 625.

STORB, R., RUDOLPH, R. H., GRAHAM, T. C. & THOMAS, E. D. (1970b) The effect of prior transfusions on marrow grafts between histocompatible canine siblings. *J. Immunol.*, *105*, 627.

STORB, R., THOMAS, E. D., BUCKNER, C. D., CLIFT, R. A., JOHNSON, F. L., FEFER, A., GLUCKSBERG, H., GIBLETT, E. R., LERNER, K. G. & NEIMAN, P. L. (1974c) Allogeneic marrow grafting for treatment of aplastic anemia. *Blood*, *43*, 157.

STORB, R., THOMAS, E. D., WEIDEN, P. L., BUCKNER, C. D., CLIFT, R. A., FEFER, A., FERNANDO, L. P., GIBLETT, E. R., GOODELL, B. W., JOHNSON, F. L., LERNER, K. G., NEIMAN, P. E. & SANDERS, J. E. (1976b) Aplastic anemia treated by allogeneic bone marrow transplantation. A report on 49 new cases from Seattle. *Blood*, *48*, 817.

THOMAS, E. D., BUCKNER, C. D., BANAJI, M., CLIFT, R. A., FEFER, A., FLOURNOY, N., GOODELL, B. W., HICKMAN, R. O., LERNER, K. G., NEIMAN, P. E., SERLE, G. E., SANDERS, J. E., SINGER, J., STEVENS, M., STORB, R. & WEIDEN, P. L. (1977) One hundred patients with acute leukaemia treated by chemotherapy, total body irradiation and allogeneic marrow transplantation. *Blood*, *49*, 511.

THOMAS, E. D., BUCKNER, C. D., RUDOLPH, R. H., FEFER, A., STORB, R., NEIMAN, P. E., BRYANT, J. L., CHARD, R. L., CLIFT, R. A., EPSTEIN, R. B., FIALKOW, P. J., FUNK, D. D., GIBLETT, E. R., LERNER, K. G., REYNOLDS, F. A. & SCHLICHTER, S. (1971) Allogeneic bone marrow grafting for hematologic malignancy using HL-A matched donor-recipient sibling pairs. *Blood*, *38*, 267.

THOMAS, E. D., LOCHTE, H. L. & LU, W. C. (1957) Intravenous infusion of bone marrow cells in patients receiving radiation and chemotherapy. *New Engl. J. Med.*, *257*, 491.

THOMAS, E. D., PHILLIPS, J. H. & FINCH, C. A. (1964) Recovery from marrow failure following isogeneic marrow infusion. *J. Am. med. Ass.*, *188*, 1041.

THOMAS, E. D. & STORB, R. (1970) Technique for human marrow grafting. *Blood*, *36*, 507.

THOMAS, E. D., STORB, R., CLIFT, R. A., FEFER, A., JOHNSON, L., NEIMAN, P. E., LERNER, K. C., GLUCKSBERG, H. & BUCKNER, C. D. (1975) Bone marrow transplantation (second of two parts). *New Engl. J. Med.*, *292*, 895.

THOMAS, E. D., STORB, R., FEFER, A., SCHLIGHTER, S. S., BRYANT, V. J. I., BUCKNER, C. D., NEIMEN, P. E., CLIFT, R. A., FUNK, D. D. & LERNER, K. E. (1972) Aplastic anaemia treated by bone marrow transplantation. *Lancet*, *i*, 284.

THOMAS, E. D., STORB, R., GIBLETT, E. R., LONGROSE, R., WEIDEN, P. L., FEFER, A., WITHERSPOON, R., CLIFT, R. A. & BUCKNER, C. D. (1976) Recovery from aplastic anaemia following attempted marrow transplantation. *Expl Hemat.*, *4*, 97.

UCLA BONE MARROW TRANSPLANT TEAM (1976) Bone marrow transplantation in severe aplastic anaemia. *Lancet*, *ii*, 921.

UCLA BONE MARROW TRANSPLANT TEAM (1977) Bone marrow transplantation for acute leukaemia. *Lancet*, *ii*, 1197.

VAN BEKKUM, D. W. (1976) Personal communication.

VAN BEKKUM, D. W., ROODENBURG, J. H., HEIDT, P. J. & VAN DER WAAIJ, D. (1974) Mitigation of secondary disease of allogeneic mouse radiation chimeras by modification of the intestinal microflora. *J. natn. Cancer Inst.*, *52*, 401.

VAN BEKKUM, D. W., VOS, O. & WEYZEN, W. W. H. (1959) The pathogenesis of the secondary disease after foreign bone marrow transplantation in X-irradiated mice. *J. natn. Cancer Inst.*, *23*, 75.

VAN ROOD, J. J. (1974) The HL-A system. II. Clinical relevance. *Sem. Hemat.*, *11*, 253.

VAN ROOD, J. J., VAN LEENWEN, A., SCHIPPERS, A., CEPPELLINI, R., MATTIZ, P. L. & CURTONI, S. (1966) Leucocyte groups and their relation to homotransplantation. *Ann. N.Y. Acad. Sci.*, *129*, 467.

VAN SOMEREN, H., WESTERVELD, A., HAGMEIZER, A., MESS, J. R., MEERA KHAN, P. & ZAALBERG, O. B. (1974) Human antigen and enzyme markers in man. Chinese, hamster, somali cell hybrids. Evidence for synthesis between the HL-A, PGM., ME and 1 PO-B loci. *Proc. natn. Acad. Sci., Wash.*, *71*, 962.

VAN VLOTEN, W. A., SCHEFFER, E. & DOOREN, L. J. (1977) Localised scleroderma-like lesions after bone marrow transplantation in man. A chronic graft versus host reaction. *Br. J. Dermat.*, *96*, 337.

DE VRIES, M. J., CROUCH, B. G., VAN PUTTEN, L. M. & VAN BEKKUM, D. W. (1961) Pathologic changes in irradiated monkeys treated with bone marrow. *J. natn. Cancer Inst.*, *27*, 67.

WEIDEN, P. L., STORB, R., THOMAS, E. D., GRAHAM, T. C., LERNER, K. G., BUCKNER, C. D., FEFER, A., NEIMAN, P. E. & CLIFT, R. A. (1976) Preceding transfusions and marrow graft rejection in dogs and man. *Transplant. Proc.*, *8*, 551.

WOODRUFF, J. M., HANSEN, J. A., GOOD, R. A., SANTOS, G. W. & SLAVIN, R. E. (1976) The pathology of graft-versus-host reaction (GVHR) in adults receiving bone marrow transplants. *Transplant. Proc.*, *8*, 675.

WRIGHT, S. E., THOMAS, E. D., BUCKNER, C. D., CLIFT, R. A., FEFER, A., NEIMAN, P. E. & STORB, R. (1976) Experience (experiments) with second marrow transplants. *Expl Hemat.*, *4*, 221.

8

Aplastic Anaemia in Childhood

D. I. K. EVANS

As in adults, most cases of childhood aplastic anaemia are acquired and the aetiology is often unknown. A few are due to rare congenital and hereditary disorders. It is important to recognize them, as the prognosis differs.

Table 8.1 shows the normal values for the blood count during infancy and childhood. The normal bone marrow in children is broadly similar to that of adults except during the early months and years of life. In the first three months, there is a physiological depression of erythropoiesis, with reduction of marrow normoblasts. During the first 5 years of life, the lymphocytosis of the peripheral blood is accompanied by a lymphocytosis in the bone marrow, and occasional lymphoblasts are seen. The normal range of bone marrow lymphocytes at this age is 15–35%. At the same time, plasma cells are scanty. As a result of the lymphocytosis, the bone marrow frequently appears more cellular than that of adults.

AETIOLOGY OF CHILDHOOD APLASTIC ANAEMIA

The congenital forms of aplastic anaemia usually present first in childhood, very occasionally after the second decade. Nevertheless, most cases of childhood aplastic anaemia are acquired; the causes are listed in Table 8.2. O'Gorman Hughes (1966) reviewed a large series of children at the Boston Children's Hospital from 1933 to 1964 and at the Royal Alexandra Hospital for Children, Sydney, from 1953 to 1961. 104 of the 140 cases (74%) were idiopathic or acquired, and only 29 (21%) were constitutional.

Constitutional aplastic anaemia is defined as a chronic form of bone marrow failure associated with other features such as congenital anomalies, a familial incidence, or preceding amegakaryocytic thrombocytopenia at birth or in early infancy, i.e. features suggesting that the disease is congenital rather than acquired. We do not know how many cases presenting as acquired aplastic anaemia should rightly be classed as constitutional, but it is clear that potential familial disease

Table 8.1. Blood counts during infancy and childhood

Age	Haemoglobin (Mean and range g/dl)	Reticulocytes (%)	White cells (Mean and range × 10⁹/litre)	Neutrophils (%)	Lymphocytes (%)	Eosinophils (%)	Monocytes (%)
Cord blood	16·8 (13·7–20·1)	5·0	18·0 (9·0–30·0)	61	31	2	6
2 weeks	16·5 (13·0–20·0)	1·0	12·0 (5·0–21·0)	40	48	3	9
3 months	12·0 (9·5–14·5)	1·0	12·0 (6·0–18·0)	30	63	2	5
6 months to 6 years	12·0 (10·5–14·0)	1·0	10·0 (6·0–15·0)	45	48	2	5
7–12 years	13·0 (11·0–16·0)	1·0	8·0 (4·5–13·5)	55	38	2	5

The absolute neutrophil count after the neonatal period is constant, usually between 3·5 and 4·5 × 10⁹/litre. A count of less than 1·5 × 10⁹/litre is neutropenia.

The platelet count in childhood ranges from 150 to 400 × 10⁹/litre. Slightly lower figures may be obtained with capillary samples.

Table 8.2. Aetiology of 140 cases of childhood aplastic anaemia

Aetiology	No. of cases	Comments
Constitutional	29	
Acquired		
Drug-induced	54	
Chloramphenicol 40		One case terminated in acute leukaemia after 5¼ years
Anticonvulsants 4		
Others 10		E.g. diphenhydramine, sulphonamides, novobiocin, miscellaneous antibiotics and bronchial antispasmodics
Chemicals	6	E.g. benzene, '2-4D', model aeroplane glues and insecticides
Infection	16	
Measles 2		
Miscellaneous 14		
Idiopathic	28	One case developed paroxysmal nocturnal haemoglobinuria 5 years later
Leukaemia in the aplastic phase	5	
With pancreatic insufficiency	1	
With osteochondrodystrophy	1	

Data from O'Gorman Hughes (1966).

may not be detected in the small families of the Western world, and minor associated defects may escape detection. The problems of diagnosing the best known type of constitutional aplastic anaemia, Fanconi's anaemia, are discussed on p. 178.

Drugs and Chemicals

The drugs and chemicals which can cause aplastic anaemia are the same for children as for adults: children are neither more nor less susceptible to their toxic effects. After chloramphenicol, sulphonamides and anticonvulsants have most frequently been incriminated. There are no drugs peculiar to paediatric practice which have unusually toxic effects on the bone marrow. The accidental ingestion of myelotoxic drugs is a particular problem of childhood, and physicians prescribing potentially myelotoxic drugs to adults should warn their patients against letting them fall into children's hands. Exposure to insecticides is a rare but well-documented cause of aplastic anaemia (Sánchez-Medal et al. 1963). Another paediatric problem has been glue-sniffing (see Chapter 2) (Massengale et al. 1963). This has resulted in a fatal case of aplastic anaemia (Powars 1965).

Viral Infections

As children are particularly prone to viral disease, and lack the specific immunity to viral infections that develops with age, it is pertinent to consider the possible role of viral infection in the acquired aplastic anaemia of childhood. There is no doubt that viruses may cause bone marrow depression (Gasser 1970). Transient thrombocytopenia may accompany or follow a variety of viral diseases such as rubella and varicella. It accompanies measles (Hudson et al. 1956) and may be accompanied by a profound agranulocytosis (Fisher & Kraszewski 1952). Virus can be detected in the megakaryocytes of mice infected with the Friend leukaemia virus (Dalton et al. 1961). Administration of the virus induces thrombocytopenia within 2 days (Dennis & Brodsky 1965). Thrombocytopenia and megakaryocyte damage also accompanies cytomegalovirus infection in the mouse, and is due to infection of the megakaryocytes with virus (Osborn & Shahidi 1973). There is also a reduction of red cells 1 week and of white cells 3–4 days after infection.

Infectious mononucleosis is often accompanied by an early granulocytopenia before the typical lymphocytosis with atypical lymphoid cells appears (Carter 1969). There is also thrombocytopenia in 50% of cases (Carter 1965) and rarely anaemia, sometimes with pancytopenia (Read & Helwig 1945). At least one case of fatal proven aplastic anaemia has followed the disease (Worlledge & Dacie, 1969). However, in many cases of temporary cytopenia following viral infections, it is likely that the marrow transit compartment, rather than the ancestral stem cell, is damaged.

One viral illness, infectious hepatitis, is a well-recognized cause of a particularly severe form of aplastic anaemia, with 88% mortality (Aljouni & Doeblin 1974) (see Chapter 3). Aplastic anaemia has also been recorded in babies with congenital rubella (Horstmann et al. 1965; Lafer & Morrison 1966). Seven cases in O'Gorman Hughes' (1974) series presented with amegakaryocytic thrombocytopenia at birth or in early infancy, which antedated aplastic anaemia by 1–12 years. Their disease may also have been secondary to congenital virus infection, as congenital infection with rubella or cytomegalovirus may lead to amegakayocytic thrombocytopenia (Oski & Naiman 1972). O'Gorman Hughes (1966) also recorded two cases where aplastic anaemia followed measles. A case seen by the author followed mumps. Her bone marrow caused marked inhibition of colony growth (CFU-C) by normal bone marrow.

Howie and Crosby (1961) inoculated human volunteers and patients with lymphoma with a modified form of the virus causing Venezuelan equine encephalitis. At 7 days there was pyrexia and a temporary pancytopenia. Bone marrow examination at this time revealed a panhypoplasia which in some cases was extreme, showing only fat, plasma cells, reticulum cells and scattered blasts. The changes were less severe in the healthy adult volunteers than in the patients with lymphoma, which suggests that pre-existing bone marrow disease, or immune deficiency secondary to the disease itself or to its treatment, may make the patient more susceptible to the effects of the virus. There was complete recovery in 3–14 days.

These effects are all temporary. The feature of acquired aplastic anaemia which contrasts markedly with these causes of temporary bone marrow depression is its greater severity and persistence. Any hypothesis which attempts to attribute acquired aplastic anaemia in childhood to viral disease must explain why an effect which is temporary in the majority of cases becomes permanent in a few. At present this question cannot be answered. Possible mechanisms are discussed in Chapters 1 and 3.

Starvation and Malnutrition

Red cell aplasia may result from severe childhood malnutrition such as kwashiorkor (Foy et al. 1961). Pancytopenia is not unusual in anorexia nervosa and severe bone marrow aplasia may be present, even in the absence of any pancytopenia (Pearson 1967). The response of the anaemia in kwashiorkor and childhood marasmus to riboflavin (Foy et al. 1961; Alfrey & Lane 1970) suggests that in some cases, bone marrow hypoplasia may be due to deficiency of specific factors.

Abnormal Folate Metabolism

A family with aplastic anaemia, neutropenia and leukaemia was reported by Branda et al. (1978). The proband had aplastic anaemia which responded to high doses of folic acid. It was suggested that this was the result of defective uptake of folic acid, but Babior (1978) postulated a defect of folate retention (see also p. 231).

Graft-Versus-Host Disease

In animal experiments, graft-versus-host disease may lead to bone marrow failure (Simonsen 1962) and there is evidence that this sequence of events may also occur in man. Hathaway et al. (1965) described two babies with progressive vaccinia necrosum who developed pancytopenia with bone marrow aplasia and histiocytosis, an erythematous rash and hepatomegaly following treatment with multiple fresh transfusions containing leucocytes. One child had Swiss-type agammaglobulinaemia (combined immune deficiency) and the other a hypoplastic thymus. It is assumed that impaired immunity, particularly of T-cell function, allows viable cells in transfused blood to proliferate, with resultant graft-versus-host disease. The exact mechanism by which marrow aplasia results is not known. A similar picture has been described in two children following intrauterine and exchange transfusions for haemolytic disease of the newborn (Parkman et al. 1974). Viable lymphocytes may survive in transfusion blood up to 3 weeks (McCullough et al. 1969), so graft-versus-host disease may complicate blood transfusion in anyone with seriously defective cellular immunity. Other possible mechanisms by which immunological mechanisms may result in aplastic anaemia are discussed in Chapter 1.

ACQUIRED APLASTIC ANAEMIA IN CHILDHOOD

The 'common' type of aplastic anaemia presents with a short illness and, frequently, a short survival. There may be a history of preceding infection, usually of a non-specific upper respiratory infection, in a previously fit child. Three of 18 Manchester cases developed aplastic anaemia after specific viral infections, two after hepatitis and one after mumps. Previous bacterial infection is rare. It is unusual for the disease to present before the age of 3 years: 50% of the cases occurred between the age of 6 and 9 years. There is no difference in the incidence for boys and girls (O'Gorman Hughes 1966).

Most children present with bruising due to thrombocytopenia and pallor due to anaemia. Clinical examination reveals no enlargement of lymph nodes, liver or spleen, and the general absence of other physical signs helps distinguish aplastic anaemia from leukaemia. The blood usually shows a complete pancytopenia. The platelet count is nearly always less than 40×10^9/litre, and in half the cases personally seen was less than 10×10^9/litre. Haemoglobin levels are usually in the range 6–9 g/dl. It is surprising that one-fifth of the Manchester cases presented with slight or no anaemia, haemoglobin levels at onset being over 10 g/dl, but there was reticulocytopenia, and the haemoglobin soon fell. White cell counts are low: two-thirds of the children had total white cell counts below $3 \cdot 5 \times 10^9$/litre with an absolute neutropenia (less than $1 \cdot 5 \times 10^9$/litre). There is no compensatory increase of monocytes or eosinophils as sometimes is seen in the isolated neutropenias of childhood. Normal blood counts for children are shown in Table 8.1.

The bone marrow aspirate is thin and hypocellular, with 40–80% lymphocytes or more, a few plasma cells, reticulum cells and mast cells, but few normal granulocytes and normoblasts. The picture may differ slightly in aspirates taken from different sites at any one time.

Bone marrow normoblasts are usually scanty: those seen may show dyserythropoiesis with morphological features, as described in Chapter 5.

Associated Features

It is important, but not always possible, to decide if aplastic anaemia is congenital or acquired, in order to advise the family about the prognosis and risks to future children. Severely affected cases may die suddenly and the physician needs to collect the maximum information quickly. The initial investigations undertaken on suspected cases of aplastic anaemia at the Royal Manchester Children's Hospital are listed in Table 8.3. There are two groups. The investigations in Group I are desirable in all cases for diagnosis and initial management. Those in Group II are useful for studying the associated abnormalities in constitutional aplastic anaemias, for elucidation of the aetiology, or for monitoring progress. At the same time the family should also be tested (Table 8.4).

Chromosome analysis may help distinguish acquired from congenital aplastic anaemia, as chromosomal defects suggest a diagnosis of Fanconi's anaemia. In suspected cases, chromosomes of the family should also be examined, as abnormalities may be found in the absence of blood disease (Zaizov et al. 1969).

Abnormal liver function tests may indicate a recent attack of viral hepatitis. Ozsoylu and Argun (1967) reported decreased tryptic activity in duodenal juice in five of six children with both acquired and congenital aplastic anaemia, with normal amylase activity. This feature, recalling the association of impaired bone marrow and pancreatic function in Schwachman's syndrome, is unexplained.

There is often a blood lymphocytopenia in acquired aplastic anaemia (see p. 69). Strauss et al. (1975) described possible graft-versus-host disease in a child with aplastic anaemia following hepatitis, attributed to the immune deficiency associated with lymphopenia. Troublesome infection seen in some cases may be a further problem.

Fetal Haemoglobin in Aplastic Anaemia

Normally, by the time a child is a year old, there is less than 2% fetal haemoglobin in the red cells. Shahidi et al. (1962) noted that in both acquired and congenital aplastic anaemia there may be in an increase of fetal haemoglobin, usually to between 3% and 15%.

An increase of fetal haemoglobin may indicate a reversion to a fetal type of erythropoiesis when the marrow is under stress. Fetal erythropoiesis may develop after successful bone marrow transplantation for aplastic anaemia (Alter et al. 1975) and after successful treatment with androgens (Brown et al. 1975). Such cases have also shown macro-

Table 8.3. Investigation of suspected bone marrow aplasia in children

Group I		Group II: Aplasia confirmed
Aplasia suspected	Aplasia probable	
Full blood counts including	Repeat bone marrow at	*Tests for haemolysis*
Haemoglobin and red cell count	second site	Autohaemolysis
Red cell indices	Bone marrow trephine	Red cell enzymes
Reticulocytes		Red cell survival (^{51}Cr)
Platelets	Haemoglobin electrophoresis	
Total white cell and differential	Alkali denaturation test	*Tests for constitutional aplasias*
counts	Kleihauer test and test for HbH	X-ray forearms and wrists
		Intravenous pyelography
Bone marrow aspiration	HLA typing	Head circumference
Blood group and Rh type	Chromosome analysis	Urine and plasma amino acids
Direct Coombs' test		IQ assessment
	Urea/creatinine	Electroencephalography
	Direct and indirect serum	Endocrine studies
	bilirubin	
	Liver function tests	*Tests for PNH*
	Proteins and electrophoresis	Ham's acid serum test
	Immunoglobulins	Sugar water test
	Australia antigen/antibody	*Tests for Schwachman's syndrome*
	Virus isolation—throat,	Faeces—trypsin and fat balance
	urine and faeces	Duodenal intubation and tests
		for malabsorption
	Urine—bilirubin, urobilin	Urine sugar chromatography
	and urobilinogen,	(galactose)
	haemosiderin	
		Miscellaneous haematological tests
		Leucocyte alkaline phosphatase
		Serum B.12

Group II: Aplasia confirmed (continued)

Red cell and serum folate
Serum iron and iron-binding capacity
Serum ferritin
Full red cell antigens
CFU—Marrow and blood
Ferrokinetics
^{99}Tm colloid marrow scan

Group I tests are desirable in all cases. Group II tests are necessary for recognition of specific syndromes and desirable for delineation of disease.

Table 8.4. Investigation of family of children with aplastic anaemia

Full blood count	HLA antigens
Platelet count	Au/SH antigen
ABO group and Rh	Other tests as indicated by propositus

cytosis, a reduction of haemoglobin A2 and carbonic anhydrase, and increased strength of the i antigen. These are all features of the red cells in the newborn, and suggest that a fetal clone may be reactivated during recovery from aplastic anaemia. However, some cases presenting as idiopathic acquired aplasia may in fact be of congenital origin, but with previously mild symptoms, too slight to bring the patient to the doctor. In such cases, a persistence of fetal haemoglobin might be expected because of marrow disorder continuing from birth.

Acquired Aplastic Anaemia and Leukaemia

Acute leukaemia is the disorder most frequently confused with aplastic anaemia on purely clinical grounds. Sometimes marrow aspirates in leukaemia are poorly cellular, in which case histological examination is essential to distinguish the two disorders. Even so, there is a small number of children who present with aplastic anaemia which is followed within a few months by frank leukaemia, and in whom the aplasia must be considered as the first symptom of leukaemia. Such cases are different from those where prolonged aplasia, and possibly drug treatment, terminates in acute leukaemia. The pre-leukaemic syndromes (see Chapters 4 and 10) which usually terminate in myeloblastic leukaemia, are extremely rare in childhood. 80% of children with leukaemia have acute lymphoblastic leukaemia. Although one-third of these cases will have anaemia, neutropenia and thrombocytopenia, occasional blast cells are often present in blood films, and only an occasional patient with pancytopenia does not have enlarged lymph nodes or hepatosplenomegaly. An enlarged spleen makes a diagnosis of childhood aplastic anaemia extremely unlikely.

X-ray of the long bones is helpful in distinguishing aplasia from leukaemia, as cases of the latter disease may show typical rarefaction or periosteal elevation. Melhorn et al. (1970) stated that aplastic anaemia might be distinguished from acute leukaemia in children by a trial of treatment with corticosteroids: the patients with leukaemia show rapid symptomatic improvement, whereas those with aplasia are unaffected.

A hypocellular bone marrow aspirate in acute childhood leukaemia may be due to a secondary reticulin fibrosis (Hann et al. 1978). The periodic acid-Schiff (PAS) reaction may be helpful, as PAS-positive granules or blocks in the lymphoid cells are typical of lymphoblastic leukaemia. In all suspect cases trephine biopsy is essential. It will confirm leukaemic infiltration in cases where aspiration is poorly cellular, and an increase of reticulin where a thin aspirate in leukaemia is secondary to bone marrow fibrosis.

Nevertheless, children may rarely present with aplastic anaemia which later progresses to acute lymphoblastic leukaemia. Two cases with histologically proven hypoplasia progressing to acute lympho-blastic leukaemia have been seen (Chang & Evans, unpublished obser-vations). In one case, relapse was preceded by a recurrence of hypo-plasia. Five children out of 465 cases with leukaemia (1·4%) in the Manchester Children's Tumour Registry presented initially with bone marrow hypoplasia before developing frank leukaemia (Marsden & Steward 1976). Several were described in the early days of the Registry when trephine biopsies were not performed: the true incidence is probably lower.

Prognosis in Acquired Aplastic Anaemia

Survival rates in acquired aplastic anaemia of childhood are poor. For the child who survives, residual haematological abnormality, pre-dominantly a persistent thrombocytopenia, is almost invariable. Even when haemoglobin levels have been normal for many years, an increase of fetal haemoglobin may be found, indicating a residual bone marrow lesion.

The results of treatment have varied in different surveys. The discre-pancies probably arise because aplastic anaemia is a rare disease and there is selection in referring cases to specialist units. Heyn et al. (1969) reported that 16 of 33 cases survived when treated with only supportive care comprising red cell and occasional platelet transfusions, and short courses of steroids. Most fatal cases died within 3 months. An unusually high number, 30 cases, were due to known causes, including many due to chloramphenicol. It is probable that this group includes children with a transient disease and mildly affected bone marrow. In most other series survival is poor. O'Gorman Hughes (1973) reported a 25% survival in 92 cases seen in Boston and Sydney. Recent results from several other large centres are summarized in Table 8.5. Approximately one-third of the children survived.

Of 15 children with acquired aplastic anaemia in Manchester, eight survive. None was due to chloramphenicol or other drugs. Two were only moderately affected, with bicytopenia rather than pancytopenia, and are in good clinical condition. Of the six who were severely affected, two have shown a partial response and one has made a good response; three show no change.

Shahidi and Diamond (1959) introduced the treatment of aplastic

Table 8.5. Some recent results in acquired aplastic anaemia of childhood

Centre	Years	No. of cases	No. of remissions	Report
Florida, USA	1961–72	11	1	Bloom (1972)
New York, USA	1966–70	7	2	Davis and Rubin (1972)
Toronto, Canada	1963–72	23	10	Freedman et al. (1974)
Manchester, UK	1966–77	15	5	Evans (unpublished)
	Total	56	18(32%)	

anaemia with corticosteroids and androgens. The initial enthusiasm for this treatment has now moderated. Approximately half the cases may show some response. Results are better in the constitutional aplastic anaemias. The experience at Boston Children's Hospital, where this form of treatment was originally introduced, are particularly revealing, and is reviewed by Li et al. (1972): 41 (71%) of 58 patients died in spite of treatment with androgens and steroids. Only 15 (26%) were alive, including three who still needed transfusions. The solitary patient who was not treated with androgen survived. There were no survivals in 11 patients treated from 1965 to 1970, at a time when greater experience was available, with better facilities for supportive care. This may have been due to selective referral of patients with a poor prognosis, as the number of cases is smaller than in previous years.

One group of patients stands out in any retrospective survey. They present with an acute onset and a severe disease. They respond poorly and die within a few months: seven of the 12 Manchester children showed this type of illness. They died within 40 weeks, four within 10 weeks. A further two died within a year; the remaining three cases have survived 4 years or more. By contrast, all patients with congenital aplasia survived for at least 2 years.

The features of the seven Manchester children with a very poor survival were as follows (median figures): age 8 years, haemoglobin 7·5 g/dl, white cells 3×10^9/litre, absolute neutrophil count $0·12 \times 10^9$/litre, and platelets 16×10^9/litre. All had less than 400 mg fetal haemoglobin per 100 ml. In five the bone marrow showed over 80% lymphocytes. There was no consistent HLA type. Immunoglobulins, Ham's test and sugar-water test were normal. Six received platelet transfusions and a similar number were treated with androgens.

The features which indicate a poor prognosis include age over 5 years, blood neutrophils less than $0·5 \times 10^9$/litre, platelets less than 20×10^9/litre, and a bone marrow with 80% or more lymphocytes. Haemoglobin levels are less important, particularly as children with a very acute onset of disease may show little anaemia. Likewise, fetal haemoglobin levels are normal, because there has been too little time for this abnormality to develop.

The prognostic importance of a raised fetal haemoglobin level was noted by Bloom and Diamond (1968): levels of over 400 mg/100 ml indicated a good prognosis. Although many of their patients had been investigated after treatment started, this finding has been confirmed by others (e.g. O'Gorman Hughes 1973). Plasma iron clearance and iron utilization may also be indicators of prognosis: Cifuentes et al. (1977) noted a significant difference in both these measurements in six children who died compared with five who survived. Such iron studies characterize the total erythropoietic activity of the marrow better than marrow aspiration.

Although the prognosis at diagnosis is much better for the patients with congenital forms of aplastic anaemia, patients with acquired aplasia who manage to survive the first year eventually may outlive the children with congenital forms of aplasia. In the international trial reported by Najean (1976) the 36 children who survived for 10 months were analysed into two groups: the 20 idiopathic cases showed a life expectancy of about 70% at six years, compared with 20% for 16 with Fanconi's anaemia. In one-third of the idiopathic cases the condition shows total or partial cure. One-third relapse when androgens are discontinued and maintenance doses are needed. One-third show progressive disease. By contrast, patients with Fanconi's anaemia show no improvement when androgens are withdrawn and need permanent treatment.

CONSTITUTIONAL APLASTIC ANAEMIA

Fanconi's Anaemia

Clinical presentation. Fanconi's anaemia (Fanconi 1927, 1967) is the best known of the congenital marrow aplasias. It is inherited in an autosomal recessive manner and bone marrow failure coexists with a wide range of congenital abnormalities. These defects may be detected at birth, but the haematological features are progressive. A normal blood count during infancy is almost invariable, but pancytopenia develops insidiously and frequently becomes symptomatic at the age of 5 years or so. Cases have rarely presented after the age of 10 years. Bruising due to thrombocytopenia is frequently the earliest symptom, but on questioning parents they will admit that the child has been pale for a long time.

The commonest associated findings are listed in Table 8.6. There is no one consistent abnormality, but over half the cases show skin

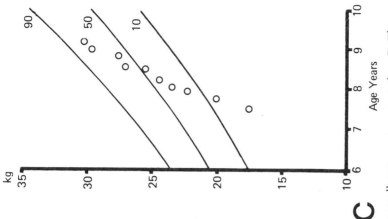

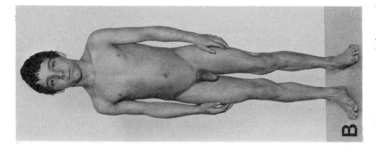

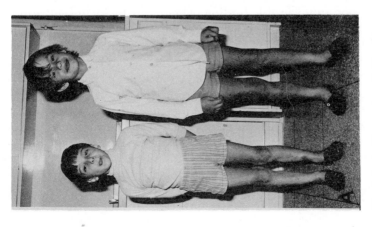

Fig. 8.1. A, The patient (left), with a normal boy of the same age (7½ years), showing the small stature at presentation. B, The same patient after treatment for 20 months with oxymetholone 50 mg/day (50 mg/m²), showing muscular development, penile hypertrophy and pubic hair. C, The patient's growth chart, showing a height increase from well below the 10th centile to between the 50th and 90th centiles after treatment with oxymetholone.

Table 8.6. Common congenital defects in Fanconi's
anaemia

Defect	Frequency (% approx.)
Skin pigmentation, generalized or localized	75
Skeletal disorders, particularly hand and forearm	60
Poor growth	55
Microcephaly	50
Renal disorders	30
Cardiac murmurs	30
Strabismus	25
Hypogenitalism	20
Mental retardation	20

pigmentation, skeletal disorders, poor growth or microcephaly. Boys predominate in a ratio of 3 : 2. The disease has been reported in several racial groups, but is rare in black children. Pigmentation may be generalized. More commonly there are café-au-lait spots or skin fold pigmentation. The skeletal defects mostly affect the hands and forearms. In the cases with skeletal defects, thumb deformities occur in over half, and radiographs of the wrists may show a reduction in the number of ossification centres in about 40% of cases. Many other skeletal abnormalities have been reported. The commonest kidney abnormality is renal aplasia, but other defects include horseshoe kidney, double pelvis and/or ureters, and ectopic kidney.

A variety of metabolic functions has been reported in Fanconi's anaemia (Bloom 1972). Normal and abnormal metabolism of folic acid and vitamin B12, adrenal function, tryptophan metabolism and plasma proteins have been described. The poor growth may be due to growth hormone deficiency (Pochedly et al. 1971; Zachman et al. 1972) but this is not an invariable finding. There may be an absent response to human growth hormone administered for treatment of small stature (Gleadhill et al. 1975). There may also be increased excretion of urinary amino acids. It should be noted that the disease is quite distinct from the so-called Fanconi syndrome of renal rickets and amino aciduria (Lignac–DeToni–Fanconi syndrome) (Fanconi 1962).

A recent case report described a 6-year-old girl with Fanconi's anaemia who showed progressive impairment of T-cell function in vitro and who developed a severe pneumonia with Pneumocystis carinii (Pedersen et al. 1977). Immunological studies have not previously been reported. Infection is usually attributed to neutropenia. The chromosome defect shown in peripheral blood lymphocyte cultures may be associated with abnormal lymphoid function.

Haematological findings. The red cells are normochromic with poikilo-cytosis and, frequently, macrocytosis, which prompted Fanconi in his original report (1927) to describe the anaemia as 'pernicious-like'. By the time the disease is diagnosed, the haemoglobin is usually 5–7 g/dl. Neutrophils are usually less than 1×10^9/litre and may show toxic granulation; platelets are likewise reduced. There is usually no reduction of lymphocytes or monocytes. The anaemia may have a haemolytic element shown by a shortened red cell survival with ^{51}Cr, and this may be reflected in a moderate reticulocytosis of 2–6%, a raised serum bilirubin and increased urinary urobilinogen. In some cases, marked reticulocytosis, as high as 60%, has been noted. As the disease progresses, reticulocytopenia predominates. The direct Coombs test, Ham's test and sugar-water tests are negative. The cells show increased sensitivity to anti-i and anti-I, and the cold antibody lysis test may be positive (Lewis 1976).

There may be an increase of fetal haemoglobin as high as 20% and the Kleihauer test shows an irregular distribution in the red cells. Analysis of the fetal haemoglobin shows the same ratio of 3 : 1 for the glycine : alanine ratio at position 136 of the gamma-chain as is found in normal babies (Beard 1976). Some cases have presented with normal levels of fetal haemoglobin. In others, an increase of fetal haemo-globin has been detected before the typical blood abnormalities have developed.

The bone marrow is typically hypoplastic, but in the early stages it may be normocellular or even frankly hypercellular, with progression to hypocellularity later. The normoblasts sometimes show dyserythro-poiesis (Fig. 8.2) (Schroeder 1966) but normoblastic erythropoiesis may also be found with only minor changes in the nuclear pattern.

A range of red cell enzyme disorders have been reported, including hexokinase deficiency (Lohr & Waller 1967). The changes have been summarized by Bloom (1972) and Beard (1976). Although variations in glycolysis, hexokinase, glucose-6-phosphate dehydrogenase, ATP and ATPase have all been reported, there is no consistent defect in the red cells and hence the anaemia and clinical symptoms cannot be attri-buted to any single metabolic abnormality.

Chromosome and cellular defects. In 1964, Schroeder et al. noted that the peripheral blood lymphocytes showed chromosomal abnormalities and this has been confirmed in many subsequent cases. The chromo-somes may show breaks, reunion figures, ring and dicentric chromo-somes, acentric fragments and endoreduplication. These findings are similar to those produced by X-irradiation. The most frequent finding is a chromatid break, usually affecting a single chromatid, associated

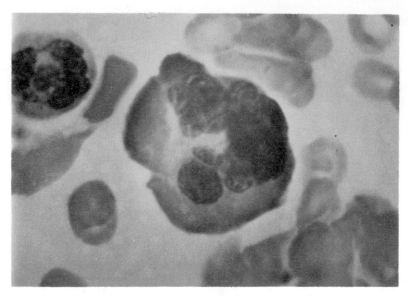

Fig. 8.2. Multinucleated giant normoblast and hypersegmented neutrophil from the bone marrow of a patient with Fanconi's anaemia.

with rotation or angulation of the distal fragment. The incidence of this finding varies from 6 to 75%. The most characteristic abnormalities are chromatid exchanges which apparently arise as a result of a break in two adjacent chromosomes followed by non-homologous reunion of the chromatids. The changes are most commonly found in peripheral blood lymphocytes, but are also present, although less obvious, in fibroblast cultures and in direct bone marrow preparations (Bloom 1972). It is possible that they are also present in other cells. Beard et al. (1973) reported one case whose fibroblast cultures on two occasions showed two different clones of cells with missing or extra chromosomes (Fig. 8.3).

The fibroblasts have a normal capacity to remove thymine dimers induced by ultra-violet irradiation (Regan et al. 1973) and lymphocytes show chromatid breaks much more readily than normal lymphocytes after exposure to ultra-violet or X-irradiation (Higurashi & Conen 1971). Fibroblasts may be difficult to grow *in vitro* and show a significantly longer population doubling time than controls. They are

Fig. 8.3. Chromosome preparations of peripheral blood lymphocytes in Fanconi's anaemia. A, Part of chromosome spread with chromatid exchange figure (arrowed). B, Multiple breaks and constrictions (arrowed). (*By courtesy of Dr H. B. Marsden and the Department of Cytogenetics, Royal Manchester Children's Hospital*)

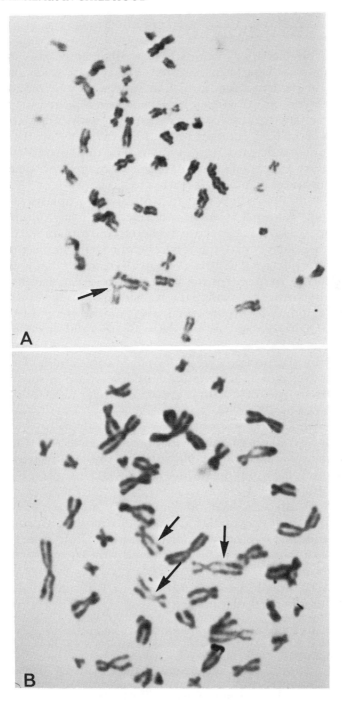

killed by lower concentrations of mitomycin C than normal cells (Swift 1976).

There is an increased incidence of malignant disease. Approximately 250 cases have been reported and at least seven cases have developed acute leukaemia, which has been of the monocytic or myelomonocytic variety. Hepatomas have been reported in five cases. Many of this latter group have had treatment with androgens, which clearly has provoked tumour formation. In one case the tumour regressed when androgens were stopped. The tumours are frequently multifocal. Several patients have developed carcinomas, sometimes in unusual sites and at an unusually early age.

Todaro et al. (1966) reported that the skin fibroblasts of patients with Fanconi's anaemia were transformed in tissue culture by the simian virus, SV40, a papovavirus related to the human wart virus. In monkeys it is a latent virus, but it may be oncogenic in the guinea-pig. There is no evidence that it is ever involved in the pathogenesis of aplastic anaemia in man. Further laboratory evidence that the cells are exceptionally prone to malignant transformation is shown by the increase of induced chromosomal aberrations when the cells are subjected to X-irradiation, ultra-violet irradiation and alkylating agents.

The parents of Fanconi children are heterozygotes and some may be recognized by the presence of abnormal chromosomes. There have been several reports of acute leukaemia developing in such families, and the heterozygote may also be at risk of a wider range of malignant disease (Swift et al. 1971).

In some families the associated abnormalities may be few and the disease may be recognized only by the chromosome defect (Zaizov et al. 1969). In the same way some family members of an affected case may have constitutional symptoms without bone marrow disease (Gmyrek & Syllm-Rapoport 1964).

Up to 2·5% of occasional random breaks may be present as an acquired finding in megaloblastic anaemia, after drug treatment, and with viral infection, in otherwise normal individuals. It is the frequency and range of abnormalities which characterize the chromosome defects of Fanconi's anaemia.

Two unrelated children with characteristic Fanconi's anaemia have shown features of particular interest:

J.S. A girl presented with thrombocytopenic bleeding at the age of $3\frac{1}{4}$ years, and a blood count of Hb 5·6 g/dl, white cells 4·5 × 10⁹/litre (polymorphs 24%, lymphocytes 76%), platelets 6 × 10⁹/litre. She was small and micro-cephalic. Abnormal skin pigmentation had been noted at the age of 3 months. Treatment with androgens and prednisone initially brought improvement which was not maintained. She developed cataracts secondary to steroid treatment. Haemorrhage became more frequent and she eventually died of pneumonia at the age of 7½ years. After 4 years' treatment with androgen including 90 g methyl testosterone and 700 g oxymetholone, autopsy revealed multiple hepatomas in the liver.

M.F. A boy aged 7 years presented with a history of pallor for 2 years and bruising for one. He was found to have pancytopenia: Hb 7·8 g/dl, white cells 3·5 × 10⁹/litre (polymorphs 23%, lymphocytes 72%, monocytes 5%) and platelets 7·0 × 10⁹/litre. In addition to small stature (height less than third centile), he had pigmented areas on the trunk and a horseshoe kidney. The tonsils were completely absent, although immunoglobulin levels were normal (IgG 690, IgA 82, IgM 60 mg/100 ml). Chromosome analysis showed breaks and endoreduplication. He has responded to oxymetholone (50 mg/m²) with growth and height gain to the 50th and 75th centiles, and a rise of Hb to 11·3 g/dl. There has been no change in white cells or platelets.

The disease is characterized by wide differences in clinical findings, haematological changes, metabolic abnormalities and other defects. The chromosome disorders are an integral feature, although there is no uniformity about which chromosomes are involved.

Tentative explanations for the defect in Fanconi's anaemia have included proposals that the disorder is due to a deficiency of essential intracellular metabolites (Schroeder 1966) or to increased breakdown by lysosomal enzymes (Swift & Hirchhorn 1966). A defect of DNA repair seems likely (Sasaki & Tonomura 1973). The cytogenetic abnormalities appear to hold the key to the basic defect. The haematological abnormalities may be the result of progressive stem-cell failure, secondary to the increased sensitivity of Fanconi cells to cytotoxic effects and to their reduced growth rate.

Other Types of Constitutional Aplastic Anaemia

O'Gorman Hughes and Diamond (1964) briefly described a group of children who presented at birth or in early infancy with amegakaryocytic thrombocytopenia and developed aplastic anaemia 1–12½ years later. The first author later described seven patients (O'Gorman Hughes 1974). Five were boys and they appeared to form a relatively homogeneous group, often with a long interval between the onset of thrombocytopenia and of aplastic anaemia. Two children developed neutropenia in the first year of life. One boy had optic atrophy and nystagmus at the age of 1 year, and was retarded. One of the two girls was microcephalic, retarded, aplastic and deaf (associated with severe bilateral otitis media). The other girl's sibling had hand deformities and anencephaly and died at the age of 3 days. There were otherwise no associated congenital deformities and no other family history suggesting a genetic predisposition.

This is a small subclassification of an already rare disorder. Few cases, and hence few consistent investigations, have been recorded. Five had slight elevations of fetal haemoglobin (3·1–5·7%). Chromosome analysis was normal in two boys. Increased breaks and gaps were found in one girl. This child had a low serum IgA and IgG and a lymphoid T-cell defect characterized by lack of reaction to skin tests for delayed hypersensitivity and a poor response to phytohaemagglutinin. She may have had Fanconi's anaemia with atypical early onset. All patients were treated with corticosteroids. Two may have shown a temporary response. All needed blood transfusions. Four were given androgens and three responded. The prognosis appears to be poor. Four patients died, one was alive but needed constant transfusions, one was in good partial remission on hormone treatment and one was lost to follow-up.

The absence of a positive family history and the nature of the defects described in the two children with other abnormalities makes it possible that the bone marrow disease in this group of children is not the result of inherited predisposition, but of some other congenital abnormality acquired *in utero* as a result of congenital virus infection or other toxic effect.

A few other patients present at the age of 5–10 years with aplastic anaemia, but without any of the usual congenital defects described in Fanconi's anaemia. Acquired aplastic anaemia may be diagnosed initially, but the slowly progressive nature of the disease and the dependence on androgens suggest a further subgroup of constitutional aplastic anaemia. Whether or not the aetiology is the same, such cases are better regarded as cases of Fanconi's anaemia, as more than one such case may occur in a family (Estren & Dameshek 1947), although not every case presenting in this way will have affected siblings.

Other rare disorders of childhood which may be confused with Fanconi's anaemia include dyskeratosis congenita, the thrombocytopenia–absent radius syndrome (TAR syndrome), and pure red cell aplasia. Perhaps the biggest problem is distinguishing between the children who present with acquired aplastic anaemia and chance congenital defects, and those with true Fanconi's anaemia. In these cases chromosome analysis may be very helpful.

Dyskeratosis congenita. Dyskeratosis congenita shares many features with Fanconi's anaemia. Patients with haematological disease may have, in addition to bone marrow failure (and occasionally a hyperplastic phase), skin pigmentation and dyschromia, lacrimal duct blockage, hypogenitalism, mental retardation and poor growth. Defects which are not shared with Fanconi's anaemia include telangiectatic erythema and atrophy, alopecia and abnormal sweating, exocrine, ungual and dental dysplasia, leukoplakia, oesophageal diverticula, and a predominance in white males. The chromosome pattern is normal. It is even rarer than Fanconi's anaemia and most cases have been reported in dermatological journals.

There are no haematological features which distinguish the two diseases. Both may have raised levels of haemoglobin F and leucocyte alkaline phosphatase. There is also an increased tendency to malignancy. Like Fanconi's anaemia, the blood disorder appears after the ectodermal abnormalities and the usual pattern has been for the ectodermal dystrophy to develop in the first decade, followed by blood disease in the second and third decades, and with carcinomatosis in the third, fourth and fifth decades (Steier et al. 1972).

In the past there was a tendency to categorize cases of dyskeratosis congenita with blood disease as instances of Fanconi's anaemia, and some of the cases of carcinomatosis reported in Fanconi's anaemia may have been due to the former. It seems probable that the basic difference in the two disorders lies in the presence of abnormal chromosomes in Fanconi's anaemia which entail a generalized predisposition to neoplasia, whereas in dyskeratosis congenita the carcinomas arise in sites previously affected by leukoplakia, as is generally the case in this abnormality.

Schwachman's syndrome. There is a rare but well-known association between failure of exocrine pancreatic secretion and bone marrow disease known as Schwachman's syndrome (Schwachman et al. 1964). The haematological presentation in most cases is a neutropenia but anaemia and thrombocytopenia may also occur, sometimes intermittently. The bone marrow may be hypocellular or show granulocyte hyperplasia. A neutrophil leucocytosis may be found during infections. There is an increase of fetal haemoglobin, evidence of a long-standing marrow disorder. Cases have been detected in infancy and a low white cell count was present on the first day of life in one case. There is failure to thrive, steatorrhoea and occasionally intermittent galactosuria. Some patients may have metaphyseal dysostosis or Hirschsprung's disease. The disease is distinct from cystic fibrosis and sweat electrolytes are normal. The patients are prone to infection and several cases have died as a result in infancy and early childhood. Multiple cases have occurred in one family, suggesting a genetic aetiology, but the basic defect is unknown.

The thrombocytopenia–absent radius syndrome. The thrombocytopenia–absent radius (TAR) syndrome was initially thought to be a partly expressed form of Fanconi's anaemia, but is now considered a separate entity. However, in this disease, thrombocytopenia is present from birth and cerebral haemorrhage is a dangerous complication in the early weeks of life. The low platelet count is secondary to megakaryocyte hypoplasia. There is aplasia of the radii, which is always bilateral, with hypoplasia of the ulnae. Associated abnormalities include dislocation of the hips, small mandible and shoulder girdle defects. There may also be a high white cell count with immature granulocytes, suggesting a leukaemoid reaction, rather than leucopenia. Anaemia is not uncommon, but chromosome analysis is normal. The thrombocytopenia tends to become less severe with age.

There is no association with thalidomide embryopathy. Radial aplasia may of course exist without thrombocytopenia and other signs of the TAR syndrome.

TREATMENT

General Management

Aplastic anaemia is a rare disease and the prognosis is poor. Facilities for general support such as platelet and granulocyte transfusion, reverse barrier nursing and bone marrow transplantation are generally only available in major centres. If any advance is to be made in diagnosis, aetiology and management of children with the disease, and if there is to be any improvement in their survival, new cases need to be referred to a centre specializing in paediatric haematology.

For the patient with severe disease but no marrow donor there is no specific treatment. So children should only be nursed in hospital if they need treatment which cannot be managed at home.

Corticosteroid and Androgen Treatment

Corticosteroids increase the red cell mass and leucocyte mobilization in normal individuals. They show a beneficial effect on capillary integrity in thrombocytopenia. Nevertheless, they have rarely produced cures in aplastic anaemia. Their use is limited by side effects, particularly the tendency to increase susceptibility to infection.

Androgens were introduced for the treatment of aplastic anaemia in children, together with corticosteroids, by Shahidi and Diamond in 1959. They have since been shown to have a beneficial effect by increasing red cell counts in patients with a wide range of refractory anaemias. The initial drug was testosterone, but non-virilizing androgens have been equally effective. Oxymetholone has been particularly widely used, but is probably no more beneficial than other non-virilizing androgens.

The customary dose of an orally active androgen such as methenolone or oxymetholone is 3–5 mg/kg/day. Prednisone is usually given concurrently at a dose of 1 mg/kg alternate days, on the understanding that it may reduce the tendency of the androgen to cause early fusion of the epiphyses and eventual dwarfing, although there is no conclusive proof of this belief. It is generally stated that treatment needs to be continued for 2 or 3 months before any response may be expected. While there is no doubt that androgens may increase the red cell mass of patients already capable of responding, it is less likely that they actually produce a cure in patients who are not also capable of making some degree of spontaneous recovery.

There is no good reason why androgens should affect the recovery of leucocytes and platelets; nevertheless, two-thirds of the children treated in an international cooperative trial (Najean 1976) showed improvement in their granulocyte counts, and one-third showed improvement of platelets. The patients whose counts improved show a better prognosis. Unfortunately, there is no evidence that these changes are due to androgen treatment, as all children in the trial receive some sort of androgen (methyl testosterone, oxymetholone or methenolone) and there is no control arm of children who receive no androgens.

Side effects of corticosteroids and androgens. Treatment with corticosteroids and androgens is discussed in Chapter 6. In childhood, some of the side effects of corticosteroid treatment may be reduced by giving the drug on alternate days, or on 4 days a week. Nevertheless, the serious complication is restriction of growth.

Androgens may be given by mouth or parenterally. Unfortunately, intramuscular injections are undesirable in thrombocytopenic children, which restricts androgen treatment to the orally active drugs.

To obtain an effect in bone marrow hypoplasia, androgens must be given in high doses. This results inevitably in some virilization, even with the 'non-virilizing' androgens. Rapid growth in height and weight, excessive muscular development, skin flushing and acne, penile and clitoral hypertrophy, increased body hair, and hoarsening of the voice are external and visible signs of androgen treatment (see Fig. 8.1). There are also less obvious effects on behaviour. Children of both sexes may show embarrassing sexual activity. Boys may become amorous with their mothers and take more than a passing interest in little girls at school. Erections and masturbation may occur. Parents and teachers need to be reassured that these are the effects of treatment, and reminded that their children's emotional development does not advance as rapidly as their physical development.

Prolonged dosage with androgens increases the rate of skeletal maturation, which may be reduced by concurrent administration of corticosteroids. The fear that rapid skeletal maturation may lead to premature fusion of the epiphyses, with eventual restriction of bone growth and body height, was not borne out in a long-term follow-up study of children treated with combined testosterone and cortico-steroids in large doses over a long period (Shahidi & Crigler 1976).

Splenectomy and Bone Marrow Transplantation

The spleen is not enlarged in the acute stage of acquired aplastic anaemia and splenectomy at this time is hazardous and offers no benefit. In the chronic stage, the operation is still hazardous. Each case should be considered on its own merits. There is an increased risk of infection and mortality in children following splenectomy for whatever reason, and the risk is higher in younger children. The risk must be increased when splenectomy is associated with leucopenia, thrombo-cytopenia and possible corticosteroid treatment.

Bone marrow transplantation is fully discussed in Chapter 7. For the congenital aplasias, the problem is to decide when and if to trans-plant. In the early stages the immediate mortality from grafting is greater than from conservative treatment. In the late stages multiple transfusions will have led to multispecific antibodies and sensitization leading to graft rejection. Successful grafts were reported for a 6-year-old girl and a 15-year-old boy both with Fanconi's anaemia (Storb et al. 1976; Barrett et al. 1977). Evidence for successful take in a patient with congenital hypoplastic anaemia was presented by August et al. (1976) although the patient died later with interstitial pneumonia.

Blood Products and Blood Transfusion

The problems of blood transfusion in aplastic anaemia are discussed in Chapter 6. The general principles are similar for children and adults. The volume of red cells and whole blood needed for transfusion in children is shown in Table 8.7.

Problems of long-term transfusion. Children who need regular blood transfusions for several years develop iron overload. Their problems are the same as seen in the long-term management of thalassaemia major, which has been reviewed by Modell (1977).

Prevention of Infection

Minor infections spread rapidly in neutropenic patients, particularly if corticosteroids have been or are being given. Steroid treatment is a contraindication to immunization with live vaccines such as BCG, rubella and measles. Exposure to the normal childhood viral illnesses

Table 8.7. Blood transfusion in children

VOLUME OF CELLS NEEDED =

$$\frac{\text{Patient's Weight (kg)} \times \text{Blood Volume (ml/kg)} \times (\text{Desired Hb} - \text{Observed Hb})}{\text{Haemoglobin concentration of cells in pack (g/dl)}}$$

Substitution in the above formula gives

$$\frac{\text{Weight in kg} \times 75 \times \text{rise of Hb needed}}{12 \text{ (whole blood) or 24 (packed cells)}}$$

Or as a rough guide:

Whole blood: Wt (kg) × 6   × rise of Hb needed = ml
Packed cells: Wt (kg) × 3·5 × rise of Hb needed = ml

Blood volume in neonates is 85 ml/kg, soon falling to 75 ml/kg which is the normal for children.

Haemoglobin concentration of whole blood is approximately 11–13 g/dl; of semi-packed cells is approximately 18–20 g/dl; and of concentrated cells is approximately 22–24 g/dl.

---

such as measles and chickenpox may be followed by extensive and serious disease. The parents should, therefore, be warned to bring the child back for prophylactic treatment with specific immune globulin (i.e. zoster immune globulin, hyperimmune measles serum) if there is any contact with such diseases. It may be advisable to keep the child away from school or from contact with other children if such diseases are circulating in the neighbourhood.

The following report illustrates the case of a boy with aplastic anaemia following hepatitis who has shown a partial recovery and now leads a normal life in spite of impaired bone marrow reserve and pancytopenia. Haemoglobin levels only improved after stopping androgen.

M.S. aged 6 years developed severe aplastic anaemia 2 weeks after onset of jaundice (Hb 8·6 g/dl, reticulocytes less than 0·1%, white cells $1·4 \times 10^9$/litre with neutrophils $0·28 \times 10^9$/litre, platelets less than 5×10^9/litre. Bone marrow showed 90% lymphocytes and only an occasional granulocytic and erythroid precursor cell. He was treated with oxymetholone, 2·2 mg/kg, but for a year transfusions were needed every 6 weeks as the haemoglobin regularly fell to 4 or 5 g/dl. He also needed regular platelet transfusions for 2 months to control bleeding. There was slight improvement of white cells to $2·0 \times 10^9$/litre (polymorphs $1·0 \times 10^9$/litre) and platelets to 20×10^9/litre. There was no severe bacterial infection, but he bruised easily and was prone to epistaxis. He returned to school with some restriction of physical activities. However, it proved impossible to curb his energy and restrictions were lifted. Oxymetholone was stopped after a year as transfusions were still needed and there appeared to be no response. Three months later the haemoglobin rose spontaneously to 8 g/dl where it has subsequently remained. Twenty months after onset he now leads a normal life with Hb 8·2 g/dl, white cells 2·8 × 10⁹/litre (polymorphs 0·39 × 10⁹/litre) and platelets 36 × 10⁹/litre.

It is essential to keep the veins of small children with pancytopenia in good condition. Routine counts should be done with fingerpricks and unnecessary venepunctures avoided. Cut-downs are never indicated and are not necessary in experienced children's units. We find 23 gauge 'Butterfly' needles (Abbott) ideal for blood collection, and use 20 or 22 gauge 'Medi-cut' (Sherwood) catheters for intravenous infusions.

Prophylactic management of bacterial infection is presently being discussed for leukaemic children. Hughes et al. (1977) gave cotrimoxazole–sulphonamide (Bactrim, Septrin) for prophylaxis against infection with *Pneumocystis carinii*. One unexpected benefit of the trial was a reduction of bacterial infections in the treated group. This may be of value in patients with aplastic anaemia and severe neutropenia.

Platelet and Granulocyte Transfusions

The indications for treatment with platelet and granulocyte transfusions and their complications are covered in Chapter 6, and only the points specifically relating to children are dealt with here.

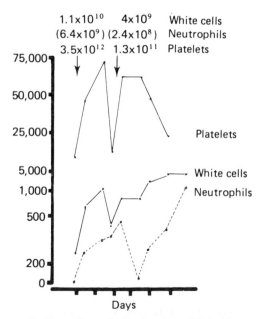

Fig. 8.4. Increments of white cells and platelets in a child after transfusions of cells from a normal adult donor collected with the Haemonetics Model 30 blood processor.

In severe thrombocytopenia a satisfactory count may be maintained by giving platelet concentrates once or twice a week. Two units are given to infants, four units to toddlers and young children. Older children are treated on a body weight basis of 1 unit/5 kg.

Granulocytes are only given for treatment of severe infections resistant to antibiotics. The benefit of granulocyte transfusions in adults is usually judged by noting a decrease of pyrexia as there is rarely any real change in the neutrophil count. However, in children the improvement in the clinical condition may be accompanied not only by a fall of temperature but also by some increase of neutrophil count.

Each granulocyte donation obtained with a cell separator contains a large number of platelets. As infected patients utilize platelets more quickly, the platelets in each granulocyte donation are a useful bonus. The changes in neutrophil and platelets counts in a child treated with granulocyte transfusions are shown in Fig. 8.4.

PURE RED CELL APLASIA (BLACKFAN–DIAMOND SYNDROME)

Clinical Features

Pure red cell aplasia, or congenital hypoplastic anaemia, was originally described in 1936 by Josephs, but is better known by the description of Diamond and Blackfan in 1938. A comprehensive review by Diamond et al. appeared in 1976. The disease presents at birth or in the early weeks of life, with anaemia, reticulocytopenia and a deficiency of bone marrow erythroblasts. The haemoglobin is often less than 6 g/dl. The red cells are normochromic but macrocytic (MCV 100–115 fl) in spite of normal B12 and folate levels. Over half the patients are pale at birth and nearly three-quarters are affected before 4 months of age. White cells and platelets are normal, although sometimes in the later stages of the disease recurrent blood transfusions lead to haemosiderosis, splenomegaly and hypersplenism. With the exception of one case (Heyn et al. 1974) the karyotype has always been normal. However, about a quarter of affected children have had other congenital defects including strabismus, hypertelorism, retinopathy, congenital heart disease, achondroplasia, webbed neck, cleft lip and palate, abnormal pigmentation, urinary tract malformations, dwarfism and skeletal abnormalities including triphalangeal thumbs. This wide range of congenital defects may lead to confusion with Fanconi's anaemia. Six patients have had pure red cell aplasia and triphalangeal thumbs, a combination which suggests a distinct syndrome. Seven had phenotypic Turner's syndrome with a short webbed neck, but no chromosomal anomaly. Fetal haemoglobin is increased, and the i antigen may persist as in other congenital bone marrow disorders. Red cell enzymes are abnormal with raised enolase, transaminase and glutathione peroxidase, resembling the pattern in cord blood cells. The erythropoietin level is high and the basic defect may comprise a defect in activating the effect of erythropoietin on the erythroid stem cell.

The inheritance appears to be dominant. There are at least 10 reports of the disease occurring in siblings, but in only three families has there been direct transmission from mother or father. In two families the father has transmitted the disease through two wives. A slight macrocytosis, or occasional cells containing haemoglobin F by the Kleihauer method may be found in a parent and be evidence of minimal disease. It seems likely that the disorder may show incomplete expression without restriction to either sex.

Cathie (1950) commented on the similarity of the facial expression: all the children had tow-coloured hair, snub noses, thick upper lips, rather wide-set eyes and an intelligent expression. This has not been the experience of most other observers. Likewise the early reports that the patients excreted an excess of anthranilic acid after a tryptophan load (Altman & Miller 1963) have not been confirmed in larger series (Diamond et al. 1961; Price et al. 1970). Mentzner et al. (1975) investigated riboflavin metabolism, because riboflavin deficiency can lead to acquired erythroid aplasia (Foy et al. 1961; Alfrey & Lane 1970). Red cell glutathione reductase showed abnormally high activation by FAD and the patients had reduced transport of radioactive riboflavin into red cells, with low red cell flavin levels. The defects were partially corrected by large doses of riboflavin by mouth, but this vitamin unfortunately is of no practical use in the management of the congenital disease.

The bone marrow shows on average only 4% normoblasts (range 0 to 13%), but different counts may be seen at different times. A small number of cells resembling lymphocytes may be seen. They have been called haematogones and are postulated to be primitive erythroid stem cells. Two cases presented with marked lymphocytosis in marrow and blood: in one case diagnosis of acute lymphoblastic leukaemia was erroneously made. The lymphocytosis remitted with steroid treatment (Miale & Bloom 1975).

The serum iron is high and the iron binding capacity is fully saturated. The serum ferritin and erythropoietin levels are also high.

There are suggestions that the disease may have an immunological basis. Spontaneous remission may occur. There is often a response to steroids, but with a dose-dependency different from other auto-

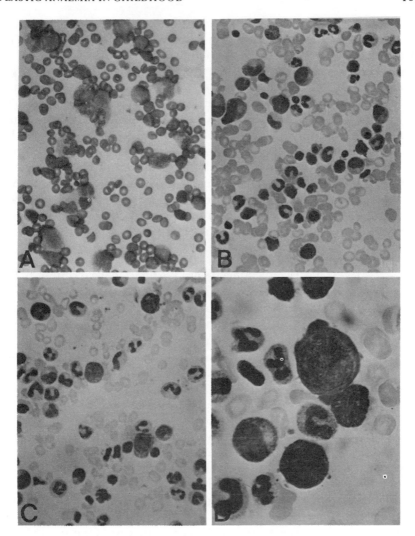

Fig. 8.5. Consecutive bone marrow aspirations in Blackfan-Diamond syndrome. The patient has required regular transfusions from the age of 18 months until his present age of 9 years. A, November 1967: marrow showed complete erythroid aplasia. B, January 1969: normal erythropoiesis. C, June 1969: the only normoblasts were large early basophilic cells. D, Enlargement of these cells.

immune diseases, and the mode of action is unknown. Two cases have remitted after treatment with 6-mercaptopurine. An inhibitor of erythropoietin-sensitive stem cells was postulated by Ortega et al. (1975); but no evidence of any serum inhibitor was found by Abraham and Scott (1967), Geller et al. (1975) or Freedman et al. (1975).

A normal number of stem cells was demonstrated by Freedman and Saunders (1977) and they responded normally to erythropoietin. These workers could not duplicate the clinical response to steroids *in vitro* and failed to demonstrate cellular inhibition of erythropoiesis, as has been reported elsewhere (see p. 16).

The disease is quite distinct from the acquired pure red cell aplasia of adults, half of whom have thymoma, often with other immunological abnormalities, and from the acquired temporary erythroblastopenia of children which may complicate chronic haemolytic anaemias or develop spontaneously in normal children (Gasser 1949). Congenital pure red cell aplasia may be distinguished from temporary erythroblastopenia by the presence of larger red cells (MCV over 90 fl) and raised haemoglobin F (Wang & Mentzner 1976). The disease usually recovers spontaneously (Wegelius & Weber 1978).

Treatment

Most success has been achieved with corticosteroid treatment. Two-thirds of the cases reviewed by Diamond et al. (1976) responded well to steroids and 14% showed a partial response. A quarter showed spontaneous remission. It is usual to start treatment with prednisone at a dose of 30–60 mg/day. Remission, if it appears, usually develops in a few weeks with a reticulocytosis and rise of haemoglobin. Diamond et al. (1961) noted that early diagnosis and treatment increased the chances of inducing remission. The dose is then reduced to the minimum maintenance level, usually in the range 5–20 mg/day. Once stabilized on prednisone, the patient usually needs to continue treatment for months or years, but the dose may need to be increased as the child grows older. The harmful side-effects of corticosteroid treatment are reduced by giving the dosage on alternate days. The dose response may be extremely critical; for instance the haemoglobin may be adequately maintained on 20 mg on alternate days, but fall if the dose is reduced to 17·5 mg.

Androgens have been used with partial success. One might expect that pure red cell anaemia would respond well to androgens. Unfortunately, the response is usually incomplete. Only half the cases reviewed by Diamond et al. (1976) responded. The side-effects of androgens in children render them undesirable for use in high dosage. However, in low doses, androgens may counteract the growth depression associated with corticosteroid treatment. Bone marrow transplantation may be considered for the occasional case with a compatible donor.

Four-fifths of cases respond to corticosteroids. For most patients who are unable to maintain a satisfactory haemoglobin, and who do not respond to steroids, it is necessary to give regular transfusions of red cells. Long-term treatment with regular transfusions over many years does not preclude spontaneous remission, even as late as 15 years. The steroid responsive children may show a fluctuating course and need varying dosage at different times. Diamond et al. (1976) collected details of 133 cases. 105 (88%) were alive (median age 5 years) and 15 (12%) were dead. The median age at death was 13 years. Two reported cases have died of acute leukaemia (see p. 231).

REFERENCES

ABRAHAM, J. M. & SCOTT, P. (1966) Red-cell aplasia. *Lancet*, *ii*, 1416.

ALFREY, C. P. & LANE, M. (1970) The effect of riboflavin deficiency on erythropoiesis. *Semin. Hemat.*, 7, 49.

ALJOUNI, K. & DOEBLIN, T. D. (1974) The syndrome of hepatitis and aplastic anaemia. *Br. J. Haemat.*, 27, 345.

ALTER, B. P., PAPPEPORT, J. M., HUISMAN, T. H. J. & SCHROEDER, W. A. (1975) Fetal erythropoiesis following bone marrow transplantation. *Blood*, *46*, 1054.

ALTMAN, K. I. & MILLER, G. (1953) Disturbance of tryptophan metabolism in congenital hypoplastic anaemia. *Nature, Lond.*, *172*, 868.

AUGUST, C. S., KING, E., GITHENS, J. H., McINTOSH, K., HUMBERT, J. R., GREENSHEER, A. & JOHNSON, F. B. (1976) Establishment of erythropoiesis following bone marrow transplantation in a patient with congenital hypoplastic anaemia (Diamond–Blackfan syndrome). *Blood*, *48*, 491.

BABIOR, B. M. (1978) Folate and aplasia of the bone marrow. *New Engl. J. Med.*, *298*, 506.

BARRETT, A. J., BRIGDEN, W. D., HOBBS, J. R., HUGH-JONES, K., HUMBLE, J. G., JAMES, D. C. O., RETSAS, S., ROGERS, T. R. F., SELWYN, S., SNEATH, P. & WATSON, J. G. (1977) Successful bone marrow transplant for Fanconi's anaemia. *Br. med. J.*, *i*, 420.

BEARD, M. E. J. (1976) Fanconi anaemia. *Congenital Disorders of Erythropoiesis. Ciba Fdn. Symp.*, *37*, 108.

BEARD, M. E. J., YOUNG, D. E., BATEMAN, C. J. T., McCARTHY, G. T., SMITH, M. E., SINCLAIR, L., FRANKLIN, A. W. & BODLY SCOTT, R. (1973) Fanconi's anaemia. *Q. Jl Med.*, *42*, 403.

BLOOM, G. E. (1972) Disorders of bone marrow production. *Pediat. Clins N. Am.*, *19*, 983.

BLOOM, G. E. & DIAMOND, L. K. (1968) Prognostic value of fetal hemoglobin levels in acquired aplastic anaemia. *New Engl. J. Med.*, *278*, 304.

BRANDA, R. F., MOLDOW, C. F., MacARTHUR, J. R., WINTROBE, M. M., ANTHONY, B. K. & JACOB, H. S. (1978) Folate-induced remission in aplastic anaemia with familial defect of cellular folate uptake. *New Engl. J. Med.*, *298*, 469.

BROWN, A. K., RAO, A. N. R. & RIEDER, R. F. (1975) Aplastic anaemia with evidence of proliferation of a true 'fetal' red cell clone following androgen therapy. *Blood*, *46*, 1053.

CARTER, R. L., (1965) Platelet levels in infectious mononucleosis. *Blood*, *25*, 817.

CARTER, R. L. (1969) Granulocytes in infectious mononucleosis. In: *Infectious Mononucleosis*, ed. R. L. Carter & H. G. Penman, p. 111. Oxford: Blackwell Scientific.

CATHIE, I. A. B. (1950) Erythrogenesis imperfecta. *Archs Dis. Childh.*, *25*, 313.

CIFUENTES, E., KINNEY, E. R., GILL, F. M. & SCHWARTZ, E. (1977) Prediction of prognosis in aplastic anaemia by ferrokinetic studies (abstract). *Pediat. Res.*, *11*, 469.

DALTON, A. J., LAW, L. W., MOLONEY, J. B. & MANAKER, R. A. (1961) Electron microscopic studies of series of murine lymphoid neoplasms. *J. natn. Cancer Inst.*, *27*, 747.

DAVIS, S. & RUBIN, A. D. (1972) Treatment and prognosis in aplastic anaemia. *Lancet*, *i*, 871.

DENNIS, L. M. & BRODSKY, I. (1965) Thrombocytopenia induced by Friend leukaemia virus. *J. natn. Cancer Inst.*, *35*, 993.

DIAMOND, L. K., ALLEN, D. M. & MAGILL, F. B. (1961) Congenital (erythroid) hypoplastic anemia. A 25 year study. Am. J. Dis. Child., 102, 403.

DIAMOND, L. K. & BLACKFAN, K. D. (1938) Hypoplastic anemia. Am. J. Dis. Child., 56, 464.

DIAMOND, L.K., WANG, W. C. & ALTER, B. P. (1976) Congenital hypoplastic anemia. Adv. Pediat., 22, 349.

ESTREN, S. & DAMESHEK, W. (1947) Familial hypoplastic anemia of childhood. Am. J. Dis. Child., 73, 671.

FANCONI, G. (1927) Familiäre infantile perniziosaartige Anämie (Pernizioses Blutbild und Konstitution). Z. Kinderheilk., 117, 257.

FANCONI, G. (1962) Physiology and pathology of calcium phosphate metabolism. Adv. Pediat., 12, 307.

FANCONI, G. (1967) Familial constitutional panmyelocytopathy, Fanconi's anaemia (F.A.). Semin. Hemat., 4, 233.

FISHER, O. D. & KRASZEWSKI, T. M. (1952) Thrombocytopenic purpura following measles. Archs Dis. Childh., 27, 144.

FOY, H., KONDI, A. & MACDOUGALL, L. (1961) Pure red-cell aplasia and kwashiorkor treated with riboflavine. Br. med. J., i, 937.

FREEDMAN, M. H., AMATO, D. & SAUNDERS, E. F. (1975) Haem synthesis in the Diamond–Blackfan syndrome. Br. J. Haemat., 31, 515.

FREEDMAN, M. H. & SAUNDERS, E. F. (1977) Diamond–Blackfan syndrome: in vitro analysis of the erythropoietic defect (abstract). Pediat. Res., 11, 471.

FREEDMAN, M. H., SAUNDERS, E. F., HILTON, J. & MCCLURE, P. D. (1974) Residual abnormalities in acquired aplastic anemia of childhood. J. Am. med. Ass., 228, 201.

GASSER, C. (1949) Akute Erythroblastopenie: 10 Fälle aplasticher Erythroblastenkrisen mit risen Proerythroblasten bei allergisch-toxischen Zustandbildern. Helv. pediat. Acta, 4, 107.

GASSER, C. (1970) Besonderheiten der kindlichen Panmyelopathien. Schweizer med. Wschr., 100, 1948.

GELLER, G., KRIVIT, W., ZALUSKY, R. & ZANJANI, E. D. (1975) Lack of erythropoietic inhibitory effect of serum from patients with congenital pure red cell aplasia. J. Pediat., 86, 198.

GLEADHILL, V., BRIDGES, J. M. & HADDEN, D. R. (1975) Fanconi's anaemia with short stature: absence of response to human growth hormone. Archs Dis. Childh., 50, 318.

GMYREK, D. & SYLLM-RAPOPORT, I. (1964) Zur Fanconi-Anämie (F.A.) Analyse von 129 beschriebenen Fällen. Z. Kinderheilk., 91, 297.

HANN, I., EVANS, D. I. K., MARSDEN, H. B., MORRIS JONES, & PALMER, M. K. (1978) Bone marrow fibrosis in acute lymphoblastic leukaemia of childhood. J. Clin. Path., 31, 313.

HATHAWAY, W. E., GRITHENS, J. H., BLACKBURN, W. R., FULGINITI, F. & KEMPE, C. H. (1965) Aplastic anaemia, histiocytosis and erythrodermia in immunologically deficient children. Probable runt disease. New Engl. J. Med., 273, 953.

HEYN, R. M., ERTEL, I. J. & TUBERGEN, D. G. (1969) Course of acquired aplastic anaemia in children treated with supportive care. J. Am. med. Ass., 208, 1372.

HEYN, R., KURCZYNSKI, E. & SCHMICKEL, R. (1974) The association of Blackfan–Diamond syndrome, physical abnormalities and an abnormality of chromosome 1. J. Pediat., 85, 531.

HIGURASHI, M. & CONEN, P. E. (1971) In vitro chromosomal radiosensitivity in Fanconi's anaemia. Blood, 38, 336.

HORSTMANN, D., BANATVALA, J. E., RIORDAN, J. T., PAYNE, M. C., WHITEMORE, R., OPTON, E. M. & FLOREY, C. DUVE. (1965) Maternal rubella and the rubella syndrome in infants. Am. J. Dis. Child., 110, 408.

HOWIE, D. L. & CROSBY, W. H. (1961) Bone marrow hypoplasia in humans experimentally induced by viral infection. Blood, 18, 800.

HUDSON, J. B., WEINSTEIN, L. & CHANG, T. W. (1956) Thrombocytopenic purpura in measles. J. Pediat., 48, 48.

HUGHES, W., KUHN, S., CHAUDHARY, S., FELDMAN, S., VERSOZA, M., AUR, R. & PRATT, C. S. (1977) (abstract) Successful chemoprophylaxis for Pneumocystis carinii pneumonitis (PCP). Pediat. Res., 11, 501.

JOSEPHS, H. W. (1936) Anaemia of infancy and early childhood. Medicine, Balt., 15, 307.

LAFER, C. & MORRISON, A. N. (1966) Thrombocytopenic purpura progressing to transient hypoplastic anemia in a newborn with rubella syndrome. Pediatrics, Springfield, 38, 499.

LEWIS, S. M. (1976) Congenital Disorders of Erythropoiesis. Ciba Fdn Symp., 37, 130.

LI, F. P., ALTER, B. P. & NATHAN, D. G. (1972) The mortality of acquired aplastic anemia in children. Blood, 40, 153.

LÖHR, G. W. & WALLER, H. D. (1967) Beitrag zur Pathogenase der Fanconi-Anämie. Blut, 15, 321.

McCULLOUGH, J., BENSON, S. J., YUNIS, E. J. & QUIE, P. G. (1966) Effect of blood-bank storage on leucocyte function. Lancet, ii, 1333.

MARSDEN, H. B. & STEWARD, J. K. (1976) Tumours in Children, 2nd ed., p. 66. Berlin: Springer.

MASSENGALE, O. N., GLASER, H. H., LeLIEVRE, R. E., DODDS, J. B. & KLOCK, M. E. (1963) Physical and psychologic factors in glue sniffing. New Engl. J. Med., 269, 1340.

MELHORN, D. K., GROSS, S. & NEWMAN, A. J. (1970) Acute childhood leukaemia presenting as aplastic anaemia. The response to corticosteroids. J. Pediat., 77, 647.

MENTZER, W. C., WANG, W. C. & DIAMOND, L. K. (1975) An abnormality of riboflavin metabolism in congenital hypoplastic anemia. Blood, 46, 1005.

MIALE, T. D. & BLOOM, G. E. (1975) The significance of lymphocytosis in congenital hypoplastic anaemia. J. Pediat., 87, 550.

MODELL, B. (1977) Total management of thalassaemia major. Archs Dis. Childh., 52, 489.

NAJEAN, Y. (1976) Androgen therapy in aplastic anaemia in childhood. Congenital Disorders of Erythropoiesis. Ciba Fdn Symp., 37, 354.

O'GORMAN HUGHES, D. W. (1966) The varied pattern of aplastic anaemia in childhood. Aust. Paediat. J., 2, 228.

O'GORMAN HUGHES, D. W. (1973) Aplastic anaemia in childhood: a reappraisal. II. idiopathic and acquired aplastic anaemia. Med. J. Aust., 2, 361.

O'GORMAN HUGHES, D. W. (1974) Aplastic anaemia in childhood III. Constitutional aplastic anaemia and related cytopenias. Med. J. Aust., 3, 519.

O'GORMAN HUGHES, D. W. & DIAMOND, L. K. (1964) A new type of constitutional aplastic anaemia without congenital anomalies presenting as thrombocytopenia in infancy. J. Pediat., 65, 1060.

ORTEGA, J. A., SHORE, N. A., DUKES, P. P. & HAMMOND, D. (1975) Congenital hypoplastic anemia: inhibition of erythropoiesis by sera from patients with congenital hypoplastic anemia. Blood, 45, 83.

OSBORN, J. E. & SHAHIDI, N. T. (1973) Thrombocytopenia in murine cytomegalovirus infection. J. Lab. clin. Med., 81, 53.

OSKI, F. A. & NAIMAN, J. L. (1972) Hematologic Problems in the Newborn, 2nd ed. Philadelphia: Saunders.

OZSOYLU, S. & ARGUN, G. (1967) Tryptic activity of the duodenal juice in aplastic anaemia. J. Pediat., 70, 60.

PARKMAN, R., MOSIER, D., UMANSKY, I., COCHRAN, W., CARPENTER, C. B. & ROSEN, F. S. (1974) Graft-versus-host disease after intrauterine and exchange transfusions for haemolytic disease of the newborn. New Engl. J. Med., 290, 359.

PEARSON, H. A. (1967) Marrow hypoplasia in anorexia nervosa. J. Pediat., 71, 211.

PEDERSON, F. K., HERTZ, H., LUNDSTEEN, C., PLATZ, P. & THOMSEN, M. (1977) Indication of primary immune deficiency in Fanconi's anemia. Acta paediat. scand., 66, 745.

POCHEDLY, C., COLLIPP, P. J., WOLMAN, S. R., SUWANSIRIKUL, S. & REZVANI, I. (1971) Fanconi's anemia with growth hormone deficiency. J. Pediat., 79, 93.

POWARS, D. (1965) Aplastic anaemia secondary to glue sniffing. New Engl. J. Med., 273, 700.

PRICE, J. M., BROWN, R. R., PFAFFENBACH, E. C. & SMITH, N. J. (1970) Excretion of urinary tryptophan metabolites by patients with congenital hypoplastic anaemia (Diamond–Blackfan syndrome). *J. Lab. clin. Med.*, 75, 316.

READ, J. T. & HELWIG, F. C. (1945) Infectious mononucleosis. An analysis of three hundred cases with three characterised by rare hematologic features. *Archs intern. Med.*, 75, 376.

REGAN, J. D., SETLOW, R. B., CARRIER, W. L. & LEE, W. H. (1973) Molecular events following the ultraviolet irradiation of human cells from ultraviolet sensitive individuals. In: *Advances in Radiation Research: Biology and Medicine*, ed. J. F. Duplan & A. Chapiro, vol. I, p. 119, London: Gordon and Breach.

SÁNCHEZ-MEDAL, L., CASTANEDO, J. P. & GARCÍA-ROJAS, F. (1963) Insecticides and aplastic anaemia. *New Engl. J. Med.*, 269, 1365.

SASAKI, M. S. & TONOMURA, A. (1973) A high susceptibility of Fanconi's anemia to chromosome breakage by DNA cross-linking agents. *Cancer Res.*, 33, 1829.

SCHROEDER, T. M. (1966) Cytogenetische and cytologische Befunde bei enzymopenischen Panmyelopathien und Pancytopenien. Familiäre Panmyelopathie typ Fanconi, Glutathionreduktasemangel-Anämie und megaloblastäre Vitamin B$_{12}$-Mangel-Anämie. *Humangenetik*, 2, 287.

SCHROEDER, T. M., ANSCHÜTZ, F. & KNOPP, A. (1964) Spontane Chromosomenaberrationen bei familiärer Panmyelopathie. *Humangenetik*, 1, 194.

SCHWACHMAN, H., DIAMOND, L. K., OSKI, F. A. & KHAW, A. T. (1964) The syndrome of pancreatic insufficiency and bone marrow dysfunction. *J. Pediat.*, 65, 645.

SHAHIDI, N. T. & CRIGLER, J. F., jun. (1967) Evaluation of growth and of endocrine systems in testosterone-corticosteroid-treated patients with aplastic anaemia. *J. Pediat.*, 70, 233.

SHAHIDI, N. T. & DIAMOND, L. K. (1959) Testosterone-induced remission in aplastic anemia. *Am. J. Dis. Child.*, 98, 293.

SHAHIDI, N. T., GERALD, P. S. & DIAMOND, L. K. (1962) Alkali-resistant hemoglobin in aplastic anemia of both acquired and congenital types. *New Engl. J. Med.*, 266, 117.

SIMONSEN, M. (1962) Graft versus host reactions: their natural history, and applicability as tools of research. *Progr. Allergy*, 6, 349.

STEIER, M., VAN VOOLEN, G. A. & SELMANOWITZ, V. J. (1972) Dyskeratosis congenita: relationship to Fanconi's anemia. *Blood*, 39, 510.

STORB, R., THOMAS, E. D., BUCKNER, C. D., CLIFT, R. A., FEFER, A., FERNANDO, L. P., GIBLETT, E. R., JOHNSON, F. L. & NEIMAN, P. E. (1976) Allogeneic marrow grafting for treatment of aplastic anemia: a follow-up on long-term survivors. *Blood*, 48, 485.

STRAUSS, R. G., BOVE, K. E., LAKE, A. & KISKER, C. T. (1975) Acquired immunodeficiency in hepatitis-associated aplastic anaemia. *J. Pediat.*, 86, 910.

SWIFT, M. (1976) Fanconi anaemia: cellular abnormalities and clinical predisposition to malignant disease. *Congenital Disorders of Erythropoiesis. Ciba Fdn Symp.*, 37, 115.

SWIFT, M. R. & HIRCHHORN, K. (1966) Fanconi's anemia: inherited susceptibility to chromosome breakage in various tissues. *Ann. intern. Med.*, 65, 495.

SWIFT, M. R., ZIMMERMAN, D. & McDONOUGH, E. R. (1971) Squamous cell carcinomas in Fanconi's anaemia. *J. Am. med. Ass.*, 216, 325.

TODARO, G. J., GREEN, H. & SWIFT, M. R. (1966) Susceptibility of human diploid fibroblast strains to transformation by SV40 virus. *Science, N.Y.*, 153, 1252.

WANG, W. C. & MENTZER, W. C. (1976) Differentiation of transient erythroblastopenia of childhood from congenital hypoplastic anaemia. *J. Pediat.*, 88, 784.

WEGELIUS, R. & WEBER, T. H. (1978) Transient erythroblastopenia in childhood. *Acta pediat. scand.*, 67, 513.

WORLLEDGE, S. M. & DACIE, J. V. (1969) Haemolytic and other anaemias in infectious mononucleosis. In: *Infectious Mononucleosis,* ed. R. L. Carter and H. G. Penman, p. 94. Oxford: Blackwell Scientific.

ZACHMAN, M., ILLIG, R. & PRADER, A. (1972) Fanconi's anemia with isolated growth hormone deficiency. *J. Pediat.*, 80, 159.

ZAIZOV, R., MATOTH, Y. & MAMON, Z. (1969) Familial aplastic anaemia without congenital malformations. *Acta paediat. scand.*, 58, 151.

9

Red Cell Aplasia

C. G. GEARY

Red cell aplasia (red cell agenesis, erythroblastopenia, 'aregenerative anaemia') is a disorder in which anaemia is associated with a selective depression of erythroid precursor cells in the marrow, reticulocytopenia in the blood, but little, if any, disturbance of granulopoiesis or thrombopoiesis. Cases fulfilling this description occur as a congenital disorder, as acute, usually transient episodes, sometimes in the course of another blood disorder, or as a chronic refractory anaemia. The first comprehensive account of red cell aplasia was probably given by Kaznelson (1922) who called it 'pure aplastic anaemia'. The epithet 'pure' red cell aplasia is still often applied to the syndrome, though in fact, a proportion of cases, particularly of the chronic type, do show other cytopenias at some stage, and a few of these eventually develop panhypoplasia. Although some haematologists might exclude the latter from consideration of the syndrome, they form an interesting link with aplastic anaemia itself. Red cell aplasia appears to be a rarer disease than aplastic anaemia, but it is possible that, since many cases recover spontaneously, they go either unnoticed or unreported. However, interest is now focussed particularly on the chronic acquired disease occurring in the adult, because of its greater autonomy and clinical importance, its intriguing relationship to autoimmunity and, not least, because this is one form of 'refractory' anaemia in which there has been notable therapeutic progress.

PATHOPHYSIOLOGY

Whereas aplastic anaemia is a disorder of the ancestral haemopoietic stem cell or its environment, red cell aplasia usually follows damage to, or inhibition of, a generation of stem cells already committed to erythroid development (see p. 4); in other words, to a specialized marrow transit compartment or its regulators. The damage producing clinical red cell aplasia may itself be of limited duration (e.g. viruses, drugs) so that temporary cessation of red cell production is rapidly followed by re-establishment of normal erythropoiesis as pluripotent cells divide to replenish the erythroid compartment; in other cases erythropoiesis is suppressed for long periods. There is evidence that in some, possibly many, of these chronic cases, this suppression occurs as a result of humoral or cellular immune processes directed against some component of the erythroid precursor cell or, rarely, its regulator erythropoietin, and this is discussed in more detail on p. 209. However, some cases are evidently the results of an intrinsic defect in the pluripotent cell, manifest first as failure of erythroid differentiation but later as panhypoplasia or leukaemia.

CLASSIFICATION

As with aplastic anaemia itself, classification of red cell aplasia is difficult because, in many cases, the precise way in which marrow erythroid precursors are damaged or inhibited is uncertain. Cases are usually grouped together according to the presence or absence of other clinical or pathological stigmata. Some authors have classified the syndrome according to its 'acute' or 'chronic' presentation, but this begs the quesion. 'Acute' in this context usually means 'self-limiting', and an acute case will eventually be labelled chronic if early remission does not occur. However, this classification does have value if combined with an attempt to identify aetiological factors. That shown in Table 9.1 is expanded from one suggested by Marmont (1974).

Table 9.1. Classification of red cell aplasia

Congenital
    Blackfan–Diamond syndrome (congenital erythroblastopenia)

Acquired

  Acute
      Associated with chronic haemolysis ('aplastic crises')
      Drugs, chemicals, infections
      Idiopathic
      Renal failure

  Chronic
      Idiopathic
        Presumed autoimmune pathogenesis*
        Pathogenesis obscure
      Associated with
        Thymoma*
        Autoimmune diseases*: systemic lupus erythematosus, autoimmune haemo-
          lytic anaemia, Hashimoto's disease, etc.
        Carcinoma,* lymphomas,* myeloma
      Drugs (?)
      Pre-leukaemia
      Severe nutritional deficiency

---

  * Autoantibodies to erythroid cells or erythropoietin demonstrated in some cases.

This emphasizes that while 'acute' cases usually result from a reversible metabolic or immunological disturbance, chronic cases occur often, though by no means invariably, in the setting of an irreversible defect in immunohomeostasis. There are three peaks in the age distribution of red cell aplasia: in childhood, corresponding to the presentation of the congenital form; at about the time of puberty; and in the over-50s. The congenital form of red cell hypoplasia is discussed in Chapter 8.

ACUTE RED CELL APLASIA

Complete cessation of red cell production is most likely to be noticed in those individuals in whom red cell life-span is already reduced, and it is not surprising that the first accounts of this form of the disorder were given in relation to patients who had hereditary spherocytosis (Lyngar 1942; Dameshek & Bloom 1948), paroxysmal nocturnal haemoglobinuria (Crosby 1953), sickle cell disease (Singer et al. 1950; MacIver & Parker-Williams 1961), autoimmune haemolytic anaemia (Eisemann & Dameshek 1954) and even haemolytic disease of the newborn (Smith 1949; Hurdle & Walker 1963). In each of these an abrupt exacerbation of anaemia in a sometimes compensated haemolytic disorder was associated with decreased jaundice, reticulocytopenia and erythroid depression in the marrow. These considerations led Ovren (1948) to postulate that the syndrome represented a temporary reduction in marrow production of red cells ('aplastic crisis') rather than—as had previously been assumed—an exacerbation of haemolysis or of hypersplenism, although it was noted that they were unusual in splenectomized individuals (Bauman & Swisher 1967). Later, cases were described, especially in children, in whom there was no antecedent history of haemolysis (Gasser 1957; Chanarin et al. 1964; Wranne 1970), and it is possible that this form of transient erythroid depression is not uncommon. In the majority, the syndrome has been associated with viral or bacterial infection, sometimes of a trivial kind; these have been reviewed by Krantz (1976). They include virus pneumonia, rubella, infectious monoucleosis, mumps, meningococcal septicaemia, viral hepatitis and even insect bites. Prodromal febrile episodes of presumed, though unproved, viral aetiology are common (Bauman & Swisher 1967). There is possibly a genetic tendency to this type of marrow depression, since several cases may occur simultaneously in siblings (Lyngar 1942; Greig et al. 1958; Hilkowitz 1960) while Gasser (1957) found that affected children frequently gave a personal or family history of allergy, such as eczema, asthma, drug sensitivity or anaphylactoid (Henoch-Schönlein) purpura. Sears et al. (1975) described a pair of identical siblings who both developed red cell aplasia during the course of viral hepatitis, but at an interval of several years. Though the anaemia was only transient, both cases progressed to 'chronic active hepatitis' with auto-antibody production. Since the causative virus was presumably of a different strain in the two cases, the occurrence of red cell aplasia in both patients suggests a genetically determined immune response, though no antibodies to erythroblasts were demonstrated.

It is possible that viruses or bacteria damage erythroid cells by direct cell-killing, as well as by an aberrant immune response, but the usually transient course of the marrow depression has made detailed studies difficult. There is evidence that a temporary increase in requirements for folic acid during infection, especially when superimposed on a subclinical deficiency associated with chronic haemolysis, can produce erythroid depression (Jandl & Greenberg 1959); there may be evidence of tissue depletion of folate during aplastic crises (Chanarin et al. 1962). Megaloblastosis, sometimes with giant proerythroblasts, has been described, though it is possible that the bizarre dyserythropoiesis frequently seen in marrows recovering from aplasia (p. 82) has occasionally been misinterpreted as true megaloblastic change (Erslev 1972). Defects in folate metabolism have been described in one form of constitutional aplastic anaemia (Branda et al. 1978) and viral infection of haemopoietic cells could conceivably produce transient biochemical derangements leading to erythroid depression. Sometimes there has been apparent response to large doses of folic acid, especially in the aplastic crises of chronic haemolysis, but true red cell aplasia probably does not respond to folic acid. For example, red cell hypoplasia (but not aplasia) has been described in two patients with pernicious anaemia and two with folate deficiency due, respectively, to alcoholism and pregnancy. All these patients suffered, in addition, from malnutrition, and two had significant renal impairment, while one had hypothyroidism. The response to the appropriate haematinic was suboptimal, as judged by the reticulocyte peak and rise in haemoglobin, but in each the erythroid marrow converted from hypoplastic to hyperplastic (Pezzimenti & Lindenbaum 1972). The biochemical lesion in the red cell hypoplasia occurring in severe nutritional states, such as marasmus and kwashiorkor, is probably due to a variable combination of deficiencies including protein, riboflavine, folic acid and ascorbic acid (Adams 1970). Specific amino acid deficiencies, such as those of tryptophan, lysine, phenylalanine and isoleucine, may be of particular importance. There is good experimental evidence that profound protein deprivation can cause failure of erythropoietin production in rats (Anagnostou et al. 1977), while there is clinical evidence that riboflavine deficiency can inhibit erythropoiesis in man (Alfrey & Lane 1970). A haemolytic component has also been demonstrated (Lanzkowsky et al. 1967). In a few patients with kwashiorkor, in which riboflavine deficiency has been particularly incriminated, administration of this vitamin has caused remission of the anaemia (Foy et al. 1961).

Profound red cell hypoplasia has occasionally been observed in both acute and chronic renal failure, usually in children (Richet et al. 1954; Gasser 1957; Pasternack & Wahlberg 1967). However, when it occurs it may be related to the cause of the renal failure, or its treatment, rather than directly to its biochemical sequelae, or failure of the kidney's 'endocrine' function. There is poor correlation between blood creatinine levels and the degree of erythroid depression. Moreover, erythropoiesis does not cease altogether, even after bilateral nephrectomy, presumably because erythropoietin is still produced in extrarenal sites; such anephric patients can still respond with a reticulocytosis to anoxia or haemorrhage (Nathan et al. 1964; de Strihon & Stragin 1969). Red cell aplasia has occasionally occurred in a child with the haemolytic–uraemic syndrome (Gasser 1957): both may have been due to a viral infection. The disorder has been noted in patients with chronic renal failure treated with azathioprine (McGrath et al. 1975).

Drugs

Red cell aplasia has been reported as a reaction to a substantial number of drugs, many of which are also suspected of causing panhypoplasia. Drug-induced red cell aplasia differs from panhypoplasia, however, in that it frequently recovers promptly after withdrawal of the drug. Although cause and effect should therefore be much easier to identify, in practice the situation is confused by the variable natural history of red cell aplasia, its tendency to spontaneous remissions, and the fact that in some reports the patient was also suffering from a disease which itself may be associated with red cell aplasia (Geary 1978). Frequently, the evidence rests with a few anecdotal reports, sometimes only one. Table 9.2 shows some of the drugs with which red cell aplasia has been associated, and the relevant case reports. In the case of phenytoin, relapse of the red cell aplasia was demonstrated on re-administration of the drug (Brittingham et al. 1964). This case was studied in detail by Yunis et al. (1967a). They found that the aplasia was reversible, but not affected by folinic acid or vitamin B12. No immunological lesion was demonstrable, but using ^{14}C labelled formate, glycine, orotic acid and uridine, it was shown that, *in vitro*, the drug inhibited DNA synthesis in erythroid cells, probably at the stage

Table 9.2. Drugs causing red cell aplasia*

Amphotericin B	Brandriss et al. (1964)
Acetylsalicylic acid	Wintrobe (1974)
Azathioprine	McGrath et al. (1975)
Carbamazepine	Hirai (1977)
Chloramphenicol	Scott et al. (1965)
	Best (1967)
Colchicine	Wintrobe (1974)
Carbimazole	Greene and Morgan (1956)
Chlorpropamide	Recker and Hynes (1969)
Cotrimoxazole	Stephens (1974)
Diphenylhydantoin	Brittingham et al. (1964)
	Jeong et al. (1974)
Gold	Reid and Patterson (1977)
Halothane	Jurgensen et al. (1970)
Isoniazid, PAS	Goodman and Black (1964)
Phenylbutazone	Swineford et al. (1958)
	Ibrahim et al. (1966)
Sulphonamides	Seaman and Koler (1953)
Tolbutamide	Schmid et al. (1963)
Benzene, benzene hexachloride	Schmid et al. (1963)

* Aspirin, butobarbitone and heparin are cited as rare causes of red cell aplasia in a report sponsored by the American Medical Association (1967). Methyl-dopa was reported to cause depression of erythropoiesis in a patient described by Devlin (1965) but no marrow aspirate was obtained.

of deoxyribotide formation, but had no effect on other haemopoietic cells. This is probably the only case in which a selective biochemical lesion, affecting exclusively the erythroid cells in the marrow transit compartment, has been demonstrated. The assumption is that other drugs can produce analogous reversible lesions, and perhaps cause red cell aplasia by mechanisms different from those which produce panhypoplasia. The confusion which surrounds this subject is well illustrated by chloramphenicol. This drug is cited as a cause of selective red cell aplasia by several authors (Ozer et al. 1960; Best, 1967) and has been noted in association with the aplastic crisis (Yunis & Bloomberg 1964); it has been suggested that the red cell hypoplasia may be a prelude to a more severe dose-related panhypoplasia (Scott et al. 1965). Although chloramphenicol undoubtedly causes a functional suppression of erythropoiesis with maturation arrest and vacuolation, probably due to a mitochondrial lesion, and this may be associated, transiently, with complete disappearance of erythroblasts from the marrow, these changes are usually rapidly reversible on withdrawing the drug (p. 30). In their careful review of 576 cases of blood dyscrasias due to chloramphenicol, Polak et al. (1972) failed to identify any cases of established pure red cell aplasia among them. If a drug were to produce chronic red cell aplasia, outlasting elimination of the drug, it would presumably do so by an immunological mechanism, since a biochemical lesion would only operate while the drug was present in the tissues. Theoretically, at least, drugs could cause chronic red cell aplasia if stem cells, committed to erythropoiesis, possess specific surface antigens, or metabolic pathways which might be vulnerable to an (auto-) immune attack (see Chapter 2). The favourable results of treatment with corticosteroids of children with the Blackfan–Diamond syndrome, and the recent finding that blood lymphocytes from such patients can suppress erythroid proliferation by normal bone marrow *in vitro* (Hoffman et al. 1976), suggests that such immunological mechanisms may exist.

CHRONIC RED CELL APLASIA

This is an uncommon disorder but it has fascinated haematologists for a quarter of a century because of its association with diseases known to have an autoimmune pathogenesis or in which disturbances of immune function are common. Although thymoma was the first of these to be recognized (Matras & Preisel 1928; Opsahl 1939), the majority of patients with thymic tumour do not show any haematological abnormality: the incidence of anaemia in thymoma is probably lower than that of myasthenia gravis. On the other hand, of the 170 or so published cases of red cell aplasia, approximately 50% have been reported to accompany a thymoma; however, as Erslev (1972) points out, this may considerably overestimate the actual incidence of thymoma in the disorder, since there is an understandable predilection to report cases in which two clinical rarities coincide. In any case, the proportion of thymoma-related cases is substantially lower in men than in women (Schmid et al. 1965). Since many cases of chronic red cell aplasia, of both the idiopathic and the thymoma-related types, are now considered to be autoimmune processes, it has been suggested that the presence of thymoma is simply an epiphenomenon of the underlying immune disturbance, and a division of the two groups may be artificial (Case Records of the Massachusetts General Hospital 1973). However, because of the frequently arresting clinical presentation of the thymoma-related cases, and the undoubted response of the anaemia to thymectomy in a proportion, there are practical, as well as historical, reasons for considering this group separately (Krantz 1976).

Red Cell Aplasia and Thymoma

Most of the literature on this subject has been in the form of anecdotal case reports, subsequently collected into major reviews to which the authors have contributed a small number of their own cases. Comprehensive reviews of the natural history of the syndrome include those of Chalmers and Boheimer (1954) Dreyfus et al. (1962), Roland (1964), Barnes (1965), Schmid et al. (1965), Hirst and Robinson (1967), Rogers et al. (1968) and Jeunet and Good (1969). The reported incidence of red cell aplasia, considering all thymic tumours, has varied from 2% in a detailed study of operative and autopsy material from 169 cases (Schmid et al. 1965) to about 10% in 31 cases in which a thymic tumour was demonstrated at surgery (Rubin et al. 1964); however, an overall incidence of about 5% seems likely (Goldstein & Mackay 1969). The syndrome is commoner in women, with a mean age in Hirst and Robinson's series of 59 years, although it does occur rarely in children (Talerman & Amigo 1968). More patients presented to the haematologist than the surgeon, the tumour being found during investigation of anaemia, but there are nevertheless well-documented cases of a thymoma being present for many years before anaemia ensued. There is no convincing report of a thymoma developing after the diagnosis of red cell aplasia, but examples of anaemia following thymectomy are quoted by Hirst and Robinson (1967) and documented by Safdar et al. (1970), Geary et al. (1975) and Bjørkholm et al. (1976). The interval between thymectomy and onset of anaemia has varied from a few months to 10 years or more. The symptoms at onset are those attributable to a refractory anaemia, but skin petechiae and occasionally even bleeding from mucous surfaces are mentioned; these patients have, as might be expected, usually shown an associated thrombocytopenia. Apart from those due to the thoracic tumour itself, such as chest pain, fever, weight loss and, rarely, superior vena caval obstruction (although this usually denotes an invasive neoplasm) (Jacobs et al. 1959), other symptoms have usually been those of associated disease. However, in Hirst and Robinson's series, 10 patients had hepatomegaly, while slight to moderate splenomegaly is mentioned by several authors.

Thymoma

The thymoma has usually been demonstrated by a conventional chest X-ray as an anterior or superior mediastinal mass (Fig. 9.1A) though, occasionally it was only found after tomography or pneumo-mediastinography. Undoubtedly, the tumour may be small enough to escape detection by all these means, for instance Green (1958) records

Fig. 9.1. Chest radiograph and histological detail from a male patient with thymoma-related red cell aplasia. Profound red cell hypoplasia followed 6 months after removal of the tumour, which weighed 300 g. The thymoma in this case showed predominantly round and oval epithelial cells, with some lymphocytes. ×600.

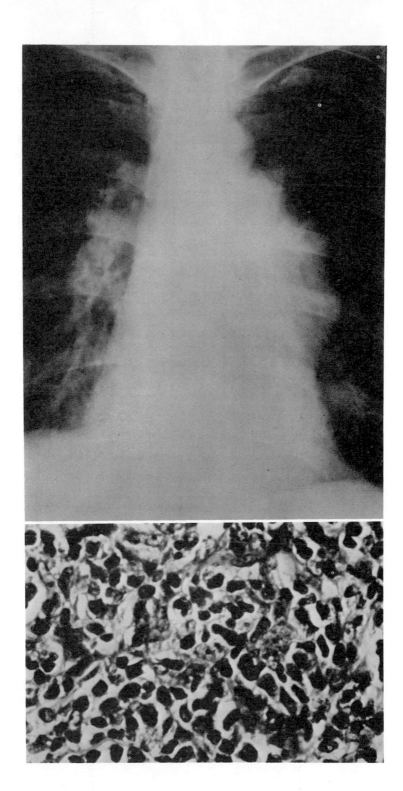

a case in which a thymoma measuring 4 cm in diameter was eventually found at necropsy. Hirst and Robinson record five cases in which the tumour was less than 5 cm in diameter; the largest weighed over 1 kg. There is no morphological feature in the thymic tumour which is pathognomonic for the presence of red cell aplasia, but in the majority of patients the tumour was encapsulated, lobulated, non-invasive and composed of epithelial cells of 'spindle' configuration; most of the remaining tumours consisted of round to oval epithelial cells (Fig. 9.1B). Occasionally, calcification is visible. The number of lymphocytes is extremely variable, but a few 'lymphocytic' tumours have been reported (Schmid et al. 1965; Rosai & Levine 1975). Hassall's corpuscles have either been absent or rudimentary. Fisher (1964) lists the rarer thymic abnormalities seen in association with red cell aplasia as thymic 'hyperplasia', mediastinal cysts and thymolipoma. Hodgkin's disease involving the thymus has been associated with red cell aplasia (Remigio 1971). Histologically malignant thymic tumours are rarely found in this syndrome, though up to 15% may show locally infiltrative features. However, patients who have multiple cytopenias, or in whom the marrow shows panhypoplasia (see p. 214) are more likely to belong to a group in whom the histological features are relatively heterogeneous, in contrast to the predominantly spindle-cell type seen in association with pure red cell aplasia (Schmid et al. 1965).

Associated Diseases

Thymoma can be associated with a wide spectrum of autoimmune disease (Souadjian et al. 1974) and it is likely that red cell aplasia can, in turn, occur with any of these (Fig. 9.2). However, the best documented associations are with myasthenia gravis (Hirst & Robinson 1967), systemic lupus erythematosus (Cassileth & Myers 1973), autoimmune haemolytic anaemia (Hirst & Robinson 1967; Eisemann & Dameshek 1954), Hashimoto's disease (Dawson 1972), the malabsorption syndrome (Gilbert et al. 1968), pernicious anaemia (Robins-Browne et al. 1977), and both hyper- and hypogammaglobulinaemia (Thiele & Frenzel 1967; Jeunet & Good 1969). Many cases also show serological stigmata of an autoimmune process, such as a positive red cell antiglobulin test, platelet or leucocyte antibodies, antinuclear antibodies, LE cells, antimitochondrial antibodies, antimuscle antibodies, cold agglutinins, or a false positive test for syphilis. Very often only one or two of these markers are found in an individual case (Krantz 1974); a positive LE phenomenon or test for antinuclear antibodies are probably the commonest. Finally, IgG antibodies inhibiting either erythropoietin, or its target cell, the primitive erythroblast, have been demonstrated in a few cases of thymoma-related red cell aplasia

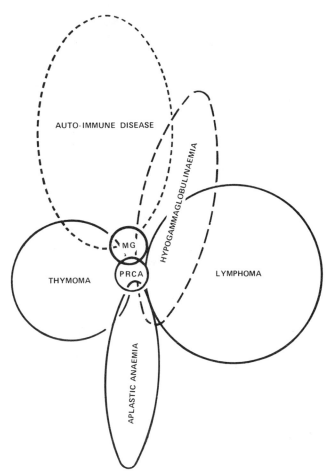

Fig. 9.2. The interrelationship of red cell aplasia (PRCA) with thymoma, myasthenia gravis (MG) and certain other disorders.

(Al-Mondhiry et al. 1971; Jepson & Vas 1974; Marmont et al. 1975).

One of the most intriguing associations is with hypogammaglobulinaemia. In one survey of thymic tumours, profound hypo-immunoglobulinaemia was found in 6% of 598 patients (Souadjian et al. 1974). Whereas the incidence of red cell aplasia in all thymomas is only about 5–6%, Jeunet and Good noted that it was much higher in patients with hypogammaglobulinaemia: of 20 patients collected from their own clinic and from the literature, seven had red cell aplasia or 'aregenerative anaemia'. In these patients, lymph node histology showed deficiency of germinal centres and plasma cells, while the thymic-dependent areas of the lymphoid organs seemed to be spared. However, functional tests have occasionally shown some depression of T-cell function, as well as those related to B-lymphocytes (Jeunet & Good 1968). Even when there was remission of anaemia after thymectomy, there was no improvement in immunological function. Frøland et al. (1976) have described significant depression of circulating surface immunoglobulin-bearing lymphocytes in red cell aplasia, with and without thymoma; by contrast T lymphocytes and those bearing Fc-receptors were normal.

Occasional patients have shown inhibitors to antigen-induced blastogenesis (Geary et al. 1975, Robins-Browne et al. 1977) while lymphocytes suppressing both immunoglobulin production and erythroid differentiation have been demonstrated in two patients with thymoma and hypogammaglobulinaemia, one of whom had repeated episodes of red cell aplasia (Litwin & Zantz 1977) though these persisted even when the anaemia was in remission, making their relationship to the clinical expression of red cell aplasia problematical.

Pathogenesis of Thymoma-Related Red Cell Aplasia

The relationship between thymoma and anaemia is perplexing, partly because the role of the thymus in normal erythropoiesis is unclear, though there is experimental evidence of collaboration between lymphoid or thymic cells and haemopoietic cells *in vivo* and *in vitro* (Schofield 1976) (see also p. 14). The thymus contains haemopoietic cells in young children (Albert et al. 1966) while Miller et al. (1965) found that thymectomy in fetal opossums not only interfered with development of lymphoid tissue but permitted persistence of splenic erythropoiesis, which normally involutes rapidly after birth. A similar effect has been described in mice thymectomized in the fetal period. The colony forming capacity of marrow from mice thymectomized in the neonatal period is reduced in comparison with that of normal animals (Zipori & Trainin 1975). An autoimmune haemolytic anaemia developed after thymectomy in certain strains of mice but paradoxically showed no reticulocytosis; these animals showed severe erythroid depression in the marrow but also often extramedullary erythropoiesis (Yunis et al. 1967*b*). It was suggested that an autoimmune process had produced both haemolysis in the blood and damage to developing erythroblasts. Although these experiments demonstrate a connection between the thymus and haemopoietic systems in the neonate their relevance to clinical red cell hypoplasia is doubtful; only one case has been described in which extramedullary erythropoiesis was conspicuous, and, although some show positive direct antiglobulin tests, in many haemolysis is not evident.

The fact that thymectomy results in remission in a proportion of cases suggests that the tumour is elaborating a substance which inhibits erythropoiesis, but attempts to extract such inhibitors from thymic tissue have usually been unsuccessful. However, Jepson and Vas (1974) showed in one case of thymoma-related red cell aplasia that an extract from thymic tissue apparently inhibited the action of erythropoietin on erythroid precursor cells, and in the case described by Al-Mondhiry et al. (1971) an inhibitor of erythropoiesis in the IgG fraction disappeared after thymectomy, although no inhibitor was isolated from the thymoma itself.

It is possible that, in patients who have hypogammaglobulinaemia, as well as red cell aplasia, in association with a thymoma, the 'tumour' arises as a result of attempts to induce or expand an involuting peripheral lymphatic system; hyperplasia—due to failure of the normal 'feed-back' homeostasis—eventually leads to metaplasia of the

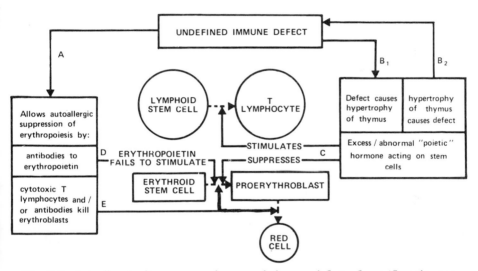

Fig. 9.3. Autoallergic diseases may be regarded as a defect of specific tolerance against 'self' components (A). There is an association between this defect and thymoma (B): the causality could run either way (1 or 2) (see text). Thymectomy in some species of mammals (C) leads to alterations in the pattern of erythropoiesis (see text), and in all mammals to a decrease in the production of new T lymphocytes. Possibly a slightly altered 'hormone' from a thymoma might suppress erythropoiesis in humans through the same hormone receptors on the stem cells. Alternatively a 'forbidden' lymphocyte clone might arise in an abnormal thymus and initiate an autoimmune attack against erythroblasts, leading to the production of antibodies to erythropoietin (D), which block its effect on the erythroid stem cell. Both cell-mediated and humoral effector mechanisms can cause cell death on the differentiation pathway from the erythroid stem cell to the mature red cell (E). This cytolytic action could occur at the CFU-C level or destroy more differentiated cells. (*By courtesy of Dr R. S. H. Pumfrey*)

thymic epithelial reticulum, which comes to resemble tumour (Jeunet & Good 1969). Such hyperactivity of the thymus might sustain the bursal equivalent system for a time before failure ensued and hypogammaglobulinaemia was observed. Possibly a 'forbidden clone' arises in the hypertrophied thymus; simultaneous red cell aplasia might then be due to autoimmune damage to erythroid precursor cells, or to elaboration of an abnormal thymic poietin which interferes with the development of erythroblasts; removal of the thymoma in this situation might improve haemopoietic function without necessarily improving B-cell function, if the underlying immunological abnormality resided in the lymphoid cells (Fig. 9.3).

Another possibility is that thymic tumour, anaemia and the immunological abnormality, when present, are all manifestations of a toxic injury or an autoimmune process which damages three tissues simultaneously but to a variable degree (Jeunet & Good 1969). The damage might be caused by lymphocytotoxins and in the early stages thymic enlargement would, again, represent an attempt to 'compensate'. The lymphocytotoxic substances could be of exogenous or endogenous origin, and might include viruses, chemicals or autoantibodies. This might explain why thymoma, red cell aplasia and hypogammaglobulinaemia may occur alone or in any combination, and the very variable temporal relationships between the three when they occur together in the same patient, as well as the results of thymectomy which might not be beneficial unless the thymus was mediating a humoral or cell-mediated antibody attack against erythroblasts.

Other Forms of Putative Autoimmune Red Cell Aplasia

Red cell aplasia with features indistinguishable from that occurring in association with thymoma, except that males and younger patients are more frequently affected, has been found as a 'primary' disorder or in the clinical context of an autoimmune or neoplastic disorder. Amongst autoimmune diseases with which red cell aplasia has been associated are systemic lupus erythematosus (Cassileth & Myers 1973), rheumatoid arthritis (Krantz 1976), autoimmune haemolytic anaemia (Eisemann & Dameshek, 1954), pernicious anaemia (Goldstein & Pechet 1965; Hotchkiss 1970), chronic active hepatitis (Zaentz et al. 1975) and hypogammaglobulinaemia (Linsk & Murray 1961). Two cases of chronic red cell aplasia have been reported in which relapses occurred during pregnancy (Skikne et al. 1976). Even in 'primary' cases in which no overt clinical evidence of another autoimmune disease is obvious, there may be serological markers of autoimmunity similar to those found in some patients with thymoma; moreover there is evidence that, in a proportion of patients, an immune inhibition of erythropoiesis is responsible for the development of red cell aplasia. A proportion of these will repsond to prednisolone or other immuno-suppressant therapy.

Amongst neoplastic disorders in which red cell aplasia has occurred are: chronic lymphatic leukaemia (Dameshek et al. 1967), myeloma (Abeloff & Waterbury 1974), Hodgkin's disease (Bauman & Swisher 1967; Field et al. 1968), lymphoma (Jepson & Vas 1974; Dumont 1974) chronic myeloid leukaemia (Frøland et al. 1976), and carcinomas of the bronchus (Entwhistle et al. 1964), breast (Clarkson & Prockup 1958; Green 1958), gastrointestinal tract (Mitchell et al. 1971; Gajwani 1976) and pancreas (Lipa & Ley 1966). Occasionally red cell aplasia is accompanied by a paraprotein in the blood without at first other evidence of an immunoproliferative disorder (Prasad et al. 1968; Fink et al. 1977). Humoral inhibitors of erythropoiesis have been demonstrated in several of these cases. However, red cell aplasia seems to be an uncommon complication of neoplasia.

The Role of Antibodies in the Pathogenesis of Red Cell Aplasia

Red cell aplasia occurs as a result of the action of hetero-, iso- and autoantibodies, and also possibly cell-mediated cytotoxic mechanisms. One of the first observations that red cell hypoplasia might be due to abnormal immunological mechanisms was that of Smith (1949), who described a case of 'aregenerative anaemia' occurring as a result of fetal–maternal ABO isoimmunization. A number of patients with chronic autoimmune haemolytic anaemia were described in whom episodes of profound erythroblastopenia and reticulocytopenia occurred (Eisemann & Dameshek 1954; Gasser 1957; Burston et al. 1959; Meyer & Bertcher 1962). Pirofsky (1969) suggested that the avidity and total amount of autoantibody in relation to the antigenic 'environment' is important in determining these. The total number of mature erythrocytes greatly exceeds that of precursor cells, and these will normally bind most of the antibody. Although the antigenic sites involved in autoimmune haemolysis are expressed most strongly on mature red cells, there is good evidence that erythroblast precursors can react with red cell antibodies (Yamamoto 1965). A sudden rise in antibody titre, or increase in its avidity, might 'swamp' the peripheral red cell mass and cause marrow damage and, occasionally, it has been shown that erythroid aplasia remits as the antiglobulin test becomes negative (Dameshek et al. 1967). This explanation might be difficult to reconcile with the comparative rarity of red cell aplasia in auto-immune haemolysis. Moreover, it is not clear why coating of intra-medullary erythroblasts with antierythrocyte IgG antibody should cause lysis *in situ* since these incomplete antibodies are not usually cytolytic and normally require the interaction of splenic or hepatic reticuloendothelial macrophages before cell death occurs. Electron microscopy shows that ingestion of marrow erythroblasts by RE cells does sometimes occur in idiopathic red cell aplasia (Böttiger 1974), but this has not been observed, specifically, in the type associated with autoimmune haemolysis. Other autoantibodies associated with the underlying immunological defect or deficiency may be responsible (Kontek 1965). It may also be significant that splenectomy is some-times effective in producing marrow remissions in this syndrome (Eisemann & Dameshek 1954), just as in primary autoimmune red cell aplasia, suggesting some splenohumoral mechanism. The role of drugs, incidental infections and folate deficiency must not be forgot-ten. It is of some interest that HLA isoantibodies can produce reticulocytopenia and probably damage erythroblasts (Zervas et al. 1972).

Schooley and Garcia (1962) produced an animal model of red cell aplasia by injecting mice with a heteroimmune antierythropoietin and producing depression of erythropoiesis. In 1966, Jepson and Lowen-stein studied two patients with red cell aplasia, one of whom had a thymoma, and demonstrated a circulating inhibitor which depressed erythropoiesis in the mouse, while Barnes (1966) showed that a factor, obtained from plasma in thymoma-related red cell aplasia, caused *in vitro* inhibition of cell growth and proliferation of normal marrow. Suppression of stem-cell colony formation in irradiated mice was also seen (Field et al. 1968). Krantz and his colleagues have shown that these inhibitors are more frequently directed against erythroblast precursors than erythropoietin itself (Krantz & Kao 1967, 1969). Two patients with red cell aplasia had a circulating inhibitor of haem synthesis, and, using an immunofluorescent antibody technique, antibody to erythroblast nuclei was demonstrated. When freed from their own plasma, marrow cells from such patients responded to erythropoietin with a large increase in haemoglobin synthesis. Moreover, an IgG globulin fraction, obtained from a patient in relapse, inhibited haemo-globin synthesis in erythropoietic marrow obtained after successful immunosuppressive therapy; his post-treatment plasma did not have this effect. Comparable results were reported by Jepson and her colleagues (1968) who also demonstrated an inhibitor of erythroblast DNA synthesis in the plasma of some patients with red cell aplasia. Demonstration of the inhibitor of haem synthesis *in vitro* correlated well with clinical response to immunosuppressants. An IgG antibody which was cytotoxic for erythroblast precursors (obtained from the same patient after remission) was demonstrated by labelling cells with ^{59}Fe and exposing them to pre-treatment serum; damage to erythroblasts was measured by release of the isotope into the culture medium (Krantz et al. 1972). Later studies suggested that erythroid depression was associated with cytotoxic complement-dependent antibodies or immune complexes, present in four of seven cases, which disappeared after successful treatment. The interrelationship of these various inhibitors of erythroblasts is problematical, but Zaentz and Krantz (1973) suggest that the inhibitor of haem·synthesis may be identical with the cytotoxic antibody; antinuclear antibody could be formed secondarily to erythroblast damage resulting from cytotoxic antibody attacking the cell surface. Antibodies might be directed against 'developmental' antigens expressed only on erythroblast precursors. Membrane-bound IgG antibody, believed specific for marrow erythroblasts, was found in a patient with thymoma-associated red cell hypoplasia whose conventional antiglobulin test was negative (Bjørkholm et al. 1976). IgG antibodies might block specific receptors on erythropoietin-sensitive cells.

Most patients of this type have high (though ineffective) levels of circulating erythropoietin (Peschle & Condorelli 1976). Peschle and Condorelli showed that the addition of anti-human gamma-globulin to the serum would usually restore its erythropoiesis-stimulating activity, thus demonstrating that there was no chemical interaction between inhibitor and erythropoietin, which would be anticipated if there were antigen–antibody linkage. Nevertheless, these workers have demonstrated occasional patients with red cell aplasia in whom erythropoietin levels were very low, using both *in vitro* erythroblast culture and the ex-hypoxic polycythaemic mouse as an assay system; boiling the serum (erythropoietin being relatively thermostable) destroyed an inhibitor and demonstrated the presence of biologically active erythropoietin. The inhibitor was, again, found to be an IgG antibody which was abolished by immunosuppressive therapy. In six of seven cases of red cell aplasia, Peschle and Condorelli (1976) found that antibodies to erythropoiesis were directed against the marrow cells (Type I). One had an IgG inhibitor of circulating erythropoietin (Type II) (Peschle et al. 1975). The marrow 'level' at which Type I antibodies act is uncertain; it may be the differentiated (morphologically recognizable) erythroblast, but Peschle has suggested primary damage to a morphologically undifferentiated precursor cell, recently formed from the erythropoietin-responsive cell, or CFU-E (Fig. 9.4); there is evidence, from agar cultural studies, that CFU-E cloning from normal marrows is inhibited by up to 50% by the sera of some patients with red cell aplasia in relapse (Ghio et al. 1976): CFU-E production from the marrows of such patients was much reduced, but not completely absent. Moreover, some cases of red cell 'aplasia' do show small

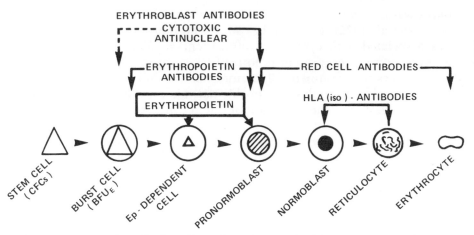

Fig. 9.4. Humoral antibodies directed against erythroblast precursors, showing possible target cells. Lymphocyte-mediated processes (see text) are not shown. These antibodies could arise as a result of iso-immunization, but in some cases seem to be related to the pathogenesis of red cell aplasia.

numbers of proerythroblasts in their marrows, suggesting that limited maturation is still possible (Zaentz et al. 1975). Gill et al. (1977) suggest that the rather variable degrees of erythroid hypoplasia seen in this autoimmune syndrome would be explicable if elevated erythropoietin levels are stimulating erythropoiesis, but with simultaneous destruction of erythroid cells by cytotoxic antibodies at the proerythroblast or polychromatophilic stage. Significantly, Jepson and Vas (1974) found that, in some patients with red cell aplasia, very high levels of erythropoietin sometimes made demonstration of an inhibitor in an *in vitro* system difficult, although it could be identified by diluting the plasma, or by physical separation.

Peschle and Condorelli (1976) summarize the evidence that these autoantibodies are pathogenetically related to the erythroid depression as follows: (*a*) the inhibitor is confined to the IgG serum fraction, (*b*) it disappears after successful immunosuppressive therapy and (*c*) experimental models for both types of human red cell aplasia have been established in rodents, while IgG fractions from some patients will inhibit erythropoiesis in normal human marrows. Nevertheless, some patients with idiopathic red cell aplasia in whom no humoral autoantibodies have been demonstrated have still responded to immunosuppressants; these patients may be of the same type but possess titres of antibodies too small to demonstrate, or may result from a different type of damage. Thus, lymphocytes capable of suppressing erythropoiesis have been demonstrated in some children with congenital erythroblastopenia who respond to corticosteroids (p. 16): some adult cases of acquired red cell aplasia might be of a similar type, or even late manifestations of the congenital form. Zaentz and Krantz (1973) suggest that certain other forms of refractory anaemia may result from autoantibodies to erythroblasts. These have been reported in a single case of acquired sideroblastic anaemia, who subsequently responded to azathioprine (Zervas et al. 1974). Interestingly, two patients with red cell aplasia responsive to immunosuppressants reported by Beard et al. (1978) initially showed marrow and isotopic pictures of dyserythropoiesis.

Other Types of Acquired Red Cell Aplasia

In some adult patients with red cell aplasia, inhibitors cannot be demonstrated and immunosuppressive drugs are ineffective (primary red cell aplasia type III). A history of exposure to myelotoxins is possibly commoner in this group. These cases include patients whose marrow abnormality is really a pre-leukaemic disorder (Pierre 1974); for example, 10% of cases of idiopathic red cell aplasia documented by Schmid et al. (1963) eventually developed acute leukaemia, and two cases, in whom no erythroblast antibodies were demonstrable, were reported by Peschle and Condorelli (1976) to develop leukaemia, while Dumont (1974) reported that in 38 cases of chronic red cell aplasia, without thymoma, observed in one clinic over a 12-year period, no fewer than 17 developed acute or 'subacute' granulocytic leukaemia. There may or may not be abnormalities of myelopoiesis or a significant increase in marrow blast cells; in one case, a persistent chromosomal abnormality was found in marrow cells for many months before the onset of leukaemia (Fitzgerald & Hamer 1971). Some patients with this type of red cell aplasia also eventually develop panhypoplasia (two of 38 in Dumont's series); they, too, usually do not show response to immunosuppressants, and the anaemia can be regarded as 'partial' stem-cell failure: progressive defects in the environment of the stem cell, or more probably in the stem cell itself, could lead from a selective cytopenia to full hypoplasia (see Chapter 1). It is of interest that in occasional cases of acquired red cell hypoplasia, marrow CFU-C are much reduced even when the peripheral granulocyte count is normal (Milner et al. 1977). These cases of gradual stem-cell failure might be regarded as the antithesis of myeloproliferative disorders, in which overproduction of the three cell lines occurs. Red cell aplasia has been recorded as a late (and usually pre-leukaemic) feature of myelofibrosis and myeloid metaplasia (Bentley et al. 1977).

HAEMATOLOGICAL DIAGNOSIS

The important diagnostic criteria of red cell aplasia are a severe, selective anaemia with minimal changes in other blood elements; profound reticulocytopenia; absence or virtual absence of erythroblasts in an otherwise cellular marrow; very poor ($< 10\%$) incorporation of ^{59}Fe into erythrocytes, and usually a high serum iron with near-saturation of the iron-binding capacity (Marmont 1974). Anaemia is normochromic and normocytic and the blood film does not show any diagnostic features: the macrocytosis often seen in the congenital form of erythroid hypoplasia is rare. In profound red cell hypoplasia, reticulocytes are completely absent and, in general, the absolute reticulocyte count is lower than in panhypoplasia, in which 'hot pockets' are often present (see p. 71). Thus in Hirst and Robinson's series of thymoma-related cases, of 48 recorded reticulocyte counts, 12 had no reticulocytes, and 31 had less than 1%; significantly, the prognosis was *worse* in those who had more than 1%, and who presumably had something other than 'pure' red cell aplasia. In a significant number of patients—possibly as least as high as 15% (Case Records of the Massachusetts General Hospital 1973)—red cell aplasia associated with thymoma has been accompanied by other cytopenia at diagnosis or later in the evolution of the disease (Rogers et al. 1968; Dawson 1972). The commonest is thrombocytopenia, which may be persistent. Granulocytopenia associated with red cell hypoplasia is less common and in such cases underlying panhypoplasia must be carefully excluded (Schmid et al. 1965).

In a review of 61 cases of anaemia associated with thymoma, Rogers et al. (1968) found that 10 patients eventually developed pancytopenia with marrow aplasia demonstrated in several; four of these had pancytopenia at diagnosis. However, pancytopenia may also occur in red cell aplasia if autoantibodies to granulocytes and platelets are present, and does not then have the same prognostic significance.

A woman of 71 presented with a history of increasing anaemia for 1 year, her haemoglobin finally reaching a nadir of 5·4 g/dl when the reticulocyte count was less than 0·1%. The granulocyte count was then 450/µl, but the platelet count was 200 000/µl. Marrow aspirate showed profound red cell hypoplasia, but granulopoiesis was active with a slight increase in primitive cells (Fig. 9.5). No thymoma was demonstrated. A pre-leukaemic disorder was at first suspected, but antinuclear antibodies were present and the red cell antiglobulin test was positive. Following prednisolone therapy, a reticulocytosis occurred, and the haemoglobin rose to 10·5 g/dl, while the granulocyte count recovered to 1200/µl. Later marrow aspiration showed the reappearance of erythroblasts and less conspicuous maturation arrest of granulopoiesis. Remission is sustained 6 months later. (Details by permission of Dr James Chang.)

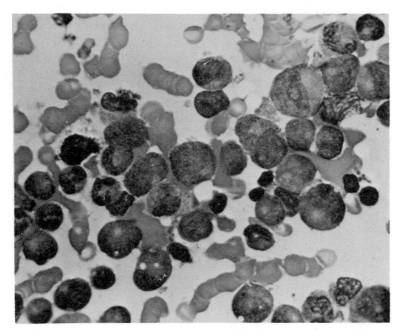

Fig. 9.5. Marrow from a patient with red cell aplasia, probably complicating disseminated lupus erythematosus. Severe granulocytopenia was present; both haemoglobin and granulocyte count rose after steroid therapy (see text).

Inhibitors of CFU-C as well as of CFU-E may be present in autoimmune disease and the marrow picture may then be hypocellular, but response to immunosuppressants has been reported in such cases (Cline & Golde 1978). Interestingly, both amegakaryocytic thrombocytopenia and agranulocytosis have been associated with thymoma (Thiele & Frenzel 1967; Sundstrom et al. 1972). Only very rarely does a patient presenting with pancytopenia revert to selective red cell hypoplasia. Lymphocyte counts are usually normal, though abnormalities of lymphocyte subpopulations may be present (see p. 206). A few patients have shown a mild blood lymphocytosis.

The marrow aspirate is typically normocellular, or even (when granulocytic hyperplasia is present) (Zaentz et al. 1975) hypercellular. Some cases show a complete or virtually complete absence of erythroblasts (Fig. 9.6). However, others do show erythroid activity—perhaps because autoimmune types run a fluctuating course—and if seen during one of these periods, erythroblasts may be present in marrow smears. Such as are present are immature but usually morphologically normal. In a study of 16 patients with red cell aplasia without thymoma, Schmid et al. (1963) found only three with complete absence

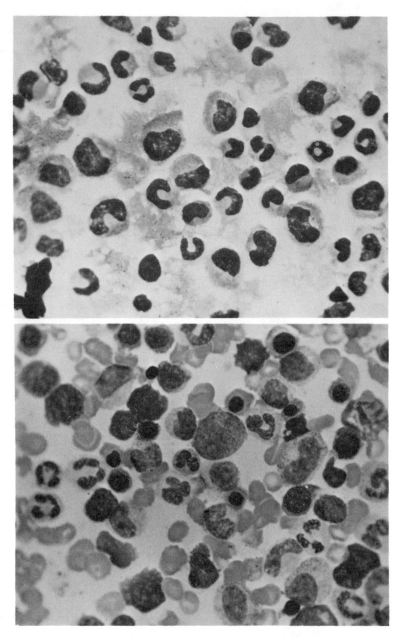

Fig. 9.6. Marrow from the second patient shown in Fig. 9.7 before and after immuno-suppressive therapy.

of erythroblasts, whereas the rest had between 0·2 and 6·2%. Gill et al. (1977) described three cases in whom the proportion of marrow erythroblasts ranged from 2 to 10%; all responded to immunosuppressants. Red cell hypoplasia may be more profound in cases associated with thymoma. The global nature of erythroid aplasia may be demonstrated by marrow scintigraphy (Bunn et al. 1976).

Although in every series, both with and without thymoma, a proportion have shown early marrow hypoplasia, these should probably be categorized separately, though cases presenting initially with selective red cell hypoplasia may develop, after a period of months or years, into aplastic anaemia (Schmid et al. 1965; Hirst & Robinson 1967; Rogers et al. 1968; Dumont 1974), so that the true diagnosis may not be obvious at the outset. Patients with marrow hypoplasia are much less likely than those with selective erythroid hypoplasia (Hirst & Robinson 1967) to respond to thymectomy or immunosuppressants.

In some cases, a conspicuous feature in the marrow has been the presence of small, densely staining cells resembling lymphocytes; on morphological grounds they have been identified as primitive haemopoietic cells ('haematogones'), abnormal myelocytes, degenerating erythroblasts or lymphocytes. Possibly they are morphological evidence of a chronic autoimmune process in the marrow, as they are especially conspicuous in some cases responsive to immunosuppressants (Marmont 1974). Nevertheless, similar cells have been noted in congenital erythroid hypoplasia, and even in nutritional anaemia. Occasionally, lymphoid follicles are present. Plasmacytosis may also be conspicuous.

^{51}Cr studies show a significant reduction in red-cell survival in some cases, and there may be evidence of splenic haemolysis in patients with positive antiglobulin tests or in those with hypersplenism associated with iron overload.

MANAGEMENT OF RED CELL APLASIA

The investigation and therapy of red cell aplasia have been well summarized by Krantz (1976) and Marmont (1976). Except in patients with haemolytic disorders, the onset of anaemia in red cell aplasia is usually insidious, since even complete cessation of haemoglobin production will result in a fall of haemoglobin of only about 1% each day. In chronic forms of the disorder, it is unlikely that erythropoiesis fails as rapidly, and since compensatory physiological changes, including increased 2,3-DPG production, occur during this time, it may be present for some time before a diagnosis is made. In children with chronic haemolysis, however, an episode of red cell aplasia will rapidly produce obvious symptoms of tissue anoxia. Jaundice usually becomes less conspicuous during the period of marrow failure, while bone pain may occur as it recovers.

Most patients with 'acute', transient, episodes of red cell aplasia recover within 2 months, and often much more quickly, so that a period of observation for this period is justifiable (Krantz 1976), particularly if there is a history of infection or exposure to drugs or chemicals known to cause aplasia; any suspected drug (see Table 9.2) should naturally be withdrawn. The blood creatinine is checked. Vitamin B12 and folate deficiency requires correction: evidence of malnutrition will prompt appropriate dietary measures. The patient often requires at least one blood transfusion, even if the disease is of a self-limiting type; the level of haemoglobin required will be dictated *inter alia* by the age of the patient and his cardiovascular status.

During this period, evidence of immunological abnormalities should be sought and thymoma excluded, if necessary using tomography; though open exploration of the mediastinum is probably not justifiable, some authorities recommend pneumo-mediastinography. Lymphoma and carcinoma are excluded as far as possible, and serum immunoglobulins examined for evidence of a paraprotein. If no recovery occurs within 3 months, it is likely that the patient has a chronic form of red cell aplasia, and if transfusions are still required, a decision about long-term management must be made. If a thymoma is present, it should be removed if possible, since, although the results are unpredictable, a significant number of patients subsequently enter remission; moreover, occasional patients may only respond to immunosuppressive therapy after thymectomy.

Response to Thymectomy

The results of thymectomy have varied: some workers have reported remission rates as high as 29% (Jacobs et al. 1959), others have had less good results, though these were improved if thymectomy was followed by immunosuppressive therapy. For example, Hirst and Robinson (1967) had an initial remission rate of 15% but this was improved to 30% if corticosteroids were used later. The time interval between surgery and remission of anaemia is also variable, from a few weeks to several months, and improvement is not always sustained. However, some very long remissions have occurred (Kaung et al. 1968), though it must not be forgotten that spontaneuous remissions occasionally occur (Anderson & Ladefoged 1963). Patients with marrow panhypoplasia rarely repond to thymectomy (Rogers et al. 1968). Most of the reports of 'aplastic anaemia' responding to thymectomy (Humphreys & Southworth 1945) appear to have been cases of red cell aplasia.

Usually surgical removal is required, and X-irradiation has rarely influenced the anaemia. In a few cases, it has been possible to demonstrate the disappearance of an immunological abnormality which might have been implicated in the pathogenesis of the disease. Thus, Al-Mondhiry et al. (1971) showed that their patient lost a serum inhibitor of erythropoiesis after thymectomy, while Robins-Browne et al. (1977) showed that in their case of thymoma associated with multiple immunological defects, including red cell aplasia, an inhibitor of haem synthesis disappeared after thymectomy had produced a remission of the anaemia. Several other markers of autoimmunity were not affected.

Immunosuppressive Therapy

If no thymoma is present, or if there is no response to thymectomy, the patient may still respond to immunosuppressants. This is probably more likely if markers of an immunological abnormality are present, particularly antibodies directed at erythroblasts or erythropoietin. If red cell aplasia has occurred in the setting of an autoimmune disease, treatment is normally directed at the underlying disorder which may, itself, be susceptible to immunosuppressive therapy. However, a proportion of patients with chronic red cell aplasia will benefit from immunosuppressants, even when no inhibitor is demonstrated. It is reasonable, therefore, to perform a therapeutic trial of these drugs even if the clinical evidence of autoimmunity is not strong. Prednisolone is often of less value in this syndrome than antimetabolites or cytotoxic drugs, though it has occasionally been effective alone (Di Giacomo et al. 1966; Böttiger & Rausig 1972; Beard et al. 1978) or after failed thymectomy (Hirst & Robinson 1967) and in younger patients (Gasser 1957; Skikne et al. 1976) in whom, in any case, prolonged administration of cytotoxic drugs may be undesirable because of the grave risk of causing sterility (Krantz 1976). Other immunosuppressants which have been employed are 6-mercaptopurine, cyclophosphamide, and cyclophosphamide in combination with prednisolone or antilymphocyte globulin (Marmont et al. 1975; Zaentz et al. 1976). Krantz (1976) has treated 8 adults with regimens of this kind and reports remissions in five. Since treatment is inevitably a therapeutic 'trial', the haematological response must be carefully monitored with twice weekly blood counts, including absolute reticulocyte counts (see p. 64). Krantz (1974) recommends a gradual increase in the daily dose of azathioprine or cyclophosphamide in the hope of administering a substantial amount before bone marrow depression occurs: up to 200 mg of cyclophosphamide a day may be tolerated for short periods, though an intractable haemorrhagic cystitis may limit its use (see p. 144). While a reticulocytosis will occasionally occur within a few days of starting therapy, there is often no response for several weeks, and it may not be seen until the drug is withdrawn following incipient bone marrow hypoplasia. Careful monitoring of granulocyte and platelet counts is therefore mandatory. Remissions induced by immunosuppressive therapy may be permanent (Gill et al. 1976), especially in younger patients, but very often relapse occurs within 1–3 years, though second and even third remissions have been obtained (Krantz 1976): presumably these patients have an irreversible change in immune tolerance which drug therapy only suppresses for a limited period. Cytotoxic drugs may have to be given for long periods to sustain remission (Zaentz et al. 1976). Occasionally morphological or serological evidence of dyserythropoiesis may persist while a patient is in clinical remission (Marmont 1974). The recent reports of successful treatment of myasthenia gravis by plasma-pheresis (Dau et al. 1977) suggest that this technique might be of value in red cell aplasia due to circulating inhibitors (Cline & Good 1978).

Splenectomy

Another form of therapy sometimes, and inexplicably, of benefit is splenectomy. The first observed successes were in patients with con-comitant autoimmune haemolytic anaemia, but there are several reports of remission in patients with apparently primary red cell aplasia or in association with thymoma (Chalmers & Boheimer 1954; Dreyfus et al. 1963; Safdar et al. 1970; Zaentz et al. 1975). The author has seen two cases of this type respond to splenectomy, and their course is illustrated in Fig. 9.7.

The first patient, a young woman of 21, presented with a refractory anaemia, associated with a variable leucopenia. The marrow was cellular but showed erythroid depression with maturation arrest at the proerythro-blast stage; there were increased numbers of lymphocytes. Although there was a moderate shortening of the ^{51}Cr red cell survival, the antiglobulin test was negative and the reticulocyte count less than 1%. It was suspected she might have a lymphoma, and this seemed more likely when, 2 years later, the spleen became palpable, although she had by then received approxi-mately 60 units of blood at 3-week intervals. Following removal of the spleen, which weighed 360 g and showed only signs of haemosiderosis, the haemoglobin rose slowly to normal and transfusion has not been required

Fig. 9.7. Two patients with red cell aplasia who responded to splenectomy. Marrow from patient R.D. showed some proerythroblasts, but there was severe maturation arrest of erythropoiesis and heavy infiltration with 'lymphoid' cells. Patient V.R. showed profound red cell aplasia.

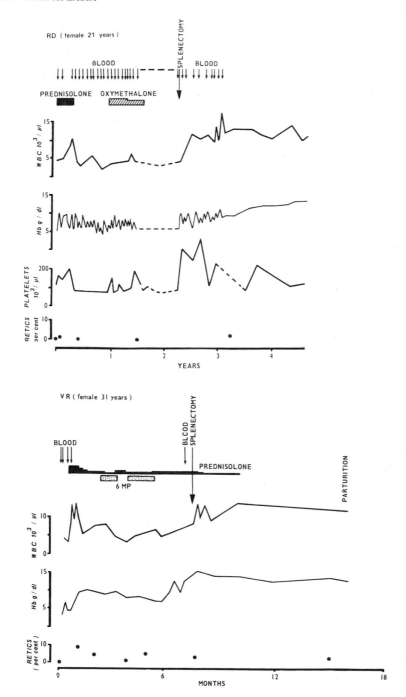

for 3 years. However, CFU-E production by this patient's marrow remains abnormally low, and there is still lymphocytic 'infiltration' of the marrow.

The second case was a woman of 31 who presented with a sudden onset of anaemia. Initial investigations (Dr R. D. Popham) confirmed a diagnosis of pure red cell aplasia. Several blood transfusions were necessary. There was good haematological response to prednisolone, with reappearance of marrow erythroblasts and a reticulocytosis. However, severe psychological symptoms necessitated reduction of prednisolone. 6-Mercaptopurine was used but caused neutropenia; the patient developed pneumonia and a severe herpes zoster infection, with a fall in haemoglobin to 7 g/dl. On withdrawal of this drug, and increasing the dose of prednisolone to 10 mg, the haemoglobin rose to 10 g/dl but then began to fall. A further blood transfusion was given, and splenectomy performed. Following splenectomy, the haemoglobin rose to normal and it was possible to discontinue prednisolone altogether. Four years later she remains in good health and has given birth to a healthy child. Although a spontaneous remission of red cell aplasia cannot be excluded in this case, splenectomy seems to have had a beneficial effect on the natural history of the disease.

Splenectomy removes a large number of antibody forming cells and is of itself a form of immunosuppression, but whether it interrupts a more specific splenomyeloid inhibition, as has been postulated (Eisemann & Dameshek 1954), is unknown. Unlike the effects in other autoimmune cytopenias, remissions after splenectomy in red cell aplasia may occur only gradually and after a delay. Krantz (1976) emphasizes that splenectomy should be carried out if immuno-suppressive therapy fails; conversely immunosuppressive therapy should be tried again after an unsuccessful splenectomy. However, many patients will not respond to the operation.

There remains a group—between a third and a half of adult patients—whose anaemia will not improve with any of these measures. Excluding those who have a progressive leukaemic disorder, survival is probably rather better than in patients with panhypoplasia, because bleeding and infections are not usually clinical problems and a few will respond to androgens, such as oxymethalone. For the rest, blood transfusion at regular intervals, as necessary, is the only therapy of value: these patients face the risks attendant on any long-term transfusion programme, such as transfusion reactions, hepatitis and haemosiderosis. Eventually it may be possible to define a group with intrinsic stem-cell defects in whom marrow transplantation should be considered.

SUMMARY

Red cell aplasia is an uncommon but not excessively rare disorder, in which there is a selective depression of erythroid precursors in the marrow, granulopoiesis and thrombopoiesis being well preserved.

Cases occur as transient episodes, often following infections, or drug exposure, but these only rarely become chronic, and may go unnoticed unless the patient has a concomitant haemolytic disorder.

Chronic red cell aplasia is of at least two main types: one occurs in the setting of a defect in immunohomeostasis, of which a thymoma is the most striking accompaniment; a proportion of these will respond to thymectomy. Other cases, not associated with thymoma, nevertheless show markers of an autoimmune process, including autoantibodies to erythroid precursors or erythropoietin: some of these will respond to immunosuppressants. A second group, probably accounting for at least a third of all chronic cases, represent an intrinsic defect in the haemopoietic stem cell or its regulatory environment, and in these, immunosuppressive therapy is usually ineffective and evolution into panhypoplasia or leukaemia more likely.

REFERENCES

ABELOFF, M. D. & WATERBURY, L. (1974) Pure red cell aplasia and chronic lymphocytic leukaemia. Archs intern. Med., 134, 721.

ADAMS, E. B. (1970) Anaemia associated with protein deficiency. Semin. Hemat., 7, 55.

ALBERT, S., WOLF, P. L., PRYJMA, I. & VASQUEZ, J. (1966) Erythropoiesis in the human thymus. Am. J. clin. Path., 45, 460.

ALFREY, C. P. & LANE, M. (1970) The effect of riboflavin deficiency on erythropoiesis. Semin. Hemat., 7, 49.

AL-MONDHIRY, H., ZANJANI, E. D., SPIVACK, M., ZALUSKY, R. & GORDON, A. S. (1971) Pure red cell aplasia and thymomas: loss of serum inhibitor of erythropoiesis following thymectomy. Blood, 38, 576.

AMERICAN MEDICAL ASSOCIATION (1967) Registry on Adverse Reactions, Panel of Hematology. Council on Drugs.

ANAGNOSTOU, A., SCHADE, S., ASHKINAZ, M., BARORE, J. & FRIED, W. (1977) Effect of protein deprivation on erythropoiesis. Blood, 50, 1093.

ANDERSON, S. B. & LADEFOGED, J. (1963) Spontaneous remissions in thymoma related pure red cell aplasia. Acta haemat., 30, 319.

BARNES, R. D. (1965) Thymic neoplasms associated with refractory anaemia. Guy's Hosp. Rep., 114, 73.

BARNES, R. D. (1966) Refractory anaemia and thymoma. Lancet, ii, 1464.

BAUMAN, A. W. & SWISHER, S. N. (1967) Hyporegenerative processes in hemolytic anemia. Semin. Hemat., 4, 265.

BEARD, M. E. J., KRANTZ, S. B., JOHNSON, S. A. N., BATEMAN, C. J. T. & WHITEHOUSE, J. M. A. (1978) Pure red cell aplasia. Q. Jl. Med., 187, 339.

BENTLEY, S. A., MURRAY, K. H., LEWIS, S. M. & ROBERTS, P. D. (1977) Erythroid hypoplasia in myelofibrosis: a feature associated with blastic transformation. Br. J. Haemat., 36, 41.

BEST, W. R. (1967) Chloramphenicol associated blood dyscrasias. J. Am. med. Ass., 201, 181.

BJØRKHOLM, M., HOLM, G., MELLSTEDT, H., CARLBERGER, G. & NISELL, J. (1976) Membrane bound IgG on erythroblasts in pure red cell aplasia following thymectomy. Scand. J. Haemat., 17, 341.

BÖTTIGER, L. E. (1974) Electron miscroscopy observations and immunosuppressive therapy in a case of adult red cell aplasia. Proc. XV Congr. int. Soc. Haemat., Jerusalem, 522.

BÖTTIGER, L. E. & RAUSIG, A. (1972) Pure red cell anaemia: immunosuppressive treatment. *Ann. intern. Med.*, 76, 593.

BRANDRISS, M. W., WOLFF, S. M., MOORES, R. & STOHLMAN, F. (1964) Anaemia induced by amphotericin B. *J. Am. med. Ass.*, 189, 663.

BRITTINGHAM, T. E., LUTCHER, C. L. & MURPHY, B. L. (1964) Reversible erythroid hypoplasia induced by diphenylhydantoin. *Archs intern. Med.*, 113, 764.

BRANDA, R. F., MOLDOW, C. F., MACARTHUR, J. R., WINTROBE, M. M., ANTHONY, B. K. & JACOB, H. S. (1978) Folate-induced remission in aplastic anaemia with familial defect of cellular folate uptake. *New Engl. J. Med.*, 298, 69.

BUNN, H. F., MCNEIL, B. J., ROSENTHAL, D. S. & KRANTZ, S. B. (1976) Bone marrow imaging in pure red blood cell aplasia. *Archs intern. Med.*, 136, 1169.

BURSTON, J., HUSAIN, O. A. N., HUTT, M. S. R. & TANNER, E. I. (1959) Two cases of autoimmune haemolysis and aplasia. *Br. med. J.*, 2, 1514.

CASE RECORDS OF THE MASSACHUSETTS GENERAL HOSPITAL (1973) *New Engl. J. Med.*, 288, 729.

CASSILETH, P. A. & MYERS, A. R. (1973) Erythroid hypoplasia in systemic lupus erythematosus. *Am. J. Med.*, 55, 706.

CHALMERS, J. N. H. & BOHEIMER, K. (1954) Pure red cell anaemia in patients with thymic tumours. *Br. med. J.*, 2, 1514.

CHANARIN, I., BANKHAN, P., PEACOCK, M. & STAMP, T. C. B. (1964) Acute arrest of haemopoiesis. *Br. J. Haemat.*, 10, 43.

CHANARIN, I., BURMAN, D. & BENNETT, M. C. (1962) The familial aplastic crisis in hereditary spherocytosis: urocanic acid and formiminoglutamic acid excretion studies in a case with megaloblastic arrest. *Blood*, 20, 33.

CLARKSON, B. & PROCKUP, B. J. (1958) Aregenerative anaemia associated with benign thymoma. *New Engl. J. Med.*, 259, 253.

CLINE, M. J. & GOLDE, D. W. (1978) Immune suppression of haematopoiesis. *Am. J. Med.*, 64, 301.

CROSBY, W. H. (1953) Paroxysmal nocturnal haemoglobinuria: report of a case complicated by an aregenerative (aplastic) crisis. *Ann. intern. Med.*, 39, 1007.

DAMESHEK, W. & BLOOM, M. L. (1948) The events of the haemolytic crisis of hereditary spherocytosis with particular reference to the reticulocytopenia, pancytopenia and abnormal splenic mechanism. *Blood*, 3, 1381.

DAMESHEK, W., BROWN, S. M. & RUBIN, A. D. (1967) 'Pure' red cell anaemia (erythroblastic hypoplasia) and thymoma. *Semin. Hemat.*, 4, 222.

DAU, P. J., LINDSTROM, J. M., CASSEL, C. K., DENYS, E. H., SHEV, E. E. & SPITLER, L. E. (1977) Plasmapheresis and immunosuppressive drug therapy in myasthenia gravis. *New Engl. J. Med.*, 297, 1134.

DAWSON, M. A. (1972) Thymoma associated with pancytopenia and Hashimoto's thyroiditis. *Am. J. Med.*, 52, 406.

DEVLIN, J. G. (1965) Methyl-dopa as a cause of erythroid depression. *Br. med. J. ii*, 1184.

DI GIACOMO, J., FURST, S. W. & NIXON, D. D. (1966) Primary acquired red cell aplasia in the adult. *J. Mt Sinai Hosp.*, 33, 882.

DE STRIHON, C. VAN Y. & STRAGIN, A. (1969) Effects of bilateral nephrectomy on transfusion requirements of patients undergoing chronic renal dialysis. *Lancet*, ii, 703.

DREYFUS, B., AUBERT, P., PATTE, D., FRAY, A. & LE BOLLOC'H-COMBRISSON, A. (1962) Erythroblastopénie chronique avec tumeur du thymus. Analyse de 43 observations. *Nouv. Revue fr. Hémat.*, 2, 739.

DREYFUS, B., AUBERT, P., PATTE, D. & LE BOLLOC'H-COMBRISSON, A. (1963) Erythroblastopénie chronique découverte après une thymectomie, Heureux effets de la corticothérapie à forte dose après échec de doses moyennes. *Nouv. Revue fr. Hémat.*, 3, 765.

DUMONT, J. (1974) Clinical studies on 38 cases of chronic red cell aplasia in the adult. *Proc. XV Congr. int. Soc. Haemat., Jerusalem*, 543.

EISEMANN, G. & DAMESHEK, W. (1954) Splenectomy for 'pure red cell" hypoplasia (aregenerative anaemia) associated with autoimmune haemolytic disease. *New Engl. J. Med.*, 251, 1044.

ENTWHISTLE, C. C., FENTEM, P. H. & JACOBS, A. (1964) Red cell aplasia with carcinoma of the bronchus. *Br. med. J.*, *2*, 1504.

ERSLEV, A. J. (1972) In: *Haematology*, ed. W. J. Williams, E. B. Beutler, A. J. Erslev and R. W. Rundles, p. 280. London: McGraw-Hill.

FIELD, E. D., CAUGHI, M. N., BLACKETT, N. M. et al. (1968) Marrow-suppressing factors in the blood in pure red cell aplasia, thymoma and Hodgkin's disease. *Br. J. Haemat.*, *15*, 101.

FINK, U., EMMERICH, B. & RASTETTER, J. (1977) Pure red cell aplasia with paraprotein-aemia. *Proc. 4th Meet. europ. Div. int. Soc. Haemat.*, 624.

FISHER, E. R. (1964) Pathology of the thymus and its relation to human diseases. In: *The Thymus in Immunobiology*, ed. R. A. Good & A. E. Gabridson. New York: Harper & Row.

FITZGERALD, P. H. & HAMER, J. W., (1971) Primary acquired red cell hypoplasia associated with a clonal chromosomal abnormality and disturbed erythroid pro-liferation. *Blood*, *38*, 325.

FOY, H., KONDI, A. & MACDOUGALL, L. (1961) PRCA in marasmus and kwashiorkor treated with riboflavin. *Br. med. J.*, *i*, 937.

FRØLAND, S. S., WISLØFF, F. & STAVEN, P. (1976) Abnormal lymphocyte populations in pure red cell aplasia. *Scand. J. Haemat.*, *17*, 241.

GAJWANI, B. (1976) Pure red cell aplasia associated with adenocarcinoma of the stomach. *N.Y. St. J. Med.*, *76*, 2177.

GASSER, C. (1957) Aplasia of erythropoiesis. *Padiat. Clins N. Am.*, 445.

GEARY, C. G., (1978) Drug-related red cell aplasia. *Br. med. J.*, *i*, 51.

GEARY, C. G., BYRON, P. R., TAYLOR, G., MACIVER, J. E. & ZERVAS, J. (1975) Thymoma associated with pure red cell aplasia immunoglobulin deficiency and an inhibitor of antigen-induced lymphocyte transformation. *Br. J. Haemat.*, *29*, 479.

GHIO, R., LOWENBERG, B. & DICKE, K. A. (1976) Cytotoxic activity in serum from pure red cell aplasia patients detected by an erythroid colony assay. In: *Leukaemia and Aplastic Anaemia*, ed. D. Metcalf, M. Conderelli & C. Peschle. Rome: Il Pensiero Scientifico.

GILBERT, E. F., HARLEY, J. B. & ANIDO, V. (1968) Thymoma, plasma cell myeloma, red cell aplasia and malabsorption syndrome. *Am. J. Med.*, *44*, 820.

GILL, P. L., AMARE, M. & LARSEN, W. E. (1977) Pure red cell aplasia: three cases responding to immunosuppression. *Am. J. med. Sci.*, *273*, 213.

GOLDSTEIN, C. & PECHET, L. (1965) Chronic erythrocytic hypoplasia following pernicious anaemia. *Blood*, *25*, 31.

GOLDSTEIN, G. & MACKAY, I. R. (1969) *The Human Thymus*, pp. 319–37. London: Heinemann.

GOODMAN, S. B. & BLACK, M. H. (1964) A case of red cell aplasia occurring as a result of anti-tuberculous therapy. *Blood*, *24*, 616.

GREEN, P. (1958) Aplastic anaemia associated with thymoma: report of 2 cases. *Can. med. Ass. J.*, *78*, 419.

GREENE, R. & MORGAN, D. C. (1956) Toxicity of the anti-thyroid drug, carbimazole. *J. clin. Endocr.*, *16*, 391.

GREIG, H. B. W., METZ, J., BRADLOW, B. A., THERON, J. J. & MORRIS, R. W. (1958) The familial crisis in hereditary spherocytosis. *S. Afr. J. med. Sci.*, *23*, 17.

HILKOWITZ, G. (1960) The 'aplastic crisis' and erythroid maturation defect occurring simultaneously in three members of a family. *A.M.A. Archs intern. Med.*, *105*, 100.

HIRAI, H. (1977) Two cases of erythroid hypoplasia caused by carbamazepine. *Jap. J. clin. Haemat.*, *18*, 33.

HIRST, E. & ROBINSON, T. I. (1967) The syndrome of thymoma and erythroblastic anaemia. *Medicine, Balt.*, *46*, 225.

HOFFMAN, R., ZANJANI, E. D., VILA, J., ZALUSKY, R., LUTTON, J. D. & WASSERMAN, L. R. (1976) Diamond–Blackfan syndrome: lymphocyte mediated suppression of erythropoiesis. *Science, N.Y.*, *193*, 899.

HOTCHKISS, D. J., jun. (1970) Pure red cell aplasia following pernicious anaemia (Abstract). *Proc. VIIIth int. Congr. Haemat.*, 133C.

HUMPHREYS, G. H. H. & SOUTHWORTH, H. (1945) Aplastic anaemia terminated by removal of a mediastinal tumour. *Am. J. med. Sci.*, *210*, 501.

HURDLE, A. D. F. & WALKER, A. G. (1963) Bone marrow hypoplasia in the course of haemolytic disease of the newborn. *Br. med. J.*, *1*, 518.

IBRAHIM, J. H., RAUSTRON, J. & BOOTH, J. (1966) A case of red cell aplasia in a Negro child. *Archs Dis. Childh.*, *41*, 213.

JACOBS, E. M., HUTTER, R. V. P., POOL, J. L. & LEY, A. B. (1959) Benign thymoma and selective erythroid hypoplasia of the bone marrow. *Cancer, N.Y.*, *12*, 47.

JANDL, J. H. & GREENBERG, M. S. (1959) Bone marrow failure due to relative nutritional deficiency in Cooley's haemolytic anaemia. *New Engl. J. Med.*, *260*, 461.

JEONG, Y.-G., YUNG, Y. & RIVER, G. L. (1974) Pure red cell aplasia and diphenyl-hydantoin. *J. Am. med. Ass.*, *229*, 314.

JEPSON, J. H., GARDNER, F. H., DEGNAN, T. & VAS, M. A. (1968) Gammaglobulin inhibitor of erythropoiesis in erythroblastopenic plasma from patients with thymoma. *Clin. Res.*, *16*, 536.

JEPSON, J. H. & LOWENSTEIN, L. (1966) Inhibition of erythropoiesis by a factor present in the plasma of patients with erythroblastopenia. *Blood*, *27*, 425.

JEPSON, J. H. & VAS, M. (1974) Decreased *in vivo* and *in vitro* erythropoiesis induced by plasma of ten patients with thymoma, lymphosarcoma, or idiopathic erythro-blastopenia. *Cancer Res.*, *34*, 1325.

JEUNET, F. S. & GOOD, R. A. (1969) Thymoma, immunologic deficiencies and hemato-logical abnormalities. In: *Immunologic Deficiency Diseases in Man*, ed. D. Bergsama, p. 192. New York: National Foundation.

JURGENSEN, J. C., ABRAHAM, J. P. & HARDY, W. W. (1970) Erythroid hypoplasia after halothane hepatitis. report of a case. *Am. J. dig. Dis.*, *15*, 577.

KAUNG, D. T., CECH, R. F. & PETERSON, R. F. (1968) Benign thymoma and erythroid hypoplasia: 13 year case following thymectomy. *Cancer, N.Y.*, *22*, 445.

KAZNELSON, P. (1922) Zur Enstehung der Blutplätchen. *Dt. Verh. ges. inner. Med.*, *34*, 557.

KONTEK, M. (1965) Ostra, odwracalna nierydolnost szpiku z komponenta hemolityezna (na tle immunologicicynynn). *Niad. Lek.*, *18*, 1263.

KRANTZ, S. B. (1974) Pure red cell aplasia. *New Engl. J. Med.*, *291*, 345.

KRANTZ, S. B. (1976) Diagnosis and treatment of pure red cell aplasia. *Med. Clins N. Am.*, *60*, 945.

KRANTZ, S. B. & KAO, V. (1967) Studies in red cell aplasia, I. Demonstration of a plasma inhibitor to heme synthesis and an antibody to erythroblast nuclei. *Proc. natn. Acad. Sci., U.S.A.*, *58*, 493.

KRANTZ, S. B. & KAO, V. (1969) Studies on red cell aplasia. II. Report of a second patient with an antibody to erythroblast nuclei and a remission after immuno-suppressive therapy. *Blood*, *34*, 1.

KRANTZ, S. B., MOORE, W. H., & ZAENTZ, S. D. (1972) Studies on red cell aplasia. V. Presence of erythroblast cytotoxicity in α-globulin fraction of plasma. *J. clin. Invest.*, *52*, 324.

LANZKOWSKY, P., MCKENZIE, D., KATZ, S., HOFFENBERG, R., FRIEDMAN, R. & BLACK, E. (1967) Erythrocyte abnormality induced by protein malnutrition. II. ^{51}Cr labelled erythrocyte studies. *Br. J. Haemat.*, *13*, 639.

LINSK, J. A., & MURRAY, C. K. (1961) Erythrocyte hypoplasia and hypogamma-globulinemia. *Ann. intern. Med.*, *55*, 831.

LIPA, M. & LEY, D. C. H. (1966) Thymoma and erythroid hypoplasia with carcinoma of the pancreas, bronchiolar hyperplasia and pulmonary tuberculosis. *Ann. intern. Med.*, *65*, 541.

LITWIN, S. D., & ZANTZ, E. D. (1977) Lymphocytes suppressing both immune-globulin production and erythroid differentiation in hypogammaglobulinaemia. *Nature, Lond.*, *266*, 57.

LYNGAR, E. (1942) Samtidig apptreden av anemik kriser hos 3 barn i en familie med haemolytisk ikterus. *Nord. Med.*, *14*, 1246.

MCGRATH, B. P., IBELS, L. S., RAIK, E., HARGRAVE, M., MAHONY, J. F. & STEWART, J. H.

(1975) Erythroid toxicity of azathioprine: macrocytosis and selective marrow hypoplasia. *Q. Jl. Med.*, *44*, 57.

MacIver, J. E. & Parker-Williams, J. E. (1961) The aplastic crisis in sickle cell anaemia. *Lancet*, *1*, 1086.

Marmont, A. M. (1974) Pure red cell aplasia. In: *Present Problems in Haematology*, ed. J. Libansky & L. Donner, p. 225: Amsterdam: Excerpta Medica.

Marmont, A. M. (1976) The immunosuppressive treatment of autoimmune erythroblastopenia (pure red cell aplasia). In: *Leukaemia and Aplastic Anaemia*, ed. D. Metcalf, M. Condorelli & C. Peschle. Rome: Il Pensiero Scientifico.

Marmont, A., Peschle, C. & Sanguineti, M. (1975) Pure red cell aplasia (PRCA). Response of 3 patients to cyclophosphamide and/or anti-lymphocyte globulin (ALG) and demonstration of two types of serum IgG inhibitors to erythropoiesis. *Blood*, *45*, 247.

Matras, A. & Priesel, A. (1928) Uber einige Gewachse des Thymus. *Beitr. path. Anat.*, *80*, 270.

Meyer, L. M. & Bertcher, R. W. (1962) Acquired hemolytic anaemia and transient erythroid hypoplasia of the bone marrow. *Am. J. Med.*, *28*, 606.

Miller, J. F. A. P., Block, M., Rowland, D. T. & Kind, P. (1965) Effect of thymectomy in hemopoietic organs of the opossum embryo. *Proc. Soc. exp. Biol. Med.*, *118*, 916.

Milner, G. R., Testa, N. G., Geary, C. G., Dexter, T. M., Muldal, S., MacIver, J. E. & Lajtha, L. G. (1977) Bone marrow culture studies in refractory cytopenia and smouldering leukaemia. *Br. J. Haemat.*, *35*, 251.

Mitchell, A. B. S., Pinn, G. & Pegrum, G. D. (1971) Pure red cell and carcinoma. *Blood*, *37*, 594.

Nathan, D. G., Schupack, E., Stohlman, F. J. V. & Merrill, J. P. (1964) Erythropoiesis in anephric man. *J. clin. Invest.*, *43*, 2158.

Opsahl, R. (1939) Thymus-karcinom og aplastisk anemi. *Nord. Med.*, *2*, 1835.

Ovren, P. A. (1948) Congenital haemolytic jaundice: the pathogenesis of the 'haemolytic crisis'. *Blood*, *3*, 231.

Ozer, F. L., Traux, W. E. & Levin, W. C. (1960) Erythroid hypoplasia associated with chloramphenicol therapy. *Blood*, *16*, 997.

Pasternack, A. & Wahlberg, P. (1967) Bone marrow in acute renal failure. *Acta med. scand.*, *181*, 505.

Peschle, C. & Condorelli, M. (1976) Physiopathology of pure red cell aplasia, types I and II. In: *Leukaemia and Aplastic Anaemia*, ed. D. Metcalf, M. Condorelli & C. Peschle. Rome: Il Pensiero Scientifico.

Peschle, C., Marmont, A. M., Marone, G., Arturo, G., Sasso, G. F. & Condorelli, M. (1975) Pure red cell aplasia: studies on an IgG serum inhibitor neutralising erythropoietin. *Br. J. Haemat.*, *30*, 411.

Pezzimenti, J. F. & Lindenbaum, J. (1972) Megaloblastic anaemia associated with erythroid hypoplasia. *Am. J. Med.*, *53*, 748.

Pierre, R. V. (1974) Preleukaemic states. *Semin. Hemat.*, *11*, 73.

Pirofsky, B. (1969) *Autoimmunisation and the Autoimmune Haemolytic Anaemias*, p. 86. Baltimore: Williams & Wilkins.

Polak, B. C. P., Wessling, H., Schut, D., Herxheimer, A. & Meyler, L. (1972) Blood dyscrasias attributed to chloramphenicol. *Acta med. scand.*, *192*, 409.

Prasad, A. S., Berman, L., Tranchida, L. & Poulik, M. D. (1968) Red cell hypoplasia, cold haemoglobinuria and M-type gamma G, serum paraprotein and Bence-Jones proteinuria in a patient with lymphoproliferative disorder. *Blood*, *31*, 151.

Recker, R. H. & Hynes, H. E. (1969) Pure red cell aplasia associated with chlorpropamide therapy. *Archs intern. Med.*, *123*, 445.

Reid, G. & Patterson, A. C. (1977) Pure red cell aplasia after gold treatment. *Br. med J.*, *ii*, 1457.

Remigio, P. A. (1971) Granulomatous thymoma associated with erythroid hypoplasia. *Am. J. clin. Path.*, *55*, 18.

Richet, G., Alagille, D. & Fournier, E. (1954) L'erythroblastopénie aigué de l'anemie. *Presse Méd., Paris, 62*, 50.

ROBINS-BROWNE, R. M., GREEN, R., KATZ, J. & BECKER, D. (1977) Thymoma, pure red cell aplasia, pernicious anaemia and candidiasis: a defect in immuno-homeostasis. *Br. J. Haemat.*, *36*, 5.

ROGERS, H. G., MANALIGOD, J. R. & BLAZEK, W. V. (1968) Thymoma associated with pancytopenia and hypogammaglobulinaemia: report of a case and review of the literature. *Am. J. Med.*, *44*, 154.

ROLAND, A. S. (1964) The syndrome of benign thymoma and primary aregenerative anaemia: an analysis of 43 cases. *Am. J. med. Sci.*, *247*, 719.

ROSAI, J. & LEVINE, G. D. (1975) *Tumours of the Thymus*. Washington, D.C.: Armed Forces Institute of Pathology.

RUBIN, M., STRAUS, B. & ALLEN, L. (1964) Clinical disorders associated with thymic tumours. *Archs intern. Med.*, *114*, 389.

SAFDAR, S. H., KRANTZ, S. B. & BROWN, E. B. (1970) Successful immunosuppressive treatment of erythroid aplasia appearing after thymectomy. *Br. J. Haemat.*, *19*, 435.

SCHMID, J. R., KIELY, J. M., HARRISON, E. G., BAYRD, E. D. & PEASE, G. L. (1965) Thymoma associated with pure red cell agenesis. Review of literature and report of 4 cases. *Cancer, N.Y.*, *18*, 216.

SCHMID, J. R., KIELY, J. M., PEASE, G. L. & HARGRAVES, M. M. (1963) Acquired pure red cell aplasia. Report of 16 cases and review of the literature. *Acta haemat.*, *30*, 255.

SCHOFIELD, R., (1976) Lymphocyte co-operation in haemopoiesis. In: *Leukaemia and Aplastic Anaemia*, ed. D. Metcalf, M. Condorelli & C. Peschle, p. 392. Rome: Il Pensiero Scientifico.

SCHOOLEY, J. C. & GARCIA, J. F. (1962) Immunochemical studies of human urinary erythropoietin. *Proc. Soc. exp. Biol. Med.*, *109*, 325.

SCOTT, J. L., FINEGOLD, S. M., BELGIN, G. M. & LAWRENCE, J. S. (1965) A controlled double-blind study of the haematological toxicity of chloramphenicol. *New Engl. J. Med.*, *272*, 1137.

SEAMAN, A. J. & KOLER, R. D. (1953) Acquired erythrocyte hypoplasia: a recovery during cobalt therapy. Report of two cases. *Acta haemat.*, *9*, 153.

SEARS, D. A., GEORGE, J. N. & GOLD, M. S. (1975) Transient red cell aplasia in association with viral hepatitis: occurrence four years apart in siblings. *Archs intern. Med.*, *135*, 1585.

SINGER, K., MOTULSKY, A. G. & WILE, S. A. (1950) Aplastic crisis in sickle cell anaemia: a study of its mechanism and its relationship to other types of haemolytic crisis. *J. Lab. clin. Med.*, *35*, 721.

SKIKNE, B. S., LYNCH, S. R., BEZWODA, W. R., BOTHWELL, T. H., BERNSTEIN, R. & KATZ, J. (1976) Pure red cell aplasia. *S. Afr. med. J.*, *50*, 1353.

SMITH, C. H. (1949) Chronic congenital aregenerative anaemia (pure red cell anaemia) associated with iso-immunisation by the blood group factor 'A'. *Blood*, *4*, 697.

SOUADJIAN, J. V., ENRIQUEZ, P., SILVERSTEIN, M. N. & PEPIN, J.-M. (1974) The spectrum of diseases associated with thymoma. Coincidence or syndrome? *Archs intern. Med.*, *134*, 374.

STEPHENS, M. E. M. (1974) Transient erythroid hypoplasia in a patient on long-term co-trimoxazole therapy. *Postgrad. med. J.*, *50*, 235.

SUNDSTROM, C., LUNDBERG, D. & WERNER, I. (1972) A case of thymoma in association with megakaryocytopenia. *Acta path. microbiol. scand.*, *80*, 487.

SWINEFORD, O., CURRY, J. C. & CUMBIA, J. W. (1958) Phenylbutazone toxicity: depression of erythropoiesis. A case report. *Rheum. Arthritis*, *1*, 174.

TALERMAN, A. & AMIGO, A. (1968) Thymoma associated with aregenerative anaemia and aplastic anaemia in a 5 year old child. *Cancer, N.Y.*, *21*, 1212.

THIELE, H. G. & FRENZEL, H. (1967) Immunoglobulin: Mangelsyndrome und Agranulocytose bei Thymom. *Schweiz. med. Wschr.*, *97*, 1606.

WINTROBE, M. M. (1974) Appendix I. In: *Clinical Haematology*. Philadelphia: Lea & Febiger.

WRANNE, E. (1970) Transient erythroblastopenia in infancy and childhood. *Scand. J. Haemat.*, *7*, 76.

YAMAMOTO, M. (1965) Experimental studies on immunological mechanisms of aplastic anaemia. I. Effects of anti-erythroblastic antibody on peripheral blood and bone marrow. *Jap. J. Allergy*, *14*, 55.

YUNIS, A. A. & BLOOMBERG, G. R. (1964) Chloramphenicol toxicity: clinical features and pathogenesis. *Prog. Haemat.*, *4*, 138.

YUNIS, A. A., ARIMURA, G. K., LUTCHER, C. L., BLASQUEZ, J. & HALLORAN, M. (1967a) Biochemical lesion in dilantin-induced erythroid aplasia. *Blood*, *30*, 587.

YUNIS, E. J., HONG, R., GREWE, M. A., MARTINEZ, C., CORNELIUS, E. & GOOD, R. A. (1967b) Post-thymectomy wasting associated with auto-immune phenomena: antiglobulin positive anaemia in A and C57BL/6Ks mice. *J. exp. Med.*, *125*, 947.

ZAENTZ, S. D. & KRANTZ, S. B. (1973) Studies on pure red cell aplasia, VI. Development of two stage erythroblast cytotoxicity method, and role of complement. *J. Lab. clin. Med.*, *82*, 31.

ZAENTZ, S. D., KRANTZ, S. B. & BROWN, E. B. (1976) Studies on pure red cell aplasia. VIII. Maintenance therapy with immunosuppressive drugs. *Br. J. Haemat.*, *32*, 47.

ZAENTZ, S. D., KRANTZ, S. B. & SEARS, D. A. (1975) Studies on pure red cell aplasia. VII. Presence of erythroblasts and response to splenectomy: a case report. *Blood*, *46*, 261.

ZERVAS, J. D., DELAMORE, I. W., CUNLIFFE, D. J. & ISRAELS, M. C. K. (1972) Observations on the survival of circulating reticulocytes. *Br. J. Haemat.*, *24*, 453.

ZERVAS, J., GEARY, C. G. & OLEESKY, S. (1974) Sideroblastic anemia treated with immunosuppressive therapy. *Blood*, *44*, 117.

ZIPORI, D. & TRAININ, N. (1975) The role of thymic humoral factor in the proliferation of bone marrow CFU-S from thymectomized mice. *Exp. Haemat.*, *3*, 389.

10

The Aplasia–Leukaemia Syndrome

GILLIAN R. MILNER and C. G. GEARY

There are numerous case reports of the evolution of leukaemia from a pre-existing state of marrow aplasia, whether the latter is considered idiopathic or drug-induced (Wetherley-Mein 1960; DeGowin 1963; Delamore & Geary 1971; Li & Nathan 1971; Koeppen et al. 1975): Pierre (1974) found 64 cases of acute leukaemia arising as a complication of 'idiopathic' aplastic anaemia in a search of the world literature. That such an evolution can, on occasion, be part of the natural history of marrow aplasia is not in question. The exact incidence, however, of a leukaemic transformation is difficult to establish. In several large series of cases of aplastic anaemia in both children and adults, totalling 656 individuals in all (Mohler & Leavell 1958; Israels & Wilkinson 1961; Lewis 1965; Najean et al. 1965; Vincent & de Gruchy 1967; Wolff 1967; Heyn et al. 1969; Sanchez-Medal et al. 1969; Williams et al. 1973) there is only one report of the development of leukaemia (Mohler & Leavell 1958). However, in some of these cases the interval of follow-up was relatively short. In contrast, in a series of approximately 100 children with aplastic anaemia from Boston, acute leukaemia developed in three idiopathic acquired cases (Li & Nathan 1971). One can only conclude that leukaemia following acquired aplastic anaemia is an entity but a relatively rare event. The interval between the initial manifestation of aplastic anaemia and evolution to leukaemia is extremely variable, ranging from a few months to many years. For example, in one reported case the interval between the two diagnoses was 20 years (Geary et al. 1974).

By contrast, leukaemia is a relatively common complication of constitutional aplastic anaemia. Fanconi's anaemia appears to carry an increased risk of leukaemic transformation although here, again, the exact incidence has not been established. One review of the literature has estimated that, of approximately 170 cases, four terminated in leukaemia (Schroeder & Kurth 1971). This, however, may be an over-estimate of the true incidence since isolated, uncomplicated cases of Fanconi's anaemia are unlikely to be reported. There is also an increased risk of leukaemia in asymptomatic relatives of individuals known to have Fanconi's anaemia. In a survey of 49 families containing 66 cases of Fanconi's anaemia the incidence of leukaemia in non-anaemic relatives was estimated to be four times that of the population in general (Garriga & Crosby 1959).

Cytogenetic abnormalities in Fanconi's anaemia are prominent and include chromosome and chromatid breaks and translocations. Such abnormalities are found in lymphocytes (and fibroblasts) as well as on direct marrow culture (see pp. 175–6). Since certain other congenital disorders such as Down's syndrome, Bloom's syndrome and ataxia telangiectasia also show an increased incidence of leukaemia and have cytogenetic abnormalities, the presence of chromosomal abnormalities in Fanconi's anaemia seems to be relevant to the pathogenesis of leukaemia in such individuals. Also of interest is the finding that when fibroblasts taken from such a patient, or their relatives, are cultured with the oncogenic virus SV40, there is an above normal degree of transformation (Dosik et al. 1970). The abnormalities in Fanconi's syndrome are not confined to the haemopoietic system although the main pathological features and usual oncogenic transformation is in the marrow. The latter may be related to the high cell turnover in this tissue, permitting increased opportunity for malignant mutation in a situation of chromosomal instability (see p. 10).

An interesting family has recently been described by Branda and his colleagues (Branda et al. 1978). The proband had aplastic anaemia and came from a large family, many members of which showed severe haematological disease, including five cases of acute leukaemia and 12 deaths due to leucopenia. The patient's marrow showed megaloblastic changes in the few erythroid precursors which remained and there was haematological response to large doses of folic acid, with increase in marrow cellularity. A defect in the uptake and retention of methyltetrahydrofolic acid by his marrow and stimulated lymphocytes was demonstrated; five other family members showed similar lesions. Whether the defect in folate metabolism is primary or secondary is not yet clear, but in this family it appears to be associated with a genetic defect predisposing to both aplasia and leukaemia.

Leukaemia arising in other types of marrow hypoplasia seems to be much less common. Hypoplasia of a single cell line is, in itself, much more unusual than is panhypoplasia. Pure red cell aplasia of the congenital variety, the Blackfan–Diamond syndrome, does not appear to predispose to leukaemia. A recent review of 133 cases had none with such an evolution (Diamond et al. 1976) but it must be remembered that, until recently, the life expectancy in this disorder has been poor. Two cases of acute leukaemia complicating the syndrome have recently been reported (Krishnan et al. 1978; Wasser et al. 1978). There are a few reports of the development of leukaemia in the acquired form of pure red cell aplasia (Soutter & Emerson 1960; DiGiacomo et al. 1966); Schmid et al. (1963) found four cases, three of acute leukaemia and one of chronic myeloid leukaemia, in a review of the world literature, but the exact incidence is not known. However, a recent review suggests it to be relatively common in patients not responding to immunosuppressants (see p. 213).

The aplastic anaemia–PNH syndrome is fully discussed in Chapter 5. PNH has been reported as preceding leukaemia in a small number of individuals (Holden & Lichtman 1969; Jenkins & Hartmann 1969; Kaufman et al. 1969; Carmel et al. 1970) and it has been suggested that this condition is analogous to certain myeloproliferative disorders which may terminate in acute leukaemia (Dameshek 1969). The main pathological feature of PNH is manifest in the red cells, but evidence of a panmyelopathy is to be found in the neutropenia, thrombocytopenia and reduction in leucocyte alkaline phosphatase commonly present. In addition, studies on PNH red cells indicate the presence of both a clone of abnormal and normal red cells (Rosse & Dacie 1966). In cases where leukaemia has developed later, the factor causing the PNH clone could also have been leukaemogenic, or regeneration in a damaged marrow might provide a soil conducive to the origin of an aberrant leukaemic clone.

PRE-LEUKAEMIA

The association between aplasia of the marrow and leukaemia may manifest itself in two different ways and it may, or may not, be pertinent to distinguish between them. In the first the initial diagnosis is that of aplasia of one or more marrow elements, followed, after a variable interval, by evolution to leukaemia. On the other hand there is a small but distinct group of patients who present with a hypoplastic marrow, but with additional features suggesting a potential progression to leukaemia from the time of initial diagnosis. This latter type of case may, by some, be given the label of pre-leukaemia, a state which was initially categorized by Block et al. (1953). The features of the pre-leukaemic state in general have been evaluated more recently in a retrospective analysis of the early stages of 132 cases of acute leukaemia (Saarni & Linman 1973). Approximately half their patients gave a clinical history of antecedent symptoms suggestive of a pre-leukaemic phase and in approximately one-third more complete haematological documentation indicated a pre-leukaemic stage. Only one of this group of patients had a hypoplastic marrow, but in a more recent review, Linman and Saarni (1974) have suggested that as many as 20% of leukaemias pass through a hypoplastic stage. The cyto-logical features which these authors consider to suggest a diagnosis of pre-leukaemia include dyserythropoietic features, in particular oval macrocytosis and megaloblastoid changes, a small excess of early granulocyte precursors, an acquired Pelger Huet phenomenon, an absolute monocytosis and morphological abnormalities in the plate-lets and megakaryocytes. Some of these, e.g. macrocytosis (although not specifically ovalocytosis) and megaloblastoid changes, are of course features of aplastic anaemia itself and may make the diagnosis of pre-leukaemia very difficult. The finding most definitely suggesting future leukaemic evolution is probably a relative though small excess of myeloblasts and/or promyelocytes, although here care must be taken to exclude the transiently similar picture which may be found in a regenerating marrow. Furthermore, the normal method of quanti-tation, by percentage of cells of a particular type present, is less valid when there is a marked reduction in cellularity of other cell types.

A prospective study of a group of cases where there was a small but definite increase in myeloblasts has been carried out jointly in three centres and recently reported (Najean et al. 1976). Of 79 patients, only one had a positive history of exposure to a myelotoxic agent (benzene). The majority had normocellular or moderately hypocellular marrows but a quarter were considered to have marrows of much diminished cellularity. Two-thirds of the patients eventually evolved to acute myeloblastic leukaemia, but the initial cellularity did not appear to influence the likelihood of such an evolution.

Such cases with a small or moderate excess of blasts are called by some authorities 'smouldering leukaemia'. The borderline between this and pre-leukaemia may be difficult to define objectively; indeed, the delineation of 'pre-leukaemia' itself has been criticized as being only really permissible as a retrospective diagnosis. However, the concept remains a useful one and ongoing studies of such patients will provide further information as to the natural history of these dis-orders and delineate the best time to begin cytotoxic as well as supportive therapy. Such a diagnosis does not necessarily imply that within the life span of the individual there will be an inevitable progression to leukaemia: the concept would remain valid even if in some cases the disorder is non-progressive or even, occasionally, reversible. Leukaemia, in effect, produces a 'functional aplasia' of the marrow, in that normal haemopoietic stem-cells are repressed or crowded out; indeed, it has been questioned whether, in some cases of fully developed acute leukaemia, any normal stem-cells remain (Killman 1970). It is conceivable that smouldering leukaemia with a hypoplastic marrow represents a similar syndrome in which the leukaemic cell mass is still very small. Moreover, the question arises as to whether cases of putative pre-leukaemia with a hypoplastic marrow are really part of the same syndrome as aplasia with no pre-leukaemic features, which, nevertheless, later develop frank leukaemia. The former may be a 'telescoped' variety of the latter, or they may be different disorders.

An example of a case showing no leukaemic features during an initial aplastic phase is shown in Fig. 10.1.

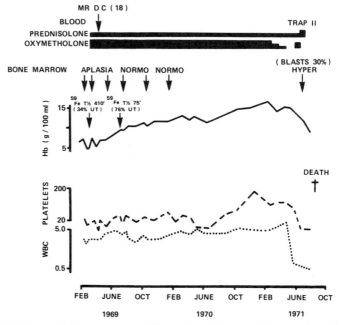

Fig. 10.1. A boy of 16 presented with a short history of anaemia and bruising. The marrow showed panhypoplasia. There was slight skin pigmentation but no other stigmata of a congenital marrow disorder, and idiopathic acquired hypoplasia seemed more likely. There was initially a good response to androgens, with improvement in blood count, marrow cellularity and ferrokinetics. Although the marrow remained cellular, the onset of leukaemia 2 years later was associated with· sudden marrow failure.

CYTOGENETIC STUDIES

Cytogenetic studies in aplastic anaemia on the marrow itself are rendered difficult by the very aplasia. Abnormal findings have been non-specific, mainly chromosomal breaks and gaps, chromatid exchanges and extra chromosomes without prominent evidence of aneuploid clones (Haak et al. 1977). In one study there were similar findings in those individuals who did, and those who did not, develop leukaemia (Dosik et al. 1970). Chromosome studies in individuals exposed to drugs which are on occasion myelotoxic and perhaps leukaemogenic have included benzene (Tough & Court Brown 1965) and phenylbutazone (Stevenson et al. 1971). The findings, again, have been those of chromosome breaks and translocations without evidence of aneuploid clones. In general, a majority of patients with aplasia have a normal marrow chromosome complement but a minority have an increased number of polyploid cells (Cobo et al. 1970). On the whole the evidence suggests that chromosome studies are of limited value in predicting a possible leukaemic evolution or potential in aplastic anaemia, but more cases need to be studied. An ongoing study of 220 patients with pre-leukaemia, of whom approximately 20% had aplastic marrows, has demonstrated a higher incidence of cytogenetic abnormalities in patients in whom leukaemia evolved, compared to those where the picture was more stable (Pierre 1974).

THE PATHOGENESIS OF LEUKAEMIA IN APLASTIC ANAEMIA

In theory, the association between leukaemia and aplastic anaemia in general could be due either to a single agent or to more than one agent. If a single agent is incriminated, it is necessary to postulate that leukaemogenesis is induced by the agent itself causing the aplasia: this may be no more than the production of a state of instability in the marrow, favouring the later evolution of a malignant clone or clones. On the other hand, if the basic damage is to the marrow environment then this may provide a more fertile soil for such cells to develop. In either of these instances the initial damage would be responsible both for the initial aplasia and the subsequent development of leukaemia.

If a multifactorial aetiology is considered, the postulate is then that the damage caused by the initial agent may thereafter make marrow cells more susceptible to the oncogenic action of another agent or agents. There are certain agents considered as potentially leukaemogenic to normal marrow and it is relevant to consider the possible influence of such agents on marrow which has passed through a period of aplasia. Candidates are radiation, viruses and certain drugs and chemicals.

The leukaemogenic effects of radiation are as well known as its effect in inducing aplasia. A great deal of information has come from the atomic bomb explosions in Japan. The acute effect on the marrow of exposure to radiation from the bombs was aplastic anaemia, the chronic effect a five-fold increase in the incidence of leukaemia beginning approximately a year after the exposure and with a peak incidence about seven years later (Brill et al. 1962). Fortunately, acute exposure to such high doses of radio-activity is a rare occurrence, but there is evidence that a lower radiation dose may be leukaemogenic in the presence of a pre-existing marrow abnormality such as poly-cythaemia rubra vera (Modan & Lilienfeld 1965) or a susceptible population such as the fetus *in utero* (MacMahon 1962; Stewart & Kneale 1970), or even in young children (Bross & Natarajan 1972). The question of the threshold of radioactivity necessary for leukaemo-genesis remains unanswered, but it seems reasonable to speculate that in situations of marrow damage this may be lowered to levels associated with diagnostic X-rays or even to levels approaching natural background in some geographical regions.

Viruses are known to be leukaemogenic in animals (for review see Gunz & Baikie 1974). Virus particles characteristic of C-type RNA viruses have been demonstrated by electron microscopy in material derived from human individuals with leukaemia (Almeida et al. 1963; Burger et al. 1964; Newell et al. 1968). Such types of virus cause, amongst others, fowl, murine and feline leukaemia. However, the specificity of such findings remains uncertain since similar particles have been seen in non-leukaemic material (Grist & Fallon 1964). Perhaps of more potential relevance to the association between leukaemia and aplasia is the recent finding of C-type virus particles in the human placenta (Kalter et al. 1973). This raises the possibility that such agents could be vertically transmitted to offspring, remain latent, but become oncogenic if abnormalities are first induced by another extraneous agent. Another possibility is the existence, perhaps in the marrow, of an 'oncogene', that is, an oncogenic virus which has been incorporated into the genome of the cell and is therefore replicated at cell division (Huebner et al. 1970). The oncogenic potential of such a virus could remain dormant, and not detectable ultrastructurally, but could possibly come into play when other extraneous factors influence the marrow.

The association between exposure to a drug or chemical and the development of leukaemia is strongest in the case of benzene. Chronic exposure to this toxic agent is well known to give rise to aplasia (Vigliani & Saita 1964) and leukaemia may develop with (DeGowin 1963) and without (Aksoy et al. 1972) a preceding episode of aplasia. Exposure to benzene may on careful questioning be found to be more frequent than is generally thought (Girard & Revol 1970; Brandt et al. 1977). Drugs which in some susceptible individuals cause aplasia, and after the use of which leukaemia has also been reported, include chlor-amphenicol (Brauer & Dameshek 1967) and phenylbutazone (Dougan & Woodliff 1965; Jensen & Roll 1965).

The theory that some cases of aplastic anaemia at least might be due to damage to the marrow microenvironment has been discussed in Chapter 1 and the conclusion drawn that a majority of cases appear to be due to stem-cell damage. The increasing evidence that immune, possibly autoimmune phenomena may play an aetiological role in some cases has also been considered. This is certainly so for some cases of pure red cell aplasia. If the aplasia is more widespread then it is necessary to postulate antibody directed against a more pluripotential, less committed, precursor. Autoimmune disorders in humans are not generally considered as increasing the incidence of malignancy in general or leukaemia in particular. Nevertheless, autoimmune disorders are more common in states of immunodeficiency and it has been suggested that a failure of immune competence is the basis for autoimmune phenomena in general (Fudenberg & Wells 1976). Both malignancy and autoimmune disorders are increased in individuals with congenital immunodeficiency, although the malignancy is more commonly a lymphoma than a leukaemia. Defects in immune capacity have been found in aplastic anaemia. These include a depletion of B-lymphocytes and subnormal response to antigenic challenge (Morley & Forbes 1974; Morley et al. 1974) and a reduction in immunoglobulin levels (Mir et al. 1977). Such defects could, however, be an accompaniment rather than an agent of the aplasia.

CYTOTOXIC THERAPY, MARROW HYPOPLASIA AND LEUKAEMIA

Drugs causing immune suppression and cytotoxic agents used in the treatment of neoplasia have been reported as increasing the incidence of leukaemia (*Lancet* 1977). An above average incidence has been reported after drug therapy in Hodgkin's disease (Rosmer & Grünwald 1975), multiple myeloma (Kyle et al. 1970; Rosmer & Grünwald 1974) and chronic lymphocytic leukaemia (Rosmer & Grünwald 1975). An increased incidence of leukaemia has also been found in similarly treated disorders, other than those of lymphoreticular tissue, such as ovarian carcinoma (Reimer et al. 1977) and bronchial carcinoma (Stott et al. 1977). Cases have also arisen after such treatment of non-neoplastic disorders such as glomerulonephritis (Roberts & Bell 1976) and Wegener's granulomatosis (Westberg & Swolin 1976). The drugs implicated as single agents include melphalan, cyclophosphamide and busulphan, but many such patients are recipients of multiple immuno-suppressive or cytotoxic agents. It has, however, been suggested that cyclophosphamide has a particular propensity as an oncogen in this situation (Puri & Campbell 1977); leukaemia is encountered most frequently after combined radiation and cytotoxic therapy (Coleman et al. 1977).

The possible mechanisms of leukaemogenesis in such situations are various. They include depression of immune surveillance, permitting the proliferation of any aberrant malignant clone which may arise, direct mutagenesis to such a clone or activation of a latent leukaemogenic virus. It is of interest that in an experimental model of chronic marrow aplasia produced by busulphan, immunological abnormalities were present (Pugsley et al. 1978). Alternatively an increased incidence of infection with chronic intense stimulation of leucocyte proliferation might increase the chance for mutations to arise.

In many of the reports of leukaemia arising after drug therapy there was no definite antecedent episode of aplasia. By contrast in a recent report of acute leukaemia arising after treatment of carcinoma of the bronchus with busulphan, all four patients with this evolution had a previous episode of pancytopenia (Stott et al. 1977). It can, however, be pointed out that some degree of hypoplasia is inevitable in a majority of patients on such therapy, where dosage is commonly controlled by keeping the peripheral blood parameters at levels indicative of myelosuppression but of an insufficient degree to cause secondary complications. Profound changes in CFU-C cloning have been found, for example, in patients receiving chlorambucil for autoimmune disease, and recovery may take many weeks (Tchernia et al. 1976). Evolution of leukaemia after myelosuppression may be qualitatively different in aetiology from that arising after more profound marrow hypoplasia, but it is also possible that the same pathogenesis—perhaps regeneration in a damaged marrow—is operative and the distinction is only a quantitative one.

The majority of cases of leukaemia arising after an aplastic episode have been of the acute 'non-lymphoblastic' variety. This is also true of those arising after radiation or drug therapy, where acute myelomonocytic leukaemia is especially common (Larsen & Brincker 1977). There are reports of chronic myeloid leukaemia in atom bomb survivors and after drug therapy (Jensen & Roll 1965) and of acute lymphoblastic leukaemia in children (Melhorn et al. 1970) but these are a minority. There is a subjective impression of a relative increase in acute erythroleukaemia. For example, in a study of 5455 patients with carcinoma of the ovary, of 13 cases of acute non-lymphoblastic leukaemia, three were classified as acute erythroleukaemia (Reimer et al. 1977). An earlier review of cases of acute leukaemia arising after drug therapy concluded that the incidence of erythroleukaemia was no higher than in published series of acute non-lymphoblastic leukaemia arising apparently *de novo* (Cardamone et al. 1974). However, inclusion of more recently reported series might lead to an opposite conclusion. If this is so, the reasons for acute erythroblastic and even of acute non-lymphoblastic predominance are not clear. Perhaps the latter is related to the age distribution of the patients at risk, though it is also possible that the 'radiomimetic' effect of cytotoxic drugs such as cyclophosphamide and melphalan predisposes to myeloid rather than lymphoid leukaemia (Geary 1976; Louie & Schwartz 1978).

With increasing use of immunosuppressive and cytotoxic agents for a greater number of disorders, more attention is being paid to the link between leukaemia and marrow depression or aplasia. At present it is impossible to distinguish between various aetiological possibilities. First, a single insult may produce more than one abnormality, the manifestations being sometimes sequential (Dameshek 1967). Alternatively more than one agent may be necessary, insult upon insult; of relevance here are the studies of Gibson and his co-workers. They have investigated the records of a large group of children with acute leukaemia and studied the possible interaction of several factors (Gibson et al. 1968). These were radiation due to diagnostic X-rays in the mother before conception or during pregnancy, a history of previous maternal miscarriages or stillbirths and a preceding virus infection in the child. When compared with a control group of children they found a statistically significant increase in the incidence of three or four, but not less than three, factors within the past history of an individual leukaemic child and concluded that there are multiple risk factors which must operate before leukaemia develops. It is also possible that both single and multiple agents may induce leukaemia on a basis of marrow aplasia.

Marrow culture studies *in vitro* usually show reduced colony formation (CFU-C) in aplastic anaemia itself (see p. 10) in pre-leukaemia or smouldering leukaemia (Sultan 1972; Milner et al. 1977) and in florid acute leukaemia (Greenberg et al. 1971; Metcalf 1973). However they may be of value in detecting the presence of any residual marrow damage after apparent clinical and haematological recovery (Howell et al. 1975). There is also evidence that a leukaemic evolution may be accompanied by changes in the cluster:colony ratio (Sultan 1976). Of considerable interest would be more sequential studies, particularly on patients under long-term therapy known to induce a higher incidence of leukaemia and in cases of aplasia where recovery seems complete but culture studies indicate residual marrow damage. New methods for assessing stem-cell capacity are being developed (Barr et al. 1975) and may well provide new information on the aetiological link between aplasia and leukaemia.

REFERENCES

AKSOY, M., DINÇOL, K., ERDEM, S. Y. & DINÇOL, G. (1972) Acute leukaemia due to chronic exposure to benzene. *Am. J. Med.*, *52*, 160.

ALMEIDA, J. D., HASSELBACK, R. C. & HARN, A. W. (1963) Virus-like particles in blood and two acute leukaemia patients. *Science, N.Y.*, *142*, 1487.

BARR, R. D., WHANG-PENG, J. & PERRY, S. (1975) Haemopoietic stem cells in peripheral blood. *Science, N.Y.*, *190*, 284.

BLOCK, M., JACOBSON, L. O. & BETHARD, W. F. (1953) Preleukaemic acute human leukaemia. *J. Am. med. Ass.*, *152*, 1018.

BRANDA, R. F., MOLDOW, C. F., MACARTHUR, J. R., WINTROBE, M. M., ANTHONY, B. K. & JACOB, H. S. (1978) Folate-induced remission in aplastic anaemia with familial defect of cellular folate uptake. *New Engl. J. Med.*, *298*, 469.

BRAUER, M. J. & DAMESHEK, W. (1967) Hypoplastic anaemia and myeloblastic leukaemia following chloramphenicol therapy. *New Engl. J. Med.*, *277*, 1003.

BRANDT, L., NILSSON, P. G. & MITELMAN, F. (1977) Non-industrial exposure to benzene as a leukaemogenic risk factor. *Lancet*, *ii*, 1074.

BRILL, A. B., TOMONAGA, M. & HEYSSEL, R. M. (1962) Leukaemia in man following exposure to ionising radiation. *Ann. intern. Med.*, *56*, 590.

BROSS, I. W. J. & NATARAJAN, M. S. (1972) Leukaemia from low-level radiation. *New Engl. J. Med.*, *287*, 107.

BURGER, C. L., HARRIS, W. W., ANDERSON, N. G., BARTLETT, T. W. & KNISELY, R. M. (1964) Virus-like particles in human leukaemic plasma. *Proc. Soc. exp. Biol. Med.*, *115*, 151.

CARDAMONE, J. M., KIMMERLE, R. I. & MARSHALL, E. Y. (1974) Development of acute erythroid leukaemia in B-cell immuno-proliferative disorders after prolonged therapy with alkylating drugs. *Am. J. Med.*, *57*, 836.

CARMEL, R., COLTMAN, C. A., YATTEAU, R. F. & COSTANZI, J. J. (1970) Association of paroxysmal nocturnal haemoglobinuria with erythroleukaemia. *New Engl. J. Med.*, *283*, 1329.

COBO, A., LISKER, R., CORDOVA, M. S. & PIZZUTO, J. (1970) Cytogenetic findings in acquired aplastic anaemia. *Acta haemat.*, *44*, 32.

COLEMAN, N. N., WILLIAMS, C. J., FLINT, A., GLATSTEIN, E. L., ROSENBERG, S. A. & KAPLAN, H. S. (1977) Haematologic neoplasia in patients treated for Hodgkin's disease. *New Engl. J. Med.*, *297*, 1249.

DAMESHEK, W. (1967) Riddle. What do aplastic anaemia, paroxysmal nocturnal haemoglobinuria (PNH) and 'hypoplastic' leukaemia have in common? *Blood*, *30*, 251.

DAMESHEK, W. (1969) Foreword and proposal for considering paroxysmal nocturnal haemoglobinuria (PHN) as a 'candidate' myeloproliferative disorder. *Blood*, *33*, 263.

DEGOWIN, R. L. (1963) Benzene exposure and aplastic anaemia followed by leukaemia fifteen years later. *J. Am. med. Ass.*, *185*, 748.

DELAMORE, I. W. & GEARY, C. G. (1971) Aplastic anaemia, acute myeloblastic leukaemia and oxymetholone. *Br. med. J.*, *ii*, 743.

DIAMOND, L. K., WANG, W. C. & ALTER, B. P. (1976) Congenital hypoplastic anaemia. *Adv. Paediat.*, *22*, 349.

DIGIACOMO, J., FURST, S. W. & NIXON, D. D. (1966) Primary acquired red cell aplasia in the adult. *J. Mt Sinai Hosp.*, *33*, 382.

DOSIK, H., HSU, L. Y., TODARO, G. J., LEA, S. L., HIRSCHHORN, K., SELIRIO, E. S. & ALTER, A. A. (1970) Leukaemia in aplastic anaemia: cytogenetic and tumour virus susceptibility studies. *Blood*, *36*, 341.

DOUGAN, L. & WOODLIFF, H. J. (1965) Acute leukaemia associated with phenylbutazone treatment: A review of the literature and report of a further case. *Med. J. Aust.*, *1*, 217.

FUDENBERG, H. H. & WELLS, J. V. (1976) Pathogenesis of autoimmune diseases. In: *Recent Advances in Rheumatology*, ed. W. W. Buchanan & W. C. Dick, p. 171. London, Churchill.

GARRIGA, S. & CROSBY, W. H. (1959) The incidence of leukaemia in families of patients with hypoplasia of the marrow. *Blood*, *14*, 1008.

GEARY, C. G. (1976) Therapy-linked leukaemia. *Lancet*, *ii*, 862.

GEARY, C. G., DAWSON, D. W., SITLANI, P., ALLISON, H. A. & LEYLAND, M. J. (1974) An association between aplastic anaemia and sideroblastic anaemia. *Br. J. Haemat.*, *27*, 337.

GIBSON, R. W., BROSS, I. D. J., GRAHAM, S., LILIENFELD, A. L., SCHUMAN, L. M., LEVIN, M. L. & DOWD, J. E. (1968) Leukaemia in children exposed to multiple risk factors. *New Engl. J. Med.*, *279*, 906.

GIRARD, R. & REVOL, L. (1970) La fréquence d'une exposition benzénique au cours des hémopathies graves. *Nouv. Revue fr. Hémat.*, *10*, 477.

GREENBERG, P. L., NICHOLS, W. C. & SCHRIER, S. L. (1971) Granulopoieses in acute myeloid leukaemia and preleukaemia. *New Engl. J. Med.*, *284*, 1225.

GRIST, N. R. & FALLON, R. J. (1964) Isolation of viruses from leukaemia patients. *Br. med. J.*, *2*, 1263.

GUNZ, F. & BAIKIE, A. G. (1974) *Leukaemia*, 3rd ed., p. 64. New York and London: Grune and Stratton.

HAAK, H. L., HARTGRINK-GROENVELD, C. A., FERNISSE, J. G., SPECK, B. & VAN ROOD, J. J. (1977) Acquired aplastic anaemia in adults. I. A retrospective analysis of 40 cases: single factors influencing the prognosis. *Acta haemat.*, *58*, 257.

HEYN, R. M., ERTEL, I. J. & TUBERGEN, D. G. (1969) Course of acquired aplastic anaemia in children treated with supportive care. *J. Am. med. Ass.*, *208*, 1372.

HOLDEN, D. & LICHTMAN, H. (1969) Paroxysmal nocturnal haemoglobinuria with acute leukaemia. *Blood*, *33*, 283.

HOWELL, A., ANDREWS, T. M. & WATTS, R. W. E. (1975) Bone-marrow cells resistant to chloramphenicol in chloramphenicol-induced aplastic anaemia. *Lancet*, *i*. 65.

HUEBNER, R. J., KELLOFF, G. J., SARMA, P. S., LANE, W. T., TURNER, H. G., GILDER, R. V., OROSZLAN, S., MEIER, H., MYERS, D. M. & PETERS, R. L. (1970) Group-specific antigen expression during embryogenesis of the genome of the C-type RNA tumour virus: implications for ontogenesis v. oncogenesis. *Proc. natn. Acad. Sci.*, *U.S.A.*, *67*, 366.

ISRAELS, M. C. G. & WILKINSON, J. F. (1961) Idiopathic aplastic anaemia: incidence and management. *Lancet*, *i*, 63.

JENKINS, D. E. & HARTMANN, R. C. (1969) Paroxysmal nocturnal haemoglobinuria terminating in acute myeloblastic leukaemia. *Blood*, *33*, 274.

JENSEN, M. K. & ROLLS, K. (1965) Phenylbutazone and leukaemia. *Acta med. scand.*, *178*, 505.

KALTER, S. S., HELMKE, R. J., HERELING, R. L., PANIGEL, M., FOWLER, A. K., STRICKLAND, J. E. & HELLMAN, A. (1973) C-type particles in normal human placentas. *J. natn. Cancer Inst.*, *50*, 1081.

KAUFMANN, R. W., SCHECHTER, G. P. & McFARLAND, W. (1969) P.N.H. terminating in acute granulocytic leukaemia. *Blood*, *33*, 287.

KILLMAN, S.-A. (1970) A hypothesis concerning the relationship between normal and leukemic hemopoiesis in acute myeloid leukemia. In: *Haemopoietic Cellular Proliferation*, ed. F. Stohlman. p. 267. New York: Grune & Stratton.

KOEPPEN, K. M., PAULISCH, R., SCHNEIDER, D. & GERHARTZ, H. (1975) Panmyelopathie, ein präleukämisches Stadium. *Klin. Wschr.*, *53*, 581.

KRISHNAN, E. V., WEGNER, K. & GARG, S. K. (1978) Congenital hypoplastic anaemia terminating in acute promyelocytic leukaemia. *Pediatrics, Springfield*, *61*, 898.

KYLE, R. A., PIERRE, R. V. & BAYRD, E. D. (1970) Multiple myeloma and acute myelo-monocytic leukaemia. Report of four cases possibly related to melphalan. *New Engl. J. Med.*, *283*, 1121.

Lancet (1977) Leading article, *i*, 519.

LARSEN, J. & BRINCKER, H. (1977) The incidence and characteristics of acute myeloid leukaemia in Hodgkin's disease. *Scand. J. Haemat.*, *18*, 197.

LEWIS, S. M. (1965) Course and prognosis in aplastic anaemia. *Br. med. J.*, *1*, 1027.

LI, F. P. & NATHAN, D. G. (1971) Therapy linked leukaemia. *Br. med. J.*, *3*, 765.

LINMAN, J. W. & SAARNI, M. I. (1974) The preleukaemic syndrome. *Semin. Hemat.*, *11*, 93.

LOUIE, S. & SCHWARTZ, R. S. (1978) Immunodeficiency and the pathogenesis of lymphoma and leukaemia. *Semin. Hemat.*, *15*, 117.

MCMAHON, B. (1962) Prenatal x-ray exposure and childhood cancer. *J. natn. Cancer Inst.*, *28*, 1173.

MELHORN, D. K., GROS, S. & NEWMAN, A. J. (1970) Acute childhood leukaemia presenting as aplastic anaemia: the response to corticosteroids. *J. Pediat.*, *77*, 647.

METCALF, D. (1973) Human leukaemia: recent tissue culture studies on the nature of myeloid leukaemia. *Br. J. Cancer*, *27*, 191.

MILNER, G. R., TESTA, N., DEXTER, M., GEARY, C. G., MULDAL, S. & LAJTHA, L. J. (1977) Studies in the refractory cytopenias. *Br. J. Haemat.*, *35*, 251.

MIR, M. A., GEARY, C. G. & DELAMORE, I. W. (1977) Hypoimmunoglobulinaemia and aplastic anaemia. *Scand. J. Haemat.*, *19*, 225.

MODAN, B. & LILIENFELD, A. M. (1965) Polycythaemia vera and leukaemia—the role of radiation treatment. *Medicine, Balt.*, *44*, 305.

MOHLER, D. N. & LEAVELL, B. S. (1958) Aplastic anaemia: an analysis of 50 cases. *Ann. intern. Med.*, *49*, 326.

MORLEY, A. & FORBES, I. (1974) Impairment of immunological function in aplastic anaemia. *Aust. N.Z. J. Med.*, *4*, 53.

MORLEY, A., HOLMES, K. & FORBES, I. (1974) Depletion of B-lymphocytes in chronic hypoplastic marrow failure (aplastic anaemia) *Aust. N.Z. J. Med.*, *4*, 538.

NAJEAN, Y., BERNARD, J., WAINBERGER, M., DRESCH, C., BOIRON, M. & SELIGMANN, M. (1965) Evolution et prognostic des pancytopeines idiopathiques. *Nouv. Revue fr. Hémat.*, *5*, 639.

NAJEAN, Y., PECKING, A. & BROQUET, M. (1976) Refractory anaemia with partial myelo-blastic medullary infiltration. Clinical study and evolution under androgeno-therapy. *Nouv. Revue fr. Hémat.*, *16*, 68.

NEWELL, G. R., HARRIS, W. W., BOWMAN, K. O., BOONE, C. W. & ANDERSON, N. G. (1968) Evaluation of virus-like particles in the plasmas of 255 patients with leukaemia and related diseases. *New Engl. J. Med.*, *278*, 1185.

PIERRE, R. V. (1974) Preleukaemic states. *Semin. Hemat.*, *11*, 73.

PURI, H. C. & CAMPBELL, R. A. (1977) Cyclophosphamide and malignancy. *Lancet*, *i*, 1306.

PUGSLEY, C. A. J., FORBES, I. J. & MORLEY, A. A. (1978) Immunological abnormalities in an animal model of chronic hypoplastic marrow failure induced by busulphan. *Blood*, *51*, 601.

REIMER, R. R., HOOVER, R., FRAUMENI, J. F. & YOUNG, R. C. (1977) Acute leukaemia after alkylating-agent chemotherapy of ovarian carcinoma. *New Engl. J. Med.*, *297*, 177.

ROBERTS, M. M. & BELL, R. (1976) Acute leukaemia after immunosuppressive therapy. *Lancet*, *2*, 768.

ROSMER, F. & GRÜNWALD, H. (1974) Multiple myeloma terminating in acute leukaemia. *Am. J. Med.*, *57*, 927.

ROSMER, F. & GRÜNWALD, H. (1975) Hodgkin's disease and acute leukaemia. A report of eight cases and review of the literature. *Am. J. Med.*, *58*, 339.

ROSSE, W. F. & DACIE, J. V. (1966) Immune lysis of normal human and paroxysmal nocturnal haemoglobinuria (PNH) red blood cells. I. The sensitivity of PNH red cells to lysis by complement and specific antibody. *J. clin. Invest.*, *45*, 736.

SAARNI, M. I. & LINMAN, J. W. (1973) Preleukaemia. The haematologic syndrome pre-ceding acute leukaemia. *Am. J. Med.*, *55*, 38.

SANCHEZ-MEDAL, A., GOMEZ-LEAL, L. D. & RICO, M. G. (1969) Anabolic androgenic steroids in the treatment of acquired aplastic anaemia. *Blood*, *34*, 283.

SCHMID, J. R., KEILY, J. M., PEASE, G. L. & HARGRAVES, M. M. (1963) Acquired pure red cell agenesis. *Acta haemat.*, *30*, 255.

SCHROEDER, T. M. & KURTH, R. (1971) Spontaneous chromosomal breakage and high incidence of leukaemia in inherited disease. *Blood, 37*, 96.

SOUTTER, L. & EMERSON, C. P. (1960) Elective thymectomy in the treatment of aregenerative anemia associated with monocytic leukaemia. *Am. J. Med., 28*, 609.

STEVENSON, A. C., BEDFORD, J. & HILL, A. G. S. (1971) Chromosomal studies in patients taking phenylbutazone. *Ann. Rheum. Dis., 30*, 487.

STEWART, A. & KNEALE, G. W. (1970) Radiation dose effects in relation to obstetric x-rays in childhood cancers. *Lancet, i*, 1185.

STOTT, H., FOX, W., GIRLING, D. J., STEPHENS, R. J. & GALTON, D. A. G. (1977) Acute leukaemia after busulphan. *Br. med. J., 4*, 1513.

SULTAN, C. (1972) In vitro studies of bone marrow in refractory anaemia. *Br. J. Haemat., 23*, Suppl. 177.

SULTAN, C. (1976) Discussion. *Nouv. Revue fr. Hémat., 17*, 122.

TCHERNIA, G., MIELST, F., SUBTIL, E. & PARMENTIER, C. (1976) Acute myeloblastic leukaemia after immunosuppressive therapy for primary non-malignant disease. *Blood Cells, 2*, 67.

TOUGH, I. M. & COURT BROWN, W. M. (1965) Chromosome aberrations and exposure to ambient benzene. *Lancet, i*, 684.

VIGLIANI, E. C. & SAITA, G. (1964) Benzene and leukaemia. *New Engl. J. Med., 271*, 872.

VINCENT, P. C. & DE GRUCHY, G. C. (1967) Complications and treatment of acquired aplastic anaemia. *Br. J. Haemat., 13*, 977.

WASSER, J. S., YOLKEN, R., MILLER, D. R. & DIAMOND, L. (1978) Congenital hypoplastic anaemia (Diamond–Blackfan syndrome) terminating in acute myelogenous leukaemia. *Blood, 51*, 991.

WESTBERG, N. G. & SWOLIN, B. (1976) Acute myeloblastic leukaemia appearing in two patients after prolonged continuous chlorambucil treatment for Wegener's granulomatosis. *Acta med. scand., 199*, 373.

WETHERLEY-MEIN, G. (1960) The myeloproliferative syndromes. In: *Lectures on Haematology,* ed. F. G. J. Hayhoe, p. 132. London: Cambridge University Press.

WILLIAMS, D. M., LYNCH, R. E. & CARTWRIGHT, G. E. (1973) Drug induced aplastic anaemia. *Semin. Hemat., 10*, 195.

WOLFF, J. A. (1967) Anaemias caused by infections and toxins, idiopathic aplastic anaemia and anaemia caused by renal disease. *Pediat. Clins N. Am., 4*, 469.

Index

Bold figures indicate a principal entry

APLASTIC ANAEMIA

Aplastic Anaemia

edited by

C. G. GEARY

FRCP(Ed), FRCPath

Consultant Haematologist, Manchester Royal Infirmary;
Honorary Lecturer in Clinical Haematology, University of Manchester

BAILLIÈRE TINDALL · LONDON

A BAILLIÈRE TINDALL book published by
Cassell Ltd
35 Red Lion Square, London WC1R 4SG
and at Sydney, Auckland, Toronto, Johannesburg
an affiliate of
Macmillan Publishing Co. Inc.
New York

© 1979 Baillière Tindall
a division of Cassell Ltd

All rights reserved. No part of this publication may be reproduced, stored in a retrieval
system or transmitted in any form or by any means, electronic, mechanical,
photocopying or otherwise, without the prior permission of Baillière Tindall, 35 Red
Lion Square, London WC1R 4SG

First published 1979

ISBN 0 7020 0698 X

Printed in Great Britain by Spottiswoode Ballantyne Ltd. Colchester and London

British Library Cataloguing in Publication Data

Aplastic anaemia.
1. Aplastic anemia
I. GEARY, C G
616.1'52   RC641.7.A6

ISBN 0-7020-0698-X